The Economics of Regional Trading Arrangements

R

The Economics of Regional Trading Arrangements

Richard Pomfret

CLARENDON PRESS · OXFORD
1997

don Street, Oxford OX2 6DP
York
Bogota Bombay
Town Dar es Salaam
Delhi Florence Hong Kong Istanbul Karachi
Kuala Lumpur Madras Madrid Melbourne
Mexico City Nairobi Paris Singapore
Taipei Tokyo Toronto Warsaw
and associated companies in
Berlin Ibadan

Oxford is a trade mark of Oxford University Press

Published in the United States by
Oxford University Press Inc., New York

British Library Cataloguing in Publication Data
Data available

Library of Congress Cataloging in Publication Data

ISBN 0–19–823335–3

1 3 5 7 9 10 8 6 4 2

Typeset by Graphicraft Typesetters Ltd., Hong Kong
Printed in Great Britain
on acid-free paper by
Bookcraft (Bath) Ltd.,
Midsomer Norton, Somerset

Preface

The Economics of Regional Trading Arrangements provides a unified analysis of policies which discriminate among trading partners. With the European Union's 1992 programme, the North American Free Trade Agreement and attempts to form or strengthen regional trading arrangements in South America, southern Africa, and Southeast Asia, regionalism became a major issue in international commercial diplomacy during the early 1990s. The proliferation of regional trading arrangements was viewed by some as a challenge, and by others as a complement, to the establishment of the World Trade Organization as the successor to GATT.

Why another book on regionalism? Much of the literature on regionalism is over-simplistic, in particular in abusing the 'trade creation is good and trade diversion is bad' distinction and in theorizing about the systemic consequences. Confronting theoretically possible outcomes with the evidence from actual regional trading arrangements has been limited, and often based on 'stylized facts' rather than hard evidence. Without agreement on likely outcomes in specific situations, polemical statements about the economic desirability of or harm from proposed regional arrangements are difficult to rebut. These points are not readily made in journal articles, which is why I have written a book.

This book analyses the new regional arrangements by relating them to geographically discriminatory trade policies in general, before asking whether the new regionalism requires new theoretical analysis. The approach is to combine in roughly equal proportions history, theory, and a review of empirical studies. This is appropriate because the key theoretical result is the welfare ambiguity of introducing discriminatory trade policies. Empirical studies can provide a sense of which of the potentially offsetting effects are more or less important, although, since the impact varies according to circumstances, no individual case sheds conclusive light on the general effects of discriminatory trade policies. Since some consequences take a long time to have their full impact and may be systemic, it is also useful to observe how regional arrangements have evolved in practice.

In all of this, some judgement is required. History never repeats itself exactly. Theory needs to be applied, and empirical work in this area is difficult because our knowledge of key parameters (especially the substitutability between imports from different trading partners) is limited. The political economy of why regional trading agreements are signed is further complicated by the intrusion of foreign policy (and other non-economic) considerations and by frequent gaps between anticipated or perceived consequences and actual outcomes.

Nevertheless, recent views that the 'new regionalism' of the 1990s is so different and that history and old 'customs union theory' are irrelevant to its assessment need to be challenged. Non-tariff barriers to trade and non-economic motives for trade policies are not unique to the 1990s, nor are hub-and-spoke arrangements and agreements which go beyond narrowly defined trade policies.

The book's origins lie in a 1988 book by me entitled *Unequal Trade* published by Basil Blackwell, and I thank Tim Goodfellow of Blackwell for permission to reproduce extensively from that book. I am grateful to Anne Krueger for encouraging me in 1994 to undertake a new edition after the Blackwell book went out of print, although what started out as a revision and update turned into an essentially rewritten and far longer book. Many contributors to the huge recent literature on regionalism helped me in discussion and by making available unpublished material. I hope that these debts are reflected in the References, and apologize for any omissions. Special thanks are due to Michael Plummer for reading and providing detailed comments on the first draft.

A sabbatical leave from the University of Adelaide in 1996 provided me with the time to write the book. I am grateful to Jonathan Pincus for supporting my leave, and to the OECD Development Centre, Vanderbilt University Graduate Program in Economic Development, and Simon Fraser University Department of Economics for hospitality during the leave. Last but not least, my thanks go to Sue Hughes for her copyediting and to Andrew Schuller at OUP for being a supportive editor.

R.P.

Contents

PART III: EMPIRICAL EVIDENCE

PART IV: POLITICAL ECONOMY

List of Figures

List of Tables

Abbreviations

In this book, GDA (geographically discriminatory arrangement) is used as a generic term synonymous with discriminatory trade policy, while RTA (regional trading arrangement) refers to GDAs identified with a particular region. In general, PTA (preferential trading arrangement) refers to a GDA in which trade barriers are lowered on imports from certain trading partners, and a FTA (free trade area) is the specific case of a PTA in which tariffs on trade among participants are eliminated. Some GDAs' names, however, incorporate 'FTA' even though they are not free trade areas (e.g. AFTA involves reduced but not necessarily zero tariffs on internal trade). A CU (customs union) is a FTA whose members pursue a common external trade policy.

The terms EEC, EC, and EU are applied without distinction to the Western European customs union, although EEC is preferred in earlier contexts, when it was normal usage, and EU in 1990s contexts. Similarly, CMEA and Comecon are used interchangeably.

ACP	African, Caribbean, Pacific (participants in Lomé)
AD	anti-dumping duties
AFTA	ASEAN Free Trade Area
AIP	ASEAN Industrial Project
APEC	Asia-Pacific Economic Co-operation
ASEAN	Association of Southeast Asian Nations
Benelux	Belgium, the Netherlands and Luxembourg
BOP	balance of payments
CACM	Central American Common Market
CAP	Common Agricultural Policy (of the EC/EU)
CARICOM	Caribbean Community and Common Market
CARIFTA	Caribbean Free Trade Association
CBERA	Caribbean Basin Economic Recovery Act
CBI	Caribbean Basin Initiative (led to CBERA)

CEAO	Communauté Economique de l'Afrique de l'Ouest
CEFTA	Central European Free Trade Area
CER	Closer Economic Relations (Australia/New Zealand)
CET	common external tariff
CGE	computable general equilibrium (models)
CIS	Commonwealth of Independent States
CMEA	Council for Mutual Economic Assistance (Comecon)
Comecon	see CMEA
CU	customs union
CUSTA	Canada-United States Free Trade Agreement
CVDs	countervailing duties
DFI	direct foreign investment
EAC	East African Community
EAEC	East Asian Economic Caucus
EAGA	East ASEAN Growth Area
EC	European Communities
ECO	Economic Co-operation Organization
ECOWAS	Economic Community of West African States
ECSC	European Coal and Steel Community
EEC	European Economic Community
EFTA	European Free Trade Association
EMS	European Monetary System
EPU	European Payments Union
ERM	Exchange Rate Mechanism (of the EMS)
EU	European Union
FTA	free trade area
FTAA	Free Trade Area of the Americas (proposed)
G7	Group of Seven (Canada, France, Germany, Italy, Japan, UK and USA)
GATT	General Agreement on Tariffs and Trade

GCC	Gulf Co-operation Council
GDA	geographically discriminatory arrangement
GEMU	German Economic and Monetary Union
GNP	gross national product
GSP	generalized system of preferences
IBRD	International Bank for Reconstruction and Development (the World Bank)
ILO	International Labour Organisation
IMF	International Monetary Fund
ISI	import-substituting industrialization
ISO	International Standards Organisation
ITO	International Trade Organization (still-born)
ITU	International Telecommunications Union
JCM	the Johnson-Cooper-Massell proposition
LAFTA	Latin American Free Trade Agreement
LAIA	Latin American Integration Association
MCAs	monetary compensation amounts (within the CAP)
MERCOSUR	Mercado Comun del Cono Sur (Southern Common Market)
MFA	Multifibre Arrangement
MFN	most-favoured nation
MRU	Mano River Union
NAFTA	North American Free Trade Agreement
NTB	non-tariff barrier to trade
OECD	Organization for Economic Co-operation and Development
OEEC	Organization for European Economic Co-operation
PTA	preferential trading arrangement
QR	quantitative restriction
RTA	regional trading arrangement
SAARC	South Asian Association for Regional Co-operation

SADCC	Southern African Development and Co-ordination Conference
SADC	South African Development Community
SAFTA	South American Free Trade Area (concept)
SEA	Single European Act (of the EC, 1985)
Sijori	Singapore, Johor and Riau
SPARTECA	South Pacific Regional Trade Co-operation Agreement
SRZ	subregional economic zone
TAFTA	Transatlantic Free Trade Area (concept)
TNC	transnational corporation
UNCTAD	United Nations Conference on Trade and Development
UNEP	United Nations Environment Programme
UNESCO	United Nations Education, Science and Culture Organisation
UNIDO	United Nations Industrial Development Organisation
VAT	value added tax
VER	voluntary export restraint agreement
WIPO	World Intellectual Property Organization
WTO	World Trade Organization (established 1995)

1

Introduction

In international trade diplomacy, the period from the mid-1980s until late 1993 saw a dramatic race between the forces of regionalism (represented by the EC92 programme and the North American Free Trade Area) and the forces of multilateralism (represented by the Uruguay Round). Tension was maintained until the last minute, when the race ended in a tie with both runners crossing the finishing line in late 1993. Did the result prove that regionalism and multilateralism are complementary and can coexist? Or has the conflict been delayed as the new defender of multilateralism, the World Trade Organization, faces continuing challenges from regionalism?

The issue is important given the widespread view that the historically rapid growth in the world economy during the second half of the twentieth century was assisted by the open GATT-based international trading system. The future of the trading system is given added importance in the 1990s as many countries that previously pursued inward-oriented economic policies have switched their development strategies towards greater participation in the world economy. Will the reforming economies of South Asia and the former USSR be integrated into the global economy, or will the process be hampered by a resurgent regionalism?

This book situates the new regional trading arrangements in the broader realm of discriminatory trade policies. The debate has shifted over recent decades from being about customs unions and other preferential tariff policies to being about regional economic integration, 'reducing the significance of national policies within a geographical area' (Anderson and Blackhurst, 1993, 1). Nevertheless, starting from a wider perspective is useful because there is a well-defined body of theory and stock of empirical studies on preferential trading arrangements. I will also include discussion of other discriminatory measures (such as voluntary export restraint agreements and other quantitative restrictions on trade) because they illustrate some of the effects of discrimination and because their proliferation is part of the story of weakened commitment to the non-discrimination principle in the 1970s and 1980s.

Discriminatory trade policies are not a new phenomenon. When rulers first intervened in trade flows they saw no necessary reason to treat all trading partners equally, and some discriminatory elements have always been present in the international trading system. Yet in the twentieth century there have been consistent efforts to purge these elements. The various international conferences of the interwar period echoed with calls for more equal trading conditions, which finally took effect in the 1947 General Agreement on Tariffs and Trade (GATT)—the legal framework for the postwar international trading system—whose cornerstone is the principle of non-discrimination.

Despite these intentions, the world saw a gradual retreat from the principle, to the extent that by the 1980s a majority of world trade was being conducted under discriminatory regimes and the GATT system was seriously threatened. The threat was highlighted in the late 1980s as the two largest trading units embarked on major regional initiatives, completing the European common market and establishing the North American Free Trade Area. The intellectual debate was intensified as arguments were developed in favour of regionalism, or in support of the view that regional arrangements were the best means to the end of global trade liberalization.

Why has this happened? The central theme of this book is that, despite the negative GATT stance which has firm roots in economic theory, there are incentives for individual groups of countries to introduce discriminatory trading arrangements. Thus, without strong multilateral commitment to maintaining a system based upon non-discrimination, such a system will gradually be undermined. Moreover, infringements of the non-discrimination principle tend to breed further infringements, creating a momentum for increasing systemic breakdown. The final outcome is uncertain because countries recognize long-term benefits from maintaining a system based on non-discrimination. Countries oppose discriminatory trading arrangements from which they are excluded, but may react by working to strengthen the multilateral system or by forming their own discriminatory arrangements.

Are regional trading arrangements (RTAs) a good thing? Economic theory can help to identify their effects, but because discriminatory trade policies by their nature exclude the global welfare optimum (which requires no barriers to trade), theory cannot provide conclusive answers about the net benefits of RTAs in a tariff-ridden world. Empirical studies are necessary to evaluate the welfare implications of any specific RTA, and reviewing the empirical literature can help to establish presumptions about the main consequences of RTAs. Since some effects take a long time to have their full impact or may be systemic, it is useful to observe how RTAs and other geographically discriminatory arrangements have evolved in practice. Thus, this book combines in roughly equal proportions history, theory, and empirical evidence in order to draw conclusions about the impact of RTAs and to evaluate their desirability.

Although the book is about the economics of RTAs, the importance of non-economic considerations in many regional arrangements is acknowledged, even if such considerations are not analysed thoroughly. The European Union and the Association of Southeast Asian Nations, for example, have important and legitimate non-economic goals, so that even if the economic consequences were found to be negative they might well be outweighed by the positive benefits from regional concord. Moreover, some economic benefits achieved by regional arrangements may represent the limits of the politically possible, so again it may make little sense to criticize them for failing to bring about the optimum economic outcome.

In this introductory chapter, I will define terms, introduce the main arguments, and then provide an outline of the book's structure.

1. Vocabulary

Discriminatory trade policies involve deliberate use of government policy to create different trading conditions for residents of various foreign nations. I will not be concerned with discrimination initiated by private agents (e.g. citizens' boycotts, international cartels, and other price discrimination by firms). Nor will I deal with trade policies that incidentally harm some countries more than others, as any product-specific import duty, for example, invariably does.[1]

There are a variety of terms used to describe the phenomena being dealt with in this book, most of them value-laden. Discrimination is intended as the most neutral term to describe different treatment for trade with different trading partners. Usually the different treatment is towards imports, but not exclusively so, e.g. the US grain embargo following the Soviet invasion of Afghanistan, Arab restrictions on oil shipments to the Netherlands and the USA after the 1973 Arab–Israeli war, or United Nations sanctions against Iraq in the 1990s. A distinction is often made between negative and positive discrimination, with the yardstick being the most-favoured-nation tariff. Negative discrimination may be in the form of sanctions (as in the above examples of export restrictions), but it also applies to almost any quantitative restriction on imports. Positive discrimination may simply involve having a separate tariff schedule for, say, developing countries, but it can also apply to attempts at economic integration.[2] Analytically there is no distinction between 'sanctions' and 'preferences' and indeed, as soon as either are introduced, most-favoured-nation (MFN) treatment itself becomes discriminatory in one direction or the other.

Economic integration does, however, pose a demarcation problem, and is also responsible for more terminology which will recur in this book. One approach is to form a *free trade area*, in

[1] Similar definitions are adopted by Patterson (1966, 20–1) and Hieronymi (1973, 7). Patterson emphasizes the distinction between discrimination among nations and discrimination among commodities, and Hieronymi emphasizes the difference between public policy and private agents' independent decisions. Riedel (1987) argues that discrimination among commodities is the most serious discrimination in US tariff policy.

[2] Semantic confusion may arise, however, because the economic integration literature frequently distinguishes between negative integration (i.e. removing barriers to integration, such as internal tariffs) and positive integration (i.e. creating union-wide markets and institutions by positive actions). This usage was popularized by Tinbergen (1954, 122), who believed that 'negative integration' may be sufficient to raise living standards but that it 'will be a slow process which may be accelerated by positive action', of which the two elements are tax harmonization and industrial policy. By the 1980s analysts of the EC, frustrated by incomplete Western European integration, had much longer lists of necessary 'positive integration' policies (e.g. Pelkmans, 1984), and the EC's 1992 programme addressed them. In the 1990s a similar distinction emerged using the terms 'shallow' and 'deep integration'.

which each country grants free access to its partners' exports but maintains its own commercial policy towards non-members. A *customs union* goes a step further in establishing a common trade policy towards non-members, while a *common market* enables free movement of factors of production (labour, capital) across members' borders. *Economic union* involves a common market plus common economic policies. These are not necessarily sequential steps, and the taxonomy does not precisely fit actual arrangements. (For example, in the USA, which is in most senses an economic union, state governments can have economic policies running counter to federal policies and purchasing arrangements which form barriers to free interstate trade, whereas the European Union is an incomplete common market which has some common economic policies.) It is, however, a useful taxonomy in highlighting the continuum from simple preferences to full economic union and pointing to the arbitrary element in focusing on trade among nations in the present context. The difference between Alberta's discriminatory treatment of Manitoban exports and French treatment of Italian exports is one of degree rather than of kind. The European Union has supranational aspirations, but in this book it will be treated as an arrangement among independent nations (along with other free trade areas, customs unions and common markets),[3] whereas federal nations such as Australia, Canada, or the USA will be treated as single trading units.

The book aims to provide a unified treatment of geographically discriminatory trading arrangements. Interest has shifted during the twentieth century. In the 1930s a major concern was the use of exchange controls and bilateral barter arrangements, but, apart from in developing countries and within the Soviet bloc, these have been of minor importance during the second half of the twentieth century and had practically disappeared by the 1990s. Similarly, the imperial preference schemes between European countries and their colonies or former colonies, which

[3] In Chs. 5 and 6, I will argue that the EC/EU is *en route* to a single federal entity, although *when* it will cross the hazy boundary will be a matter of dispute. Meanwhile, Canadian policy-makers, concerned about the consequences of growing provincial powers, signed an Agreement on Internal Trade which took effect in 1995 and sought to address obstacles to the flow of goods, services, labour, and capital within Canada (Trebilcock and Schwanen, 1995).

were a major issue in the original GATT negotiations of the 1940s, have diminished in importance with decolonization. The 'new protectionism' of the 1970s and 1980s involved discriminatory protective devices and spawned a large literature, but interest subsided in the 1990s as some of the more dramatic measures (e.g. voluntary export restraint agreements) were rolled back. In the 1990s, following the completion of the EU's internal market and the negotiations for a North American Free Trade Area, the focus shifted to regional trading arrangements (RTAs). The theory of geographically discriminatory arrangements (GDAs) can be applied to all of these policies, but given the contemporary emphasis on RTAs this book's main focus is on regionalism.

Regionalism typically involves a geographical dimension. The nature of this dimension, however, varies greatly from small localized organizations such as the Central American Common Market to groupings spanning the largest ocean in Asia–Pacific Economic Co-operation (APEC). In popular debate in the 1990s regionalism became shorthand for the segmentation of the global economy into a few large blocs. An important distinction, emphasized by Detlef Lorenz (1991), is between regionalism and regionalization: the former refers to policy, the latter to trade flows. Regionalization occurs when trade among members of a region increases relative to their trade with outsiders. Regionalization may be a consequence of regionalism, but it can also have other causes.

Trade policy debate during the 1990s featured several other 'isms' whose usage was often an imprecise shorthand. *Multilateralism* became shorthand for the GATT trade negotiations and, after completion of the Uruguay Round, for working through the World Trade Organization. *Unilateralism* is self-explanatory, apart from when US 'aggressive unilateralism' to open up other countries' markets in the 1980s was achieved by bilateral negotiation. *Bilateralism* was usually reserved for more amicable negotiations, although it then blends into 'regionalism'.[4] In this book, bilateralism is used in the specific sense of negotiating two-way trade

[4] Irwin (1993) distinguishes between *progressive bilateralism*, represented by the treaties of the 1860s which produced freer non-discriminatory trade by including MFN clauses, and *pernicious bilateralism*, represented by the exclusive trade arrangements of the 1930s. I avoid this terminology because these two types of arrangement are too diverse to justify a common label.

flows, usually in balance and effectively as a barter arrangement. Such bilateral arrangements are the antithesis of the open multilateral trading system embodied in the GATT rules.

2. Arguments

The theory of discriminatory trade policies and its application will be analysed in the main parts of the book. This introductory section provides a brief survey of the main arguments, without necessary caveats and reservations. The basic ambiguity arises because preferential trade policies reduce one price distortion —that between domestic and partner country products—but introduce another—between partner and third-country products. The classic exposition of this ambiguity was by Jacob Viner (1950). In the third quarter of the twentieth century economists tended to emphasize the costs of discrimination, by contrasting preferential tariffs with unilateral tariff reduction. In the 1980s and 1990s more positive arguments in favour of regionalism were advanced.

The basic economic cost of discriminatory trade policies is the possible misallocation of global resources. By distorting the relative prices of imports from different sources, such policies may encourage purchase from a trading partner that is not the least-cost producer. In the presence of other distortions a discriminatory trade policy can be welfare-improving, but the first-best solution involves removing all distortions (which precludes discriminatory policies). This was the thrust of the economic analysis of preferential trading arrangements after Viner's (1950) book, culminating in the proposition that, since non-discriminatory tariff reductions are always superior, discriminatory arrangements can be explained only by non-economic motives (the Johnson–Cooper–Massell, or JCM, proposition).

Discriminatory trade policies will typically involve higher transaction costs than non-discrimination. For non-preferred countries there is an incentive to source their exports through a preferred trading partner, to use false labelling, etc., in order to avoid the higher duty (or other trade barriers). From the importing country's perspective, such practices are more difficult to monitor than evasion of non-discriminatory trade barriers. Both the attempted evasions and the costs of determining and enforcing rules of origin involve uncompensated welfare losses from a global perspective.

Less precise, but potentially more serious, are the political consequences of abandonment of the MFN principle. Discrimination politicizes international trade in several ways. Negotiating preference margins on a case-by-case basis promotes hard bargaining and, when outcomes are seen relative to other preference recipients, leads to frequent feelings of grievance.[5] If discriminatory policies are determined by national legislatures as reprisals against trading partners who do not play fair, then they are likely to proliferate but to be seen in a different light by the reprisal-taker and by the object of the reprisal.[6] Finally, since discriminatory measures normally affect geographical trade patterns, they can be used to create or cement spheres of influence. Competitive bargaining and influence spheres add to mercantilist tendencies to see international trade as a zero-sum game, in contrast to the GATT/WTO philosophy of promoting mutual gains through freer trade. Such a change in attitude opens up the prospect of economic disputes leading to political conflict, as happened in the 1930s.

Contrary to the JCM proposition, discriminatory trading arrangements can benefit members more than unilateral tariff reduction. In mainstream customs union theory this result arises from terms of trade effects, and members' gains are therefore at the expense of outsiders; thus, from a cosmopolitan perspective, the JCM proposition still holds, and the argument for

[5] Recognition of the 'frequent controversies' caused by discriminatory policies was one reason for the United States embracing unconditional MFN treatment after the First World War (United States Tariff Commission, 1919, 42). After accepting Greece as an associated member in 1961, the EC came under strong pressure from Turkey for equal treatment, and much of the later progress of the EC's Mediterranean policy can be explained by similar concerns about relative position (Pomfret, 1986a). The Lomé Convention between the EC and its African, Caribbean, and Pacific associates has also seen recurring disputes over origin rules, preference margins, etc. (Stevens, 1984).

[6] In the early 1980s several 'reciprocity' bills came before the United States Congress with the aim of taking retaliatory measures against trading partners who did not offer US exports as easy an access to their markets as their imports received in American markets. Specific criticisms were aimed at Japan (ignoring US sources of the bilateral trade deficit), but they illustrate a general assymetrical conception of foreign markets as more intricately organized and more difficult to penetrate than one's own markets (Cline, 1982; Pomfret, 1984).

international rules to prevent such 'beggar-thy-neighbour' policies is strengthened. In the new trade theory of the 1980s, models with imperfect competition reinforce this conclusion; regional integration can lead to reduced marginal costs for insiders benefiting from the larger market, at the expense of competing firms located outside the integrated market. More controversially, in light of traditionally negative views of discriminatory trade policies, the new trade theory could also identify possibilities for global-welfare-enhancing preferential trading arrangements; in the absence of a global antitrust policy, trade barriers may improve global welfare by offsetting distortions resulting from imperfect competition. Nevertheless, the practical case for global free trade remains strong.

Regionalism can reduce the bargaining costs of reaching international trade agreements. Especially as the number of GATT/WTO members increased and their composition diversified, reaching agreement in that global forum may have become more difficult. Decline in US hegemony may also have impaired the capacity of GATT as a force for multilateral trade liberalization. Especially on complex or controversial issues, which have come to the fore as simple trade barriers such as tariffs or quota have shrivelled, global agreement may be impossible. Regional groups, in contrast, may reach agreement and introduce desirable measures among themselves without harm to outsiders.

The biggest area of disagreement between supporters and opponents of regionalism in the 1990s is over the best means to the agreed end of global trade liberalization. If regional arrangements are easier to negotiate, then they can permit experimentation and eventual extension of codes on trade-related measures such as investment, intellectual property rights, trade and the environment, and so forth. In this view, they are building blocks to a better world trading system. If regional arrangements evolve into exclusive blocs which disrupt multilateral trading patterns, then they are stumbling blocks in the way of creating a better world trading system (and may be a retrograde step).

This debate over means to an end has become sharper both because of the actual developments referred to at the start of this Introduction, and also because economists have become more aware of the importance of path dependence. Especially in international trade policy formation, the past matters and one thing often leads to another.[7] That lesson emerges very strongly from Part I of this book.

3. Outline of the Book

This book takes a four-part approach to analysing geographically discriminatory arrangements (GDAs).

Part I provides a narrative history of the world economy, in order to show how GDAs have evolved in response to current economic and political conditions and to perceptions about their impact. Chapters 2 and 3 describe the establishment of a world trade system based on non-discrimination in the mid-1800s, followed by the decline of this system and its dramatic collapse in the 1930s. The 1947 General Agreement on Tariffs and Trade (GATT) made non-discrimination the cornerstone of the postwar international trade regime (Chapter 4), but the practice of the next four decades saw a gradual erosion of the non-discrimination principle as more and more exceptions occurred (Chapter 5). The conflict between the GATT principle and practice came to a climax during the 1986–94 Uruguay Round of multilateral trade negotiations, when the two major trading units, the United States and the European Union, were simultaneously working on regional trading arrangements (Chapter 6). In the end the Uruguay Round did reach a positive conclusion, and the establishment of the World Trade Organization signalled a new era in world trade.

Part II presents the theory of GDAs. The mainstream Vinerian analysis and its extensions are presented in Chapters 8 and 9. Although this literature is often derided for its lack of unambiguous results, that attitude is wrong. The fundamental ambiguity of the welfare effects on a preference donor and on the world is an important result. Other conclusions about the distribution of gains and losses or about the effects of alternative forms of

[7] Krueger's (1990) classic exposition of the 'life of their own' approach concerns US sugar policies, a good example of discriminatory trade policies being perverted to achieve a succession of aims and ending up as a complex and costly arrangement, which would never have taken the form it had by the late 20th c. had it been designed afresh. Pomfret (1987) makes a similar point about the evolution of Canadian policy towards automobile imports during the 1980s. The comparative static and taxonomic approaches underlying the theories in Part II are poorly equipped to address path dependence.

GDAs (e.g. customs union versus free trade areas) are both important and unambiguous. Chapter 10 deals with newer research topics, introducing imperfect competition and new policy areas, as well as the problem of complexity. Chapter 11 deals with fundamental issues in international trade theory by questioning the normal practice of assuming nations to be massless points floating in space; especially with respect to regional trading arrangements (RTAs) geography may matter, and with regional integration it is important to ask when an economic union ceases to involve independent trading units (a question that is especially relevant to treatment of the EU).

The empirical evidence on discriminatory trading arrangements is assessed in Part III. This is organized by region and by type of GDA, although the purpose is to seek generalizations about the relative importance of the various effects of GDAs. European integration has dominated the literature, but it is difficult to measure the effects of such a major and evolving arrangement as the EU because it is difficult to know what would have occurred in the EU's absence. North American RTAs are also given a separate chapter because of the large number of empirical studies, often with innovative techniques, made since the mid-1980s. The trade and welfare effects of other RTAs and of trade preferences for developing countries are reviewed in Chapters 14 and 15, and are important for casting light on why GDAs usually fail to last, or become unimportant. Chapter 16 deals with some global issues, although these are difficult to address with economists' measurement tools. In general, the empirical literature is hampered by our lack of knowledge of the elasticity of substitution between imports from different countries, which is the crucial parameter where discrimination is concerned, but some findings do recur. The most common empirical results are that GDAs can have a substantial impact on the direction of trade, but the welfare effects are generally small (apart from a few cases where trade preferences offered by a large country to a small country provide substantial benefits to the latter).

Finally, in Part IV theory and practice are combined to provide explanations for the existence of discriminatory trading arrangements, and to examine the prospects for the world trading system. The distribution of costs and benefits underlying the small net welfare effects helps to explain the existence of GDAs, because the beneficiaries (i.e. producers from inside the GDA) are likely to be more aware of the effects and more politically influential than the losers (i.e. consumers and taxpayers in the GDA and producers in third countries). Non-economic and foreign policy considerations may also be important, as political influence is often related to economic influence (so the direction of trade matters to policy-makers), and perceptions play a role, as policy-makers often exaggerate the potential impact of GDAs. In the long run mistaken perceptions will be shown up and the net costs of GDAs may be more apparent, so that governments may be induced to reach agreement to reverse the proliferation of GDAs.

The concluding chapter summarizes the findings. The biggest issue of all—whether the world trading system can flourish on the basis of non-discrimination or whether it will inevitably collapse into a morass of GDAs—is difficult to answer because we have only one historical episode (i.e. that from the 1860s to the 1930s) to draw upon. That episode can be explained by the tendency of GDAs to proliferate owing to political economy and foreign policy considerations. The outcome, however, is not inevitable and depends critically on institutional and other ambient factors. The GATT helped to prevent a rerun of the collapse of the international trading system, and a broader commitment to liberal trade policies by WTO members augurs well for the future. Indeed, if global trade liberalization is on the agenda for the first decades of the twenty-first century, then discriminatory trade policies could become a thing of the past.

PART I

HISTORY

Introduction to Part I

Part I provides a narrative history of the role of discriminatory trading arrangements in the world economy. Chapter 2 deals with the system established in the 1860s and its operation until 1929, while Chapter 3 describes the collapse of that system in the 1930s. Chapter 4 examines the treatment of discriminatory trade policies in the General Agreement on Tariffs and Trade (GATT), which contained the rules governing international trade after 1947. Chapter 5 discusses the erosion of adherence to the non-discrimination principle between 1947 and 1985, while Chapter 6 deals with the conflict between regionalism and multilateralism during the Uruguay Round of multilateral trade negotiations. Chapter 7 examines the treatment of these matters in the World Trade Organization (WTO) and the main regionalism-related issues facing the WTO.

The political background and proximate causes and effects of policies and trading arrangements will be analysed, but more systematic analysis and evaluation will be done later in the book after looking at the relevant theory and empirical evidence. The main purpose of Part I is to present the material, which will be analysed in depth in the remainder of the book, and to impart a sense of the dynamics of international trading arrangements.

At no time in the past two centuries has the nature of the world trading system been static. The pressures towards non-discrimination are strong, since all countries benefit from buying from the cheapest source and from having no worse access to export markets than their competitors have. There is also a presumption that non-discrimination is the most efficient and probably most harmonious basis for international trade, a presumption that was strong among the architects of the post-1945 international economic system. Nevertheless, discriminatory trading arrangements have had a tendency to proliferate, and this part seeks to identify the facts of the proliferation process.

2

Evolution of the Most Favoured Nation Principle up to 1929

A history of discrimination in modern tariff policy can usefully begin in the nineteenth century. Although commercial treaties since the sixteenth century and perhaps even earlier had contained the most-favoured-nation (MFN) pledge, it was not until the second half of the nineteenth century that its general use became the basis of international tariff policies. Indeed, before the 1780s no major nation had uniform tariff treatment over its entire national territory, so that not even all nationals received equal access to the national market.

The history of the adoption of non-discrimination as the basis for most international trade in the third quarter of the nineteenth century and of the subsequent adherence to this principle up to 1929 provides the background for the collapse of the multilateral trading system during the 1930s and the revival of the non-discrimination principle in the GATT. The pre-1930 experience also provides examples of discriminatory trade policies being adopted and illustrations of their intended purpose and of their unforeseen disadvantages, which extends the empirical base for analysis of such arrangements in Part IV.

1. The MFN Clause up to 1870

From the end of the Napoleonic Wars until the 1870s, internal tariff unification was accompanied by a long movement towards freer external trade by the major European nations. The free trade movement was led by Britain, whose almost total elimination of tariffs by 1860 simultaneously eliminated discrimination among trading partners. Britain did not seek to impose universal free trade, and acquiesced in the introduction of protective tariffs by British colonies (e.g. Victoria in 1851, Canada in 1858–9, and the South African colonies in 1866–7), and in the 1854–66 preferential trading arrangement between the North American colonies and the USA. Nevertheless, British influence on other European countries' tariff policies was strong, and they reduced their tariffs (Kindleberger, 1975). The instrument for ensuring that tariff reduction was accomplished by diminishing discrimination among trading partners was the inclusion of the most-favoured-nation clause in commercial treaties.[1]

The MFN clause took two forms: unconditional and conditional. The unconditional form obligated a treaty signatory to extend to its co-signatory any trade concessions granted to third countries now or in the future without reservation. The conditional MFN clause granted the co-signatory opportunity to enjoy the same treatment as a third country provided that it offered the same compensation as the other country had given to obtain favoured treatment.

In Europe the conditional form was often used between 1820 and 1860, but was similar in effect to unconditional MFN treatment because of the prevalence of single-schedule tariffs and rarity of special concessions. Moreover, a single treaty with an unconditional clause rendered inoperative any conditionality in MFN clauses of treaties involving the same countries; that is, if country A has a conditional MFN clause in its treaty with B and an unconditional MFN clause in its treaty with C, then a tariff concession granted by A to D for compensation must be granted to C without compensation and, although B cannot claim the concession automatically because D receives it, B can do so because C receives it—which amounts to B's obtaining MFN treatment without having to offer compensation to A equal to that given by D. The last European attempt to use the conditional form as a way to withhold automatic extension of MFN treatment was by Sardinia in 1851, but before the year's end Sardinia found it necessary to concede unconditional MFN treatment in order to obtain a commercial treaty with Austria, which had the effect

[1] Earlier commercial treaties which did not include the MFN clause were explicitly discriminatory (e.g. the 1703 Methuen Treaty favoured Anglo-Portuguese trade by discriminating against France) and were for this reason strongly criticized by economists (see the chapter on commercial treaties in Smith, 1776). The criticisms no longer applied when the unconditional MFN clause was inserted in treaties (i.e. after 1823 in the case of Britain).

of making the MFN provisions in previous Sardinian treaties unconditional; meanwhile, Sardinia had probably received poorer terms in the earlier treaties than if it had been willing to grant unconditional MFN treatment (Viner, 1931). By the time of the 1860 Anglo-French commercial treaty the unconditional MFN clause had become the norm in European tariff treaties; the continental European nations tended to have, at most, two-tier tariff schedules with one rate for treaty partners and one for the rest of the world.

The sole important practitioner of conditional MFN treatment was the United States.[2] From its first commercial treaty, with France in 1778, until 1923 the USA maintained that MFN pledges must be interpreted as conditional, even when the precise wording of a treaty was unclear. In the only case where the USA recognized that an unambiguously unconditional MFN pledge had been granted (the 1850 treaty with Switzerland), as soon as other countries claimed privileges granted by the USA for compensation to one country but then granted freely to Switzerland, the United States refused further gratuitous extension of the privileges and served notice of termination of the clause in the Swiss treaty (US Tariff Commission, 1919, 428). At the same time, the USA did not hesitate to claim from treaty partners benefits that were granted freely in consequence of unconditional MFN pledges to third countries. Since all other major trading nations had signed unconditional MFN clauses, the USA was claiming MFN treatment unconditionally but offering it conditionally. Moreover, the conditionality of US offers was open to varying interpretations. In connection with favourable treatment given to Cuba and Hawaii, the USA appealed to 'special circumstances' as justification for refusing other countries the opportunity to make similar bargains. In 1897 the USA gave special tariff reductions to several European countries in return for minor reductions in their high tariffs, but withheld them from Britain which did not have tariffs to reduce; earlier the USA had passed on to Bremen favours given to Belgium on precisely the grounds that Bremen already had lower duties than Belgium in the area of

[2] The Latin American countries and Japan, following the American example, also used the conditional form, but since they had single-schedule tariffs and made no special concessions to other countries they rarely, if ever, had occasion to invoke the conditional provision.

Belgian compensation and was thus entitled to the favours under the conditional MFN clause of the treaty with the USA.[3] Given such arbitrary interpretation of the equivalent compensation required, the American conditional MFN pledge could scarcely be considered most-favoured-nation treatment at all.

Several customs unions were formed during the second and third quarters of the nineteenth century. Almost all were associated with the formation of new nations and, as such, were a counterpart to the tariff unification which had made customs boundaries correspond to the political boundaries of established nations during the previous half century.[4] The most important were the German Zollverein, the Italian post-unification free trade area (a customs union after 1887), the Canadian Confederation, and the union of Moldavia and Wallachia (future Romania); the later Australian and South African customs unions fall into the same category. A few customs unions involving a large and a small country guaranteed the smaller country's independence and were motivated by administrative convenience. (The Italy–San Marino and France–Monaco customs unions both involved small independent states turned into enclaves after Italian unification.) These departures from MFN treatment aroused little foreign opposition. The proposed Franco-Belgian customs union of 1840, on the other hand, invoked protests from Britain and Prussia, although the complaints were of violating Belgian neutrality obligations rather than being directed at MFN commitments.[5]

In sum, tariff history from 1820 to the 1870s was dominated by two trends: the consolidation of national tariff areas, and the movement towards freer trade among nations. The former trend introduced some new discrimination, but discrimination in favour

[3] These and other examples are given in Viner (1924). He concludes that 'the right to receive . . . concessions granted to a third country for compensation is of little practical value. The grantor of concessions . . . is itself the judge of the equivalence of the compensation offered for the same concessions by other countries. If it does not wish to extend its concessions to third countries, it need only deny the equivalence of the compensation offered.'

[4] Customs union had been completed by the USA in 1787, France in 1790, Britain and Ireland in 1826 and Spain and Switzerland during the 1840s. It came later in the century in Denmark and Austria-Hungary, and Czarist Russia never had a uniform tariff throughout its territory.

[5] The French response that a commercial treaty could not threaten political independence was accepted by Austria, but Britain and Prussia were opposed to any increase in French influence over Belgium (Viner, 1950, 87).

of fellow-nationals was acceptable. The latter trend was associated with diminishing discrimination in international trade as tariff reductions were passed around immediately in accord with MFN pledges. Both trends came to a rapid climax between 1860 and 1871, when Italian and German unification were complete and France abandoned protectionism by signing with other Europeans commercial treaties containing unconditional MFN clauses. By the 1870s almost all intra-European trade was being conducted at the MFN treaty tariff rates, with 'the almost complete disappearance of discrimination against particular countries' (Haight, 1941, 38). The only major exceptions to these trends were the hodge-podge of tariff regimes that characterized the Austrian and Russian Empires and the American conditional MFN interpretation.

2. From 1870 to 1914

Among the European countries that dominated nineteenth-century international trade, 1870 marked a high point in free trade and in the absence of discrimination among trading partners.[6] Between 1870 and 1914 trade became less free and discrimination became more common. Both Germany and France had high and rising tariffs by 1914, and only Britain and some small countries remained committed to free or almost free trade. In practice, the situation with respect to discrimination was not so different in 1914 from half a century earlier, but the commitment to liberal non-discriminatory trade policies had been eroded and this paved the way for the international economic order (or disorder) of the interwar period.

The forces behind increased protectionism were growing nationalism and the long depression which took up most of the last quarter of the century. Growing nationalism led several countries to reverse the pre-1870 commitment to low tariffs embodied in treaties containing MFN clauses. Reclaiming of tariff autonomy (i.e. freed from international commitments) was a prelude to more protective tariffs for agriculture, as world grain prices began to decline rapidly after 1873,[7] and then for national industries.

[6] Bairoch (1989) argues that free trade peaked in Europe during the period 1866–77.

[7] National responses to falling grain prices are analysed in Kindleberger (1951).

French commitment to the 1860s treaty system had never been very deep. Napoleon III negotiated the 1860 Anglo-French treaty with the political objective of inducing English non-intervention in Italy, and there was strong opposition within the French Parliament both to the treaty's content and to the principle of Parliament not being involved. After the fall of the Empire in 1870, the Third Republic's leadership favoured protectionist trade policies and decision-making was returned to Parliament where protectionist interests were strong. By 1892 the treaty system of tariffs set for twelve years and extended on an MFN basis had been replaced by an autonomous two-tariff system, whereby partners receiving MFN treatment faced the lower of the two tariffs (but had no guarantee against changes in its level), and this treatment could be revoked upon twelve months' notice. The new system was associated with rising tariff levels, but in itself did not involve increased discrimination. In 1913 most of France's imports (involving some twenty-five countries, including all of Europe) entered at the lower rate, while all imports from several South American states and British Dominions faced the higher rates and imports from the USA, Canada, and some tropical countries were subject to the lower tariff on a fixed list of products and to the higher tariff on unlisted goods (Haight, 1941, 70). There were, however, some temporary episodes of discrimination: major tariff wars with Italy and Switzerland, and minor disputes involving Romania, Spain and Belgium. The Franco-Italian trade war was the economic repercussion of Italy's decision in the early 1880s to ally with Germany and Austria-Hungary rather than with France. The Franco-Swiss trade war arose from Swiss opposition to France's 1892 tariff increases.

More important than actual discriminatory trade policies was the philosophical distancing of the French leadership not only from free trade, but from the MFN principle. Inclusion of the MFN clause in the 1871 Treaty imposed on France by a victorious Prussia was a source of guilt by association (Viner 1931)—although, ironically, the French negotiators had wanted this guarantee against German discrimination (Haight, 1941, 65). The attraction of the American conditional interpretation also grew, as the USA became more competitive in industrial goods and seemed to be gaining the benefits of MFN treatment without paying the full price (although, as we have just seen, even in

French markets the USA was not receiving full most-favoured treatment). Thirdly, the growing practice of designing tariff classifications so detailed as to discriminate in effect against specific supplying countries induced the belief that MFN obligations were not yielding France all the benefits that it should receive in other markets. Underlying these specific reservations, the growth of nationalism and of international tensions were succouring the view that commercial policy should be an instrument of foreign policy (as used against Italy in the 1880s and 1890s), and MFN obligations were an obstacle to such use.

Germany also stressed autonomous tariff-making and, beginning in 1879, this was associated with increased protection. After the initial tariff increases, and again after the 1902–5 tariff increases, however, Germany signed long-term commercial treaties (usually for twelve years) containing unconditional MFN clauses. Thus, the MFN principle was not abandoned, although it was undermined by an increasingly detailed tariff schedule. The 1902 tariff enumerated 1446 items, compared with the 387 enumerated in the previous tariff.[8]

One frequently quoted item in the 1902 tariff, which allowed special treatment for Switzerland without violating MFN obligations to countries exporting cattle from lower altitudes, was: 'Large dapple mountain cattle or brown cattle reared at a spot at least 300 metres above sea level and having at least one month's grazing each year at a spot at least 800 metres above sea level.' After quoting this item, Viner (1931) argues that isolated examples offer no proof that tariff specialization had been carried to absurd lengths, but he goes on to make the important point with respect to MFN treatment 'that no formula is proof against bad faith'. Unfortunately, in the increasingly tense atmosphere among European nations during the years leading up to the First World War, good faith was in diminishing supply and each country was willing to read the worst into others' behaviour. Germany

[8] These figures are from von Matlekovits (1906, 251–2), quoted by the US Tariff Commission (1919, 483). Delle-Donne (1929, 19) makes the same point but gives different figures: an increase from 394 items in the 1879 tariff to 946 in the 1902 tariff. The discrepancy may arise from inclusion of subdivisions incorporated into the tariff schedule as the post-1902 treaties were being negotiated—a process which, according to von Matlekovits, was deliberately aimed at subverting the spirit of MFN treatment.

in particular was accused of unfair trade practices aimed at achieving political goals, e.g. predatory dumping to hamper industrialization in other countries and to dominate their trade. Although these accusations had some foundations (especially with respect to German dealings with Italy), much of the dispute seems to have arisen from Germany's rapid export growth, which was due in part to better (but fair) commercial practices.[9]

Elsewhere in Europe, Spain and Italy pursued protectionist policies, while the Netherlands, Belgium, and Denmark retained low single tariff systems. Great Britain remained committed to free trade, but domestic opposition from protectionists and Imperialists (who wanted general tariffs in order to grant Imperial Preference) was growing in strength, especially after the turn of the century.

The United States shared in the trend towards higher trade barriers, but maintained the conditional interpretation of the MFN clause. There was, however, growing dissatisfaction over failure to obtain best possible access to foreign markets. The United States, with the conditional MFN bargaining tool, received less favourable treatment for exports to continental Europe than did free trade Britain, which had nothing to offer in return for MFN treatment. This had been unimportant before the late nineteenth century, when American exports had been primary products facing low non-discriminatory trade barriers, but as its comparative advantage shifted into industrial products, unfavourable treatment of US exports became more damaging. Moreover, the situation was likely to get worse rather than better as the policies of both the government and large US corporations came under growing criticism in Western Europe, and proposals for concerted European action against American commercial competition started to circulate around the turn of the century (Viner, 1950, 22–4). Thus, just as the European nations were losing faith in MFN pledges, the USA was moving towards reform of commercial policy based on adoption of unconditional MFN treatment.

By 1914 tariffs were higher than half a century earlier everywhere except in Britain and the smaller north European countries.

[9] See Hirschman (1945, 54–8); German emphasis on personal contact, studying national variations in consumer tastes, and learning foreign languages were frequently noted in the contemporary French and British literature.

Increased protective tariffs paved the way for increased discrimination among trading partners. The trade wars between Switzerland and France (1893–5), Germany and Russia (1893–4), and Russia and the USA (1901–5) all involved discriminatory tariff retaliation against higher trade barriers. Recognition of the damage done to the protagonists (with benefits going to neutrals) was the main reason for these trade wars' short duration.

In other trade wars a stronger economy tried to impose its political will on a weaker one. Of these, the 1888–98 Franco-Italian trade war was the most important; it reduced their mutual trade by over 60 per cent and was believed to have hurt Italy more than France (Delle-Donne, 1929, 29), but it did not induce a reversal of alliances by Italy (France's political goal); and the consequent reorientation of Italian trade in this and the next decade, which contributed to Germany becoming Italy's main source of imports and market for exports by 1913, was presumably contrary to French foreign policy interests. Where the trade link was of minor importance to the smaller economy, a trade war could linger on for years without the larger power achieving its goal, e.g. Germany's trade wars with Spain (1892–1906) and with Canada (1897–1910).[10] Against these failures, it was widely believed that Germany had used commercial policy successfully to achieve political influence in geographically closer trading partners, although in the final analysis Germany was unable to secure Italy's co-operation when war broke out. The net result of 1870–1914 trade policy changes was probably some increases in discrimination accompanying higher trade barriers, but more importantly a growing willingness to use discriminatory trade policies for political purposes—even though the track record of such attempts was rather poor.

The pre-1914 period has been interpreted by Irwin (1993) as an example of progressive bilateralism providing building blocks for globally free trade. He divides the period at 1860 in order to distinguish between the failure of British efforts to encourage free trade by example and the rapid expansion of treaty-based

[10] The German attempt to force Canada to abandon Imperial Preferences failed miserably, as was obvious when Germany did not extend the trade war to the other Dominions when they granted Imperial Preferences during the following decade; but the trade war dragged on until Germany could extricate itself without too much loss of face.

liberalization after 1860. In fact, much of European trade during the 1850s was covered by treaties containing MFN clauses, and French embracement of the MFN principle in the 1860s was the final step. That this was a high point rather than a starting point is recognized by Irwin in a footnote (p. 116, n. 7), but he does not acknowledge the fragility of a multilateral system based on renewable and reversible treaties with no other constraints on national policy autonomy. Although international trade remained reasonably free and non-discriminatory between 1870 and 1914, signs of strain and fragility were accumulating.

3. From European War to Global Depression

With the outbreak of war in 1914, European governments controlled international trade by prohibiting trade with the enemy, regulating trade with neutrals, and favouring trade with allies. The full extent of the breakdown of European commitment to non-discriminatory trade policies was revealed not so much in these reactions to total war, but more fundamentally in the plans for a postwar international economic order. While the war's outcome was still uncertain, both sides were making commitments for a postwar trading system based on discrimination. Meanwhile, two forces were working in the opposite direction: American conversion to unconditional MFN treatment, and Britain's continuing (albeit weakened) commitment to free trade. The first of these forces was, however, nullified by the American delegation's unwillingness to consider plans for economic reform at the Versailles Conference; only Britain argued for their inclusion in the League of Nations Covenant, but the constraints were too weak to bind national policy-makers.[11] Succeeding international conferences called for the adoption of unconditional MFN treatment as the basis for international trading relations, but the calls were consistently ignored. On the whole, the decade after Versailles continued the post-1870 trend of increasing tolerance for discriminatory trade policies, preparing the way for

[11] Art. 23 of the Covenant contained 'the empty because ambiguous and indefinite formula pledging all the member countries to grant each other "equitable treatment"' (Viner, 1931). The subsequent history of international conferences and their ignored resolutions is analysed in an almost posthumous report (League of Nations, 1942).

wholesale abandonment of non-discrimination as a guiding principle after 1930.

During the war both sets of European allies were concerned with establishing closer postwar economic relations and discriminating against their wartime enemies. Negotiations between Germany and Austria-Hungary culminated in the Salzburg Treaty of October 1918, which provided for partial free trade between the signatories (Viner, 1950, 105–8). Whether the provisional internal tariffs covering about half of Austro-German trade would have been removed later to complete a Mitteleuropa free trade area remains hypothetical, as the treaty was cancelled by military defeat.

Meanwhile, Britain, France, Italy, and Russia had also been making plans for postwar economic co-operation. Especially among the continental European allies, the belief was strong that German economic policies had paved the way for war, and indeed had almost achieved the German political goal without war.[12] Briand, the French prime minister, opened the 1916 Paris Economic Conference by referring to 'the economic slavery into which the enemy sought to drag us' (Hirschman, 1945, 58). The Conference Resolutions called for postwar discrimination against the enemy and for mutual aid, but they masked disagreements about the extent of German exclusion from trade and of postwar economic co-operation among the allies.[13] The Paris Resolutions also aroused misgivings among neutrals, who would be outside the allied bloc, and especially in the USA, where President Wilson viewed 'exclusive economic leagues . . . no proper basis for a peace of any kind'.[14]

With American entry into the war and growing confidence of ultimate victory among America's allies, there was some backsliding from the Paris Resolutions. In particular, it became clear that discrimination against the enemy would be transitory. In

[12] Among the influential commentaries appearing on the eve of or early in the war were *La Germania alla conquista dell'Italia* by Preziosi (1914) and *Les Méthodes allemandes d'expansion économique* by Hauser (1915).

[13] Russia and Italy relied more than Britain or France upon German markets and were more fearful of economic retaliation, while all participants were concerned about relinquishing any sovereignty over commercial policies.

[14] Reported in the *New York Times*, 29 August 1917, and quoted in Hirschman (1945, 64); Wilson's original draft referred to such trading arrangements as 'childish'.

Britain the Balfour Committee on Commercial and Industrial Policy after the War, reporting in December 1917, envisaged no more than a brief period of prohibition against the enemy and was less concerned with economic co-operation among the wartime allies than with national commercial autonomy (e.g. to protect British industries, to grant Imperial Preference, and to reject decimalization of the currency). The prospects for postwar economic co-operation became even bleaker during 1918, and shortly after the Versailles Treaty was signed in June 1919 the Supreme Economic Council of the Allies was dissolved.

The commercial policy issue at the peace negotiations was no longer postwar co-operation against the enemy, but the conduct of national trade policies. The French and American positions were directly contradictory. French Minister of Commerce Clémentel declared in December 1918:

> the Government has denounced all commercial conventions which embody the most-favoured-nation clause. The clause will not reappear. It will never again poison our tariff policy. (quoted by Viner, 1931)

while the third of President Wilson's Fourteen Points required:

> The removal so far as possible of all economic barriers and the establishment of an equality of trade conditions among all the nations consenting to the peace and associating themselves for its maintenance,

i.e. unconditional MFN treatment as the basis of postwar trade. In the end the peace treaties evaded the conflict; the vanquished states were required to grant unconditional MFN treatment for a limited period,[15] while the victors' commercial policies were mentioned only in perfunctory terms. This outcome left the victorious nations (and, as it turned out, the vanquished after 1925) complete freedom of action in determining their commercial policies.[16] At international economic conferences during the 1920s

[15] For Germany the period was five years from January 1920 with possible extension by the League Council, and for Austria and Hungary, three years.

[16] Hirschman (1945, ch. 7) describes the outcome of economic sovereignty which was not subject to any international constraints (neither the common action of the Paris Resolutions nor the general rule of the Fourteen Points) as the worst of all possible outcomes. There seems, however, to have been no desire to place trade issues high on the Versailles agenda. (Reparations and war debts were more pressing economic questions.) The American delegation 'poured cold water on proposals for planning a charter for a better world economic order' (Viner, 1951, 285), perhaps because Wilson foresaw the added difficulties this would pose for Senate ratification of the Treaty.

attempts were made to re-establish unconditional MFN treatment as the guiding principle for international trade relations, but despite apparently positive communiqués the major trading nations would make no commitment compromising their tariff autonomy, including their power to discriminate among trading partners.

Despite the lack of an international economic code, European trade was on balance liberalized during the 1920s.[17] The French experience was crucial. In addition to renunciation of the unconditional MFN clause, French policy-makers were concerned with maintaining, or regaining, export markets, and after the collapse of Allied economic co-operation they were unwilling to risk losing markets by unilateral adoption of a state-managed trade policy; 'more important than the wish to discriminate was the desire for reciprocity' (Haight, 1941, 126), which led to adoption of conditional MFN treatment as French policy. The gap between minimum and maximum tariff rates was widened in 1921 from 50 to 300 per cent with the possibility of levying intermediate rates. The change was aimed mainly against Germany, who had to face the maximum rate but could not retaliate,[18] and was also intended to give greater bargaining space for negotiating bilateral treaties. In practice, the latter aim was unsuccessful because treaty partners demanded the minimum rate even more adamantly now that the spread was so large; of the fifty or so commercial treaties negotiated by France between 1919 and 1927, only a dozen involved intermediate rates and these covered only a limited list of goods (Haight, 1941, 129). The threat of retaliation limited discriminatory trade practices, and at the same time ad

[17] The main exception to this statement concerns the new nations created after the war. The political settlement, by raising the number of separate customs units in Europe from 20 to 27, itself increased trade discrimination. Attempts to maintain free trade among the successor states of south-eastern Europe (e.g. the Portorosa Protocol of 1921) failed, mainly because of nationalist desires to control trade policies, although revenue needs, protectionist lobbies, and internal regional conflicts also contributed. All of the south-east European states had 1927 tariff rates well above the 1913 Austro-Hungarian and Serbian average tariff rates of 22–3%: Czechoslovakia 31%, Hungary 30%, Yugoslavia 32%, Bulgaria 68%, and Romania 42% (Drabek, 1985; tariff rates from Liepmann, 1938, 415).

[18] The wide spread generated fears that German goods were being routed via Czechoslovakia or Austria to qualify for lower tariff rates. French administrative capacity for dealing with such evasion was not very great—in contrast to the complex rules of origin criteria included in post-1960s discriminatory trade arrangements—and rerouting may have reduced the policy's efficacy in hurting German exports.

valorem tariff rates were reduced by the postwar inflation.[19] In 1923 France began preparations for tariff reform but was overtaken by events, i.e. the 1925 monetary crisis and the January 1925 release of Germany from the obligation of granting unconditional MFN treatment, which was accompanied by imposition of the highest German duties on French exports. In consequence, France reverted to a conventional policy, initiated by the 1927 trade treaty with Germany and followed in 1928 by treaties with Switzerland, Belgium, Italy, Austria, and Czechoslovakia, so that by 1929 the situation was similar to that of 1867 in so far as a large part of the French tariff schedule was consolidated in international agreements. France's 1927 treaty with Germany played a similar role to the 1860 treaty with England in ushering in a system of conventions which established in effect non-discriminatory trade among the major European trading nations.

Britain and the United States were both outside this conventional system of non-discrimination, and both pursued (predominantly) non-discriminatory trade policies unilaterally. There were, however, trouble signs ahead in the form of shifts towards protectionism. Britain had been since 1860 a free trade country with import duties for purely revenue purposes on a dozen articles, notably tobacco, tea, and wines and spirits. The first protective tariffs—on cars and motorbikes, clocks and watches, musical instruments, and film—were the 1915 McKenna Duties, introduced to save cargo space for importing necessities but retained after the war. They were followed by the 1921 'Key Industries' Duties for infant industries (e.g. precision instruments, wireless valves, and some chemicals), and minor protective tariffs on hops and silk (1925) and on buttons and hollow ware (1928). The incidence was not great, and at the elections of 1906 and 1923, in which tariffs were a major issue, the protectionist party was defeated. Nevertheless, the free trade principle had been breached, and this was accompanied by discrimination as Empire-made imports were subject to preferential tariff rates.

US policy on tariff discrimination went in exactly the opposite direction to that of France. After rejecting the unconditional MFN

[19] The French tariff consisted mainly of specific duties and, although the duties were increased, a 1926 Parliamentary Committee reported that the postwar increase in duties did not compensate for more than half of the increase in prices (Condliffe, 1950, 480).

clause throughout its previous history, the USA embraced this clause in its war aims and in practice after 1923. At the Versailles peace talks the USA made no effort to force unconditional MFN treatment on to other countries, and afterwards tried to convert by example. Unfortunately, the example was flawed by some minor exceptions of countries receiving better than MFN treatment (e.g. Cuba) and, more importantly, by America's high tariff policy. The American position was that tariff levels were a domestic matter, but once they had been set all trading partners should be treated equally. Critics of this position, most vociferous in France, argued that a country that excluded one's exports could not expect MFN treatment of its own exports—essentially the prewar American position! It was only after the retaliation following the 1930 American tariff hike that the USA was again willing to consider this argument seriously.

Jacob Viner (1951, 259) has claimed that the general trend of trade barriers from the late 1870s to the Second World War was an increase in the discriminatory character of trade policies. The 1920s, however, formed an intermission in this process. Apart from the creation of new customs units in Eastern Europe following the postwar territorial rearrangements, there was little net change in the height or discriminatory character of the major trading nations' tariffs (Table 2.1). By the late 1920s there was even optimism in some quarters about the prospects for reducing trade barriers through international actions. Co-operation had yielded substantial results in the areas of refugee settlement, public health, fighting the drug traffic, and the financial reconstruction of Austria and Hungary. When League of Nations officials summoned the 1927 World Economic Conference, 'they realized that they were attacking the citadel of economic nationalism. Success had seemed to lie within their grasp' (Condliffe, 1950, 487). In fact, they were deluded: delegates of the fifty nations unanimously adopted a final Conference report condemning protectionist tariff policies and calling for tariff reduction, but the numerous trade treaties signed between 1927 and 1929 tended to consolidate existing tariffs, and only a few small countries (e.g. Austria, Belgium and Czechoslovakia) actually lowered any tariffs.

Within a few years the same officials were facing a hopeless salvage operation. The nationalistic forces building up in all countries, the willingness to use trade policies to further political

TABLE 2.1 Average Tariff Levels, 1913 and 1925 (%)

	1913	1925
Netherlands	3	4
Denmark	9	6
Belgium	6	8
Switzerland	7	11
Germany	12	12
France	18	12
Austria	18	12
Sweden	16	13
Italy	17	17
Spain	33	44
UK	—	4
India	4	14
Canada	18	16
Australia	17	25
Argentina	26	26
USA	33	29

Note on method: The *ad valorem* equivalent of duties imposed on the 20 representative exports of 14 countries were calculated for each importing nation; the average tariff levels are unweighted arithmetic means. As the source document recognizes, the sampling, calculation of prices and weighting procedure are all open to criticism, but when tariff schedules were in no way standardized and most duties were specific, any calculation of 'average' tariff rates involved heroic assumptions. Alternative estimates for the European nations are given in Table 3.1.

Source: League of Nations (1927, 15, method B1); Eastern European countries that were not independent tariff areas in 1913 are omitted.

goals, and the absence of any strong national or international defender of a trading system based on non-discrimination proved overwhelming. Rather than marking a new dawn, the late 1920s were a twilight phase in the sixty-year trend towards more discriminatory trade policies.

4. The Colonial Question

Although discriminatory trade arrangements existed between various metropolitan powers and their colonies, the trade arrangements in themselves were not a major source of conflict between 1860 and 1930. Before the 1850s most colonial arrangements had been based on exclusivity or, at least, strongly preferred treatment for the imperial country in its colonies. As Britain adopted free trade, British colonies were permitted an 'open door' policy with respect to their imports; this did not necessarily involve free trade (Canada and Victoria in particular adopted protective tariffs), but it did mean no discrimination among import suppliers.[20] The Netherlands and France followed suit during the 1850s and 1860s. In addition to unilaterally opened doors, non-discriminatory import policies were imposed by international treaty in 1885 for many African countries and later for Morocco, American Samoa, the Panama Canal Zone, the Philippines, and Korea (the last two for a ten-year period only). After the First World War similar conditions were attached to League of Nations 'B' Mandates (Tanganyika, Togoland, Cameroons, and Ruanda–Urandi).

Some colonies were assimilated into the metropolitan country's customs area, i.e. with internal free trade and a common external tariff. France adopted this approach towards Algeria as it gradually came under French control in the second half of the nineteenth century, and extended it to Indo-China in 1887–8 and to some small colonies in 1892. In practice, France retained some duties on imports from these colonies until 1928, when complete internal free trade was established and the colonies were given some flexibility in tariff setting for a list of foreign products.[21] Similar arrangements existed between Japan and Korea and Formosa and between the USA and Puerto Rico, Hawaii, and Alaska.

Finally, some colonial relations followed an intermediate path involving trade preferences but less than complete customs assimilation. Italy, Spain, and Portugal adopted this approach, as did France with her Pacific colonies, West Africa and Somaliland, and St Pierre and Miquelon, and the United States with the Virgin Islands, Guam, and the Philippines.[22] The revival of Imperial

[20] The Dominions gradually assumed full commercial policy autonomy and occasionally used this to make discriminatory trading arrangements, e.g. the 1854–66 Canadian–US Reciprocity Treaty described in the Appendix, and the Imperial Preference schemes described later in this chapter.

[21] At this time Tunis was also assimilated into the French customs area.

[22] The USA also had preferential trade arrangements with Hawaii (1875–1900) and Cuba (after 1903), although these were not described as colonies, and the USA received preferential tariff treatment from Brazil after 1904 (in consequence of a threatened tax on American coffee imports). After adopting unconditional MFN treatment in 1923, the USA requested that Brazil cease these preferences.

Preference within the British Empire also took this form as Canada (in 1897), New Zealand (1903), South Africa (1904), and Australia (1907) offered tariff preferences to Britain, which were reciprocated on a small scale after 1919. Some parts of the Empire, e.g. India and Newfoundland, gave no preferences to Britain before the late 1920s, and 'All the various preferences granted by Great Britain before 1931 did not amount to very much' (Benham, 1941, 89–90).

5. Conclusions

Between 1860 and 1930 the principle of non-discrimination governed the commercial policies of the major trading nations. First, the most important of these nations before the First World War, Great Britain, had almost totally free trade which left no room for discrimination; even when minor protective duties were introduced and Imperial Preference granted in 1919, the preference margins were small. Secondly, the continental European nations gave priority to not being discriminated against in their export markets, and to this end incorporated the unconditional MFN clause into their commercial treaties. Up to 1930 this practice survived the post-1870s protectionism, pre-1914 aggressive competition from Germany, and the post-1914 renunciation of the unconditional MFN clause by France. Thirdly, the United States, which had been outside the system of unconditional MFN treatment before 1917, made an about-turn because the USA felt that its bargaining approach was ineffective in securing favourable access to export markets and was the source of frequent controversies in international relations.

At the same time, there were frequent deviations from non-discriminatory policies. The USA before 1919 and France after 1919 tried to use differentiated tariff treatment as a bargaining lever to open export markets. More commonly, the goal was political, as in Germany's use of discriminatory export policies to create spheres of influence during the early twentieth century, in the 1888–98 Franco-Italian tariff war, in Britain's acceptance of Imperial Preference after the First World War, and in the 1916 Paris Resolutions. Although the deviations were not predominant before 1930, they provided evidence of governments viewing discriminatory trade policies as serving national purposes, while the Versailles Peace negotiations and various international conferences of the 1920s showed the lack of commitment to international enforcement of a world trading system based upon non-discrimination. The potent mixture of discriminatory trade policies being viewed as serving national goals and being unfettered by international constraints exploded after 1930, and the multilateral trading system went into severe decline.

3

Commercial Policies in the 1930s

Between 1929 and 1939, government policies disrupted the flow of international trade, turned it increasingly into bilateral channels, and frequently determined which channels should be strengthened and which weakened. The result was a reduction of global welfare as opportunities for specialization were forgone and the world's resources misallocated. The process by which this occurred is less easy to describe; adverse conditions existed in all the major trading nations, and once the process had begun it tended to be self-reinforcing as the effects of one measure became the cause of others. Similarly, the nationalism, which was one of the causes of growing government intervention, was itself fanned by discriminatory trade measures which contributed to the deterioration of international relations which would lead to world war.

Assigning blame for the breakdown of the international trading system based on non-discrimination is a difficult task. By the late 1930s, it was clearly continental European countries that had most comprehensively rejected the MFN principle, but they can scarcely be seen as originators of the breakdown—neither German nor Italian trade policy became obviously discriminatory before 1934. The initial impetus for the MFN clause falling into disrepute was actions by the USA and Britain—ironically, two countries that claimed continuing adherence to unconditional MFN treatment until the outbreak of war.

Despite resolutions that 'commercial treaties should contain the unconditional most-favoured nation clause in its broadest and most liberal form' (Final Report of the 1927 World Economic Conference), several continental European countries were reluctant to apply tariff reductions to imports from countries with high non-negotiable tariffs. When the butt of this criticism, the USA, embarked in 1929 on the process of raising already high tariffs, trade liberalization within Europe was killed by the prospect of having to pass on any tariff reductions to the USA. Among the immediate political consequences were proposals for a United States of Europe, and among the more durable economic consequences were a retaliatory wave of protection and growing dissatisfaction with the MFN principle.

Britain did not retaliate in 1930 and remained committed to the MFN principle, but when Britain joined the protectionist tide in late 1931 this involved strengthening the largest preferential trading arrangement, covering about a third of world trade. Britain claimed that Imperial Preference was not inconsistent with MFN pledges because the participants were 'British' and MFN claimants received the best treatment among foreigners—a distinction viewed by other countries as unconvincing when applied to the Dominions.[1] Britain's adherence to the MFN principle was also rendered somewhat hypocritical by the overt use of bargaining pressure to gain better treatment than others in British export markets, especially for coal sales to northern Europe; the benefits from these arrangements were small, but in negotiating them Britain has been blamed for starting the fashion for bilateral bargaining.

The international monetary crisis from 1931 onwards provided an even greater stimulus for discriminatory trade policies than the increased protectionism of the early 1930s had done. Faced with severe shortages of means of payment for foreign transactions, country after country introduced exchange controls, which were accompanied by other non-tariff barriers to trade and by attempts at bilateral balancing of international transactions. By 1934–5, when the worst of the depression was over and some monetary stability had been restored, administrative controls of international trade had become so well developed that many countries decided to maintain them as tools of national policy and, within continental Europe and parts of Asia at least, there was no halt to the decline of multilateral non-discriminatory trade practices. At this stage the USA and, less decidedly, Britain stood for liberalization and non-discrimination, but their capacity for economic leadership was limited and they were powerless to reverse the trend before the outbreak of war.

[1] France adopted a similar argument in assimilating various colonies, but aroused less opposition. The difference seemed to lie in the independence of Australia, Canada, New Zealand, and South Africa in almost all areas, including commercial policy, and in the size of the Dominions' trading activities.

The chronology and conjuncture of events are important for understanding trade policy developments of the 1930s. In many instances one thing led to another, and the situation was not easily reversible once new vested interests had been created or new possibilities perceived. On other occasions policy innovations passed fortuitously unchecked because they were overshadowed by contemporaneous events. Nevertheless, a narrative approach to the decade would be too unwieldy for present purposes and this chapter will be organized by topics: tariff barriers, non-tariff barriers, Imperial policies, and then an assessment of the consequences of the commercial policies of the 1930s.

1. Higher Tariffs

During the first decade after the First World War the net direction of tariff changes was unclear. The 1927 World Economic Conference had raised hopes that tariffs might be reduced, but in 1928–9 the movement was in the opposite direction. The stimulus was falling primary product prices. Among major grain importers, Germany raised MFN duties on wheat by 29 per cent and Italy by 87 per cent between the beginning of 1928 and July 1929; over the following twelve months these duties were further increased by 134 and 18 per cent, while French duties on wheat went up by 128 per cent (Gordon, 1941, 23).[2] In the face of mounting balance of payments crises, Argentina and Australia left the gold standard, while the agricultural counties of eastern Europe imposed higher general tariffs.[3]

Meanwhile, and more important, early in 1929 a highly protectionist tariff bill began its slow progress through the American

[2] Many European grain importers also introduced milling requirements (specifying a minimum domestic grain content for flour), which were varied according to the competitive pressures on domestic farmers. Italian government funds had been used to promote agricultural efficiency since Mussolini declared the Battaglia del Grano in 1925.

[3] The actions described in this paragraph were generally non-discriminatory, but in at least one case a bilateral trade war broke out. Czechoslovakia's introduction of 90% cereal duties led to an open trade war with Hungary after their commercial treaty expired in December 1930; Czechoslovakia's imports from Hungary fell from $47 m in 1930 to $7 m in 1931, while Hungarian imports from Czechoslovakia fell from $51 m to $15 m and never recovered (Drabek, 1985, 441 and 490–1).

legislative system. Despite many international protests at every stage (with thinly veiled threats of retaliation) and a famous warning letter from American economists, Congressmen paid attention only to domestic interests, and when the bill became law in June 1930 US tariffs were raised well above their already high level. Upward tariff revision followed almost immediately in Canada, Cuba, Mexico, France, Italy, Spain, Australia, New Zealand, and other countries.

Why did the 1930 tariff, unlike previous US tariff revisions, provoke rapid and widespread retaliation? First, depression and a lack of new loans from the USA left debtor countries with trade deficits little alternative to reducing imports; the spectacle of the leading creditor nation running a trade surplus and adopting a highly projectionist tariff was absurd, but the debtors had to respond and since all countries could not run simultaneous trade surpluses a vicious circle was set in motion. Secondly, there had been few competing suppliers of the main US exports (i.e. cotton, wheat, meats, wood, and oil products) before the late nineteenth century, but since then American exports had become more vulnerable to retaliation as the share of manufactured goods increased and as US raw materials faced competition from other suppliers. The highly visible boom in American automobile exports during the second half of the 1920s offered one obvious target for retaliation. At the same time, there was less fear of losing a trade war with the USA, since trading partners considered the 1930 tariff already close to prohibitive on many of their important exports.

The American tariff posed a threat to the non-discrimination principle because an appropriate response was to retaliate selectively against US exports. The French foreign minister, Briand, tried from 1929 on to organize concerted European action through the establishment of a United States of Europe, but in the face of political opposition to French-led federalism the idea made no progress. Plans for regional tariff arrangements among Eastern European countries were forestalled by British and American insistence on their MFN rights. Countries were thus left to make national responses, and proved reluctant to abandon their MFN clauses. Only Spain, which had already announced in 1927 that the USA might not receive MFN treatment on future tariff revisions,[4] explicitly withdrew MFN treatment from the USA by raising tariffs on imports of special interest to the USA (e.g. automobiles, tyres, and radios) and then negotiating with France reductions of these tariffs which were passed on to other non-US suppliers.

Other countries maintained the letter of their MFN pledges, but found ways to discriminate in effect against American exports. Immediately after the US tariff increase, Italy raised duties on automobiles, and within five weeks had negotiated a treaty with the USSR, trading cars, trucks, and ships for Russian wheat, coal, wood, and oil products. Using either public procurement or pressure on private importers, the Italian government also made agreements to obtain copper from Belgium and Chile and cotton from Egypt and Turkey. In consequence, while Italian exports to the USA fell from $90 million in 1929 to $55 million in 1931, imports from the USA dropped from $186 million to $70 million. European carmakers exploited not only their tariff advantage in Spain but also the widespread anti-Americanism aroused by the 1930 tariff, to end American exports' strong market position for ever.[5] The Canadian elections, held a month after the US tariff became law, returned a Conservative government which immediately raised import duties; increased general protection fell most heavily on imports from the USA, the largest supplier, as imports from the second largest supplier, Britain, entered at Imperial Preference rates. American firms tried to evade the obstacles by investing in Canada and by sourcing their exports via Canadian

[4] Spanish exports had been especially hurt during the 1920s by American policies, sometimes unintentionally but in other cases by design. Spain's main prewar export, alcoholic beverages, was eliminated by Prohibition. When Spanish exporters shifted to grapes, these were banned on the grounds of preventing the Mediterranean fruit fly from reaching the USA, and the ban was maintained on imports of all Spanish fruit even after adequate safeguards had been proven. With wine and fruit excluded, Spain's main export to the USA in the 1920s was cork, and this was hampered by an American requirement that 'Made in Spain' be stamped on each cork—a process allegedly costing more than the cork itself (J. M. Jones, 1934, ch. 2).

[5] American automobile sales in Spain and Italy were decimated, from 13,930 units in 1929 to 1436 in 1931 (J. M. Jones, 1934, 61 and 82). In Switzerland opposition to the new US tariff on watch and clock imports led the public sector to cancel orders for American cars. Jones reports how Swiss agents for an American vacuum cleaner company carried statements signed by the British Consul attesting that their models had been made in Canada.

branch plants or European assembly points, but such practices increased costs and could be shortcircuited.

The 1930 Hawley–Smoot tariff and its aftermath illustrated the dangers of a world trading system based on autonomous tariff policies. Reaction to an unreasonably large tariff increase may be so strong that unconditional MFN pledges are insufficient to prevent discriminatory retaliation. On this occasion most countries were careful not to contravene explicitly their MFN obligations, but instead found ways to bypass them. Flouting the spirit of MFN treatment would alone have contributed to diminishing respect for the principle of non-discrimination, but in the atmosphere of the early 1930s the situation was made even worse by the absence of any willingness to admit that steps had been taken in a wrong direction. The United States would not admit that other countries' tariff hikes were retaliatory since this would throw into question the view that tariff levels are solely a domestic matter, while some of the retaliating countries were happy for an excuse to increase tariff barriers and hopefully protect domestic employment. The whole episode increased the barriers to world trade, exacerbated the depression,[6] fuelled economic nationalism, and legitimized unilateral tariff actions which bent the non-discrimination principle.

A second momentous tariff increase was that introduced by Great Britain as an extraordinary measure in November 1931 and consolidated in the February 1932 Import Duties Act. The Act established a general 10 per cent tariff on foreign goods, with provision for higher rates on luxuries or where British production was threatened, and for higher or lower rates on imports from countries discriminating against or favouring British exports. The penalty duties were applied rarely and briefly, so that in practice

[6] The role of the Hawley–Smoot tariff in the Great Depression is debated. Initially, the impact may have been positive for the USA (via Keynesian multiplier effects) but harmful to the rest of the world, but retaliation would feed back negative effects on the US economy so that in the long run all countries were worse off. Meltzer (1976, 469) ascribes a larger role, concluding that 'the Hawley–Smoot tariff . . . worked to convert a sizeable recession into a severe depression' by impeding the equilibrating specie flow mechanism (the US balance of payments went from deficit to surplus and prices fell less there than elsewhere, when a larger fall was required for adjustment) and then, after retaliation hurt the farm sector, by causing bank failures in agricultural regions. For comments on Meltzer's argument see Brunner (1981, 82, 150, 158 and 332).

the tariff was non-discriminatory among non-Empire countries.[7] Nevertheless, by abandoning free trade Britain opened the door to meaningful Imperial Preference (agreed upon at Ottawa in the summer of 1932) and to the possibility of other discriminatory trading practices. In addition, Britain abdicated any position of leadership or attempt to provide an example, as British trade policy for the rest of the decade was characterized by opportunism and vacillation.

Why did Britain abandon free trade? Capie (1983) has argued convincingly that for some years, and especially after the First World War, domestic producers and Empire-free traders had been gaining support for widespread protection. Although the Conservative Party lost the 1923 election on the tariff issue, important party leaders remained committed to protection, and when they gained power at an opportune moment (October 1931) the tariff was rapidly introduced. The worldwide increase in tariffs during 1930 and 1931 (plus the adoption of import quotas by France in summer 1931) and the international financial crisis facilitated Britain's resort to protection, but they appear to have been subsidiary as causes.[8]

[7] The Irish Free State occupied a peculiar position. Up to 1932 both Ireland and the UK had essentially free trade policies, and in that year both embraced protection. More important for their bilateral trade was the outbreak of a trade war in 1932, when the Irish government withheld payment of annuities due under pre-independence land reform schemes and the British government responded with levies on agricultural imports from Ireland to recoup the amount withheld. Quotas and retaliatory duties by both sides lasted until the 1938 Anglo-Irish Trade Agreement, which gave most Irish goods free entry to the UK and preferential treatment for most British exports to Ireland.

[8] In both cases, timing suggests no close casual link. The 1931 financial crisis precipitated renewed debate over the need for a general tariff on balance of payments grounds, but the government abandoned the gold standard in September before any decision in favour of a tariff had been taken. After the October election the financial crisis could be dealt with (and was being dealt with) by devaluation of the pound. Eichengreen (1981) argues that the decision to introduce the general tariff was dominated by concern that devaluation alone would not be sufficient to remove the external constraint on recovery, but the key policymakers whom he quotes (e.g. Chamberlain, the Chancellor of the Exchequer after October) were long-time protectionists utilizing any favourable argument, rather than new converts under the pressure of recent events. It is even clearer that Britain was not retaliating against other countries' trade barriers, although frustration over a lack of bargaining chips had been rising with the height of those barriers. The Hawley–Smoot tariff had an indirect impact by helping to put into power in Canada a Conservative prime minister vociferously committed to converting Britain to meaningful Imperial Preference. The view expressed by the

The direction of British trade policy between 1932 and the outbreak of war is unclear. Tariff revisions were generally upward, some quantitative restrictions and bilateral agreements were introduced, and in 1933 the government warned that unconditional MFN treatment would not be granted indefinitely to countries refusing concessions to British exports (Gordon, 1941, 409 n.). The last threat was rarely exercised,[9] but Britain did succeed in obtaining from the Scandinavian and Baltic countries guaranteed purchases for exports (especially coal) which far exceeded recent market shares.[10] Lewis (1949, 85 and 168) blames 'the British urge to bilateralism . . . exploiting bargaining power' for starting a fashion, but these discriminatory actions were relatively mild. Towards imports, Britain maintained unconditional MFN treatment for foreign goods, apart from restrictive quotas on imports of Japanese textiles into home and colonial markets. Despite negotiating some bilateral clearing agreements, Britain remained in the camp of the free exchange countries—as reflected in British participation in the 1936 Tripartite Agreement and co-operation with the USA during the late 1930s (including their 1938 trade agreement). There was, however, lingering doubt as to the strength of Britain's commitment to an open multilateral trading

French minister, Bonnet—'One fact is evident: it is that Britain is not free. Its dominions and in particular Canada whose Prime Minister Bennett is a man of extraordinary violence have a predominant influence on her, to the point of modifying totally her opinion in the space of a few seconds' (Kindleberger, 1986, 303 n.)—is overdrawn, but makes the point that British decisions were not taken in a trade policy vacuum.

[9] The most important case was the 20% surtax imposed on imports from France for five months in 1934, because French import quotas failed to give Britain a 'fair' market share (Haight, 1941, 173–4; Benham, 1941, 130).

[10] Agreements in 1933 set market shares for British coal at 80% of Danish coal imports, 70% of Norwegian coal imports, and 47% of Swedish coal imports; the 1932 actual shares had been 58%, 43%, and 30%. If compared to a remote enough base year (i.e. at least before Britain's 1926 strike) it could be claimed that no discrimination was intended, but clearly the agreements reflected British bargaining power rather than current 'free market equilibrium' shares (Gordon, 1941, 411–12). Similar agreements guaranteed British coal 77% of Iceland's coal imports, 75% in Finland, 85% in Estonia, 70% in Latvia and 80% in Lithuania (Benham, 1941, 131). These agreements helped British market shares in the countries concerned (most clearly in Denmark, whose bargaining position was weakest), but there may not have been a net gain as competitors' redirected exports displaced British coal exports to other countries (Lewis, 1949, 84). Rooth (1984; 1986) has argued that Britain's dismal export performance outside the Scandinavian and Baltic regions was due to other factors; the problem is that we have no well-specified model of the counterfactual situation.

TABLE 3.1 Average Tariff Levels, European Countries, 1913, 1927, and 1931 (%)

	1913	1927	1931
Germany	16.7	20.4	40.7
France	23.6	23.0	38.0
Italy	24.8	27.8	48.3
Belgium	14.2	11.0	17.4
Switzerland	10.5	16.8	26.4
Sweden	27.6	20.0	26.8
Finland	35.0	31.8	48.2
Spain	37.0	49.0	68.5
Austria	22.8 (Austria, Czechoslovakia, Hungary)	17.5	36.0
Czechoslovakia		31.3	50.0
Hungary		30.0	45.0
Bulgaria	22.8	67.5	96.5
Poland	(a)	53.5	67.5
Romania	30.3	42.3	63.0
Yugoslavia	(b)	32.0	46.0

Note: Liepmann excluded Great Britain, Holland, Denmark, and Norway because of their extensive free lists. His 1913 figures for (a) Poland was the Russian tariff of 72.5% and for (b) Yugoslavia was the Serbian tariff of 22.2%. The caveat to Table 2.1 applies here too.

Source: Liepmann (1938, 415).

system. In the first three months of 1939 there were signs of a comprehensive trade agreement with Germany based on market cartelization, but after the occupation of Prague these plans were shelved (Benham, 1941, 134). In sum, Britain's behaviour does not deserve Lewis's opprobrium, but Britain had clearly ceased to provide a principled lead on free trade and non-discrimination.[11]

The early 1930s movement towards higher tariffs ended up being worldwide. Liepmann's estimates of European tariff levels (Table 3.1) show a sharp contrast in Western Europe between

[11] In addition, Britain's insistence on MFN treatment when other countries considered withdrawing it (e.g. British opposition to 1930–1 proposals for granting Eastern European cereal exports preferential access to Western European markets, to the March 1931 Austria–German customs union proposal, and to the July 1932 Ouchy Convention establishing tariff preferences among the Benelux countries led to all three plans being abandoned) was seen as hypocritical in light of the 1932 Ottawa Conference's agreements on Imperial Preference. Irwin (1993) cites Britain's opposition to the Ouchy Convention as an example of commitment to multilateralism threatening a promising bilateral initiative aimed at trade liberalization.

the, on balance, unchanged tariffs of 1913–27 and the sharp increase between 1927 and 1931, while in Spain and Eastern Europe the already upward trend accelerated after 1927. In Canada a forty-year decline in average customs duties from 31 to 24 per cent was reversed in the four years between 1929 and 1933.[12] Even Australia, widely believed to have the highest tariffs in the world before 1929, managed to raise tariffs still further. Among the more important trading nations, only Japan stood outside the trend.[13] In what would later be called the underdeveloped economies of Latin America, Africa, and Asia, decisive steps towards the development strategy of import-substituting industrialization behind highly protective tariffs were being taken.[14]

Despite the potential for greater discrimination inherent in higher tariffs, governments hesitated to discriminate. Indeed, in 1931 and 1932, as the main goals of tariffs became the raising of revenue, the reduction of aggregate unemployment, and the maintenance of a balance of payments equilibrium, rather than the protection of specific economic activities, tariffs tended to make less and less distinction between products or trading partners (with the exception of Imperial Preference). After 1931, however, many governments came to believe that tariffs were inadequate to achieve any of these goals, and they turned to exchange controls and to other non-tariff barriers against imports. The USA (wholly) and the UK (largely) remained outside the new trend, but they had contributed to its emergence by insisting on national autonomy in trade policy-making and by their unwillingness to support cooperative solutions to the problems of the international economy before the mid-1930.

[12] Young's (1957, 33) figures are the ratio of duty collected to dutiable imports, a downward-biased measure of average tariff rates, and are not comparable with Liepmann's European figures based on estimated prices and actual tariff schedules of selected individual products.

[13] The Netherlands and Denmark, which are not included in Table 3.1, followed Britain's lead and adopted across-the-board tariffs in late 1931, although they remained among the least protectionist European countries.

[14] The chronology here is rather mixed; e.g. India already had protective tariffs during the 1920s, which were raised in the early 1930s. The stimulus to protection being adopted at this time was in some cases exogenous; e.g. Egypt did not have tariff autonomy before 1930. And for export-oriented economies like Argentina, the collapse of world grain prices was the decisive influence. Nevertheless, among all these cross-currents, the climate of the times established in North America and Europe surely helped to legitimize tariff protection elsewhere.

2. Non-tariff Barriers to Trade

Disruption of the international monetary system in summer 1931 provided the stimulus to commercial policy innovation. In Austria and Germany, devaluation was initially ruled out for fear of starting a vicious inflationary circle and deflation was unpopular with socialist government members in view of the already depressed economic conditions, so exchange controls were adopted to deal with their short-term balance of payments problems. The agricultural exporting countries of Eastern Europe also turned to exchange controls, apart from Poland, which pursued strict deflationary policies. In Britain the main weapon was devaluation, reinforced by a tariff. After Britain's devaluation Austria abandoned strict exchange controls in favour of a *de facto* devaluation, while Germany continued to support the mark by exchange controls accompanied during 1932 by deflation. France had no balance of payments problems in the early 1930s; however, when faced with falling import prices (a trend reinforced by deflationary policies and devaluation elsewhere) quantitative restrictions (QRs) on imports were introduced in summer 1931 to help domestic producers.

The monetary instability continued through 1933, when the USA left the gold standard.[15] At the 1933 Economic Conference the European countries placed restabilization of exchange rates at the top of the agenda and, when President Roosevelt refused to commit the dollar to a new par value, the conference broke up without tackling trade policy issues. Of the countries still faithful to the gold standard, France, the Netherlands, Belgium, and Switzerland retained freedom of exchange, strengthened their QRs, and deflated, but by 1936 all four had given up the struggle to avoid devaluation. Italy and Poland retained their official exchange rates but abandoned the gold standard spirit in favour of exchange controls. In doing so they joined Germany and most

[15] The USA does not feature in this section because the USA did not adopt exchange controls and the only QR before 1939 was the sugar quota introduced in 1934, which reserved all but 0.4% of the US market for domestic growers plus Hawaii, Puerto Rico, the Virgin Islands, Cuba, and the Philippines. The USA did, however, use tariff quotas on some agricultural imports and other NTBs such as the health and labelling requirements mentioned earlier in the context of Spanish goods.

east European countries, which had tightened their controls in 1934.

To bring some order into a consideration of the idiosyncratic national policies of 1931–9, I shall distinguish between the non-tariff trade barriers (NTBs) of the free exchange countries and the policies of exchange control countries.[16] Both groups of countries contributed to the breakdown of the non-discrimination principle. Although the NTBs of the free exchange countries were introduced as non-discriminatory and temporary, they were almost inevitably discriminatory in incidence, and with time governments were tempted to use this feature actively. Exchange controls could likewise be introduced without discriminatory intent, but they too became discriminatory in practice, especially after 1934, in part because, as official exchange rates became increasingly overvalued relative to the market-clearing rate, effective exchange controls required total control of all transactions involving foreigners, so that government authorities determined with whom trade was carried out and on what terms.

NTBs in the free exchange countries

Quantitative restrictions on imports (QRs) had largely disappeared from use by the late nineteenth century. They were revived during the First World War, but were mostly dismantled after the war. The first country to reintroduce QRs on a large scale during the 1930s was France.[17]

France had been sheltered from the early impact of the depression and monetary crises by an undervalued currency. Nevertheless, there was concern over how to deal with rapidly falling import prices and a belief that tariffs were inadequate to protect domestic producers under the circumstances. Thus, although tariffs on agricultural imports had been raised substantially since

[16] In practice, most of the 'free exchange countries' outside North America had exchange controls, but these were generally of a mild type aimed against short-term capital flight. The exchange control countries also had import quotas and other NTBs which in 1931–4 helped them deal with balance of payments problems; but as controls over the means of payment were tightened, these other trade restrictions became redundant.

[17] More limited QRs had been introduced in 1930 by Australia on a list of manufactured goods and by some European countries (e.g. Czechoslovakia and Spain) on agricultural imports (Haberler, 1943, Chapter 3).

1929, in summer 1931 they were supplemented by QRs. Initially the number of quotas was not large, but the timing was important; with the world's eyes turned to the financial crisis in Vienna, Berlin, and London, the commercial policy innovation in Paris went unprotested. A precedent having been established, when quotas were extended to manufactured imports in the following year and gradually spread to about 3000 goods by 1934 (covering about 65 per cent of all French imports by the mid-1930s, according to Haight, 1941, 178), complaints from abroad were about size and distribution rather than principle. The French action was contagious, and by the end of 1932 eleven European countries had fully fledged import quota systems.[18]

Initially most of the QRs were not intended to be discriminatory. There were exceptions, e.g. Italy's retaliatory quotas on imports from France,[19] but the QRs were usually aimed at reducing imports in general to ease balance of payments difficulties or to protect specific domestic activities. Nevertheless, by their nature QRs tend to be discriminatory. Global QRs favour geographically closer countries; with lower transport costs and shorter travel times, risk of refused entry was smaller and less costly for them. This feature encouraged countries with QRs to require that importers obtain licences before goods were shipped, but how were licences to be allocated in a non-discriminatory way? Equal shares discriminate against more efficient producers; e.g. after negotiating a tariff quota of 5000 tons for Finnish butter, Germany applied the same absolute values to Danish butter despite much larger imports of butter from Denmark than from Finland.[20] Base-year shares discriminate against fast-growing

[18] QRs were also used by Japan, Iran, and the British and Dutch Asiatic colonies, but were less common elsewhere. Australia and South Africa actually abolished most of their QRs in 1932 (Haberler, 1943, 17).

[19] In 1932 Italy imposed QRs on wines, perfumes, automobiles, and other products of France. France retaliated with QRs on meat, sausage, and cheese from Italy, who countered with QRs on cotton yarn, lace, and machine tools from France (Heuser, 1939, 43).

[20] This episode had more serious consequences when Germany tried to extend QRs on this basis to fruit and vegetable imports from Belgium, Denmark, and the Netherlands, and incited boycott movements against German industrial exports. Röpke (1934, 61–2) saw this episode, by its failure to satisfy both agricultural interests and export industries in Germany, as one of the factors leading to the overthrow of the von Papen government in November 1932—and bringing Hitler one step closer to power.

TABLE 3.2 Imports subject to Quotas in the European Countries not using Exchange Controls, 1937 (%)

Country	% of imports subject to quotas
France	58
Switzerland	52
Netherlands	26
Belgium	24
Ireland	17
Norway	12
UK	8
Sweden	3

Source: League of Nations, *World Economic Survey, 1938–1939*, p. 189; quoted in Gordon (1941, 253).

exporters—Japan in particular suffered from this approach.[21] Moreover, given the fluctuations in trade flows during the late 1920s and early 1930s, the choice of base year would make a substantial difference to quota allocations and could be used to favour any trading partner.

After 1933 the free exchange countries relying most heavily on QRs (see Table 3.2) attempted to use quotas to favour countries giving better market access to their exports. France, for example, withheld 75 per cent of 1934 quotas to countries outside the gold bloc and the USA, pending negotiations with each country for special concessions to French exports.[22] Britain immediately imposed a 20 per cent surcharge on imports from France, which was removed five months later only when France granted Britain the full import quota. Germany introduced new QRs on French exports, and a new arrangement was worked out only after months of negotiation. In general the concessions gained for French exports were meagre and mostly from smaller trading

[21] Britain set textile quotas for its colonies' imports on the basis of 1927–31 average import levels, which favoured Lancashire at the expense of Japan. Dutch QRs introduced in 1933 reversed the rapidly increasing market share of Japanese textiles in the Dutch East Indies to the benefit of American and European exporters.

[22] The account in this paragraph is based upon Haight (1941, 172–90). Irwin (1993) emphasizes the macro rather than the micro aspects of the QR regime, so that, after France finally devalued in 1936, the QRs became less necessary.

partners. The episode can be seen as a return to France's 1919 opposition to the unconditional MFN clause because it hindered differential treatment of France's trading partners, and again, the position was abandoned because other countries were ready to adopt countermeasures to make discrimination against their exports costly to France. Carrying out this policy through QRs had the added disadvantage of requiring frequent detailed negotiations about quota levels. A committee to consider reform of the quota regime was set up in 1935, but action was delayed by the 1936 devaluation of the franc, the 1937 recession, and 1938 stabilization of the franc. In August 1939 about one-fifth of the quotas on manufactured imports were removed, and the process would likely have continued had war not broken out a month later.

The 1930s also saw growing resort to other NTBs, which were not always new, but which became more restrictive. Labelling requirements, health standards, etc., used by the USA *inter alia* during the 1920s (*see* fn. 4) became more of a hindrance to exporters. Isaacs (1948, 648–9) cites many instances from an American government guide to labelling requirements: for example, the origin of razor blades exported to France had to be marked on each blade; Britain required imported eggs to be labelled in lettering not less than 2mm high; Argentina required envelopes and other paper products to be individually marked (although an exception was made for confetti, whose origin needed to be identified only on the wrapper); Canada required the nationality of every toothbrush to be marked on its handle. Customs valuation procedures had been used before to adjust the actual value of duties paid under *ad valorem* tariffs,[23] but Canada in the 1930s gave customs officials such discretion over import valuation that in effect they could set the duty rate on a consignment-by-consignment basis. Government spending, especially where used as a conscious contracyclical policy, was allocated to favour domestic products, and was occasionally used to discriminate

[23] For example, Austria had set its own valuation of German and American cars during the 1920s to favour the former (i.e. American cars were valued at well above their market price so that they were subject to higher duty than an equal-priced German car). The French administration of Syria and the Lebanon undervalued imports from France and the French colonies to undermine the uniform tariff rate required under the mandate (Gerig, 1930, 160–1).

among trading partners.[24] There is little purpose in detailing further practices which acted as trade barriers, of which who knows how many passed undocumented; suffice it to say that widespread use of NTBs permitted fine-tuning of the nature and source or destination of foreign trade.

Just as the extent of the NTBs other than QRs is difficult to monitor, so is the degree to which they were used to discriminate among trading partners. Nevertheless, some NTBs were clearly designed for that purpose. In 1930 government procurement policies by Italy and Switzerland and customs valuation procedures by Canada—to mention only three transparent cases—were used to retaliate against the USA without increasing barriers against other countries' imports or formally breaking MFN commitments to the USA. In 1931–2 Italy, Austria, and Hungary agreed to subsidize their exports to one another, which was equivalent to preferential tariff reductions.[25] After 1933 discrimination seems to have become still more widespread. The opaqueness of NTBs also increased and secret trade arrangements became more common (Gordon, 1941, 380). With NTBs gaining in importance, the MFN principle declined in significance.[26]

Working in the opposite direction were two factors limiting discrimination among free exchange countries. First, fear of retaliation discouraged too harsh a curtailment of another country's exports. France's experience with QRs was repeated with respect to other countries' NTBs. Trading partners perceiving discrimination against their exports retaliated against the offending country's exports. Opaqueness was one attraction of NTBs, as tools for discrimination and secret trade arrangements were also signed to avoid retaliation by third countries, but exporters

[24] As a supplement to the 1933 UK–Denmark trade agreement, there was an 'understanding' that first offer of Danish municipal government orders would be made to British firms and that on Danish central government orders British firms were to receive a preference of 10% (Viner, 1943).

[25] QRs could also be used more easily than tariffs to form regional pacts because their relationship to MFN obligations was less clear. The Ouchy Convention had been torpedoed in 1932 because powerful outsiders insisted on their MFN rights, but the 1937 Oslo Convention by which Belgium, Luxembourg, and the Netherlands abolished QRs on imports from one another and from Scandinavia did take effect (although it was allowed to lapse a year later).

[26] Even the USA, for whom MFN tariffs remained the main trade policy instrument, used tariff specialization to restrict MFN benefits to third countries from bilaterally negotiated tariff cuts (Beckett, 1941, 24–30).

would eventually sense what was happening and encourage action by their government. Important trading nations thus tended to forestall discrimination against their exports and, while smaller countries had less bargaining power, the scope for discriminating among them was often too limited to be worthwhile. Second, NTBs could be evaded by false labelling or other innovative methods. Japan was the target of many complaints about 'illegal' trading practices,[27] but this was because Japan suffered most from NTBs designed around 1920s market shares and had little bargaining power, so guile was the only peaceful recourse. Such practices imposed enforcement costs on the importing country, and administrative costs were one reason for free-exchange countries turning against a too complex system of NTBs.

In the earlier discussion of tariffs a distinction could be made between their level and their discriminatory impact; the MFN clause was the key to separating the two by preventing discrimination when tariffs existed. In the realm of NTBs, the distinction is less operational and the meaning of MFN treatment less clear. Some NTBs by their nature tend to discriminate among trading partners (e.g. QRs), while others are not necessarily discriminatory but can be used to discriminate. More opaque NTBs are attractive instruments for discrimination, not only because they can be held to be consistent with MFN obligations, but also because the likelihood of retaliation is less if their incidence is hidden. In the non-cooperative international economic environment of the 1930s, countries searched for new NTBs and were suspicious of their trading partners' practices. As discriminatory measures proliferated, administrative, economic, and political costs were incurred, whose distribution was complex but which at global level represented definite losses in welfare and stability.

Exchange controls

Exchange controls introduced during the First World War had largely been removed by 1925. In the second half of 1931, in the

[27] After the Netherlands introduced QRs on Japanese textiles exported to the Dutch East Indies, Japanese shirts (not covered by the QRs) had tails up to three meters long which could be detached and sold as cotton piece goods to textiles consumers (Gordon, 1941, 271 n.). Before origin requirements were specified as having to be by country rather than by region or city, Japanese exports to America were assembled in the town of Usa in order to have a confusing label.

wake of the international monetary crisis, many European countries and some Latin American countries reintroduced exchange controls. Some of these restrictions were mild and temporary, introduced to cover a period of currency depreciation and relaxed shortly after (e.g. in the UK, Norway, and Sweden). Others, particularly in central and Eastern Europe and in some Latin American countries, involved severe restrictions and became permanent.

Faced with balance of payments deficits too severe for short-term financing, countries had the choice among devaluation, deflation, and exchange controls. The debtor countries never seriously considered devaluation, at least not as the initial step, because it would increase the burden of foreign debt (if assets were dominated in domestic currency and liabilities in foreign currencies) and because of fear that devaluation would inaugurate a vicious circle of inflation as rising import prices were passed on via demands for higher wages to higher prices. These concerns were especially important in the central European countries which had recently experienced hyperinflations. After the Austrian and German banking crises (and associated capital flight) of summer 1931, exchange controls were introduced by Germany and Hungary in July and by Czechoslovakia, Yugoslavia, and Austria in October; all were initially viewed as temporary measures to meet extreme crises of confidence.

The initial exchange controls typically involved requiring foreign exchange earnings to be turned over to the central bank (or other government agency), which allocated it to importers and other *bona fide* demanders of foreign exchange. In this mild form, exchange controls permitted restriction of capital flight without disruption of other international transactions. The situation was, however, unstable because at the existing exchange rate demand for foreign exchange exceeded supply, and the controls were evaded on black markets and by false invoicing, smuggling, and legal evasions via loopholes in the regulations. Only a fraction of foreign exchange earnings reached the competent authorities, disbursements to importers were a small proportion of their requested amounts, and trade was restricted and often determined by idiosyncrasies of the control system rather than by economic or national priorities.

The possible reactions were illustrated by Austria and Hungary. In February 1932 Austria gave permission for private currency deals at negotiated rates and these were gradually spread to cover more transactions until 'by the end of 1932 the most vigorous features of exchange control had vanished' (H. S. Ellis, 1941, 51) and *de facto* devaluation had taken place. Hungary, dependent on agricultural exports (and thus facing adverse terms of trade changes) and heavily indebted, avoided devaluation by tightening exchange controls to cover every transaction and in effect establishing an individual exchange rate for each transaction. Traditional trade policy instruments became redundant in Hungary after 1933 as the conditions under which imports entered were ultimately determined by 'secret and arbitrary' administrative decisions about how much foreign exchange was available for each import transaction.[28]

The most important trading nations to adopt exchange controls were Germany and Italy, who both had strict controls by 1934. The German exchange controls introduced in July 1931 to restrict capital flight were accompanied in 1931–2 by deflationary policies. After Hitler's accession to power in January 1933 expansionary macroeconomic policies were adopted, and at the official exchange rate imports became more and more attractive and exports less competitive; the large trade surplus of 1930–2 diminished in 1933 and turned into a deficit in 1934. Devaluation was rejected and exchange controls had to be tightened, culminating in the September 1934 New Plan, whereby any acquisition of foreign exchange required a prior licence; i.e. there was complete authoritarian control of what should be imported and exported, in what quantities, at what terms, and with which countries. Italy came by a different route. Apart from post-1927 agricultural tariff increases and 1931 retaliatory quotas on imports from France, Italy pursued a liberal trade policy up until 1934. After the dollar's departure from gold, however, Italy was unwilling to undertake the deflationary measures required to maintain the old lira parity and in 1934 exchange controls were introduced instead.[29] The policy was consolidated when the

[28] On Hungary see H. S. Ellis (1941, ch. 3); the quote is from p. 155.

[29] Welk (1937) identifies severe balance of payments problems as the reason for Italy's adoption of exchange controls, but the other gold bloc countries faced similar problems after 1933 and reacted differently; Poland initially deflated, while France, Belgium, the Netherlands, and Switzerland used QRs to relieve pressure on the exchange rate, although the last four countries had all devalued by 1936. Italy's more interventionist government philosophy presumably encouraged acceptance of the administrative solution.

League of Nations imposed sanctions in October 1935 after the Italian invasion of Ethiopia; Italy already had a well-developed machinery for controlling trade and in December a single government office was given a monopoly over foreign exchange transactions.[30] Enforcement remained a problem in both countries, despite the extension of the death penalty in Germany in 1936 and in Italy in 1939 to offences against the foreign exchange regulations.

The international counterpart to exchange controls was bilateral payments arrangements. As exporters to exchange control countries became reluctant to make further shipments without guaranteed payments in their home or another convertible currency, governments sought methods of balancing bilateral payments to eliminate the need for international currency flows. A simple clearing arrangement involved an importer making payments into a special account at his own national bank, which would use the proceeds to pay exporters to the country from which the imports had come; a similar arrangement in the other country would ensure that exporters received payment from importers. More sophisticated arrangements would make allowance for non-trade transactions and perhaps for a net capital flow. Creditor nations were particularly anxious to negotiate bilateral arrangements as a way of earmarking some of the exchange control countries' foreign exchange for debt servicing. Thus, international trade was increasingly pushed into bilateral channels.

Limits to bilateral agreements were, however, imposed by the fundamental dilemma of how to react when desired transactions differed from predicted transactions. For the free exchange countries, it was especially difficult to forecast the precise pattern of international transactions with a specific country. Thus, although many bilateral arrangements were negotiated between 1932 and 1935, few new ones were signed after that. The free exchange countries continued to trade multilaterally. Agreements between two exchange control countries could be more closely controlled and they continued in effect, but even these countries

[30] The League's sanctions failed, partly because of Italy's activist trade policy, but even more because sufficient countries continued their Italian trade (including such major trading nations as the USA and Germany) that switching markets involved little hardship to Italy.

had to abandon bilateralism when trade shocks occurred.[31] In consequence, bilateral arrangements became a feature of the 1930s international economy and led to increased bilateralization of the exchange control countries' trade, but they governed a minority of international trade.[32]

Exchange controls had their own momentum. To be effective in the face of rapidly changing relative national price levels, they had to be ever tightened, until they became synonymous with total foreign trade control. In the end other trade policy instruments became irrelevant, and trade policy by administrative decision became secret in detail and subservient to political will—and totally discriminatory. Germany, in particular, was accused of using trade to dominate Eastern Europe and prepare for war, a topic I shall return to later in this chapter.

3. Imperial Preference

The open door principle in colonial territories collapsed during the 1930s. France had already abandoned the principle by an assimilation policy, which brought most of the French colonies into a free trade area with France in 1928. Britain had adopted Imperial Preference in 1919, but with few tariffs the practical importance of this step was limited. Britain's adoption of the general tariff paved the way for a meaningful system of Imperial Preference to be agreed with the autonomous tariff members of the Commonwealth at the 1932 Ottawa Conference. The Netherlands mildly closed the open door to the Dutch East Indies by introducing import quotas which worked against Japanese goods. All other colonial arrangements were dominated, both in scale and in their impact on thinking about the international trading

[31] For example, bad harvests in 1937 and 1938 forced Germany to satisfy part of the increased demand for food imports on the world market (Röpke, 1942, 42).

[32] Gordon (1941, 132–3) quotes figures showing about one-eighth of world trade being conducted under bilateral clearing agreements in 1937, of which 39% involved Germany and 9% Italy. As she points out, however, the definition of bilateral arrangements adopted is a restrictive one, and international comparisons based on gold values are 'of doubtful significance' for 1937 given the multiple exchange rates and varying depreciations; i.e. the figures are underestimates and rough approximations at that. The countries with the highest percentages of imports covered by clearing arrangements were Bulgaria (88%), Romania (75%), Turkey (72%), Yugoslavia (61%), Hungary (60%), Greece (56%), Germany (53%), Italy (45%), Latvia (37%), Estonia (36%), Switzerland (36%), and Chile (34%).

system, by British Imperial Preference, and after brief consideration of the other cases this section will deal primarily with the British Empire's preferential trading arrangement.

The general tendency among the imperial powers was towards a greater orientation of their trade towards their dependencies, accompanied by a shift from surplus to deficit in this trade. During the 1920s trade with colonies, protectorates, and mandated territories accounted for 11 per cent of French imports and 16 per cent of French exports; by 1936 these percentages had increased to 29 and 33 per cent and, although the colonial share fell after the 1936 franc devaluation, it was still 27 per cent of both imports and exports in 1938 (Haight, 1941, 263). Portugal, Belgium, and the Netherlands also conducted a greater share of their trade with their overseas dependent territories, especially on the import side (Thorbecke, 1960, 100–02), although the percentages and value were smaller than for France. The Italian overseas empire was extended by the invasion of Ethiopia in 1935, and the share of Italian exports going to dependencies increased from 5 per cent in 1934 to 14 per cent in 1935 and to 31 per cent in 1936 (US Tariff Commission, 1941, 108). Japan also was carrying on a substantial trade with newly acquired dependencies by the late 1930s.

The deterioration in foreign countries' access to British Empire markets was striking. In 1930 over four-fifths of imports from foreign (i.e. non-Empire) countries entered the UK duty-free, whereas after the Ottawa Conference the proportion was reduced to a quarter (Gordon, 1941, 221). MacDougall and Hutt (1954, 237) have calculated that the preference margin on British exports to the Commonwealth increased from 5 per cent in 1929 to 10–11 per cent in 1937, while the preference margin on British imports from the Commonwealth rose from 2–3 per cent in 1929 to 10–12 per cent in 1937.[33] This discriminatory trading arrangement caused resentment in Europe, especially in the Low Countries (whose preferential trading arrangement under the Ouchy Convention was prevented by British insistence on MFN rights) and in countries without colonial empires. Most of all, it aroused strong opposition in the USA on grounds of principle (both the MFN clause and American dislike of colonialism were at issue)

[33] They define the preference margin as the difference in percentage points between the *ad valorem* duty paid on trade with the USA and with the UK.

TABLE 3.3 Proportion of British Trade with Empire Countries, 1931 and 1938 (%)

	UK exports		UK imports	
	1931	1938	1931	1938
Canada	5.3	4.8	3.8	8.6
Australia	3.7	8.1	5.3	7.8
New Zealand	2.9	4.1	4.4	5.1
South Africa	5.6	8.4	1.5	1.6
India	8.3	7.7	4.3	6.1
Irish Free State	7.8	4.3	4.2	2.5
Rest of Empire	10.1	12.5	5.2	8.7
Total Non-Empire	56.3	50.1	71.3	59.6

Source: Glickman (1947, 447).

and on the practical matter that in the two largest US export markets major competitors received preferential treatment.

Glickman has estimated that the Empire's share of British exports rose from 43.7 per cent in 1931 to 49.9 per cent in 1938, while the Empire's share of British imports went from 28.7 to 40.4 per cent in the same period (Table 3.3). Glickman interprets these share data with caution; the biggest impact lies in the growing market share of primary product exports from Australia, New Zealand, and Canada to Great Britain, which may have been due only in part to tariff preferences. The volume of British wool imports, for example, rose 70 per cent between 1928 and 1938—well above the growth of commodity trade in general, and mainly of benefit to Australia and New Zealand, who did not need tariff preferences in order to dominate the market (Thorbecke, 1960, 137–9). On the other hand, tariff preferences certainly helped these same two countries to maintain their dairy and meat exports to the UK, at the expense of non-preferred suppliers (Denmark and Argentina in particular). Even allowing for the difficulty of isolating the impact of tariff preferences from other influences on market shares, the 1931–8 changes are substantial.[34] This is

[34] Another problem with observing market shares for before and after Ottawa dates is that Empire shares of British trade had been increasing since 1870 without much Imperial Preference (Capie, 1983, ch. 2), but as Capie also mentions, some of the pre-1914 increase reflected the doubling in size of the Empire. During the 1930s the Empire's size was fairly constant.

even more so if the Irish shares are removed from the Empire category in Table 3.3; considering that the Irish Free State and the UK were involved in a trade war between 1932 and 1938, their mutual trade should not be included under the Imperial Preference umbrella during those years. Excluding Ireland, the Empire share of British exports increased from 36 per cent in 1931 to 46 per cent in 1938 and of British imports from 25 to 38 per cent. These are big shifts, and consistent with the greater increase in preference margins on the import side.

Similar shifts in market shares occurred in the Dominions.[35] Canada obtained 17 per cent of imports from the UK, Australia, and New Zealand in 1928 and 20 per cent in 1938, while 35 per cent of Canadian exports went to these three trading partners in 1928 and 46 per cent in 1938. Australia and New Zealand received 46 per cent of their imports from Britain and Canada in 1928 and 50 per cent in 1938, while sending 49 per cent of their exports in 1928 and 64 per cent in 1938 to those two countries. The African colonies and Dominion also strengthened their imperial trading ties, although again it is difficult to separate the impact of tariff preferences from other changes such as copper discoveries in Northern Rhodesia, US agricultural control policies (which helped Kenya and Uganda gain markets for their cotton exports), and the place of gold in South African exports. All told, even without a well-defined counterfactual of what trade patterns would have been in the absence of Imperial Preference, the shifts in market shares seem large enough to justify the conclusion that the post-Ottawa tariff preferences did affect trade flows.

The welfare consequences of Imperial Preferences are more difficult to establish. Undoubtedly there was trade diversion as some non-Empire suppliers lost markets. Ironically, in light of strong US opposition, America does not appear to have been a major sufferer—US share of British imports actually increased from 12 to 14 per cent between 1931 and 1938 (Glickman, 1947),[36] and a post-1932 decline in the US share of Canadian imports was reversed after the trade agreements of 1935 and 1938. Discrimination against US manufactured exports to other imperial

[35] The figures in this paragraph are taken from Thorbecke (1960, 40, 59 and 139–41).

[36] Glickman (1947, 468) concludes that 'The United States was not greatly injured by the Imperial Preference system. Only a few products were affected . . .'.

markets was countered by establishing subsidiaries in Canada as export platforms, e.g. for automobile sales by the large US producers to New Zealand.

Among the imperial participants, there was considerable discontent with the functioning of the preferences. British farmers opposed free entry for the Dominion's meat and dairy products, while British manufacturers were dismayed by the high levels of even the preferential tariff rates when Dominion industries demanded protection, and the British government felt its hands tied by imperial pledges when negotiating with foreign countries.

Although the Dominions' primary product exports benefited from favoured access to the British market, the Dominions were soon disappointed at the lack of growth in this market. On both sides there were complaints that Imperial Preferences raised the cost of living, by keeping up food prices in Britain and the price of clothing, shoes, and other manufactured goods in the rest of the Empire.[37] A contemporary commentator concluded that 'By 1939 there was not much enthusiasm for imperial preference either in Great Britain or in the rest of the Empire' (Benham, 1941, 108).

4. Consequences of 1930s Trade Policies

The economic consequences of the trade policies of the 1930s are universally seen as adverse. One fundamental cost—higher trade barriers reducing the level of trade and eroding the gains from trade—is not our direct concern. Increased bilateralism and regionalization are bad because they cut off possibilities for triangular trade and thus reduce the level of and gains from international trade—in the 1930s context, reinforcing the negative effects of higher trade barriers. In addition, they were seen by many as contributing to the growth of political tensions and thus to the outbreak of war.

Bilateralism

The evolution and limitations of bilateral arrangements have been described earlier in this chapter. The movement was strongest

[37] Britain's imperial partners were encouraged to raise trade barriers against Japanese manufactured exports in order to protect British exports whose competitiveness was declining.

TABLE 3.4 Bilateral Trade Indices, Germany 1929–1938 (%)

	1929	1930	1931	1932	1933	1934	1935	1936	1937	1838
Index (G)	77.2	76.0	66.9	67.1	71.9	75.4	79.4	83.4	82.4	83.9

Note: $n = 39$ up to 1937; in 1938 Austria is included in Germany ($n = 38$). The non-requited trade (100–G) consists of multilateral trade among the 39 plus the balance on trade with other countries and on non-trade items in the balance of payments.

Source: calculated from League of Nations *International Trade Statistics*; data also available in Child (1958, 159–161, 172–174, 180, 182–183, 187–88, 192, 199–200).

during the years 1932–5, and in the second half of the decade the only important trading nations still making heavy use of bilateral arrangements were Germany and, to a lesser extent, Italy. Most of the remaining south-east European countries' trade was carried out under bilateral arrangements, but they were less common elsewhere.[38] At this point a summary index will be utilized to give a quantitative guide to these developments.

A suitable index of the degree of bilateralism in a country's actual trade is the following variant on the Grubel–Lloyd intra-industry trade index:

$$G = 1 - \frac{\sum |X_i - M_i|}{\sum (X_i + M_i)} \times 100, \tag{3.1}$$

where X_i and M_i are exports to and imports from the i th trading partner. The index G runs from 0 (no bilateral trade) to 100 (all bilateral trade flows in exact balance).

Values of G for Germany between 1929 and 1938 are given in Table 3.4. The increase after 1931 and again in the mid-1930s supports the proposition that growing bilateralism accompanied changes in German trade and payments regimes. What also emerges is the presence of other forces, especially between 1929 and 1931. The increased multilateralism of 1929–31 reflected a dramatic decline in German exports to the USA while imports from the USA (Germany's biggest supplier) fell more slowly, and a corresponding increase in the share of German exports to France, the Netherlands, and, especially, the USSR.[39] The 1930

[38] See fn. 32.

[39] The USA supplied 12–13% of German imports in all years from 1929 to 1932, but the percentage of German exports going to the USA fell from 7.4% in 1929

American tariff hike played a role in upsetting Germany's bilateral trade flow, and thus presumably contributed to the German search for new trade policies. Another feature of Table 3.4 is that, despite the progressive tightening of exchange controls and expected continuing increases in bilateralism, the *G* index flattens out in 1937 and 1938. The explanation lies in the inability of rigid controls to meet all eventualities; two bad harvests forced Germany to import food from non-exchange-control countries, and these imports were not balanced by equal increases in exports to those countries. In sum, the index not only captures in a clear synthetic manner the increasingly bilateral nature of Germany's foreign trade after 1931, but it also reveals that in the late 1930s the urge to bilateralism could still be limited by exogenous shocks.

The 1938 German bilateral trade index is compared with indices for other countries in Table 3.5. The first five countries are listed in order of total trade and, among these five largest trading nations of 1938, Germany's trade was conducted on the most bilateral pattern. The Netherlands and Italy represent two Western European countries pursuing alternative paths, the former retaining free international payments mechanisms and the latter using exchange controls; the indices indicate greater bilateralism in Italian trade.[40] Finally, indices are given for four east European countries.

Table 3.5 suggests for free exchange countries a normal range of bilateralism in the late 1930s between 65 and 72 per cent of total trade. Germany had a similar ratio between 1931 and 1933, but by the mid-1930s German trade had become considerably more balanced bilaterally and the multilateral portion had fallen

to 5.1% in 1931 and 4.9% in 1932 (the value of German exports to the USA fell from RM991 m in 1929 to RM281 m in 1932); depression affected the values, but US protectionism seems the best explanation of the falling export share. The share of German exports going to Britain rose in 1929–31, but fell sharply after British abandonment of gold. The gold bloc countries were the only remaining free exchange countries offering reasonably open markets for German exports to offset the deficit with the USA, but, since Germany already had trade surpluses with the gold bloc members, increasing focus on their markets raised measured multilateralism (100–*G*) in German trade. The sudden, and short-lived, increase in (unrequited) German exports to the USSR in 1931–2 accentuated this.

[40] The Italian index is less reliable because a larger part of Italy's trade is not specified by trading partner. I had hoped to include Japan and some South American countries in Table 3.5, but the individual country data covered only 74% of Japanese trade and 84% of Chilean trade.

TABLE 3.5 Bilateral Trade Indices, Selected Countries, 1938 (%)

Country	*n* (coverage)	*G*
Great Britain	85 (95.4)	66.7
USA	79 (97.6)	68.5
Germany	47 (88.9)	82.4
France	54 (95.8)	71.5
Canada	64 (95.8)	64.9
Netherlands	75 (96.0)	71.4
Italy	70 (86.2)	76.2
Bulgaria	26 (97.6)	83.8
Hungary	45 (97.6)	78.0
Romania	28 (94.4)	80.2
Yugoslavia	48 (98.2)	84.1

Note: coverage = % of total trade accounted for by the *n* identified trading partners; *n* is determined by the number of separately entered trading partners in the source.

Source: calculated from UN *Direction of International Trade*, Statistical Papers, Ser. T, vol. VIII, no. 7 (October 1957), pp. 82–201.

below a fifth. The south-east European countries had a bilateral emphasis similar to that of Germany. Italy occupies an intermediate position between the free exchange and the exchange control countries, which in part is due to the unbalanced trade with Italy's African colonies.

The index used in this section illustrates the dramatic shift away from multilateralism by Germany between 1931 and 1936 (and the limits to this movement), and the split between free exchange and exchange control countries in terms of the degree of bilateralism in their actual trade relations. Röpke (1942, 15) has made the important distinction between actual and virtual multilateralism; the former can be measured,[41] but the 'ever-present latent possibility to change from bilateral to multilateral interchange' is at least as crucial and cannot be measured. By withdrawing a larger part of their international trade from the open world market, the exchange control countries reduced the virtual multilateralism even of the free exchange countries, so that the analysis in this subsection can be only a lower bound

[41] Röpke refers to estimates by Hilgerdt giving 'about 20% as normal'. Table 3.5 suggests that this is too low a figure; for Britain, the USA, and Canada about a third of trade was multilateral, and for France and the Netherlands almost 30%.

guide to the full scope of forgone trading opportunities resulting from the retreat from multilateralism.[42]

Regionalization

Another characteristic of international trade during the 1930s was the emergence of trading blocs or commercial empires. The initial step was the decline of the open-door principle analysed above, and its replacement by preferential trading arrangements within the French, British, and other European-centred empires. The impact on the direction of French and British trade was large: for both countries the share of imperial trade in total trade increased by at least ten percentage points in the decade after 1928 (Anderson and Norheim, 1993). Other countries, notably Japan and Italy, sought to acquire political empires and having done so turned them into preferential trading areas (PTAs); the impact on trade patterns was especially striking in the case of Japan (Table 3.6). This regionalization of international trade was separate from the bilateralism just described, because, while some PTAs existed within bilateral regimes, others (notably British Imperial Preference) did not. The two phenomena did, however, come together in the most controversial case of regionalization, the increased German economic domination of south-Eastern Europe.

The growth in Germany's share of the south-east European countries' trade, especially after 1933, was dramatic: from 4.5 per cent of their imports and 4.9 per cent of their exports in 1929, the German share increased to 7.0 and 5.4 per cent in 1933, and to 12.3 and 11.4 per cent in 1935.[43] The first bilateral arrangement involving the area, the 1932 Hungo-German clearing agreement, was in response to German determination to secure the release of credits tied up by Hungarian exchange controls (H. S. Ellis,

[42] Eichengreen and Irwin (1995) apply a gravity model to 1920s and 1930s trade flows and conclude that 'standard determinants of bilateral trade flows (income, proximity and contiguity) had a diminished influence in the 1930s, as if commercial policies increasingly overrode their effects' (p. 3). They also conclude that regional trading blocs and currency blocs did not have a consistent impact, implying that the problem was the cocktail of protectionist and discriminatory policies rather than any one specific ingredient.

[43] From League of Nations trade statistics for Bulgaria, Greece, Hungary, Romania, Turkey, and Yugoslavia, as reported in Child (1938, 159–61).

TABLE 3.6 Regionalization of World Trade, 1929–1938 (%)

	Share of regional bloc In imports		In exports	
	1929	1938	1929	1938
UK	30.2	41.9	44.4	49.9
France	12.0	27.1	18.8	27.5
Belgium	3.9	8.3	2.6	1.9
Netherlands	5.5	8.8	2.6	1.9
Portugal	7.9	10.2	12.7	12.2
Italy	0.5	1.8	2.1	3.3
Japan	20.2	40.6	24.1	54.7
Germany	16.7	27.6	12.8	24.7

Note: regional blocs are defined for the UK as the Commonwealth, colonies, and protectorates; for France, colonies, protectorates, and mandated territories, for Belgium, the Belgian Congo; for the Netherlands and Portugal, overseas territorities; for Italy, colonies and Ethiopia (Abyssinia); for Japan, Korea, Taiwan, Kwantung, and Manchukuo; for Germany, six southeast European countries plus Latin America.

Source: League of Nations data quoted in Irwin (1993, 110).

1941, 202). Further development of the process was related to the south-east European countries' desperate search for markets for their agricultural exports and Germany's willingness to make purchases at favourable prices and sometimes under long-term contracts. By 1934 a systematic orientation of German trade policy towards securing dominant market positions in the south-east European countries' foreign trade is discernible.

There are two competing explanations of the motives behind German trade policy in south-east Europe, one emphasizing market power and the other emphasizing geopolitical motives. The economic benefits to the south-east European countries are straightforward; by joining a German-led trade bloc, they could share in Germany's relatively rapid post-1933 economic recovery, and through exchange controls and bilateral payments arrangements they could prevent leakages to the free exchange countries and maximize the multiplier effects. The market power argument explains German acquiescence in terms of bargaining power *vis-à-vis* the south-east European countries which enabled Germany to garner the lion's share of the benefits. Child (1958), for example, states that Germany was able to improve terms of trade and, at least in 1934 and 1935, import on credit. The theoretical analysis is plausible, but Child provides no empirical support for the hypothesized use of market power.[44]

Neal (1979) has attacked the market power hypothesis on the grounds that Germany's terms of trade with the south-east European countries deteriorated rather than improved between 1934 and 1938. In light of this fact, Germany can scarcely be said to have exploited a growing market share in south-east Europe to gain monopoly profits. Instead, Neal argues that Germany suffered economic losses by importing south-east European goods at higher than world prices, but accepted these losses as the cost of gaining greater political influence in the region. When the south-east European countries had trade surpluses in 1934–5, they could choose between allowing their exchange rate to appreciate *vis-à-vis* the mark (as Romania and Yugoslavia did) or to finance the blocked mark accounts and thus stimulate domestic economic activity (as Hungary and Bulgaria did); the short-run macroeconomic benefits were greater in the latter case, but at the cost of increased dependence upon trade with Germany. In Neal's view there was no exercise of market power; Germany offered the opportunity for expansionary Keynesian policies plus terms of trade benefits to any south-east European country prepared to accept closer economic ties with Germany.

Hirschman (1945), although writing before both Child and Neal, brought together the monopoly and influence aspects in a convincing way. His index of large countries' preferences for smaller trading partners indicates that this preference was particularly strong in the case of Germany during the 1930s. He also measured the country concentration of small countries' trade, and found this to rise for the south-east European countries during the same period. He contrasted this last phenomenon with results for two other groups of smaller European countries:

1. Belgium, the Netherlands, Switzerland, Austria, Czechoslovakia, and Poland, whose trade was more equally spread across

[44] Earlier, H. S. Ellis (1941) and several writers in the late 1930s had also emphasized German use of market power. These commentators seem to have been influenced by the contemporary imperfect competition revolution in economic theory. In the early 1940s, patriotism coloured the debate in England over Germany's prewar trade policies (e.g. Benham, 1940; Einzig, 1941).

several trading partners and who kept this diversification throughout the decade, helped by the low commodity concentration of their exports;

2. the Baltic and Scandinavian countries, whose foreign trade was characterized by an Anglo-German duopoly and who actively worked to maintain this balance.

Because of geography, the south-east European countries had a more restricted choice among major trading nations as trading partners, and Germany was able to fulfil the goal of dominating some smaller countries' trade because of potential monopoly position in the region.[45] Thus, while market power was an enabling factor, Hirschman saw German motives in terms of increasing political influence rather than economic gain.

By its nature, political influence is harder to define or measure than monopoly profits. In the longer run German trade policies paved the way for total control over the region after the outbreak of war. Emphasis is, however, usually placed on the role of these policies in preparing for war, e.g. by enabling Germany to secure access to food and raw materials supplies and to pressure south-east European trading partners to modify their output mix according to German requirements. Britain and France offered little resistance to the growing German influence in the region, partly because their empires made them less desperate for south-east Europe's commodity exports and partly because their less centralized trade policy regimes were less suited to fine-tuned discrimination among trading partners. Kaiser (1980, 317–18) has described this as a 'fundamental political miscalculation' on the part of France and Britain, permitting Germany secure access to raw materials in the late 1930s which in turn led to military victory in 1940, and he is scornful of official British justifications for non-discriminatory trade policies towards south-east Europe.

[45] The argument could be extended to explain why Hungary and Bulgaria were more willing to accept the German bargain than Romania or Yugoslavia were; the former were smaller and their exports were specialized towards agricultural goods, while the latter's more diversified exports (especially Romania's oil) gave them greater opportunity to maintain a greater variety of trading partners. It is, however, difficult to discriminate between this hypothesis and the purely political explanation that Hungary and Bulgaria shared with Germany the status of vanquished nations and hopes for border revision, whereas Yugoslavia, Greece, and Turkey had no such hopes, and Romania (justifiably, as it turned out) had a positive fear of territorial loss.

Nevertheless, it is debatable just how well-prepared Germany was for war, especially in terms of stockpiles and access to raw materials, and within a few years it was evident that Germany's decision to go to war was an even more fundamental miscalculation than British policy in the 1930s.[46] In sum, Germany's trade policies added to German political influence in south-east Europe and to economic preparation for war, but the extent of these gains can be overstated—it was certainly less than a guarantee of ultimate victory in war with Britain.

Whatever the political benefits from regional preferential trading arrangements, they involved economic costs. During the 1930s the approach to PTAs was not to reduce trade barriers for preferred trading partners, but rather to increase trade barriers on non-preferred trade, so that instead of trade creation and trade diversion the outcome was trade destruction and trade diversion, both involving resource misallocation costs. There were also administrative costs, at a maximum those of totally directing foreign trade and at a minimum the need to establish rules of origin for trade within imperial PTAs. Underlying the net economic costs, however, there were distributional effects, i.e. gainers as well as losers. Exporters in south-east Europe were strong supporters of close ties with Germany because of the favourable markets for their goods, and they were often influential enough to get their governments to shoulder the burden of debt collection.[47] In the Dominions, primary product exporters were strong supporters of Imperial Preference, and they received some sympathy from British farmers who saw Imperial Preference as a way partially to overturn the repeal of the Corn Laws.

[46] The other side of this coin is the fact that Britain, even apart from any loyalty to the MFN principle, was right not to be tempted to grant preferential treatment for south-east European food exports, since this would have conflicted with Imperial Preference arrangements which in turn helped secure the political loyalty of a far more important granary and raw material supply source.

[47] The point is made by Röpke (1942, 40 n.), and some south-east European examples are given in Child (1958, 153 and 157). On the other hand, the bilateral arrangements hindered industrialization in south-east Europe and this led governments at times to restrict their supply of primary products or their scale of purchases from Germany. Bilateral trading arrangements can also have a differential impact on a country's various exporting regions; e.g. Britain's coal export arrangements with Baltic and Scandinavian countries benefited the English coalfields located near east coast ports but harmed the Welsh coalfields which now faced stronger competition from Polish and German coal exports to Western and southern Europe.

Finally, however the political gains and the economic costs and benefits fell out, there was one generalized political cost in so far as regionalization heightened international tension. The ability of Britain, France, *et al.* to fall back on their colonial markets and to call in imperial debts during the early 1930s surely contributed to the desire of Italy, Japan, and Germany for their own commercial empires. Yet the acquisition of such empires was bound to cause conflict and disagreement by reducing the areas open to trade on equal terms. The League of Nations attempted to halt the process by economic sanctions, but with the USA, Germany, Japan, and many other nations not participating, sanctions caused little economic discomfort to Italy and certainly not enough to deter the Italian takeover of Abyssinia.[48] The sanction-imposing countries lost their Italian trade to non-sanction countries, and soon abandoned the experiment. After that failure of policing by economic pressure, the 'have not' nations were encouraged to further commercial and political expansion, while the 'have' nations, to their increasing frustration, could find no peaceful method of resisting these moves.

5. Looking Ahead

As important as the actual consequences of 1930s trade policies was the perception among designers of the postwar international economic order that these policies had been disastrous. This perception coloured the Anglo-American plans for postwar institutions, which were tailored to avoid repetition of the 1930s. The IMF's mandate on convertibility (i.e. to encourage removal of exchange controls) was aimed at promoting freer trade. The emphasis in the ITO Charter and the GATT was on non-discriminatory trade policies; trade barriers were permissible, but the appropriate instrument was MFN tariffs (with quotas only for temporary use as emergency weapons). The disagreements that did arise between British and American negotiators were minor relative to the scope of their shared positions on the foregoing topics.

[48] Sanctions were imposed in October 1935 and withdrawn in July 1936. For a brief account of the episode see Hufbauer *et al.* (1985, 142–9).

The USA had already pointed the way towards the postwar trade regime by the 1934 Reciprocal Trade Agreement Program, which granted the President authority to negotiate tariff reductions with the principal supplier of a commodity—a key innovation to restrict free-riding on the MFN clause. In practice, however, American negotiating policy was cautious during the remaining prewar years, constantly fearful of the latent power of domestic pressure groups favouring protection. Duties collected, as a percentage of dutiable imports, had by 1938 fallen back to pre-1930 levels, but America was a high-tariff country even then, and Beckett concludes 'that the reciprocal trade agreements programme has not produced any spectacular change in trade' (1941, 113).[49] In addition, the USA was ready to use higher tariffs as a weapon against countries considered to be not treating American exports fairly; for example, MFN concessions were withheld from Australia (between 1936 and 1938) and from Germany, and countervailing duties were applied to imports of certain goods from Germany and Italy before 1939 (Gordon, 1941, 399 and 408), and, despite denunciation of colonial PTAs, the USA continued to trade with Cuba, Puerto Rico, Hawaii, and Alaska outside the MFN framework.

Nevertheless, however slow the progress towards lower tariffs, and despite continuing deviations from the non-discrimination principle, the United States was moving away from the isolationist 'autonomous' economic policy-making of the early 1930s. The Reciprocal Trade Agreements were one aspect. Another example is the contrast between Roosevelt's unilateral decision to leave the gold standard and his refusal to discuss dollar stabilization in 1933 and his co-operation with Britain and France in the 1936 Tripartite Agreement which permitted the franc's

[49] The import-weighted average US tariff was 38.5% after the 1922 Act, 44.9% after Hawley–Smoot, and 38.2% in 1938 (Beckett, 1941, 67). The degree of import liberalization was limited by not negotiating many tariff reductions, by restricting their spread under MFN obligations through reclassification (i.e. specialization of the tariff code), and by refusing negotiations with some countries (e.g. Australia, whose wheat, butter, milk, and other agricultural exports were feared by American farmers). Any assessment of the programme has to balance its success in reversing the protectionist trend against the limited movement away from the very high pre-1934 tariffs, but the cautious conclusion of Beckett seems more appropriate than Gordon's unsupported statement that the programme 'has been remarkably successful' (1941, 407).

devaluation without retaliation or ill-will. By 1941 American representatives were ready to enter seriously into negotiations for a liberal trading system.[50] The Second World War gave them the opportunities to take the leading role.[51]

[50] In addition to the revulsion against the 1930s experience, the American situation was favourable to a liberal trade policy in several respects. The Reciprocal Trade Agreement programme had shifted trade policy authority from Congress to the Executive (a shift which, according to Robert Baldwin (1985), would not be reversed until the 1980s), which is more concerned with international relations and less beholden to domestic sectional interests. The presence of Cordell Hull, a fanatical free-trader, as Roosevelt's secretary of state helped to maintain the administration's momentum for trade liberalization. Even with these temporary advantages (and huge US trade surpluses in the early postwar years), congressional suspicion of trade liberalization measures and of international commitments which might limit America's protectionist elbow-room remained strong enough to prevent ratification of the ITO Charter and leave the more informal GATT as the legal basis for the postwar international trade regime.

[51] The Anglo-American wartime negotiations on the postwar economic arrangements are described in Gardner (1956).

4

Non-Discrimination in the GATT

The negotiations that led to the 1947 General Agreement on Tariffs and Trade (GATT) were strongly influenced by the interwar experience.[1] Many politicians saw restrictive commercial policies in general, and bilateralism in particular, as having contributed to the economic depression of the 1930s and to the outbreak of the war. These perceptions led to a strong will to create a postwar international economic order based on a liberal non-discriminatory trading system. Thus, Article I of the GATT requires that:

> any advantage, favour, privilege or immunity granted by any contracting party to any product originating in or destined for any other country shall be accorded immediately and unconditionally to the like product originating or destined for the territory of all other contracting parties.

In sum, the cornerstone of the GATT is the extension of unconditional most-favoured-nation (MFN) treatment to all fellow-signatories.

Despite the commitment to unconditional MFN treatment, the GATT did not exclude all discriminatory trade policies, and the exceptions illustrate the practical difficulties of legislating against such measures. Notwithstanding Anglo-American agreement on the principle of non-discrimination, British Imperial Preferences were a stumbling block. On British insistence, a 'grandfather' clause permitting continuation of existing preferential

[1] These negotiations were intended to lead to an International Trade Organization (ITO), playing a role akin to that of the IMF; but the ITO Charter was never ratified by the negotiating countries. The provisional trade rules of the ITO were incorporated into the GATT in order to provide a multilateral framework for bilaterally negotiated trade agreements. This interim arrangement was desired by the USA because the Truman Administration wanted concrete results during the three-year extension of the Reciprocal Trade Agreements Act granted in 1945 in order to persuade Congress to ratify the ITO Charter. The goal was not achieved, but by historical accident the more flexible GATT survived to provide the basis for postwar international trade law (Curzon, 1965, 27–33).

TABLE 4.1 Chronology of the GATT

Date	Event
Apr. 1947	Geneva Round (23 countries sign the GATT)
Nov. 1947	March 1948; Havana Conference (ITO Charter)
1949	Annecy Round
1950–1	Torquay Round (30 GATT signatories, accounting for 80% of world trade)
1956	Geneva Round
1960–2	Dillon Round
1964–7	Kennedy Round
1971	GSP incorporated as a derogation from the GATT
1974	First Multifibre Arrangement
1973–9	Tokyo Round
1986–94	Uruguay Round
1995	GATT superceded by the World Trade Organization (WTO)

arrangements was written into the GATT. A second exception arose over the customs union issue, and GATT Article XXIV permits customs unions and free trade areas so long as they involve free trade for substantially all of the participants' goods. Article XIX, permitting temporary actions to deal with market disruption, also allows measures likely to be discriminatory in effect. The grandfather clause had by the 1970s become a dead letter with respect to British Imperial Preferences, but all three loopholes were to provide wedges for undermining the non-discrimination principle during the postwar period.

The operation of the GATT was characterized by a succession of rounds of multilateral trade negotiations (Table 4.1). The early rounds were concerned primarily with achieving reciprocal reductions in the bound (i.e. legal maximum) tariff levels of the major trading nations. The two final rounds lasted longer because they addressed more difficult issues associated with non-tariff barriers to trade. The Tokyo Round led to a significant revision of the GATT by adding an Enabling Clause, which allowed developing countries to adopt preferential tariffs under less stringent conditions than in Article XXIV. The Uruguay Round led to the creation of the World Trade Organization, whose rules essentially incoporated GATT and which will be dealt with in Chapter 7.

1. The Grandfather Clause

Preferential tariffs featured in the Anglo-American negotiations behind the GATT not only as a matter of principle but also around the specific issue of Imperial Preferences—indeed, the negotiations almost broke down on this point. On the American side, easier access to the British, Canadian, and other Commonwealth markets was considered important as a counterweight to protectionist lobbies in selling a more liberal trade policy to the American public. On the British side, the major concern was over protectionist trends in the United States, especially if the Republican Party were to win the 1948 election, and the UK was unwilling to take any initiative in modifying tariff preferences before the level of American tariffs was reduced. There was also a political motive behind Britain's defence of Imperial Preferences; the war effort had strengthened pro-Commonwealth public sentiment, and the tariff preferences provided a means of maintaining ties during the era of growing political independence of Commonwealth members. Thus, although the United States could see a simple economic cost to itself from Imperial Preferences in the form of trade diversion, the British defence of Commonwealth preferences was in terms of bargaining counters and political implications rather than any narrow economic criterion of static welfare maximization.

The USA agreed to the inclusion in the GATT of a grandfather clause permitting continued application of existing preferential trade arrangements (Article I, paragraph 2) in return for British agreement not to increase preference margins. In practice, Britain found that this commitment reduced future bargaining power, because, as long as Britain maintained zero duties on Commonwealth goods, all MFN tariffs were *de facto* bound by the requirement not to increase preference margins. In 1953 Britain even went so far as to obtain a waiver permitting the raising of some unbound duties, but it was little used and closely monitored by other GATT contracting parties (Curzon, 1965, 66).

Ironically, this issue, which had been so emotional in the late 1940s, rapidly lost practical significance as British policy became oriented towards Europe, and Commonwealth preferences formally ended when Britain joined the European Community in 1973. The grandfather clause did, however, play some minor role in justifying the extension of French and Belgian colonial preferences after the formation of the EC to all six EC members (although this clearly created new preferential arrangements too). Perhaps more important, although no legal precedent was established, the grandfather clause condoned politically motivated PTAs which did not meet Article XXIV standards.

2. The Customs Union Issue

The most significant exception to MFN treatment set out in the GATT is contained in Article XXIV, which states conditions under which GATT signatories may form customs unions and free trade areas. The three main conditions are:

1. Trade barriers facing non-members must not 'on the whole' be higher than those previously in effect.
2. Trade barriers must be eliminated on 'substantially all' trade among members.
3. Interim arrangements to permit scheduling the customs union or free trade area must be completed over a reasonable period of time.

The last two conditions were aimed at preventing Article XXIV's use as a cover for less thorough-going preferential trading arrangements.

Article XXIV represents the GATT-drafters' attempt to resolve the potential conflict between their ultimate goals of freer and non-discriminatory trade policies: as long as trade barriers exist, a preferential tariff reduction is a step towards the first goal and away from the second goal. Under what conditions should this step be allowed, as better than no change? Article XXIV accepts that such conditions exist but gets them wrong, because of 'a fundamental misconception of the nature and consequences of the conflict between regional arrangements and non-discriminatory free trade' (Dam, 1963, 615).[2]

[2] Dam quotes a statement by Clair Wilcox (1949, 70–1), a US Department of State official who played a role in drafting the GATT, as typifying the 'confusion of thought' at the time; he, rightly, castigates the statement as a 'nonargument' (Dam, 1963, 633). The same statement also came in for criticism from Viner (1950).

Allowing 100 per cent discrimination of 'substantially all' trade among customs union members and forbidding all partial discrimination has no economic justification;[3] the former could worsen global resource allocation while some partial preferential arrangements could improve it. Even though clarification by economists of the conditions for welfare-improving PTAs only really began after 1950 (see Chapter 8), which perhaps offers some excuse for the GATT's drafters' misconceptions, GATT practice failed to take account of preferential trading theory. There was no attempt to revise Article XXIV. In sum, Article XXIV as drafted was a useless guide to the desirability or undesirability of a PTA, and remained so.

In addition to being poor economics, Article XXIV was not good law; the apparently precise conditions are in practice imprecise. Comparing the average 'height' of a customs union's common trade barriers and its members' previous trade barriers can be done in many ways. How much intra-union trade constitutes 'substantially all', and how fast a transition satisfies the 'reasonable period of time' condition? The latter questions were central to discussions within GATT about the admissibility of EFTA (which excluded the agricultural sector) and the EC–Greece association agreement (which envisaged a twenty-two-year transition period). The tariff height issue arose in the context of the EC whose common external tariff supposedly averaged the generally high French and Italian tariffs and the generally low German and Benelux tariffs,[4] but debates failed to address the yet-to-be-decided common agricultural policy which fostered some astronomical

[3] Indeed, it could be argued that this condition gave a licence for trade-diversion-biased customs unions, because the excluded trade presumably would be in goods where uncompetitive domestic producers had political influence and the trade-creating impact thus would be reduced. Dam (1963, 635) argues that from this perspective a condition requiring substantial reduction in barriers on all intra-union trade would make more sense.

[4] Tariff averaging makes little economic sense because higher tariffs are likely to contain more water, but, even if averages are taken, there remains the problem of how to weight each tariff rate. Despite the protestations by non-members, the EC's common external tariff on manufactured imports gave outsiders better access than earlier customs unions which had tended to adopt the tariff levels of the most protectionist member (e.g. Canadian Confederation and incorporation of the Prairie provinces; South Africa; the inclusion of Tanganyika in a customs union with Kenya and Uganda during the 1920s; and the Benelux agreement of the 1940s—the German Zollverein, in which Prussia to some extent converted to free trade, is the main exception).

effective rates of protection. The consequence of these ambiguities was to render Article XXIV practically unenforceable. As Dam (1963, 619) noted, after reviewing the sources of imprecision, 'the dismaying experience . . . has been that no customs union or free-trade area agreement presented for review has complied with Article XXIV and yet every such agreement has been approved by a tacit or explicit waiver'.[5]

The scathing critique of Article XXIV by Kenneth Dam and others (e.g. Dam, 1963 and 1970; Lortie, 1975) suggests why GATT proved unable to contain increased discrimination in international trade. Article XXIV offers a gaping loophole in the unconditional MFN treatment announced in Article I. Nevertheless, by requiring the reporting and study of proposed customs unions and free trade areas, and by having a clear philosophy of opposition to made-to-measure preferential trading arrangements, it is a loophole rather than a *carte blanche* for discrimination.

3. The Market Disruption Issue

Article XIX permits GATT signatories, in cases of market disruption by imports, to 'suspend the obligation [of the GATT] in whole or in part'. This permits the importing country to avoid the Article XI prohibition on import quotas, and in those safeguard actions sanctioned by GATT quotas were the preferred response. Whether the quotas must be non-discriminatory is not specified, but the general interpretation of international trade lawyers has been that the MFN principle still applied (e.g. Jackson, 1969). There was, however, a major exception to this principle under the GATT aegis, as well as increasing discriminatory safeguard measures outside the GATT purview.

GATT waivers for quantitative restrictions on cotton textile imports by the United States from specified Asian suppliers, which blossomed into the 1961 Short-term Arrangement followed

[5] Almost 30 years later, the chairman of one of the last GATT working parties (on the Canada–USA Free Trade Agreement) introduced the report to the GATT Council in 1991 by observing that 'Over fifty previous working parties on individual customs unions or free trade areas had been unable to reach unanimous conclusions as to the GATT consistency of those agreements. On the other hand, no such agreements had been disapproved explicitly' (World Trade Organization, 1995, 11).

by the 1962 Long-term Arrangement and eventually the Multi-fibre Arrangement (MFA), came to cover virtually all textiles and clothing trade between high-wage and low-wage countries. The MFA and its predecessors are contrary to the GATT spirit not only in their obviously non-temporary nature as safeguards, but also because the MFA mechanism of bilaterally set quotas clearly contravenes the non-discrimination principle.

While the MFA was established under GATT auspices, the more common practice of importing countries has been simply to avoid GATT rules and procedures when it comes to safeguarding industries threatened by disruptive imports. Instead, they have negotiated orderly marketing arrangements with principal suppliers or imposed pressure for 'voluntary' export restraint. The net effect of the multiplying presence of such measures was 'the breakdown of international rules governing safeguard and escape-clause actions' (Pearson, 1983, 4). Attempts to bring market disruption measures back within the GATT framework during the 1973–9 Tokyo Round failed, mainly because of disagreement over the permissibility of selectivity. France and Britain in particular pressed for selectivity in a new safeguard clause, while their opponents stuck by the non-discrimination principle. In the absence of any agreement, Article XIX remained in effect, while bilateral restraints flourish in practice.

The main economic argument against the selective aspect of voluntary export restraints and their like is the same as that against discriminatory trade policies in general. Such measures encourage imports from unrestrained (typically less efficient) suppliers, in place of imports from the restrained supplier, i.e. trade diversion. Of course, to the extent that trade diversion occurs, the measures are failing in their primary purpose of protecting the import-competing industry. Thus, although some protection is afforded in the short and medium term, the long-term effect is likely to be either extension to more and more suppliers (as with textiles and clothing) or abandonment of the measures.[6] Despite these flaws, voluntary export restraints continued to be popular

[6] One reason for the non-renewal by the USA of orderly marketing arrangements with South Korea and Taiwan for footwear in the late 1970s was the rapid growth of imports from other sources (Hong Kong and the Philippines in particular) which made it apparent that continued protection would ultimately require an MFA-type framework covering all low-wage suppliers (Pearson, 1983).

when a principal supplier could be bullied into compliance without antagonizing important trading partners who are minor suppliers of the good in question;[7] they provided a quick fix to satisfy domestic pressures for protection while bypassing the GATT constraints on such action.

The new protectionism based on bilateral non-tariff barriers, which is illustrated by the MFA and which spread to dozens of other goods after the mid-1970s, was a key phenomenon in the erosion of MFN treatment. It will, however, receive only passing treatment in the remainder of this book. The main reason for this omission is that such measures are introduced for protectionary rather than discriminatory motives, and, indeed, if they are truly discriminatory they will have to be dropped or extended to cover all significant (and potentially significant) suppliers—at which point they cease to be truly discriminatory.[8] The preferential trading arrangements dealt with in greater detail in the remainder of this book involve cases where discrimination was itself a principal aim. Nevertheless, it must be kept in mind that the resolution of the market disruption issue contrary to the spirit (and for the most part outside the letter) of GATT contributed to the erosion of the General Agreement's prestige, and hence reduced the force of its inducement to making unconditional MFN treatment the basis for international trade policies.

4. Other GATT-Approved Discrimination

Two other GATT articles permitted discriminatory trade policies,[9] but their influence was felt only during the first decade after 1947. Article XIV authorized imposition of discriminatory QRs by countries facing acute balance of payments problems. During

[7] Condoning such attitudes and approaches to trade policy was itself a major cost in so far as it engendered political discord and undermined confidence in the co-operative approach of the GATT to international economic issues.

[8] This is an overstatement in so far as blocking the most threatening imports may be sufficient; e.g. the MFA now covers almost all low-cost suppliers and obviously discriminates in favour of countries not covered by that label (most notably Italy).

[9] Other articles could support discriminatory measures (e.g. Article XXIII, defining the complaints procedure, allows discriminatory sanctions in the last resort), but they are minor (Curzon, 1965, 66–7) and have proven insignificant in practice.

the immediate postwar period Article XIV provided legitimacy to the prevalent European practice, but as countries approached long-term external balance and their currencies became convertible, BOP-motivated QRs were abandoned (see Chapter 5). Article XXXV authorized non-application of the GATT to a new contracting party. Originally included at India's request (to avoid being bound by the GATT in India's trade relations with South Africa), Article XXXV was invoked by fourteen GATT signatories when Japan became a contracting party in 1955. All the major trading nations involved disinvoked Article XXXV over the next decade, but the episode revealed the unwillingness of many industrialized countries to abide by the non-discrimination principle when faced by fast-growing manufactured imports from low-wage countries.[10]

5. Conclusions

The GATT is an easy institution to criticize. It had little or no enforcement power, and indeed it was not intended to govern world trade policies—only with the abortion of the more ambitious International Trade Organization (ITO) did the GATT assume this role. The GATT rules make a strong opening statement on non-discrimination, but then permit several loopholes, some of which are poorly defined.

The GATT was shaped by its times. The interwar years had shown that no statements from Geneva could by themselves break the stranglehold of bilateral arrangements on intra-European trade; after 1947 GATT principles held no authority in Eastern Europe, while in Western Europe currency convertibility was an essential prerequisite to their functioning. The architects of the postwar system expended too much time and goodwill on the issue of British Imperial Preferences,[11] whose subsequent

[10] This episode is described by Patterson (1966, ch. 6), who concludes that: 'The practices and the policies of the rest of the world toward Japan in the two decades following the end of World War II built up a substantial amount of case law precedent and hazily qualified international approval for the use of discriminatory measures for sheer protectionist purposes' (p. 317) '. . . This was one of the more unsavory chapters in post-war international commercial policy' (p. 318).

[11] Even allowing for wartime strengthening of emotional bonds, it is surprising that continuation of Imperial Preferences was taken so seriously by both British and American architects of the postwar system. Their existence after 1932

importance faded rapidly despite their GATT legality. The customs union issue was taken less seriously than it should have been, because few postwar customs unions or free trade areas were anticipated.[12] The market disruption issue was also not satisfactorily covered within the GATT, which led to discriminatory trade measures under Article XXXV, by special waivers or, more commonly, outside the GATT framework altogether. The rapid industrialization of parts of the Third World based on manufactured export expansion was not foreseen in 1947, and indeed the whole question of the developing countries' role in the international trading system was not addressed in the GATT beyond the American crusade against colonial preferences.[13]

Given these predictive failures and the unpropitious circumstances of the immediate postwar years, it is surprising how durable the GATT proved to be. With few subsequent revisions, it emerged as the guidepost for international trade policies. Despite the many deviations from non-discrimination described in this and the next chapter, Article I of the GATT remained a potent force by placing the onus of justification on the nation introducing a discriminatory trade policy. Nevertheless, if nations were intent on pursuing such policies, there was little that the GATT Secretariat and dispute procedures could do beyond providing adverse publicity. Precisely for this reason, it is important to understand why all the major trading nations subscribed to GATT principles, and yet were increasingly prepared to contravene them. This is the task of the remainder of the book.

had yielded few economic benefits (cf. the concluding assessment in s. 3.3), and more importantly, the second largest trading nation in the preference system had reversed the pro-imperial trade policy of the early 1930s. Canada in the 1940s became a leading proponent of multilateralism, and non-discrimination and, given Canadian presence at most of the international economic negotiations of that decade, this position can hardly have been unknown to the USA and UK (Plumptre, 1977, 17–35).

[12] The four European customs unions (France–Monaco, Italy–San Marino, Switzerland–Lichtenstein, and Belgium–Luxemburg) and the African customs unions among British and Belgian colonies were all seen as special cases, as was the Benelux customs union agreed upon by the three governments-in-exile in September 1944 and consolidated over the following 16 years. Meade *et al.* (1962) provide case studies of the Belgium–Luxemburg and Benelux unions.

[13] Article XV of the ITO Charter permitted tariff preferences for developing countries' exports, subject to certain conditions. This article was not included in the GATT, and Chile's proposal in 1954–5 to incorporate it was rejected.

5

Discrimination in International Trade, 1947–1985

The post-1947 evolution of discriminatory trade policies can be divided into five phases. Between 1947 and the mid-1950s the dominant economic issue was currency convertibility, and during this period the Western European countries, for balance of payments reasons, used discriminatory removal of quantitative trade restrictions to favour intra-European trade over intercontinental trade. After the dismantling of the quantitative restrictions and easing of exchange controls, there was a decade when discrimination was not a major trade issue; although the EC and the generalized system of preferences (GSP) were being negotiated, there was substantial agreement among the major trading nations over their desirability. Renewed proliferation of discriminatory trade agreements after 1967 brought the MFN principle back into the limelight, and opened up controversies between the EC and the USA on this issue. During the 1980s the USA abandoned the principled support of non-discrimination and began following its own discriminatory trade policies. This major change triggered a global debate over the merits of regionalism versus globalism, which coincided with the Uruguay Round of multilateral trade negotiations and is dealt with in the next chapter.

The account in this chapter will be a narrative, with analysis of economic consequences and motivation contained later in the book. The focus will be primarily on Western Europe and the USA. With a few minor exceptions, other major trading nations did not devise discriminatory trade policies of their own and were less active than the USA in opposing deviations from the MFN principle. The many preferential trading arrangements among developing countries will be briefly summarized; like the Council for Mutual Economic Assistance (Comecon), their significance for the international trading system was small.

1. BOP-Motivated Discrimination, 1947–1958

The postwar international economic order negotiated among the wartime allies fell into abeyance after 1947. The IMF and the International Bank for Reconstruction and Development (IBRD) survived, but the ITO never came into existence, and the less ambitious GATT was left to govern trade relations. Between 1947 and 1958, however, the role of the IMF and the GATT in setting the framework for international economic relations among the major trading nations was severely limited by the widespread absence of currency convertibility. The IMF played no role in resolving the acute postwar dollar shortage, because the USA prevented activation of the scarce currency clause and because of the constraints on deficit countries' access to IMF resources,[1] and the IMF remained subordinate to purely European institutions in that continent's monetary arrangements until it co-operated with European governments' moves towards convertibility after 1953 (Patterson, 1966, 113–19). The GATT remained little more than a discussion chamber during the first half of the 1950s because the two largest trading nations, the USA and the UK, would not give serious attention to European-inspired plans for across-the-board tariff cuts or for liberalization of intra-European trade.[2]

[1] Triffin's assessment of the IMF in 1947–56 is representative: 'The record of these ten years is a grim and dismal one . . . The Fund's failures must be recognized' (1957, 116); but in his April 1957 Postscript he presciently saw signs of dramatic change (pp. 339–40). Gardner's history of the wartime and postwar negotiations provides an illuminating perspective; in the original 1956 edition he saw his task as one of explaining the failure of these negotiations to produce lasting results, whereas in the 1969 edition a long new introduction fudges the issue, because by then it was apparent that the creators of these institutions must have done something right.

[2] This debate culminated in the Benelux delegation's formal proposal in 1954 for a GATT amendment to permit regional discrimination. The proposal was withdrawn in the face of strong US-led opposition (Patterson, 1966, 105–7). The most important GATT contribution during its first decade was the deep tariff cuts of the early 'rounds' of negotiations (Geneva in 1947, Annecy in 1948, and, to a lesser extent, Torquay in 1951), which were agreed to by the European nations because the impact on their imports was nullified by QRs; but when the QRs were removed during the next decade they left behind 'only a tattered tariff barrier' (Curzon, 1965, 71). Curzon also emphasized the role of discussions at GATT in familiarizing national ministers and officials with trade policy issues and with other nations' attitudes (p. 95), and he ascribes the decision by the six signatories of the Treaty of Rome to form a GATT-conforming customs union rather than a looser preferential trading arrangement to fear of a negative response in GATT (pp. 68, 96).

The year 1947 was a fateful year for Europe. Britain, still the world's largest importing nation, tried to fulfil its obligation (under the 1945 Loan Agreement with the USA) to restore sterling convertibility in July 1947, but after five weeks convertibility was abandoned as Britain's reserves fell rapidly. Continental Europe continued to run a large trade deficit as the ravages of war were accentuated by a harsh winter. And in the east it became increasingly apparent that the Soviet Union was establishing political domination over the countries liberated by the Soviet army. The USA reacted with a new policy directed at promoting economic reconstruction in Western Europe.

In June 1947 Secretary of State Marshall announced America's willingness to provide financial support for a recovery programme drawn up jointly by European countries. The Western European nations responded enthusiastically through a series of committees which co-ordinated their aid requests, and, after American approval of the programme, the Organization for European Economic Co-operation (OEEC) was established in April 1948. The most specific trade commitments were contained in Article 4 of the OEEC Convention, where the signatories agreed to:

> achieve as soon as possible a multilateral system of payments *among themselves*, and [to] cooperate in relaxing restrictions on trade and payments *between one another*, with the object of abolishing as soon as possible those restrictions which at present hamper such trade and payments. (emphasis added)

Commitment to the ITO principles in Article 6 was vaguer, while the objective of general convertibility passed unmentioned in the OEEC Convention. Although the Marshall Plan was in part prompted by European trade deficits, and although continuing discriminatory QRs in Europe could thus have been justified at least in the short term as GATT-consistent, there was a fundamental difference in orientation between the regionalism of the OEEC Convention and the globalism of the GATT and the IMF. This switch in orientation was supported by the USA because it aided the US political objective of increasing Western European economic interdependence. Also, because the level of Marshall Plan aid was linked to the size of the Euro-American trade deficit, trade diversion at the expense of American exports to Europe was viewed positively by the US Administration as evidence of

European co-operation in keeping the programme within reasonable financial limits. After the financial aid ceased, the USA continued to support the European Payments Union and regionally discriminatory European QRs as anchors of Western Europe political solidarity and as stepping stones to full convertibility, but after 1951 the USA opposed new discrimination.[3]

The group discrimination envisaged in the OEEC Convention was given theoretical support by Frisch (1947; 1948) and Fleming (1951). Their argument is a variant on the theory of the second-best; in the presence of convertibility restrictions, discrimination against imports from hard currency countries may promote additional trade with welfare gains to the importing and soft-currency exporting countries and without harm to third countries. Thus, if a country had excess demand for convertible dollars and excess supply of non-convertible francs, discrimination in favour of imports from France would permit increased mutually beneficial trade with France and would either leave trade with the USA unchanged or reduce the dollar BOP deficit. Given that countries were unwilling to use changes in exchange rates or in domestic economic activity to deal with BOP disequilibria, Fleming advocated clearing unions 'to provide governments with an incentive to apply quantitative import restrictions with the right degree of severity and discrimination' (p. 67) as 'the nearest approximation to the ideal' (p. 69).

Although valid on its own assumptions, the Frisch–Fleming argument for discrimination has had no lasting impact because, as Meade (1951, 423–5) pointed out at the time, exchange rate or macroeconomic policies are superior to direct controls as tools for dealing with BOP disequilibria. These theoretical contributions explain why group discrimination was appealing to European countries facing a chronic dollar shortage and unwilling to

[3] When in 1951 Belgium imposed new restrictions on imports from the dollar area as part of a package to reduce a trade surplus with EPU countries, the USA and Canada expressed concern but accepted the logic that, given the EPU arrangements, Belgium did have a case for at least temporary discrimination against dollar imports. Belgium moved voluntarily to relax the discriminatory measures a few months later, at which point other EPU members led by France spoke against Belgian reduction of discrimination against dollar imports as damaging to the interests of other EPU members. The USA and Canada expressed 'shock' at this position and, although the debate stopped there, it was now clear that the USA saw the EPU and existing BOP-motivated discrimination as transitional measures (Patterson, 1966, 93–7).

sacrifice domestic employment goals during the late 1940s, but was gradually abandoned as alternative BOP adjustment policies were considered in the less crisis-ridden atmosphere of the 1950s.

The practical implementation of group discrimination in Western Europe took the form of liberalizing QRs on intra-European trade but leaving them on trade with non-OEEC countries.[4] Convertibility among OEEC members' currencies was established through the European Payments Union, while they remained non-convertible into non-members' currencies. These measures appear to have had a big impact on OEEC trade patterns, especially before 1953 when the degree of discrimination began to be reduced.

The share of imports from the USA in the OEEC countries' total imports fell from 23 per cent in 1947 to 9 per cent in 1953 and then picked up again in the mid-1950s; the 1958 share, 11 per cent, was the same as that of 1938. Meanwhile, the share of intra-OEEC imports in the OEEC countries' total imports rose continually, from 30 per cent in 1947 to 43 per cent in 1953 and 47 per cent in 1958; the 1938 share had been 40 per cent.[5] Although some of this changing pattern would have accompanied European reconstruction even without group discrimination, the magnitude of the changes and the more stable shares in European countries with only limited discrimination against imports from the USA (e.g. Switzerland and Belgium) suggest a significant impact of discriminatory trade policies on OEEC trade patterns.

Despite the success of group discrimination in promoting intra-OEEC trade, the EPU–OEEC system was abandoned during the 1950s. The permanent dollar shortage feared by many in the late 1940s had been exposed as a short-run phenomenon by 1952, and the resource misallocation costs of non-convertibility and discriminatory QRs no longer seemed worth bearing. Britain and France faced more or less continuous BOP deficits during the 1950s, but the source was not specific to their dollar accounts, and when they tightened import controls they were inclined to

[4] In essentials the effects of discriminatory QRs are similar to those of discriminatory tariffs analysed in Chs. 8 and 9; in both cases the source of resource misallocation is the possibility of encouraging imports from other than the least-cost supplier (Hieronymi, 1973, 14–23).

[5] Figures in these two sentences are from OEEC *Statistical Bulletin: Foreign Trade*, reported in Hieronymi (1973, 128–54).

do so on all imports.[6] Surplus countries like West Germany and the Benelux nations also felt constrained by the EPU, which obliged them either to grant ever-increasing credits or to allow their own inflation rates to rise, neither of which they desired to do. After mid-1953 several EPU members took national steps towards convertibility which reduced the need for special credit arrangements on intra-OEEC trade and led to negotiations in July 1953 for the EPU's dissolution (Triffin, 1957, 212–20), although formal dissolution was delayed until 1958 by renewed inflation and the aftermath of the Suez Crisis. Discriminatory trade barriers for BOP reasons were then removed, although the process took about five years before they ceased to be a significant feature in international trade relations.[7]

The other important case of BOP-motivated group discrimination was the operation of the Sterling Area between 1939 and 1958. During the war, members sold their hard currency earnings to the British Treasury for sterling and confined their dollar purchases to items not readily available within the Sterling Area. The dollar pool should have been phased out when sterling became convertible in 1947, but after the failure to maintain convertibility Sterling Area co-operation on trade policies was intensified instead; for example, in July 1949 each member agreed to cut its dollar expenditure during the following twelve months to 25 per cent below their calendar 1949 level in order to halt the drain on the dollar pool. At the 1950 GATT session in Torquay there was a bitter debate over the Sterling Area policies; an IMF report concluding that BOP-motivated discrimination was no longer justifiable for some Sterling Area members was supported by Belgium, Canada, Cuba, and the USA, but contested by the UK, Australia, and New Zealand. The outcome was inconclusive,

[6] The desire to import from the cheapest source was stronger in the presence of BOP deficits, but this motive lay behind all countries' dissatisfaction with BOP-motivated discrimination both in Europe and elsewhere; South Africa, for example, cited this as the motive for abandoning the practice in 1953 (Patterson, 1966, 40).

[7] Dismantlement was slow because some of the trade barriers had had a protective effect and hence had created domestic interest groups opposed to their immediate removal. Trade with Eastern Europe continued to be governed by bilateral agreements. Within Western Europe the OEEC Code for Trade Liberalization became a dead letter—especially with the division of OEEC members between the EC Six and the EFTA Seven—and formally went out of force when the OEEC was transformed into the OECD in 1960.

and the episode was a low point for international co-operation based on sound principles.[8] It was also unnecessary as the UK moved towards convertibility in 1953; thereafter there was some continuing co-operation among Sterling Area countries, but this had ceased to be a source of significant dispute by 1958.

The discrimination involved in the Sterling Area's operation varied over time and across countries. Patterson (1966, 68) describes it as 'extensive', and this is supported by Thorbecke's evidence that intra-area imports increased from 40 per cent of total Sterling Area imports in 1938 to 50 per cent in 1953. During the next three years, however, this share slipped to 44 per cent, and Thorbecke concludes that 'the trend towards regionalization within the Sterling Area had come to an end in 1954'.[9] As in the case of Western Europe, this experience indicates that the rise and fall of group discrimination did have an impact on trade flows.

With the re-establishment of convertibility among the major trading nations' currencies, monetary arrangements ceased to play any part in the story of discriminatory trade policies after 1958. Although Frisch and Fleming had demonstrated a theoretical case for trade discrimination to deal with BOP problems, in practice, countries abandoned these policies once their resource misallocation costs became apparent. There are superior policies for dealing with BOP disequilibria once the Frisch–Fleming assumptions of non-convertibility (or fixed exchange rates and no use of domestic macroeconomic policy to achieve external balance) are relaxed. In the absence of these assumed constraints, countries see no BOP reason to justify purchasing imports from other than the cheapest source. Thus, the current relevance of the Frisch–Fleming case for discriminatory trade policies is nil, and it will receive little consideration in the remainder of this book. Nevertheless, the pre-1958 episode did have one important long-term implication, in that the decade-long intensification of intra-OEEC

[8] The IMF's decision not to press its case highlighted its impotence. The USA refused to discuss the argument that Sterling Area arrangements were a stepping-stone towards convertibility—not surprisingly, as the USA was simultaneously supporting the EPU on precisely these grounds. The UK reasserted the non-negotiability of institutional ties binding the Commonwealth together, just as these ties were about to diminish.

[9] Thorbecke (1960, 131–2); trade between India and Pakistan is excluded to maintain pre- and post-independence comparability.

trading paved the way for some continental European countries to consider economic integration as part of a political integration movement.

2. Western European Economic Integration

Western European economic integration occupies a prominent role in the postwar history of discriminatory trade policies. By the sheer size of the individual countries' international trade, a preferential trading arrangement involving France, Germany, Italy, and the Benelux nations (and later Britain, Spain, and other smaller countries) was bound to be an important step. Moreover, the European Economic Community of the Six provided an example for customs unions elsewhere in the world (especially in Latin America), and upset predictions about customs unions' insignificance in the postwar world.

The Anglo-American negotiators, who had drawn up blueprints for the postwar international economic order, failed to devise a satisfactory solution to Europe's security problems. The two major European powers invaded by Germany were unwilling to rely either on the United Nations for collective security or on a liberal international economic order to remove the source of revived German expansion. For the USSR the solution was a simple one: the conquered territories of Eastern Europe became satellites which provided a wide buffer zone between the Soviet Union and Germany. For France the problem was more difficult; initially favouring stringent restriction on Germany's industrial recovery and international control of German key resources, France made the crucial policy decision to work for a Franco-German *rapprochement* after a repressive peace had been rejected by the British and the Americans. Italy and the Benelux countries had opposed economic suppression of Germany (their major trading partner), and were willing to join in the new French policy.[10] This line-up set the stage for an economic split in Western Europe, as Britain, the Scandinavian countries, and the neutrals opposed

[10] Italy and France had negotiated, but not approved, a customs union in 1948, the same year as Benelux was formed. Both of these arrangements could have been important trade policy developments, but they were overshadowed by and became submerged in the European Economic Community.

formation of an exclusive West European trading bloc, but proved powerless to stop the Six from moving in that direction.

The first big step in the new French policy came on 9 May 1950, when Foreign Minister Robert Schuman announced his government's proposal 'that the entire French–German production of coal and steel be placed under a common High Authority, in an organization open to the participation of the other countries of Europe'; this would be 'the first step in the federation of Europe' and would 'make it plain that any war between France and Germany becomes, not merely unthinkable, but materially impossible' (quotation in English from Diebold, 1959, 1). Britain and others refused to participate in negotiations based on granting supranational power to the High Authority, but France, Germany, Italy, and the Benelux countries went ahead and the European Coal and Steel Community (ECSC) Treaty was signed in April 1951. The Treaty was submitted to the GATT in October, before going to the national parliaments of the Six for ratification.

The ECSC clearly failed to meet GATT requirements; by eliminating barriers to trade in coal and steel products among the Six but retaining barriers to trade with outsiders, the ECSC was discriminatory, and it was obviously not covered by the 'substantially all trade' requirement of GATT Article XXIV.[11] Moreover, several small European nations expected to suffer economic damage from the ECSC's formation, either through loss of export markets (e.g. Austria and Sweden) or through cartel behaviour by their suppliers (e.g. Denmark, Norway, and Sweden), while other countries worried about the precedent and loss of GATT authority if such an outright breach were condoned. Nevertheless, in November 1952 GATT waivers were formally granted for the ECSC, with only Czechoslovakia opposing. The crucial factors were that the ECSC members had already ratified the Treaty during the summer and would go ahead regardless, and that the US government had supported their case 'with uncritical enthusiasm' (Patterson, 1966, 128); under such conditions a negative vote was

[11] Although failure to fulfil the letter of GATT was inevitable, the Six did try to reduce the potential conflict by having complete free trade within the ECSC, despite Belgian and Italian pressure for internal protection for their coal and steel industries respectively (Frank, 1961, 27). According to Diebold (1959), the USA exerted pressure for this outcome—as well as for German participation when Germany had second thoughts in early 1951.

more likely to destroy GATT than to prevent the ECSC. Despite this capitulation, by requiring the ECSC High Authority to make annual reports to GATT, the principle of accountability for trade policies was affirmed, and ECSC policies do seem to have been modified during the next five years in response to complaints at GATT by trading partners who would otherwise have been without influence.

The years 1951–3 were a high point for European federalists; establishment of the ECSC was followed by the European Defence Cooperation plan and proposals for a European Parliament to control these and future federal institutions. In 1954, however, the French Assembly rejected the European Defence Cooperation plan; military and political unification was postponed indefinitely, and further unification would be through economic channels. Despite this setback, the European integration process soon regained momentum. The 1955 Messina meeting of the Six's foreign ministers set up the Spaak Committee to report on the possibility of a common market and sectoral integration in transport and energy. The Committee's work culminated in the 1957 Rome Treaties establishing the European Economic Community and Euratom.

From our present perspective, the key aspect of the Rome Treaties was the establishment of a customs union among the Six. Discussion within the GATT focused on whether the proposed common external tariff (CET) fulfilled the Article XXIV requirements of fairness.[12] The EEC proposed a simple average of their four tariff rates (Benelux counting as a single unit), but other countries argued that they would be hurt more by the increases in low tariffs than they would gain from reductions in high tariffs.[13] The EEC's position seemed even more suspect when they used their legal maximum tariffs, rather than their actual tariffs, as the basis for calculating the CET. There was, however, no doubt that with strong US support the EEC would gain GATT

[12] The EEC's treatment of associated overseas territories incurred even stronger opposition, but the EEC avoided discussion of this policy (see S. 5.3).

[13] The fundamental problem that there is no meaningful average of, say, a 30% and a zero tariff was discussed in Ch. 4. Later commentators on the EEC's simple average approach expressed conflicting views about its fairness; Patterson (1966, 165–9) criticized the EEC's position, while Frank (1961, 294) considered it a good practical way of conforming to GATT requirements.

approval, and in fact the CET issue was defused by the Six accelerating the alignment of their national tariffs and reducing the CET by 20 per cent on many industrial goods during the Dillon Round.

With the benefit of hindsight, we can see that the GATT discussion was misfocused; the CET would not be a significant source of future conflict, as its rates fell in the Kennedy and Tokyo Rounds. The real problem of access to EEC markets has concerned agricultural products, but, since the Common Agricultural Policy was not specified in the Rome Treaty and its nature decided upon only in the early 1960s, this was not a serious issue in 1957.

The Treaty of Rome was an important milestone towards Western European integration, but its immediate effect was to create a rift among the OEEC countries. The EEC involved discrimination by the Six against other OEEC members, breaching the OEEC Code. When negotiations for an OEEC-wide free trade area (incorporating the EEC) broke down, seven non-EEC countries in November 1959 signed the Stockholm Convention creating the European Free Trade Association (EFTA).[14] Despite concern over the establishment of a new regional bloc, EFTA contained little that could be objected to within GATT; the main objection was the omission of agricultural trade,[15] but with over 90 per cent of EFTA's total trade covered, it was hard to deny that 'substantially all trade' was included.

For a brief spell in the early 1960s, there was bloc competition in Western Europe. Initially, it was unclear whether this was to be a source of lasting trade discrimination, or a debate over the relative merits of a customs union including agriculture or a free trade area excluding agriculture as the basis for Western European economic integration. Meanwhile, both blocs soon gained

[14] Although the OEEC lost any effective purpose, there was uncertainty about the stability of the EEC and EFTA arrangements which replaced the OEEC trading system. One reason for the OEEC's metamorphosis into the OECD in 1960 was a desire by the USA and Canada to keep open alternative channels for European trade liberalization.

[15] More damaging to GATT principles were bilateral guarantees given for Danish agricultural exports in order to grant some measure of reciprocity. These primarily involved pork and dairy exports to Britain and Switzerland, where Denmark already had an established market position, and hence invoked little protest from third countries, although Patterson (1966, 217–18) argues that the guarantees did divert some trade in favour of Denmark.

new associate members. Finland's association with EFTA in 1961 practically involved it as a full member and posed no new problems within GATT, although the USSR as a non-GATT-signatory demanded MFN treatment (i.e. the same free access to Finland's markets as its EFTA partners would receive) and Finland was constrained to renegotiate its treaty with the USSR.[16] Greece's 1961 association agreement with the EEC conformed less clearly to Article XXIV, because the envisaged transition to full membership could take as long as twenty-two years, but protests were in vain—and ironically, full membership was achieved more speedily despite an eight-year hiatus in the process when Greek democracy was suspended. A consequence of Greek association was that the Six felt obliged to grant Turkey's request for similar status, and Turkey became an associate in 1964, although the EC seemed insincere about the future goal of full membership and the timetable to customs union was vague.

Apart from the completion of the EC's customs union in July 1968, the main event of the 1960s and 1970s was the rapprochement between EFTA and the EC, with Britain playing the crucial role. During the 1950s Britain had consistently opposed any supranationality, and for this reason had remained outside the ECSC and the Rome Treaty negotiations, but after 1960 it decided not to continue to remain outside the mainstream of Western European integration, which was increasingly obviously centred in Brussels. In 1961 Britain (accompanied by Denmark and Norway) applied for EC membership, promising EFTA colleagues that it would not join until satisfactory arrangements had been made to meet the legitimate interests of all EFTA members. The initial application was vetoed by France in January 1963, but a later application was successful, and Britain (accompanied by Denmark and Ireland) joined the European Community at the beginning of 1973. In July 1972 the EC signed bilateral free trade agreements in non-agricultural goods with the remaining EFTA countries and Iceland. After the end of dictatorships in Greece, Portugal, and Spain in 1974 and 1975, these southern European

[16] Although this in turn contravened Finnish MFN obligations to other non-EFTA countries, it was accepted as a special case. The USSR also compromised in recognition of geopolitical realities when accepting British and Swedish rejection of Soviet demands for MFN (i.e. intra-EFTA) treatment in their markets (Curzon, 1965, 285–6 and 65; Patterson, 1966, 60 and 225; Camps, 1964, 351–2).

countries applied successfully for full EC membership, which took effect in 1981 for Greece and in 1986 for Spain and Portugal. The European Community of Twelve now included all of Western Europe, apart from the 'neutrals' (i.e. the five EFTA members: Austria, Switzerland, Finland, Sweden, and Norway) and the island economies (Cyprus, Iceland, and Malta), which were linked to the EC by free trade agreements. For trade policy purposes, the economic integration of Western Europe was essentially complete.[17]

The various intra-European arrangements described in this section all involved discriminatory trade policies, whose economic effects will be assessed in Chapter 12. Many of the individual steps contravened GATT rules, but in fact they were largely unopposed by non-European GATT contracting parties. Initially, at least, the transition from the OEEC group discrimination to the EEC and EFTA seemed to involve little new discrimination against imports from outside Europe, and this was reinforced by the EEC's active participation in the Dillon and Kennedy Rounds when the common external tariff was lowered substantially. Another reason for the smooth passage of the ECSC and EEC during the 1950s was the firm support given by the USA, with the political goal of creating a strong bulwark against Soviet expansion.[18] These were both short-run motives, whose influence faded during the 1960s as the EC's agricultural policy aroused protests from non-members and as an easing of East–West tensions led to a waning of unqualified US support for the Community; by then, however, the mould of Western European integration had been set and the EC was able to stand up for itself against outside criticism. Nevertheless, as it turned out in the long run, Western European economic integration has not itself posed a serious challenge to GATT principles (unlike the EC policies

[17] The word 'essentially' is of course subjective. Many non-tariff barriers to imports were still administered at the national level, and many barriers to free trade within Western Europe remained, but the coverage of the EC's common commercial policy was now more similar to that of federal states than to that of any other group of independent nations.

[18] Although American pressure at critical moments may have helped to push forward Western European integration during the 1950s, the strongest influence was on the form that this integration took, as the USA consistently worked against the British/Scandinavian vision of turning the OEEC into a European free trade area with no supranational organization.

described in the next section); the EC appears increasingly as a definitive step towards some form of Western European unification, and prior consolidation of its customs area can then be viewed in similar light to the earlier national consolidations described in Chapter 2.

3. The European Community's External Trade Policy

Both the EC and EFTA tried to make their basic customs union and free trade area arrangements as GATT-compatible as possible.[19] The same cannot be said for the EC's external trade policy, which became the most flagrant breach of the non-discrimination principle. The Rome Treaty itself contained the seeds of a discriminatory external trade policy, although the amount of trade immediately affected by preferential trading arrangements with non-members was small. The initial transgressions were, however, not prevented, and the geographically discriminatory application of the EC's external trade barriers became chronic after the late 1960s.

The greatest conflict between the Rome Treaty and GATT rules arose over the Treaty's provision for associated overseas territories, by which each member's colonies would enjoy a preferential trading arrangement with the entire Community. Such an extension of colonial preferences could not be justified by the grandfather clause, and an expert committee (in the Haberler Report—GATT, 1958) emphasized that, given the absence of European production of the African colonies' export goods, only trade diversion could be expected and the main external sufferers would be poor countries. Britain (acting on behalf of British colonies) and several Latin American countries spoke against the association agreements, but the USA let it be known from the outset that it supported the agreements,[20] and the EC took the position that they were non-negotiable (although the Six promised

[19] Curzon (1965, 68 and 96) argues that the Six would have adopted a looser preferential trading arrangement had it not been for the threat of US and UK retaliation against such an obvious breach of GATT rules. The EFTA Convention included an article (XXXVII) stating that nothing in the Convention exempted EFTA members from their GATT obligations.

[20] Machiavellian, or political ineptitude, or just political preoccupation with getting the Common Market off to a flying start? Curzon (1965, 280) does not answer his question about American motivation.

to envisage action should serious damage to third countries occur). Thus, 'the association of the overseas territories had to be accepted for political reasons, though it was contrary to all GATT rules' (Curzon, 1965, 289).

Upon the associated overseas territories gaining political independence during the early 1960s, their preferential trading arrangements with the Six were formalized in the Yaoundé Convention. To limit discrimination against other African countries, the EC offered them special trading relationships. Nigeria signed an association agreement in 1966, but because of the civil war over Biafra it was never implemented. Kenya, Uganda, and Tanzania signed the Arusha Agreement with the EC in 1968, and Mauritius acceded to the Yaoundé Convention in 1972. With Britain's successful application for EC membership in the early 1970s, associate status was offered to Commonwealth countries having similar economies to the Yaoundé associates (thus excluding the populous Asian Commonwealth members) and to other African countries with no colonial past. After lengthy negotiations, the Lomé Convention was signed in 1975.

The 1975 Lomé Convention between the EC and the associated African, Caribbean, and Pacific (ACP) states was heralded as a new form of North–South co-operation.[21] Twitchett (1978, 164), for example, felt that 'the duty-free access enjoyed by the ACP states to EEC markets could be potentially decisive for their economic development'. On examination, however, the Lomé trade preferences did not offer much to countries whose exports are overwhelmingly primary products. Goods covered by the EC's Common Agricultural Policy were largely excluded, while the EC's common external tariff on other primary products was low and often zero. The only significant trade impact was likely to concern sugar, for which the EC guaranteed minimum purchases from ACP countries; as it turned out, these guarantees helped to limit the ACP exporters' market loss as the EC approached sugar self-sufficiency, rather than stimulating additional exports.

[21] The Lomé Convention has since been renewed, and expanded to include 70 African, Caribbean and Pacific States. Grilli (1993, 9–10) lists the participants in the Yaoundé Convention and the first four Lomé Conventions. As well as free access to EC markets for virtually all exports not covered by the CAP, the Lomé Convention provides for development aid and a commodity export earnings stabilization scheme.

Manufactured exports received more substantial preference margins, but were restricted by rules of origin requiring 50–60 per cent local value added and by a safeguard clause. The rules of origin are onerous for countries with limited local infrastructure and intermediate goods industries, and especially work against the labour-intensive assembly activities in which poor countries may have a comparative advantage (McQueen, 1982). I do not know of any actual use of the safeguard clause, but the threat of its use in 1979 encouraged Mauritius voluntarily to restrain textile exports to the EC; the important point here is that the EC's perceived readiness to withdraw duty-free access even at low levels of supply creates uncertainty, which is harmful to export-oriented investment, and illustrates the hollowness of the EC's promotion of the Lomé Convention as an equal partnership.

At the same time as it was granting special tariff preferences to the Yaoundé countries, the EC was supporting the developing countries' demands at UNCTAD for generalized tariff preferences applicable to all developing countries. When the GATT waiver permitting GSP was agreed in 1971, the EC was the first to put its scheme into action (see next section). The EC's GSP scheme was, however, carefully constructed so as to limit erosion of the value of tariff preferences for the associated African states (Stordel, 1977). The Latin American and Asian GSP beneficiaries were granted preferential treatment relative to the EC's common external tariff, but received worse treatment than the Lomé countries.

The EC entered into preferential trade agreements with almost all the Mediterranean countries by the early 1970s. In 1957 Algeria was part of France and the Rome Treaty provided for special relations with independent countries of the franc zone (i.e. Morocco and Tunisia), although the legal basis of these three countries' EC relations remained confused through the 1960s and the actual treatment of their exports varied from one EC member to another. Greece and Turkey signed association agreements (in 1961 and 1963 respectively) providing for customs union with the EC over long transitional periods, but apart from these two agreements and the Yaoundé Convention the EC was not particularly active in promoting discriminatory trading arrangements during the early and mid-1960s. Requests for associate status from Iran, Israel, and Spain were refused. A more active Mediterranean policy emerged towards the end of the decade.[22] Association agreements were concluded with Morocco and Tunisia in 1969, with Malta in 1970, and with Cyprus in 1972. Preferential trade agreements were signed with Spain and Israel in 1970, and to maintain an Israeli–Arab balance the EC offered favourable consideration to any request for a similar agreement from a Mediterranean Arab country; Egypt, Lebanon, Jordan, and Syria responded to the offer. Meanwhile, Yugoslavia had signed a non-preferential trade agreement with the EC, so that by 1972 Albania and Libya were the only Mediterranean countries without interest in special trade relations with the European Community.

To bring order into the unplanned chaos of the EC's bilateral arrangements with Mediterranean countries, in 1972 the EC Commission proposed a 'global' Mediterranean policy. The trade-related feature of the proposal was the creation of a free trade area, similar to that with Portugal under the 1972 EC–EFTA agreement, with the EC phasing out its tariffs on manufactured imports from the Mediterranean countries by 1977 and granting concessions covering at least 80 per cent of each Mediterranean country's agricultural exports to the EC, while the Mediterranean countries would remove their trade barriers on EC exports at a pace reflecting their individual levels of development. The proposal was subsequently modified in many respects, but the EC tariff preferences were introduced more or less intact in 1977 (although the southern Mediterranean countries were not required to reciprocate with preferential treatment for EC exports).[23] These

[22] During the earlier part of the 1960s completion of the internal customs union, the CAP, and the Kennedy Round negotiations took up more of the EC's attention, and the controversy surrounding France's 'empty chair' in 1965 made the Commission cautious about taking up new policy initiatives. By 1967 the customs union and agricultural policy had been practically achieved and the Kennedy Round had shown that the Six could pursue a common commercial policy. The Arab–Israeli war and Greek colonels' coup drew the EC's attention to the Mediterranean in that year (Pomfret, 1986a, 19–20).

[23] The non-trade elements of the original proposal were cut back further. There was some debate at the time over just how 'global' the actual policy was (Tsoukalis, 1977; Tovias, 1977), but in its trade aspects the common economic core of free access for manufactured exports and preferred treatment for agricultural exports from the Mediterranean countries applied to all participants (Pomfret, 1986a, 23 and 106). Yugoslavia remained a partial exception in so far as the 1980 PTA gave duty-free treatment to only 70% of Yugoslav industrial exports, but most remaining exports (including important agricultural items) received preferential access to EC markets.

are far-reaching discriminatory trade arrangements which, especially before Greek, Portugese, and Spanish accession to the EC, involved larger trading nations than the Lomé Convention. They are blatant contraventions of GATT, but protests from many third countries (including the USA) had no preventive impact.[24]

Considering the number of countries covered by the Global Mediterranean Policy, the Lomé Convention, the EC–EFTA free trade area, and GSP, how many countries were left facing the EC's common external tariff by the second half of the 1970s? The state-trading countries made special arrangements, reflecting the diminished role of market prices in their dealings. Thus, only a handful of market economies faced the purportedly MFN tariffs of the EC: Australia, Canada, Japan, New Zealand, South Africa, Taiwan, and the USA. And with the prevalence of discriminatory non-tariff barriers on imports from Japan and Taiwan and the threat of sanctions against South Africa, true MFN treatment was even more limited[25]—a situation which made a mockery of GATT Article I.

4. Developing Countries and GATT

One of the casualties of the ITO's death was its special provisions for development-inspired trade policies; the original GATT

[24] As mentioned in the previous section, the American attitude towards the EC became less positive during the 1960s. The EC's Mediterranean agreements contributed to this disenchantment; the USA saw in them no political benefits, a clear challenge to GATT principles, and discrimination against American exports. (The Florida citrus industry complained vociferously about agreements granting Israeli, Moroccan, and Spanish oranges preferential access to the large EC market—eventually to the exclusion of non-Mediterranean imports.) The complaint initiated by the USA in 1982 against the EC's treatment of citrus imports from certain Mediterranean countries was the first case brought before GATT dispute setlement procedures with respect to Article XXIV; although the panel supported the US complaint and recommended compensation, the EC and the preferred suppliers blocked adoption of the panel's report.

[25] Admittedly, none of the EC's preferential trade agreements covered all goods, but if any non-discriminatory EC trade barriers existed they covered few items. (The most likely cases are prohibitive barriers against agricultural imports.) Also, some EC preference recipients were discriminated against by non-tariff barriers; e.g. the MFA ensured better treatment for developed country textile and clothing exports to the EC than for such exports from GSP beneficiaries. These exceptions to the 'pyramid of privilege', as the EC's external trade policies have been labeled (Stevens, 1981), do not overturn my conclusions—they only show how complex discriminatory trading systems tend to become.

contained only one article (XVIII) on economic development, and it was sharply circumscribed.[26] Developing countries were reluctant to become contracting parties to the GATT, although the number of non-signatories gradually declined. Their main concern was to retain commercial policy autonomy, including the flexibility to increase trade barriers in order to protect infant industries. Although totally against the spirit of GATT, these concerns become relevant to the present book only when they are used as arguments for discriminatory trade policies to create larger sheltered markets. A second concern of the developing countries was to obtain preferential access to developed countries' markets for their exports—a cause that was pursued effectively within the United Nations framework during the 1960s and ratified by the 1971 GATT waiver permitting a generalized system of preferences (GSP) for developing countries' exports.

Preferential trade arrangements among developing countries

The dominant development strategy of the 1950s was import-substituting industrialization. Under the influence of the United Nations Economic Commission for Latin America, the independent countries of Latin America sought to overcome the problem of small domestic markets by integration schemes, which hoped to encourage investment for the entire regional market while providing protection from extra-regional imports.[27] After several years of negotiations, the Latin American Free Trade Area, or LAFTA (involving Mexico and all the South American republics) and the Central American Common Market were both established by treaties signed in 1960. The timing also reflected the example of the European Common Market, but LAFTA was a far looser arrangement than the EEC. By 1967 disenchantment with its progress led to fragmentation as five Andean nations began

[26] Initially, opponents had worried that Art. XVIII offered a huge loophole for most countries in the world to avoid GATT obligations, but early cases, in which the UK (on behalf of Northern Rhodesia) and Cuba invoked Art. XVIII unsuccessfully, discouraged further use (Curzon, 1965, 212–14).

[27] Abortive negotiations in the early 1940s had had similar aims; e.g. the five River Plate countries had agreed in 1941 on preferential tariff reductions on goods for which there was little competition among themselves, but the agreement was not ratified.

negotiations, which culminated in the 1969 Cartagena Agreement creating the Andean Pact, and as other LAFTA members made bilateral arrangements. In 1980 LAFTA was replaced by the more 'flexible' (i.e. with little binding content) Latin American Integration Association.

The source of LAFTA's instability was the wide range of size and level of development among its members, from smaller poorer countries like Bolivia and Paraguay to larger and relatively highly developed countries like Argentina, Brazil, and Mexico. Within the more industrialized LAFTA countries, the manufacturing sector had sufficient political power to block the national tariff reductions required for a true free trade area.[28] And, to the extent that LAFTA did stimulate new industrialization, the less advantaged countries felt they were unable to attract their fair share and thus were falling further behind, while the richer LAFTA members opposed redistributive measures to compensate the poorer members.[29] The more homogeneous Andean Pact was initially more dynamic, but in late 1975 a crisis arose over the external tariff, sector plan, and election of new Pact authorities, after which the integration process slowed down. The Central American Common Market functioned reasonably well for most of its first decade, but in 1968 Nicaragua introduced discriminatory measures against the other CACM members and in 1970 Honduras seceded (Edwards and Savastano, 1989, 196–7).[30]

[28] See Vaitsos (1978, s. A). Willmore (1972, 660) reports similar reservations about the CACM in Costa Rica.

[29] There were also worries that LAFTA might attract direct foreign investment, as the EEC was perceived to have done. Grunwald *et al.* (1972, 14 n.) state that Servan-Schreiber's *Le Défi Américain* 'allegedly sold more copies in Brazil than in France'. By its Decision 24, the Andean Pact countries made a common policy towards foreign investment a central feature of their agreement. During the 1980s some Pact members began weakening the content of Decision 24 because it discouraged foreign investment too strongly, and by the 1990s they were encouraging foreign investors.

[30] Whether Honduras's secession arose from dissatisfaction with the CACM or from independently determined conflicts with El Salvador is unclear. Nugent (1974, 9 n.) states that 'This drastic action was partially based on growing concern in Honduras that it was not receiving its fair share of the benefits of the CACM'; but he also traces it back to Honduran expropriation of illegal Salvadorean immigrants' land and El Salvador's military reaction in 1969. Wionczek (1972), who had given an optimistic report in 1968 on the CACM, explained the 1969 'soccer war' in terms of rising economic and social tensions, but the actual CACM

Other integration schemes among developing countries during the 1950s and 1960s were more backward looking, trying to retain close economic ties forged by a common colonial heritage.[31] The British West Indies Federation (1958–62) was followed by the Caribbean Free Trade Association (CARIFTA) in 1965. Antigua, Barbados, and Guyana, the original CARIFTA members, were joined by Dominica, Grenada, Jamaica, Montserrat, St Kitts–Anguilla, St Lucia, St Vincent, and Trinidad and Tobago in 1968, and by Belize in 1971. CARIFTA was succeeded in 1973 by a customs union, the Caribbean Community (CARICOM), which also envisaged harmonization of fiscal and monetary policies, and co-ordinated the planning of agricultural and industrial development. Introduction of import licencing by Guyana and Jamaica in response to the 1973–4 oil shock, however, immediately undermined the customs union.

In Africa, Kenya, Uganda, and Tanzania formed the East African Community (EAC) after independence, but this was disbanded in 1977. Since the collapse of the French West African Federation, its constituent states have made three attempts to reconstitute some degree of economic integration, most recently in the Communauté Economique de l'Afrique de l'Ouest (CEAO). The francophone states of central Africa are linked in the Union Douaniere et Economique de l'Afrique Centrale, while further south Zaire, Burundi, and Rwanda formed the Community of the Great Lakes, and Botswana, Lesotho, Swaziland, and South Africa the Southern African Customs Union.

rupture arose after the war's end when a proposed special development fund to channel additional resources to Honduras was vetoed by El Salvador. In general, war between member states does not augur well for a customs union's survival (the Tanzanian–Uganda war preceded the final breakup of the East African Community), although the Southern African Customs Union survived many acts of military aggression by the largest member on smaller members. Soccer games also seem unhealthy; in December 1979 a friendly match between Liberia and Sierra Leone ended in a free-for-all fight between players, supporters, and officials of both teams (Onwuka and Sesay, 1985, 132), and relations between these two Mano River Union (MRU) members remained strained through the 1980s, although the 1980 Liberian military coup was a more fundamental source of tension.

[31] Some schemes predated independence; e.g. Southern Rhodesia's 1948 customs union with South Africa was the first Art. XXIV case submitted for GATT approval, but it terminated when Southern Rhodesia joined Northern Rhodesia and Nyasaland in another short-lived customs union in 1955.

Later African schemes, however, cut across colonial backgrounds;[32] in particular, the Economic Community of West African States (ECOWAS) established by the 1975 Lagos Treaty contains sixteen anglophone and francophone countries. The 1973 Mano River Union between Liberia and Sierra Leone (joined by Guinea in 1980) and the nine-member Southern African Development and Coordination Conference (established 1980) also crossed historical lines.[33] Despite their profusion, the African integration schemes have had little impact on world trade; the sub-Saharan African economies are (except for Nigeria and South Africa) small, their trade is mainly with non-African countries, and the schemes themselves have been ravaged by distributional conflicts as new nations have been jealous of their policy-making autonomy.

Asia, in contrast to the Americas and Africa, was almost devoid of preferential trading arrangements. In South Asia and Northeast Asia this reflected political antagonisms between formerly integrated trading units. In Southeast and Southwest Asia the regional treaty organizations formed as bulwarks against communism introduced economic components, but with little real content. Iran, Pakistan, and Turkey signed the Treaty of Izmir in 1977, but the envisaged economic co-operation ceased after the Iranian revolution of 1978–9. The Association of Southeast Asian Nations (ASEAN) was formed by Indonesia, Malaysia, the Philippines, Singapore, and Thailand in 1967 and joined by Brunei in 1984, but ASEAN had no economic content until after its 1977 summit and the trade preferences and co-ordinated

[32] The East African Community may have done this earlier had it not been for the Amin coup. Between 1968 and 1971 a negotiating team met to consider membership applications from Zambia, Somalia, Ethiopia, and Burundi, but the meetings ceased after 1971. The 1968 Union of Equatorial African States (Zaire, Chad, and the Central African Republic) lost the CAR in less than a year, and the two remaining members' geographical non-contiguity reduced the union to a purely symbolic entity.

[33] Although the SADCC provided for economic co-operation, it did not directly affect members' trade policy. Most SADCC signatories joined the Preferential Trade Area for Eastern and Southern Africa established in 1984 under the aegis of the UN Economic Commission for Africa. Such overlapping institutional affiliations are common in Africa; e.g. CEAO and MRU countries are also members of ECOWAS despite some conflicts in the institutions' operation. On this, and for assessments of the various African integration schemes, see the essays in Onwuka and Sesay (1985), the study of West Africa by Robson (1983), and the more recent survey by Foroutan (1993).

industrial policies introduced in the late 1970s and early 1980s were ineffective (Pomfret, 1996b).

The general characteristic of the various preferential trading arrangements among developing countries during the 1960s and 1970s was the goal of import-substituting industrialization (ISI). Thus, although many of these PTAs were seen as comparable to the EC customs union, they differed fundamentally in their external trade policies. Almost all developing countries imposed high barriers to imported manufactures, while the EC had moderate non-agricultural trade barriers, which were reduced substantially during the 1960s and 1970s. The ISI orientation led to the problems of LAFTA, the CACM, and the EAC, as disagreements arose over the distribution of the benefits (i.e. the location of protected industries) and of the costs (i.e. paying higher prices for what were often lower-quality goods from PTA partners) associated with the ISI strategy. These problems were less pronounced elsewhere in Africa, because of the limited industrial development, and in Southeast Asia, because of the more limited commitment to ISI among ASEAN members, but the corollary was that these other PTAs had little economic impact at all.

As long as development strategies centred on ISI, developing country customs unions were doomed. Jagdish Bhagwati graphically describes the problem of those PTAs which had an impact:

> The problem was that, rather than use trade liberalization and hence prices to guide industry allocation, the developing countries sought to allocate industries by bureaucratic negotiation and to tie trade to such allocations, putting the cart before the horse and killing the forward motion. (Bhagwati, 1993, 28)

Robert Baldwin notes in his comments (Baldwin, 1993, 52–3) that bureaucratic allocation was necessary owing to the realization that, if distribution of the benefits from ISI policies were left to the market, then they would be scattered unevenly. This dilemma was practically insoluble, and the customs unions in developing countries failed because the planners were too intrusive or because they could not reach agreement and the market outcome was unacceptable to some members.

The 1979 Enabling Clause, added to the GATT after the Tokyo Round, eased the requirements for PTAs among developing countries. They did not have to cover substantially all trade or to reduce internal tariffs to zero, leaving from Article XXIV only the condition of not raising external trade barriers. Various schemes in the 1980s made use of this legal flexibility (e.g. LAIA, ASEAM, and the Gulf Cooperation Council) to make sectoral or incomplete free trade areas, although none of these had much impact.

Tariff preferences for developing countries

Tariff preferences for developing countries had been explicitly permitted in Article XV of the ITO Charter (although as a result of US opposition they were subject to stringent conditions), but were not included in the GATT. When in 1954–5 Chile proposed incorporating ITO Article XV into the GATT, it was blocked by the industrialized countries.[34] Pressure for special treatment continued to be exerted by developing countries, especially after the Rome Treaty's preferential treatment for the EC's African associates left other developing countries discriminated against in the Six's markets. One safety valve within GATT would have been to accept Nigeria's proposal to eliminate tariffs on tropical goods, which was discussed at the 1961 GATT ministerial meeting; the proposal was attractive to the USA because it effectively eroded the value of colonial preferences, and Britain could not easily oppose a Commonwealth country's suggestion, but the francophone African countries and colonies were afraid of losing their preference margins in EC markets and France succeeded in defusing the proposal (Curzon, 1965, 238).

GATT's continuing failure to reform itself in response to developing countries' demands led the latter to operate through the United Nations.[35] Special UN conferences on trade and development (UNCTAD) were called in 1964 and 1968, at which trade preferences were a major item. At UNCTAD I the USA and

[34] Despite their opposition to the general principle, developed countries had obtained GATT waivers to offer tariff preferences to specific developing countries; e.g. the USA in 1948 with respect to ex-Japanese colonies now under administration by the USA as a trustee, Italy in 1951 with respect to Libya, and Australia in 1953 with respect to Papua New Guinea. These three cases involved very small trade volumes with little effect on third countries, but they did undermine the principled opposition of 1954–5.

[35] In November 1964 three articles on economic development were added to the GATT, but they failed to meet developing country demands; specifically, they did not fully exempt the developing countries from reciprocity.

Sweden opposed such a deviation from the MFN principle, but they reversed their position at UNCTAD II, which paved the way for agreement in 1971 on a GATT waiver permitting a generalized system of preferences (GSP) for developing countries. The initial waiver was for ten years, but it was extended indefinitely by the November 1979 Enabling Cause.[36]

The introduction of a GSP not only legalized a new departure from the non-discrimination principle, but also departed from the GATT practice of negotiating bound tariff reductions which had contractual force. Individual GSP schemes were designed by the developed countries, the 'donors', who could later modify their schemes in any direction without needing to compensate developing countries for any withdrawal of benefits. Thus, discriminatory trade policies were permitted with no international control or accountability.[37]

The various GSP schemes were introduced between 1971 and 1976, and they all differed from one another (Murray, 1977). First of all, there was no consensus over the list of beneficiaries. The general principle was self-selection, and although most countries' beneficiary lists contained most of the 'Group of 77' developing countries, there were country exclusions, particularly involving the more competitive developing countries (e.g. Taiwan was excluded from the EC scheme, Hong Kong from the Japanese scheme, Greece from the US scheme). Rather more countries were excluded from the American scheme, which contained a list of political and other prerequisites for potential beneficiaries, and rather fewer from the GSP schemes of smaller donors like Australia and New Zealand. Secondly, all GSP schemes had many product exclusions: few agricultural items were included, and many labour-intensive manufactured items either were excluded or else tariff preferences were counterbalanced by non-tariff barriers. Thus, the goods in which the developing countries had a comparative advantage were left out and the goods in which they did not were left in. The donor-design feature of the schemes also meant

[36] The Enabling Clause, added to the GATT at the end of the Tokyo Round, also permitted developing countries to grant preferences to one another in order to promote economic development, which legitimized preferential trading arrangements failing to meet the Art. XXIV conditions.

[37] UNCTAD prepares reports on GSP schemes' operation, but these are simply informational and without the peer group pressure of a GATT/WTO session.

that, if a developing country did introduce a new export line, this could always be added to the product exclusions. Thirdly, the preference margins varied from scheme to scheme; for example, American GSP tariffs were invariably set at zero whereas those of the EC were seldom zero.[38] Fourthly, most GSP schemes included ceilings, i.e. volume limits beyond which MFN tariffs would apply. The American scheme had automatic triggers (the 'competitive need' provision) for removal of GSP benefits when GSP imports of a product, or the share of a single developing country in total GSP-covered imports of a product, reach specified levels. Finally, rules of origin and administrative details differ from scheme to scheme, and in some cases (e.g. the EC) deliberately restrict the availability of GSP treatment for some goods.[39]

All of these restrictions drastically reduce the coverage of GSP. Moreover, its aim of aiding export-oriented economic development is crossed by the ceilings and by the lack of binding guarantees, both of which discourage long-term investment calculations based upon GSP tariff rates. Instead, the design of the GSP schemes encourages planning on the basis of MFN tariff rates, with windfall gains on exports arriving before ceilings are reached or benefits are withdrawn. Despite these drawbacks, during the 1970s and early 1980s developing countries continued to support the GSP as better than no preferential treatment and to be suspicious of further rounds of multilateral trade negotiations to reduce developed countries' MFN tariffs (and hence erode the GSP preference margin). In sum, GSP fell far short of initial hopes for wide-ranging free access to developed countries, but it had sufficient impact to foster vested interests against globally desirable MFN tariff cuts which would reduce the GSP margins of preference.

[38] As mentioned in the previous section, the EC was concerned to retain a preference margin for African associates.

[39] Two examples from EC practice are described by Langhammer (1983). Among the rules of origin for radios or TV sets to qualify for GSP treatment, the transistors must be produced in the exporting country; this effectively excludes such exports from Southeast Asia because those countries import transistors from Japan and the USA and the EC knew of this division of labour when they laid down the rule. Many 'sensitive' items reach their EC GSP ceilings in January, but the EC publishes the annual details of its GSP scheme only in late December so beneficiaries have little idea at the time of shipment whether or not their exports are likely to qualify for GSP treatment.

5. American Attitudes towards Discriminatory Trade Policies

The United States played a central role in the postwar history of discriminatory trade policies, because the USA was the largest single trading nation and the strongest supporter of an international economic order based on non-discrimination. Between 1941 and 1947 the USA insisted on making non-discrimination the central principle of the IMF Articles and the GATT, with only a few permissible exceptions, of which the grandfather clause, grudgingly conceded under British pressure, was then seen as the main one. In this crusade the USA was supported by Canada and some of the smaller European nations, but, given the lopsided balance of economic power in the immediate postwar world, America exercised the greatest influence by far.

Between 1947 and the late 1950s Cold War preoccupations continually overrode American trade policy principles. The USA refused MFN treatment to communist countries; US tariff reductions under the Reciprocal Trade Agreements Act and negotiated in GATT rounds were not passed on to these countries, whose exports with few exceptions continued to face the 1930 Hawley–Smoot tariffs. This was permissible towards non-signatories of GATT; but in 1951 the USA suspended GATT obligations towards Czechoslovakia. Raising bound tariffs on imports from a fellow contracting party contravened both the letter and the spirit of GATT, but, while no other country followed America's lead, the action was accepted as a *fait accompli*. The US position towards communist countries was not totally consistent in that no objection was raised to Yugoslavia's application for associate GATT membership in 1958 (Curzon, 1965, 298–300). Such cavalier treatment of GATT principles could not help their credibility, although, in view of the Comecon members' withdrawal from the international trading system, these American departures from the non-discrimination principle were not too serious.

Cold War considerations also lay behind American encouragement of intra-OEEC group discrimination, the ECSC and the formation of the EEC. Although West European integration may have been an idea whose time had come, with another approach to the dollar shortage and a more critical US attitude to the terms of the Rome Treaty (e.g. on agricultural policy) a different international economic order with greater EC commitment to the MFN principle may have emerged. The clearest example of American compromising on the non-discrimination principle was US unwillingness to oppose the associated overseas territories provision in the Rome Treaty. This provision clearly contravened GATT on a point of maximum US sensitivity (i.e. colonial preferences) and was not universally approved among the Six (for example, Germany and the Netherlands favoured a global, rather than a regional, approach towards developing countries), but the USA did not wish to risk threatening the EEC's consummation. The decision stored up future trouble both because the desire to regain equality with the EEC's associates was one motive behind developing country demands for GSP and because a precedent was created which led almost inexorably to the Lomé Convention and the whole pyramid of EC preferential trade agreements. When the USA returned to a more consistent position on the MFN principle and opposed the EC's proliferating association agreements and the GSP proposals, this position was undermined by the earlier precedents which the USA had supported.[40]

Considerations closer to home led the USA to depart from the MFN principle in the use of non-tariff barriers against imports from low-wage countries and in the 1965 Autopact with Canada. Between 1955 and 1957 the USA encouraged Japan voluntarily to restrict cotton textile exports to the USA, and, when exports from other low-cost producers replaced Japanese goods, the USA brought the market disruption issue before GATT late in 1959. The 1961 GATT Short Term Arrangement permitted temporary import restrictions on cotton textiles, and the scope of GATT-permissible bilateral quotas on textile and clothing imports from low-wage countries was subsequently extended to cover almost all materials in the Multifibre Arrangement. The United States

[40] Ironically, as a reversal of their positions in the Anglo-American negotiations of the mid-1940s, Britain was often left replacing the USA as leader of the defenders of non-discrimination during the 1950s. On the issue of Western European group discrimination, Britain was afraid to be either inside a European PTA or outside one, and in the dispute over the EEC's associated overseas territories was responding to British colonies' interests. Nevertheless, by the late 1950s Britain was articulating more consistent pro-non-discrimination trade policies than the USA, although Britain's global stature had fallen too far for UK influence to carry much weight.

does not bear sole responsibility for this huge derogation from the MFN principle, but the US government's willingness during the late 1950s to promote the domestic textile industry's sectional interests did set the process in motion.

The Autopact, which provided for limited free trade in automobiles and their components between the USA and Canada, also tarnished the American image as a supporter of non-discrimination, but its global consequences have been minor. The Autopact is a special case largely involving three corporations' rationalization of production on both banks of the Detroit River, and, although sometimes seen as a precedent for bilateral sectoral trade arrangements, it so far remains unique.[41]

During the 1960s the USA reassumed the role of principal advocate of non-discriminatory international trade policies. The USA was a reluctant convert to GSP, accepting it only when all other OECD countries had done so. In contrast to the EC's immediate introduction of GSP after the 1971 waiver,[42] the American GSP scheme was not established until 1976. Although the US scheme has relatively generous preference margins, its country exclusions are more numerous than those of other GSP schemes and its ceilings are restrictive. In 1981 a product-specific graduation policy was introduced to remove from GSP eligibility countries whose exports were sufficiently competitive not to need preferential treatment; although a stated goal was to help poorer developing countries whose exports were being squeezed out by exports from richer GSP beneficiaries, the mechanism for activating graduation is petitions from US producers, so that the replacements for graduated products are more likely to come from American factories than from remaining GSP beneficiaries. In 1984 the American GSP scheme was renewed until 1993 but with tighter restrictions; for example, on imports from 'sufficiently competitive' countries the competitive need limits were set at 25 per cent of the previous year's total US imports or $25 million rather than the normal limits of 50 per cent or $63.8 million

[41] The Autopact only applied to qualified producers. Consumers and independent retailers were still bound by Canadian and US national trade restrictions, which included a ban on the import of non-antique used cars into Canada.

[42] Australia had unilaterally introduced tariff preferences for developing countries in 1966. Most other GSP schemes were introduced in 1971–2; Canada (in 1974) and the USA (in 1976) were the major laggards.

(with the dollar value indexed to US nominal GNP). Thus, with respect to this GATT-permissible discrimination the USA was dragging its feet, although by the 1980s this had less to do with support for the MFN principle than with domestic pressure for protection against import from low-wage countries.

During the 1960s and the 1970s the USA became increasingly frustrated by the inability to temper the EC's disregard for the MFN principle. By 1972, with the announcement of the Global Mediterranean Policy and the EC–EFTA free trade area, the EC had created a worldwide hierarchy of tariff preferences with only a handful of countries facing the Community's MFN tariffs. Although American pressure was occasionally able to slow down the introduction of discriminatory measures (e.g. to delay Florida citrus exporters' loss of EC market share to Mediterranean suppliers), the USA was constrained to accept the end result as a *fait accompli*.

Weakening US commitment to unconditional MFN treatment became visible in the 1973–9 Tokyo Round. On several non-tariff issues (e.g. subsidies and countervailing duties, and government procurement) the outcome was a code applying only to signatories and not to all GATT contracting parties; i.e. the codes involved conditional MFN. The importance of this deviation from non-discrimination was limited, however, by the weak impact of the codes, to the extent that this approach to non-tariff areas was essentially abandoned in the next GATT round. The Tokyo Round outcome was also characterized by failure to address the proliferating discriminatory safeguard actions such as voluntary export restraints (VERs).

By the early 1980s American policy-makers were talking about exploring new approaches to US trade policy.[43] In February 1982 President Reagan unveiled the Caribbean Basin Initiative, whose centrepiece was duty-free access of nearly all exports from eligible Caribbean countries to the USA for twelve years. The initiative was attacked from all sides in Congress, although not

[43] Weintraub (1985, 167) places the abandonment of unconditional MFN treatment a few years earlier, when the USA supported conditional MFN in non-tariff codes negotiated in the Tokyo Round. I prefer to emphasize the CBI, because discriminatory non-tariff barriers had been a grey area for some time but the USA had adamantly opposed discriminatory tariffs.

because of its discriminatory nature.[44] A watered-down version eventually became law in August 1983 as the Caribbean Basin Economic Recovery Act (CBERA); the tariff preferences remained, but to the original product exclusions (textiles and clothing and sugar) a long list had now been added. The economic significance of the CBERA for the world economy is minimal, but it signalled a dramatic change in policy and a new exception to the MFN principle within GATT. The CBERA waiver was based on a footnote to the 1979 Enabling Clause (Benedek, 1986);[45] the footnote allows for *ad hoc* consideration by GATT of any proposal for differential treatment for developing country exports, and successful first use in the CBERA gave *carte blanche* for any discriminatory trade policies towards any subset of developing countries.

A second step in the new US trade policy was the November 1983 decision to take up an earlier Israeli proposal for a USA–Israel free trade area. The following October the two countries signed an agreement which provided for the elimination by 1995 of duties and non-tariff barriers on substantially all products traded between the USA and Israel. The close political alliance between the two countries makes this something of a special case.[46] Nevertheless, the American decision bilaterally to negotiate a discriminatory trading agreement marks a break with past policy, which had emphasized multilateral negotiations over MFN tariffs.

[44] Liberals attacked the amount of aid for El Salvador, conservatives attacked the investment tax credit provisions, and labour worried about jobs.

[45] The 1980 SPARTECA scheme involving Australia, New Zealand, and some small Pacific islands had been notified to GATT under this same footnote but no formal waiver had been requested. The EC justifies its preferential trade arrangements under Art. XXIV, although the GATT findings about compatability were always inconclusive and the USA usually opposed the EC claims of GATT legality because the schemes were too partial. (In particular, Lomé and agreements with southern Mediterranean countries had little prospect of leading to full free trade areas.) The CBERA, unlike the 1984 USA–Israel free trade area, could not be justified under Art. XXIV because the tariff preferences were unilateral (as well as selective).

[46] The 1975 EC–Israel free trade agreement provided a further twist by placing US exports at a disadvantage in Israeli markets, a situation that suited neither Israel nor the USA. The USA–Israel free trade area effectively turns Israel into a country with few trade barriers and open access to major export markets (except for EC agricultural markets)—an enviable trade policy situation for a small open economy.

The CBERA and USA–Israel free trade area provided a signal that the USA was now open to offers for preferential trading arrangements. The most active negotiations were with Canada, whose late-1983 trade policy review[47] recommended new sectoral free trade arrangements with the USA along the lines of the Autopact, and after a positive US response, negotiations for sectoral trade liberalization began in 1984. In April 1985 the USA signed a bilateral agreement with Mexico on subsidies and countervailing duties. If these initiatives were to proceed, they would dwarf the previous US deviations from the MFN principle. Canada and Mexico are America's first and third largest trading partners, and to take substantial parts of these bilateral trade flows out of the GATT orbit would be a serious blow to the ideas of a world trade system based on non-discriminatory trade policies.

A second element of the new US approach to trade policy in the 1980s was an increased willingness to use discriminatory trade measures as levers to open up other countries' markets for US exports or to protect foreign investment or intellectual property rights. Bhagwati (1990) labelled this as aggressive unilateralism, because it contains highly publicized threats of unilateral withdrawal of trading rights if the partner does not change the practices which the USA deems unacceptable. Aggressive unilateralism replaces the multilateral negotiation of GATT rights and obligations and the consensus nature of GATT dispute settlement by bilateral trade negotiations in which unilateral demands are backed by threats of action based on economic strength.

Demands for a more activist US trade policy came from Congress in the early 1980s. Although the administration's response was muted until 1985, this episode contributed to the background to the Uruguay Round and thus will be analysed here rather than in the next chapter.

In 1985 President Reagan announced a Trade Policy Action Plan, which led to a flurry of more aggressive actions under Section 301 of US trade law (which authorizes retaliation against unfair foreign trade practices) and the 1985–6 market-oriented sector-specific talks with Japan. Unimpressed by the Reagan

[47] External Affairs Canada: *Canadian Trade Policy for the 1980s* (Ottawa, 1983). This decision reversed a longstanding Canadian desire to find counterweights to increased trade with the USA; the Appendix surveys the historical background to these bilateral relations.

Administration's commitment to establishing a level playing field for US traders, Congress attempted to codify the more aggressive stance in the 1988 Trade Act, which created super and special variants of Section 301 requiring the administration to identify unfair foreign trade practices. Super 301 legislation tightened the negotiating deadlines in 301 case, required the US Trade Representative to designate priority target countries and practices, and made action against such practices more automatic (although discretionary waivers were included in the final version of the Act).[48] The omnibus Trade Act also authorized retaliation against countries that do not open their telecommunications markets to US exports, against countries that are not in compliance with the GATT government procurement code or are significantly discriminating against the USA in government procurement, and against countries that discriminate against US financial firms in government bond markets (Bayard and Elliott, 1994, 16–22).

In May 1989 the US Trade Representative named the first six priority practices: Japanese government procurement practices in (1) supercomputers and (2) satellites and (3) technical barriers to forest products trade; (4) Brazilian quantitative restrictions on imports; (5) Indian trade-related investment measures; and (6) closure of insurance markets to foreign firms. On the same day President Bush announced a bilateral Structural Impediments Initiative to address systemic trade barriers in Japan. The Trade Representative also reported that South Korea and Taiwan had agreed to implement market opening measures in return for non-inclusion on the priority practices list.

The effectiveness of aggressive unilateralism in achieving the specific targets will be assessed in the section on bargaining motives for discrimination in Chapter 17. The cases of the six priority practices, however, illustrate the possibility for differing perceptions about impact. The Japanese cases were all resolved with some degree of success in changing the practices concerned; however, especially in the supercomputers case (and with the South Korean and Taiwanese agreements), there are doubts about the effectiveness of implementation and about the extent to which subsequent changes would have occurred even in the absence of

[48] Retaliation under super 301 was described by former US trade representative Robert Strauss and Senator Robert Packwood as 'mandatory but not compulsory' (quoted in Bello and Holmer, 1990, 59 n.).

US pressure. Brazil and India refused to negotiate under duress, although in both cases the policy changes desired by the USA were implemented by reformist governments in the 1990s.

The international reaction to super 301 was extremely negative. To many countries, especially in the Third World, the selection of targets in 1989 resembled politicized bullying rather than an objective list of the world's most unjustifiable trade practices. The administration had to include Japan to assuage domestic pressures and seemed to pick on Brazil and India because they opposed US goals in the Uruguay Round, while the EC was left off the list despite the CAP's eligibility because the USA feared EC retaliation and sabotage of the Uruguay Round. US retaliation against Brazil in a special 301 case on intellectual property rights in pharmaceuticals was unanimously condemned at a February 1989 GATT Council meeting. The resort to GATT illegal measures (raising bound US tariffs on imports from Brazil) and attempts to block formation of a GATT panel to hear Brazilian complaints undermined US standing as an advocate of reform of the dispute settlement mechanism.

In the early 1990s pressure for aggressive unilateralism subsided in the USA as nobody wanted to appear as a scapegoat for the breakdown of the Uruguay Round negotiations. When the super 301 measures were extended by President Clinton in 1994, they were amended to remove the possibility of targeting a country's entire set of policies. With this step, the super 301 measures aimed against specific trade practices resembled the old section 301 rather than especially aggressive unilateralism. Although the 1988 legislation represented a genuine threat to the GATT-based international trading system, the US executive's response (under three different presidents) can be viewed as a successful defusion of domestic dissatisfaction over GATT dispute resolution procedures and over the US bilateral trade deficit with Japan until the WTO was established and the deficit began to shrink. Bayard and Elliott (1994, 69–73) argue that, despite the high-profile exceptions, the USA was guilty of few GATT-illegal measures in the name of section 301.

6. Other Discriminatory Trade Policies

This section briefly covers three sets of discriminatory trade policies which do not fit readily into the mainstream of this chapter. The Council for Mutual Economic Assistance (CMEA, also known as Comecon) was sometimes seen as the Eastern European counterpart of Western European integration, but, given the CMEA countries' inward-looking development strategies, the overwhelming consequence of East European trade policies was the forgone gains from trade which accompany autarchy rather than resource misallocation arising from discrimination; i.e. the CMEA was the most extreme case of the ISI-based PTAs described in Section 4 above. Secondly, use of discriminatory non-tariff measures to safeguard domestic manufacturers from market disruption involves discrimination as an incidental consequence of seeking protective trade barriers without alienating developed country trading partners or without meeting GATT norms, rather than having discrimination as the primary purpose. Finally, economic sanctions differ from the policies described in the rest of this chapter by their explicit subservience to specific foreign policy goals, which typically leads to a limited life-span.

Without necessarily minimizing the importance of the CMEA, discriminatory non-tariff barriers, or economic sanctions, they are all tangential to this book's central theme. They did, however, play some role in so far as the presence of these additional discriminatory trade policies contributed to the MFN principle's diminished standing. Discriminatory non-tariff barriers in particular eroded the legitimacy of GATT and in the short run contributed to growing insensitivity to MFN violations. In the long run, however, the proliferation of discriminatory quotas on textiles and clothing and the costs of similar restrictions on trade in cars and steel contributed to persuading policy-makers that GATT reform was necessary and desirable.

The CMEA

The Council for Mutual Economic Assistance (CMEA) was established in 1949 by the USSR, Bulgaria, Czechoslovakia, Hungary, Poland, and Romania. Albania joined later in 1949 (but became an inactive member in 1961) and East Germany became a member in the following year. The CMEA's goal was to promote economic integration, but for most of the 1950s it was not a serious policy-making body and trade among its members was dominated by a large unrequited flow of resources from Eastern Europe to the USSR. As the 1950s progressed, however, the USSR adopted a more co-operative position on trade. The CMEA assumed a trade-facilitating role, operating the clearing mechanism based on the transferable ruble.

Attempts after 1956 to develop a measure of planned international specialization as the basis for intra-CMEA trade foundered on the reluctance of the less industrialized members to restrict themselves to their traditional activities. Especially controversial was the Galati steel project, which Romania pressed ahead with in 1961 over Soviet objections. This episode is reminiscent of the customs unions among developing countries (Section 4), and the CMEA represented the extreme case of an ISI-based regional trading arrangement. Without planning of industry location, there is little scope for a multilateral trade agreement among non-market economies whose payments are settled in non-convertible currency, so the CMEA turned into a forum for bilateral bargaining where the important negotiations were between the USSR and each individual CMEA member. The bilateral agreements tended to favour trade between the signatories over non-CMEA trade,[49] but the need for detailed negotiations when prices differ substantially in the signatories' economies (and both diverge from world prices) and the predilection for inward-looking national development strategies restricted trade within the CMEA.

The USSR was already a closed economy before the Second World War, but the East European countries' trade–GNP ratios dropped sharply from their prewar levels after joining the CMEA. Thus, although some 'customs union' features of the CMEA can be detected, i.e. promotion of trade among members at the expense of trade with non-members, the overwhelming effect was to stifle CMEA members' overall trade and leave them on the margin of the global economy.

Several non-European countries joined the CMEA (Mongolia in 1962, Cuba in 1968, and Vietnam in 1978). The influence of these poorer countries to the CMEA's working was slight, although they all benefited from unrequited imports which were essentially aid flows.

[49] There are examples of bilateral deals favouring trade outside rather than within Comecon; e.g. Hungary imported salt from Algeria under an arrangement not requiring hard currency, while neighbouring Romania exported salt to hard currency countries including the USA—the salt-using chemical complex in Hungary is some 35 miles from the Romanian salt mine (Marer and Montias, 1982, 112).

Discriminatory measures to avoid market disruption

Voluntary export restraints (VERs) on specific manufactured exports were an unanticipated postwar trade policy innovation. Although administered by the exporting country, their implementation is monitored by the importing country with the scarcely veiled threat that non-compliance will result in imposition of import quotas. Thus, VERs are voluntary only in the sense that the exporting country prefers them to the alternative of unilateral import quotas.

The initial VER cases involved cotton textiles, and textiles and clothing remains the area of widest coverage and most restrictive conditions.[50] Facing demands for protection from imports of Japanese cotton textiles, the American government negotiated voluntary export quotas with Japan in 1955. Other low-wage countries (especially Hong Kong) replaced Japan in supplying these goods to the US market, and other industrialized countries negotiated VERs on cotton textiles (e.g. the UK with Hong Kong in 1959 and with India and Pakistan in 1960). American moves to bring these bilateral measures within GATT led to general waivers contained in the 1961 Short-Term Arrangement and 1962 Long-Term Arrangement for Cotton Textiles. With the rapid expansion of developing countries' textile and clothing exports during the 1960s and their diversification into synthetic fibres, protectionist pressures began to mount once more and culminated in the 1973 Multifibre Arrangement (MFA). Like its predecessors, the MFA permitted discriminatory quantitative restrictions in the form of bilaterally negotiated quotas, and established procedures and minimum growth rates for quotas. The procedures and quota growth rates were made more restrictive in subsequent

[50] Nogués *et al.* (1986) provide estimates of different non-tariff barriers' coverage in 1983; the position of textiles and clothing stands out, even allowing for the problems of monitoring these opaque policies. I will make no distinction here between VERs, orderly marketing agreements, and other arrangements whose distinctive feature is product-specific quantitative restrictions administered by the exporting country at the behest of the importing country. Some of the early VERs involving Japan in the early 1950s and early 1960s were negotiated in return for Japan's trading partners' disinvoking of Art. XXXV (see Ch. 4; the episode is reported in Patterson, 1966, 293–300); this does not apply to the USA, which provided the main impetus for the 1961 Arrangement for Cotton Textiles. Keesing and Wolf (1980) analyse the history up to 1980 of textile quotas against developing countries.

renewals of the MFA, but individual developing countries were unwilling to denounce the MFA for fear that without it the barriers to their textile and clothing exports would be set at even lower quantitative levels.

While negotiated under GATT auspices, the MFA clearly contravenes the spirit and letter of the GATT because:

1. it is discriminatory, permitting restrictions only on developing country exports, and the quotas are set by bilateral agreement;
2. it allows unilateral action for up to two years by the importing country; and
3. it makes no provision for the exporting country to be compensated for loss of market access.

Despite the avowedly temporary nature of the 1961 Arrangement, the MFA continues to exist as a massive deviation from the non-discrimination principle.[51]

Discriminatory regulation of trade in textiles and clothing at least occurred within a framework negotiated under GATT auspices. The same is not true of other measures to avoid market disruption by imports from developing counties. Even in the late 1950s some manufactured exports, particularly from Japan and Hong Kong, were being subject to VERs, but the great expansion of these measures came after 1973. The long boom of the 1960s saw successful manufactured export expansion by a number of developing counties, and when, during the depression of the mid-1970s, protectionism regained force in the industrialized countries, the exports of the newly industrializing countries were a prime target.

Use of VERs covered a wide range of labour-intensive and standardized products, most heavily concentrated on footwear and electronics goods. It is difficult to assess the extent of these

[51] The MFA members (the USA, EU, Canada, Norway, Switzerland, and Japan—although the last two do not apply MFA restrictions and Sweden withdrew from the MFA between 1988 and 1994) include all major trading nations; Australia and New Zealand have similar non-MFA bilateral arrangements. Leadership in tightening the MFA screw has alternated with the EC taking the lead between 1976 and the early 1980s and the USA taking a hard line in the 1986 MFA negotiations; because other developed countries never offer much opposition to the most protectionist country's position, this alteration of leadership exerted a ratchet effect in increasing the MFA trade barriers. C. Hamilton (1986) estimated trade barriers against Hong Kong textile and clothing exports to have a tariff equivalent of 32–35% in the EC and 54% in the USA.

measures, because they are frequently agreed upon behind closed doors and receive little or no publicity.[52] There is, however, no doubt that by the 1980s they had become a pervasive feature of the OECD countries' trade policies towards developing countries.

Successful use of VERs to protect domestic producers from developing countries' exports encouraged their spread to other trade conflicts. The American steel industry received protection in the form of VERs in 1968, but these became more important after the 1978 trigger-price mechanism was replaced by a 1982 VER with the EC and then by a policy of imposing VERs on nearly all suppliers in order to maintain a maximum import penetration ratio.[53] Similar steps by other established steel-producing nations effectively turned intra-OECD steel markets into an area for managed trade, with trade flows determined by bilateral bargaining rather than by market forces. Protection of American and European automobile industries moved in a similar direction. The biggest VER of all in terms of the trade value affected was the Japanese restraint of auto exports to the USA, introduced in 1981 in response to American requests and retained by Japan after the US government declined to seek its renewal in 1985. Most West European countries and Canada had similar VER agreements with Japan, some following the American lead and some more restrictive.[54] Although the auto VERs clearly distorted

[52] Other problems in making a general assessment arise from the detailed product description of most VERs, which means that any measure of their overall restrictiveness would involve a highly disaggregated economic model or a large number of partial equilibrium studies. Simple counts or measures of the percentage of imports covered fail to make allowance for varying degrees of restrictiveness, although they may provide some indication of which importing nations have been most ready to demand VERs (e.g. the World Bank survey by Nogués *et al.* (1986) found import coverage to be highest for France, Switzerland and Australia). A further problem in the 1980s was the growing subtlety, which allowed the mere mention of surveillance by an importing country to encourage self-restraint by exporters in order to avoid a formal request for VERs; the fact that such bullying could succeed was a sad commentary on the ability of international trade law to offer hope of legal redress to weaker nations.

[53] Compliance was scarcely voluntary, however, as the September 1984 policy involved US administration of an import licence scheme in order to enforce VER limits (K. Jones, 1985 and 1986).

[54] Italy's agreement with Japan was a two-way arrangement dating from the 1950s when Japan feared competition from Fiat for an infant Japanese automobile industry. Although conditions changed over the subsequent three decades, Italy insisted on maintaining an arrangement which limited Japanese car sales in Italy to a few thousand per year (the 1981 US-Japan VER was for 1.68 m cars per year).

world trade patterns during the first half of the 1980s, their efficacy as protectionist measures was eroded by challenges to the Japanese car makers from the newly industrializing countries' auto industries.

The net effect of proliferating VERs was to remove entire product groups from the realm in which GATT's non-discrimination principle applied. International trade in textiles and clothing, steel and automobiles was increasingly being conducted within a framework set by bilateral agreements.[55] The threat of new VERs induced uncertainty and fear that other products would be added to this list. Major questions for the international trading system in the mid-1980s were whether the US and EC governments would extend their VER networks to cover South Korea and future car suppliers, and whether steel VERs would be exteneded to a multimetals arrangement. Another challenge was the EC Commission's move to replace EC member governments in administering a common VER policy,[56] although whether this signalled a less opaque policy was itself obscure.

Other measures aimed at preventing market disruption include anti-dumping (AD) and countervailing duties (CVDs), which are also discriminatory in impact (often targetted at individual foreign firms) and whose use increased during the 1980s after AD and CVD codes were adopted during the Tokyo Round. Although the major trading nations' procedures were for the most part GATT-consistent, they often led to other outcomes, such as VERs which contravened the spirit of GATT by overriding the non-discrimination principle. In the USA about a third of AD petitions have been withdrawn 'after the domestic industry has achieved some type of out-of-court settlement with the foreign rival' (Prusa, 1992), and Messerlin (1989) reports similar outcomes in the EC. In some instances, the mere threat of AD petitions has brought a response from the exporter.[57]

[55] Kostecki (1987, 429) estimates that VERs, virtually unknown in the early 1970s, covered 'not less than ten per cent of world trade' by the mid-1980s. Laird and Yeats (1990) conclude that 'hard-core non-tariff barriers' applied to as much as 18 per cent of OECD imports in 1986.

[56] The February 1983 negotiation with Japan for a VER on Japanese VCR exports was the first step (Hindley, 1986).

[57] Rosendorff (1996) models US AD procedures as a signalling game, leading to VERs or other administrative actions; the outcome need not discriminate among suppliers, e.g. the 1986 USA–Japan semiconductor agreement was essentially a market-sharing agreement involving the relative shares of domestic and imported products in the Japanese market.

All of these measures are aimed primarily at protecting domestic producers, and their proliferation in part reflected the success of GATT negotiations in binding the high-income countries' tariff rates; governments could not respond to the post-1973 slowdown in growth by raising tariff barriers so they resorted to new protectionist measures. The new measures may also have been used by the EC to smooth internal market integration; as internal competition intensified in cars or steel, the competitive pressure on EC producers could be alleviated by limiting third-country supplies (Pomfret, 1986e; Bhagwati, 1993, 36–7). Nevertheless, they were derogations from the non-discrimination principle, and failure to deal with selective safeguards during the Tokyo Round fed developing countries' mistrust of GATT, even as many of them were adopting more liberal trade policies during the 1980s.

Economic sanctions

Economic sanctions involve the application of economic measures (including trade policy) in order to change the conduct of another nation. The goals have included disruption of military adventures, destabilization of foreign governments, protection of human rights, limiting nuclear proliferation, combating international terrorism, etc. (Hufbauer and Schott, 1985, 4–7). Use of economic sanctions is not new and, if anything, their use has declined relative to the level of international trade in the second half of the twentieth century, although the issue revived in the mid-1990s (see Section 6.4).

Sanctions are explicitly discriminatory, but because their goal is political and fairly specific the criterion for assessing them differs from that for the discriminatory trade policies dealt with in the rest of this book. The impact of sanctions on the world trading system is seldom a major concern, in part because they are perceived as special cases without application to normal trading relations. Their economic consequences for the imposing nation(s) are usually seen as negative, but the costs are worth bearing if the political objective is achieved. Thus, economic analysis is relevant, but in the limited sense of providing a guideline to the likely distribution of costs between the imposing and the target country—there is rarely any claim that any participant will gain economic benefits (in contrast to customs union, GSP, or even VERs).

Restrictions on imports or exports are most likely to be successful economic sanctions when there are few alternative markets for the target country. On the other hand, if markets with prices that differ little from those of the imposing country remain open to the target country, then the economic costs will fall almost entirely on the sanctions-imposing country. One reason for the speedy withdrawal of some unsuccessful trade sanctions has been the protests of exporters who have lost markets in the target country to close competitors (e.g. in the cases of the 1980–1 US grain embargo and the 1981–2 pipeline sanctions against the USSR). Even when the number of sanctions-imposing countries is large, there are incentives for individual traders to circumvent their governments' restrictions on trade with the target country (e.g. in the case of United Nations sanctions against Rhodesia).

In all cases where resistance by the target country is firm, trade sanctions have proved insufficient to bring major political change, as has been illustrated by such failures as the League of Nations sanctions against Italy, the USSR's sanctions against Yugoslavia, and American sanctions against Cuba, although they may have contributed in the long run to undermining the Rhodesian regime or apartheid in South Africa. Some studies (Hufbauer and Schott, 1985; D. Baldwin, 1985) argue that economic sanctions can be a cost-effective weapon in a country's foreign policy armory to obtain limited objectives or to send signals to foreign and domestic observers. On the whole, however, sanctions were not viewed positively by politicians or economists in the 1980s and their use appeared to be in decline.

7. Overview and Review

By the mid-1980s the number of discriminatory trading arrangements was large, but clearly they varied in relative importance. Many customs unions had been formed (and unformed) among developing countries, yet their impact on world trade was dwarfed by that of the European Common Market. Voluntary export quotas on South Korean and Taiwan footwear exports to the USA between 1978 and 1981 were important for the industries concerned, but were far less significant in terms of the trade involved than, say, the Autopact with Canada or the 1981 voluntary export quotas on Japanese autos.

To give an idea of the relative importance of the major discriminatory measures in 1985, I will now compare the value of trade conducted under these arrangements with total trade. This is of course a rough approximation, and there are obvious biases involved in so far as negative discrimination reduces trade while positive discrimination stimulates trade, so the trade under the latter measures is overstated relative to a non-discriminatory world and, in the extreme case, discriminatory prohibitions will suppress trade. Nevertheless, the orders of magnitude are striking.

Cline (1982) estimated non-MFN imports to comprise about one-tenth of total US imports in 1980. The categories covered by Cline were the MFA (3.8 per cent), the Autopact (3.0 per cent), GSP (2.9 per cent), and Comecon (0.3 per cent). Among other trading nations, the European Community's position is crucial because of its members' quantitatively dominant role in world trade (34 per cent of global imports, and 20 per cent even if intra-Community trade is excluded—see Table 5.1). Japan and other Northeast Asian newly industrialized economies adhere almost totally to the MFN principle.

Table 5.2 breaks down EC members' 1985 imports by country of origin. Half of the total consists of intra-EC trade, and about half of the remainder comes from countries to whose exports the EC grants preferential access. Not all exports from the EFTA, Mediterranean, Lomé, and GSP countries received preferential access,[58] but the only items systematically excluded were EC-produced agricultural goods, and under the Common Agricultural Policy imports of these products have dwindled in importance. Tariff preferences are, of course, non-existent on duty-free imports, and I have listed the OPEC members as a separate category because, although many of these receive preferential

[58] Nor do their preferred exports receive equal treatment by the EC; in particular, preference margins are smaller for GSP, which is also subject to ceilings beyond which MFN tariffs apply. The Mediterranean agreements were more important before Greece, Portugal, and Spain became EC members; reallocating their approximately $19 bn worth of exports to the EC(9) from intra-EC trade to the Mediterranean category in Table 5.2 would reduce the former to 50% and increase the latter to 7%.

TABLE 5.1 World Imports by Importing Country, 1985

Importing countries	Value of imports ($ bn)	Share of total specified imports (%)
European Community (12)	664	34
Intra-EC trade	353	
USA	362	19
Japan	131	7
Canada	81	4
Australia–New Zealand	30	2
EFTA	110	6
Comecon	75	4
Europe n.e.s.[a]	26	1
Middle East	105	5
Africa	60	3
W. Hemisphere LDCs	81	4
Asia n.e.s.[a]	200	10
Total world imports	1947	

[a] Not elsewhere stated.

Note: The source includes Portugal and Spain in the EC, although the data are for 1985. Categories are as in the source apart from Hungary and Romania, which are included in the USSR etc. group to form a Comecon category; the remaining n.e.s. European group consists mainly of Yugoslavia and Turkey. The column total is greater than the sum of individual entries because of unspecified trade.

Source: IMF, *Direction of Trade Statistics Yearbook*, 1986.

treatment on manufactured exports to the EC, their total exports are dominated by petroleum products.[59] This proportion of duty-free trade plus imports from countries granted MFN treatment by the EC accounts for less than one-fifth of total EC imports, leaving over 80 per cent of EC imports on non-MFN terms.[60]

[59] The OPEC/GSP dichotomy probably understates the share of EC imports from developing countries that entered on MFN terms. Laird and Sapir (1987, Table 1) quote UNCTAD data showing about 60% of EC imports from GSP beneficiaries as not MFN dutiable, and only just over 10% (or less than $9 bn in 1984) as GSP preferential. On the other hand, the EC imposes a range of discriminatory non-tariff barriers (notably under the MFA, but also on other products) on imports from developing countries so that the share of these imports not receiving MFN treatment is much larger than that of GSP preferential imports alone.

[60] This type of exercise can provide only approximate magnitudes. In addition to agricultural products, there are other exceptions to preferential treatment which

TABLE 5.2 European Community (EC12) Imports by Country of Origin, 1985

Exporting country	EC imports ($ bn)	% share
Intra-EC trade	353	53
EFTA	63	9
Mediterranean countries[a]	25	4
Lomé signatories	23	3
GSP beneficiaries[b]	44	7
Comecon	27	4
OPEC[c]	37	6
MFN[d]	93	14
Total EC imports[e]	664	

[a] Excluding Albania and Libya, which do not have preferential agreements with the EC.
[b] Excluding countries listed under other headings.
[c] Except Algeria.
[d] US (53), Japan (23), Canada (6), South Africa (6), Australia (4), and New Zealand (1); Taiwan is not listed in the data source used.
[e] The entries cover all EC imports but do not sum exactly to the total because of rounding.

Source: as Table 5.1.

Thus, for the EC at least, departures from unconditional MFN treatment had become dominant for trade policies.

Other major trading nations showed a greater commitment to the MFN principle, but the degree of commitment varied. The EFTA members had not the same array of preferential arrangements as the EC, but because their trade is dominated by intra-European trade their imports largely receive non-MFN treatment. (Out of $110 billion total imports, $90 billion came from EFTA, EC, or Comecon members.) Canada's discriminatory measures were similar to those of the USA, while Japan, Australia, and New Zealand only have GSP plus the Australia–NZ Closer Economic

would have to be covered on a product-by-product basis. At the same time, the seven countries ostensibly granted MFN treatment do in fact receive preferential treatment on MFA goods, as well as suffering discrimination against almost all other dutiable exports to the EC (and Japan has been particularly discriminated against by the imposition of 'voluntary' export restraints on exports of autos, electronic goods, and other products). These caveats aside, however, Table 5.2 illustrates that the EC's explicitly preferential arrangements cover a large part of total imports.

Table 5.3 Percentage of Total Imports Entering on other than MFN Basis, Major Trading Nations, 1985

	Total imports ($ bn)	Non-MFN ($ bn)	Percentage (non-MFN ÷ total)
EC[a]	664	535	81
USA[b]	362	36	10
Japan[c]	131	8	6
EFTA[d]	110	92	88
Canada[b]	81	8	10
Australia[e]	24	3	13
New Zealand[f]	6	1	17
Total	1378	683	50

[a] From Table 5.2.
[b] Cline's percentage.
[c] GSP $6 bn plus Comecon $2 bn.
[d] Intra-EFTA $18 bn, EC $64 bn, Comecon $8 bn, GSP $2 bn.
[e] NZ $1 bn plus GSP $2 bn.
[f] Australia $1 bn.

Source: As Table 5.1; GSP figures for EFTA, Japan, Australia, and NZ are from Laird and Sapir (1987, table 1).

Relations Agreement.[61] Putting this information together gives an estimate of over half of the major GATT signatories' imports being granted other than MFN treatment in 1985 (Table 5.3). Although there may be some upward bias on individual items, the overall percentage in Table 5.3 is a conservative estimate because it includes only the main overtly discriminatory measures. Moreover, the grand totals are relatively insensitive to adjustments in the non-MFN figures for non-European countries, and are dominated by the EC position.

The gap between the GATT blueprint for a world trading system based on non-discriminatory trade policies, described in Chapter 4, and the mid-1980s reality of a majority of world trade

[61] The 1965 Australian–New Zealand free trade agreement provided for preferential tariff reductions on specific items, but few significant reductions were agreed upon. The January 1983 Closer Economic Relations agreement (CER) reversed the procedure by setting out across-the-board tariff reduction, exceptions to which had to be negotiated, and covering non-tariff issues (see S. 6.3). Australia and New Zealand also grant duty-free or concessional access to a wide range of exports from 11 members of the South Pacific Forum under the 1981 SPARTECA agreement, but the trade volumes involved are tiny.

being conducted on other than MFN terms was large. The twenty-three countries covered by Table 5.3 account for about two-thirds of world trade. As the most prominent GATT signatories, they might be expected to provide the lead in supporting the principle of unconditional MFN treatment. This had clearly not happened. The European Community in particular had shown little regard for the principle, and given the size of its trade this was a major deviation; but the other major countries were also showing a far from firm commitment. The overall picture by 1985 was one in which the bulk of these countries' trade was carried out on a basis other than unconditional MFN treatment.

This chapter's narrative shows that discriminatory trade policies did not arrive suddenly, but rather were the outcome of a slow cumulative process; the net effect was growing disregard for the MFN principle, increasingly justified by the self-fulfilling argument that nobody else observed it. Bhagwati's (1993) distinction between the first regionalism of the 1950s and 1960s and the second regionalism of the 1980s and 1990s captures the waves of PTA formation during those decades and the differences in their nature, but hides the links between the two episodes. Although it took four decades to evolve, a continuous thread links the ECSC and the Treaty of Rome, bloc competition between the EC and EFTA, the Greek and then Turkish association agreements and the EC's Global Mediterranean Policy, and US reaction with the CBERA and USA–Israel free trade area, paving the way for NAFTA.

That, however, is to anticipate the next chapter, which examines the twin approaches pursued in the decade after 1985. Should the GATT-based system be strengthened and extended to new areas, or should regional trade arrangements be embraced and accepted as a good thing?

6

Regionalism versus Multilateralism during the Uruguay Round

United States trade diplomacy moved on a dual track after the mid-1980s. The Reagan administration wanted a new round of multilateral trade negotiations. When other trading nations responded unenthusiastically at the late-1982 GATT ministerial meeting, the USA pushed ahead with the bilateralism begun with the Caribbean Basin Initiative and the USA–Israel free trade agreement. By the time a new round was finally launched in Uruguay in 1986, negotiations for a Canada–USA free trade area were already well advanced. The momentum of US bilateralism was maintained when Mexico initiated discussions for a free trade agreement with the USA, which led to consideration of regional trading arrangements covering the entire Western Hemisphere.

Meanwhile, economic integration in Western Europe, which had appeared to be losing momentum in the early 1980s, was restimulated by the 1985 White Paper which launched the programme for creating a single market by 1992. This programme, together with the unexpected collapse of communism in Eastern Europe in 1989, ushered in a new expansion of the EC, together with a new set of associated non-members (who aspired to future membership).

The timing of these developments was important. In 1989–90 the Uruguay Round appeared to be languishing, while the EC and USA were extending and deepening regional trading blocs. The relative merits of regionalism and multilateralism were actively debated, reinvigorating the analysis of discriminatory trading arrangements (Chapters 10 and 11). At the practical level, countries in other parts of the world reassessed their international trade policy options. This coincided with (or in many cases followed) conversion to more liberal trade policies, and the main reaction was for smaller trading nations to play a more active part in the Uruguay Round than in any previous multilateral trading negotiations. At the same time, especially as the outcome of the Uruguay Round remained in doubt until late in 1993 (given the possibility of non-ratification by the US Congress), countries considered their fall-back positions. This underlay the proliferation of new regional trading arrangements (or the revitalization of existing ones), as well as debate over 'open regionalism' in the Asia–Pacific region.

1. Europe

Following a 1985 White Paper by the EC Commission, the Single European Act (signed in 1986 and ratified in 1987) laid the basis for the completion of the single European market by the end of 1992. The SEA improved EC decision-making by introducing qualified majority voting on most economic matters, rather than unanimity among member states, and removed regulatory barriers on the movement of goods, services, labour, and capital within the EC. The slow progress of passing national legislation in support of the EC92 programme meant that the deadline was missed, but substantial reduction of non-tariff barriers was taking place.[1] The EC92 programme both completed the economic integration foreseen in the 1957 Rome Treaty and liberalized areas not covered by the original treaty (e.g. government procurement and service sectors with state monopolies). Non-tariff barriers which substituted for the tariffs on internal trade and other border controls were dismantled. Other measures, such as health or safety requirements, which might act as non-tariff barriers to trade were addressed by harmonization and by mutual recognition.

An important shift in emphasis during the 1980s was to rely increasingly on the mutual recognition principle; any product that could legally be sold in one EU member country should be able to be sold in another. This built upon the 1979 *cassis de dijon* case in which the European Court had ruled that a French alcoholic beverage could not be excluded from German markets because its alcohol content failed to match German regulations. Mutual recognition is a more effective path because it

[1] By November 1994 the EC Commission reported that 91% of national measures needed to implement the SEA had been adopted (WTO, 1995, 31 n.).

avoids the detailed haggling over standards which is necessary for harmonization, although its scope is limited in areas where there are irreconcilable differences concerning what is considered acceptable.

The EC92 programme provided a further push in the continuous progress towards the economic integration of EC members, reinforcing its claim to be treated as one unit for international trade purposes. This was recognized by GATT treating the EC as a single unit in its *1991 Trade Policy Review* and by the EC's common membership in international organizations (starting with the Food and Agricultural Organization of the United Nations). The December 1991 Treaty on European Union (the Maastricht Treaty) extended the scope of this process to include monetary union, a common foreign policy, common citizenship, and co-operation on justice and social affairs. A symbol of the changing self-image was the replacement of the name 'European Community' by 'European Union' (EU).

The deepening of the EC's integration had implications for the EFTA countries, all of whose trade was heavily oriented towards EC markets. At a 1984 ministerial meeting in Luxembourg, agreement was reached on 'parallelism', i.e. that the EC92 programme would not result in new obstacles to EC–EFTA trade. This ultimately led in 1992 to the signing of the agreement on the European Economic Area (EEA), which provided that many of the features of the EC's Single Market would apply to the geographic area covering the EC and EFTA. The EEA Treaty was rejected by a referendum in Switzerland in December 1992, and entered into force for the remaining EFTA members at the start of 1994.

The governments of four EFTA members, Austria, Finland,[2] Norway, and Sweden, decided that full EU membership, with a seat at the decision-making table, was preferable to the EEA. In

[2] Finland, which had been linked to EFTA since 1961 and had a FTA agreement with the EC since 1973, became a full EFTA member in 1985. The rapid shift in EFTA attitudes towards EU membership was in part conditioned by the collapse of communism in Eastern Europe in 1989 and the disolution of the USSR at the end of 1991, which removed the neutrality argument for keeping the Western European bloc at arm's length. Austria's formal application for membership was lodged in 1989, followed by Sweden in 1991 and Finland, Norway, and Switzerland in 1992. Iceland's government, initially deterred from applying by the EU fisheries policy, changed its mind in 1994, but was informed by the EU that it would be too late to be considered in the current round of accesions, so no formal application was made (Richard Baldwin, 1995, 34).

Norway the decision was reversed by a referendum, but the other three countries joined the EU in January 1995. The states of the former German Democratic Republic had already become part of the EC customs territory in 1989. Thus, the deepening of Western European economic integration was accompanied by a substantial northward and eastward shift in the European Union.

The network of external preferential trade agreements established by the EC in the 1960s and 1970s declined in economic importance in the 1980s and 1990s. The EC–EFTA free trade area covered only Switzerland and Leichtenstein once the EEA came into effect, and the EEA applied only to Iceland and Norway among EU non-members after the 1995 EU enlargement. The Mediterranean policy covered fewer countries after Greece, Portugal, and Spain joined the EC in 1981 and 1986, and its impact on trade with North Africa and with the former Yugoslavia has declined.[3] Cyprus, Malta, and Turkey all have agreements with the EU leading to eventual customs union, in various stages of implementation; Turkey and the EU agreed to implement their customs union in 1996, while Cyprus and Malta are in the queue for accesion.[4] The Euro-Mediterranean agreement signed with Tunisia in July 1995 is expected to be a prototype for agreements with Morocco, Egypt, and Jordan (Hoekman and Djankov, 1996a, b), which would create a Euro-Mediterranean Economic Area with regional free trade in manufactures. The main innovation is to replace the one-way preferences of earlier agreements by reciprocal free trade in manufactures, which could benefit Tunisia by locking-in recent trade liberalization. Unless the new Euro-Med agreements offer more financial assistance or better access to EU markets for agricultural exports (which is unlikely), they are not offering anything that the Mediterranean non-member could not realize unilaterally, and unilateral tariff elimination would not involve discrimination against manufactured imports from non-EU sources.

[3] The declining importance for the North African countries is due to growing EU self-sufficiency in agricultural products from the Mediterranean region, especially after the enlargement of the 1980s.

[4] The Labour Party's victory in the October 1996 Maltese elections was associated with second thoughts on EU membership. Although Malta, Cyprus, and Iceland are usually considered European, their absence from the EU is of little global significance, given that their combined population is only just over 1 m people.

The GSP scheme and the Lomé Convention remain. The Fourth Lomé Convention, covering 1989–99, is clearly viewed as an aid rather than a trade agreement by the seventy ACP countries, and it is expected that in the year 2000 Lomé will finally be replaced by a regime of MFN treatment with financial transfers to the ACP countries. Both of these preferential schemes have fallen under the general cloud encompassing tariff preferences for developing countries, although some small ACP countries benefit from product-specific access to the EU market. The most controversial special regime concerns bananas, and in the 1990s this became a *cause célèbre* as non-ACP suppliers in Latin America, with US support, lodged complaints with GATT.

Before 1993 the EU banana regime allowed ACP bananas to enter duty-free while the common external tariff was 20 per cent, but implementation was complicated by a maze of special cases. Greece banned all external bananas to protect Cretan producers. France, Portugal, and Spain offered special privileges to overseas departments (Guadeloupe, Martinique, Madeira, and the Canary Islands), and France, Italy, and the UK used import licences to favour former colonies. Germany, on the other hand, by a special protocol of the Rome Treaty, imported all bananas duty-free. Only Belgium, Denmark, Ireland, Luxembourg, and the Netherlands implemented the simple tariff preferences. The differing national policies had to be supported by restrictions on intra-EU banana mobility.

The banana regime introduced in July 1993 created a single EU market in bananas, but in attempting to satisfy the many conflicting interests it created a complex administered trade policy. 'Internal' suppliers were allocated production quotas (Crete 15,000, Canary Islands 420,000, Madeira 50,000, Martinique 219,000, and Guadeloupe 150,000 tonnes), which would be eligible for price support under the CAP. 'Traditional' ACP suppliers were allocated national import quotas (summing to 857,700 tonnes), which could enter the EU duty-free, and which were linked to aid for marketing and compensation for earnings instability. A consolidated quota of 2 million tonnes was divided into 66.5 per cent for 'established' non-ACP suppliers and 'non-traditional' ACP suppliers, 30 per cent for internal or traditional ACP suppliers exceeding their preferential treatment quotas, and 3.5 per cent for new suppliers; within this consolidated quota, internal and

ACP bananas would pay no duty, while other bananas would be subject to a levy of 100 ecus per tonne (equivalent to a 20.8 per cent tariff at 1991 prices). Above the consolidated quota, ACP bananas would be subject to a levy of 750 ecus per tonne (equivalent to a 113 per cent tariff at 1991 prices) and non-ACPs to a levy of 850 ecus (177 per cent). The regime is further complicated by differential import licencing requirements.

The EU banana regime has been heavily criticized for its lack of transparency and discriminatory nature (Borrell and Yang, 1990; 1992). The 1993 reform may be more liberal than the preceding national regimes (Read, 1994), but it was opposed by Germany, whose consumers were made worse off, and by the low-cost Latin American producers. The logical solution is to replace the preferential tariffs, quotas, and licences by aid payments to the preferred internal and ACP suppliers; Raboy *et al.* (1995) have made some calculations of the potential magnitudes. The situation is exacerbated by the high dependency on banana exports of many of the preferred suppliers, small poor islands which would become aid-dependent without their Lomé banana benefits. The EU appears unwilling to renounce its use of preferential trade policies which spread some of the burden of influence-sphere maintenance on to EU consumers and non-preferred external suppliers, despite the large resource misallocation costs of the banana policy resulting from the greater suitability of Latin American production locations.

The collapse of communism in Eastern Europe created new problems for the EC's external trade policy.[5] The EC concluded 'Europe' agreements with the Czech and Slovak Republics, Hungary, and Poland in 1991, and with Bulgaria and Romania in 1993. The Europe agreements provide for establishment of a free trade area between the signatories within ten years and contain special protocols on 'sensitive' sectors (agriculture, steel, and

[5] The process of creating special relations with Eastern European countries in the late 1980s and early 1990s was frequently overtaken by the pace of political and economic change in the CMEA countries. The EC signed trade and co-operation agreements with Hungary in 1988, Poland and the USSR in 1989, and the Czech and Slovak Federal Republics, Bulgaria, and Romania in 1990. Romania had enjoyed GSP status since 1972, and this was granted to Poland and Hungary in 1990 and to the Czech and Slovak Federal Republic and Bulgaria in 1991. By 1991 these steps already seemed too cautious following the extensive reforms in Eastern Europe and collapse of the CMEA.

textiles).[6] After gaining independence in 1991, Estonia, Latvia, and Lithuania signed free trade agreements with Finland and Sweden (as well as with Norway and Switzerland) in 1992, and these were incorporated in free trade agreements signed with the EU in June 1994, with transition periods of four years for Latvia, six years for Lithuania, and none for Estonia. Slovenia also negotiated an association agreement in 1995, but Italy, which had delayed the negotiations, used its veto over formal approval of the agreement.[7]

The various new agreements with Eastern European countries are similar but not identical. Thus, in essentials they reproduce the pyramid of preferences, which characterized EC external trade policy in the 1970s. There has also been concern about the hub-and-spoke nature of the arrangements (Richard Baldwin, 1994; WTO, 1995, 52–3). A key issue in the 1990s was whether these would turn out to be temporary resting places on the road to EU membership, or a serious source of discrimination in world trade.[8]

[6] Quotas on textile and steel imports from several CMEA countries had been imposed by the EC in the late 1970s, and in all the subsequent agreements they were grandfathered together with a range of 'voluntary' restriction agreements on CAP products (Grilli, 1993, 312). Ironically, one of the main recommendations being made to formerly centrally planned economies in the early 1990s by Western advisers and international institutions was to remove export taxes and quotas; those following this advice were left only with quotas on specified exports to the EC sticking out like sore thumbs.

[7] With the highest per capita income of all the Eastern European non-members and an official target of EU membership by 2001, Slovenia's accession negotiations should be the simplest, but Italy's obstruction placed Slovenia tenth instead of first in the queue. Italy's condition for acquiescence is restitution or guaranteed priority in repurchase of property owned by Italians in territory acquired by Slovenia in 1945, a position opposed by Slovenia on the grounds that territorial and property disputes between Italy and Yugoslavia had been resolved in a series of bilateral treaties, and that Italy is using its leverage over EU accession negotiations to obtain unrelated benefits for some of its citizens.

[8] The July 1993 Copenhagen summit of the EU gave a strong commitment to open the EU to Eastern European countries, but the process lost momentum in the face of opposition from German taxpayers, the poorer EU members who benefit from EU structural funds, and the farm lobby. The budgetary costs of admitting poor and agricultural countries dominated the debate (Bofinger, 1995), although there were also concerns about the adequacy of EU political structures (e.g. disproportionate representation of small members, use of national veto, lack of parliamentary control, and unclear allocation of powers). At the EU's December 1995 Madrid summit it was announced that accession negotiations with the 8 East European applicants, Cyprus, and Malta would begin within 6 months of the conclusion of the EU intergovernmental conference, which was scheduled to end in mid-1997.

In sum, although the picture remains cloudy, the EU appears to be moving away from using one-way preferences. At the same time it is unwilling to renounce the use of tariff preferences as an instrument of foreign policy. The ongoing banana preferences and new arrangements in Eastern Europe contain the seeds of international discord, especially if the USA supports its Central Anmerican neighbours and becomes upset by EU influence-sphere-creating in the larger East European and former Soviet republics.

2. North America

The USA was ostentatiously pursuing three sets of discriminatory trade policies in the mid-1980s. Protectionist measures such as the VER covering imports of Japanese automobiles since 1981 were in response to domestic pressures and occupied a grey area with respect to GATT, against its spirit if not against the letter of GATT law. The aggressive unilateralism which had been adopted in 1985 and codified in super 301 by the 1988 Trade Act posed a more explicit challenge to GATT, by threatening unilateral withdrawal of MFN treatment without observing the agreed dispute settlement procedures. Thirdly, the USA had ended its abstention from preferential trading arrangements by pursuing the Caribbean Basin Initiative and signing the 1985 free trade agreement with Israel.

These aspects of US trade policy provided a spur for other countries to come to the GATT negotiating table by reminding them that the rule of law protects the weak rather than the strong, who can better survive by the law of the jungle. Even GATT director general Arthur Dunkel is reported to have remarked that super 301 was the best thing that the USA did for GATT, 'unifying an outraged and alarmed world behind the trading regime' (Bayard and Elliott, 1994, 74). From the US perspective, its unilateral measures succeeded in kickstarting the Uruguay Round and in putting trade-related investment measures, intellectual property rights, and trade in services on the agenda, overcoming initial strong opposition orchestrated by Brazil and India. As the multilateral negotiations progressed, the US administration scaled back its resort to discriminatory bilaterally negotiated protection and aggressive market-opening. Nevertheless, the momentum of preferential trading arrangements accelerated as agreement was reached first with Canada and then with Mexico.

Negotiations for the Canada–United States Free Trade Agreement (CUSTA) were formally initiated in 1986, and the agreement was signed in January 1988. CUSTA extends tariff-free treatment to all USA–Canada trade, and also has articles covering dispute settlement, sectoral arrangements, and other areas. CUSTA went beyond the GATT, as it then stood, by including commitments to liberalize trade in services, to grant national treatment to investors from the other country, and to permit temporary movement of businesspeople. CUSTA also covered NTBs in agriculture, with an agreement to harmonize or make equivalent sanitary standards, although CUSTA does not cover other NTBs (such as support schemes). The procurement agreement reached in the Tokyo Round is included in CUSTA and extended to additional government agencies, and the threshold for covered purchases is lowered.

In going beyond tariff reduction, CUSTA represented an important component of what came to be referred to as the new regionalism. In this respect, it could be claimed that such North American moves were following European precedent in regional integration, but the crucial difference is the absence of any desire to use economic integration as a means towards political integration in North America. Indeed, fear that economic and political integration may be inevitably linked in some way is a principal reason for Canadian indecisiveness towards preferential trading arrangements with the USA (see the Appendix).

Canada's main goal, at a time of growing pressures for unilateralism in US trade policy, had been to achieve some exemption from or recourse against US unfair trade remedies. CUSTA granted mutual exemption from safeguard actions under GATT Article XIX. Canada, however, failed to secure exemption from US unfair trade legislation or to negotiate a common understanding on the use of anti-dumping and countervailing duties. The agreement did contain extensive dispute settlement provisions, including review by a binational panel of anti-dumping and countervailing duty determinations. Based on the first thirty cases (twenty-four against US agencies and six against Canadian agencies) initiated by November 1992, Grant and Winham (1995) conclude that the panels are effective in resolving in a legal non-partisan fashion whether the determinations had followed due process as laid down in the appropriate national legislation, without commenting on the fairness of the legislation.

For the United States, a concern was to place discipline on some Canadian policies, which were viewed as providing implicit subsidies, notably in energy and in wines and spirits. A particular interest to large US firms was liberalization of Canadian foreign investment rules, and Canada agreed no longer to screen acquisitions of companies valued at less than C$100 million, except in the energy and cultural sectors, and to cease imposing local content or export requirements on US companies still subject to screening.

The most important sectoral agreement in CUSTA concerned automobiles. Chapter X grandfathered arrangements contained in the 1965 USA–Canada Autopact, but also tightened the domestic content requirements. By changing the rules (e.g. with respect to inclusion of overhead and indirect costs), CUSTA raised the old 50 per cent content requirement to about 70 per cent, according to Canadian government estimates (quoted by Whalley, 1993, 374 n.). These technical negotiations were not central to the public debate, but they led to the first major dispute under CUSTA when Honda cars assembled in Canada were treated as external imports by the US customs service; the US interpretation hinged on excluding overheads and interest payments from the domestic component of costs. This interpretation was contested by Canada, but it indicated how rules of origin could be used to exclude items from a free trade agreement. Such technical engineering within the treaty set a precedent for NAFTA.[9]

Other sectoral arrangements, e.g. for agriculture, and the services and procurement chapters were of less practical significance. Whalley (1993, 356) terms these long and complex chapters with seemingly little of substances as 'empty Chapters'. The procurement provisions do not apply to state/provincial or local governments. The services chapter makes general statements (including

[9] Even within CUSTA, such technicalities were not trivial. Hufbauer and Schott (1993, 5) report US Office of Management and the Budget estimates that 18% of US imports from Canada do not benefit from the free trade agreement and continue to pay import duties; without rules of origin, this percentage would be zero.

promises to guarantee MFN treatment) but grandfathers or exempts most services.

The CUSTA negotiations were of some interest to outsiders, since they involved the world's largest bilateral trade flow and for that reason alone posed a challenge to the multilateral trading system based on non-discrimination. Nevertheless, the economic impact was expected to be minor, as most of USA–Canada trade was already subject to low tariffs. Moreover, until the eleventh hour the outcome of the negotiations was in considerable doubt given the past history of US–Canadian free trade negotiations (see Appendix). The 1987 Candian election was a close-run thing, but the pro-CUSTA party won.

In 1990 negotiations on a Mexico–US free trade agreement were launched. A major Mexican motive, like Canada's in CUSTA, was to limit the scope for US unilateral actions against its exports. Unlike Canada, Mexico wanted to use a trade agreement to promote foreign investment.[10] Both the USA and Mexico saw a bilateral agreement as a means of locking in place the recent liberalization of the Mexican economy.

With Canada's participation in 1991, negotiation of a North American Free Trade Agreement (NAFTA) essentially entailed the extension of CUSTA.[11] Although CUSTA provided an initial framework, there were important differences in the issues involved. Mexico had far lower incomes than the USA and Canada and, although major trade liberalization had recently taken place, its tariffs were on average significantly higher than those of the USA or Canada. Although some issues were common, the North American Free Trade Agreement would have to address new areas such as labour and environmental issues.[12] Moreover,

[10] President Salinas was reportedly much influenced by a trip to Europe in which he observed the EU countries looking only east towards Central Europe (Fishlow and Haggard, 1992, 23).

[11] Although the direct impact of a Canada–Mexico trade agreement was likely to be insignificant, Canada wanted to participate in order to defend any benefits from CUSTA and to reopen some aspects of CUSTA that were considered unsatisfactory, as well as to keep informed on USA–Mexico negotiations. For the Mexican negotiators Canada's presence provided some shelter against domestic criticism that they were being dictated to by the USA.

[12] Environmentalist lobbies in the USA were galvanized by a 1991 GATT dispute panel ruling in favour of Mexico, which had complained against US import bans on tuna imposed because of allegedly dolphin-unfriendly methods used by Mexican tuna fishers.

the negotiations on sectoral issues (i.e. automobiles, textiles, agriculture, and petrochemicals) were more intense, as US vested interests feared job losses or competition from Japanese transplant factories in Mexico—fears that had been far less with respect to Canada.

Concerns about labour adjustment were addressed by including a transition period of up to fifteen years for the elimination of trade barriers. The transition arrangements are product-specific, applying mainly to agriculture and to sensitive manufactured imports into the USA and Canada (e.g. glassware, footwear, ceramic tiles, brooms, and watches). Safeguard clauses permit the reintroduction for up to four years of trade barriers in the face of import surges which threaten serious injury. For sensitive agricultural items tariff rate quotas were established, such that the MFN tariff would be applied above a certain import quantity.

The major instrument for resolving the contentious sectoral issues was detailed rules of origin, often drafted with the assistance of the industries concerned so that they could be tailor-made to achieve the desired results.[13] Rules of origin on automobiles and apparel were the last two items to be agreed upon in the NAFTA negotiations, and in the final agreement two hundred pages are devoted to rules of origin.

Agreement was reached in August 1992 and NAFTA was signed by the three countries' political leaders in December, but the US election and the need for ratification by Congress added uncertainty. In October 1992 presidential candidate Clinton endorsed the agreement, ruling out the possibility of any renegotiation if he won the November election, but he also emphasized the need for side agreements in areas of labour and the environment and for safeguards before he would send the agreement for congressional ratification. The side agreements were completed in August 1993, but this process and the need to encourage

[13] Clothing produced in Mexico gains duty-free access to the USA only if it meets the 'yarn forward' rule, which for many products requires virtually 100% sourcing of inputs from North America (WTO, 1995, 48); Mexican suppliers thus face the choice between forgoing NAFTA status or diverting trade from least-cost non-NAFTA input suppliers to Canadian and US textile firms. The rules of origin on automobiles were tailored to favour US-owned suppliers rather than use of inputs produced in North America (see Ch. 12).

wavering voters in Congress to support NAFTA led to some additional concessions to US interest groups (notably on sugar, citrus, and fruit and vegetables). Congressional approval was granted in November 1993, despite considerable opposition from US labour and environmental lobbies.

The North American Free Trade Agreement (NAFTA) entered into force at the start of 1994. As with CUSTA, the centrepiece is the elimination of tariffs and most non-tariff barriers on intra-regional trade. Some extensions to CUSTA were made in the areas of agriculture, financial services, and the protection of intellectual property, while Mexico was exempted from the provisions on government procurement (because it was not a signatory of the GATT code) and energy (a state monopoly in Mexico).[14] Cross-border transportation access (for trucks and buses) was improved, although it may be impaired by differing safety and technical standards (Hufbauer and Schott, 1993, 66–73).

The debate in the USA over NAFTA was between advocates of freer international trade and groups wishing to limit trade liberalization for various reasons, and the November 1993 vote in Congress was a victory for trade liberalization. Among academic observers, however, there were doubts about why free trade required such a long text as the NAFTA and its side agreements. In part, NAFTA's length was a result of including new issues and non-tariff barriers which may by their nature require lengthy legal treatment in order to be enforceable, but it was also a result of the complex rules of origin and transition clauses. The rules of origin issue is more serious, since they are intended to be a permanent feature, and will be addressed at several later points in this book (e.g. sections 7.2 and 10.4), but the transition arrangements also open up the prospect of managed rather than free trade.

Sugar provides an example of NAFTA both reducing international trade and obstructing market forces. In the NAFTA negotiations Mexico agreed to raise its MFN tariff so that a common market in sugar could exist with the high US price as the internal price; Mexico was attracted by access to the highly protected US

[14] Mexico did, however, agree to open up procurement of energy-related goods by the national oil company, Pemex, and the State Electricity Commmission, and to abide by GATT standards in its interventions in energy-related trade.

market, and in return was willing to trade off liberalization of its own protected corn industry. During 1993 the US negotiators, in response to pressure from the sugar lobby, tightened up restrictions on Mexican access to the US market during the fifteen-year transition period. In November 1993 the US Trade Representative confirmed that Mexico had agreed to include corn sweeteners in the determination of Mexican supply to the USA during the transition period.[15] More blatantly, a cap of 250,000 tons was placed on Mexican sugar sales in the USA from the seventh to the fourteenth year of the agreement, i.e. the years when the quantitative restrictions were supposed to be gradually phased out. These last-minute revisions were believed to be crucial in securing the votes of at least a dozen members of the US House of Representatives in support of NAFTA and thus may have been necessary for NAFTA's approval, but they contributed to the extension of a managed trade regime for sugar. Similar but less restrictive last-minute adjustments were made to the NAFTA regimes for citrus and other fruits and vegetables.[16]

The 1993 revisions in NAFTA's operating procedures highlight the dangers of bilateralism for the weaker partner and the fragility of commitments made by the stronger partner. The July 1992 agreement represented the result of trilateral negotiations, including cross-sectoral trade-offs. The subsequent revisions were *de facto* unilateral, imposed by the USA in response to domestic pressures and after initial resistance grudgingly accepted by Mexico. By contrast, attempts by other US interest groups to reopen grievances with Canada in 1993 were far less successful; for example, US wheat producers' concerns over Canadian transport subsidies and Wheat Board pricing policies were met by an

[15] The US Trade Representative's letter to Mexico's Secretary of Commerce ingenuously claimed that substitution of corn syrup for sugar could 'result in effects not intended by either party' and thus should be included in calculations of Mexican sugar supply to the US market (Orden, 1996, 369–70). The substitution of high-fructose corn syrup for sugar had been a market response to artificially high sugar prices in the USA during the 1980s, and a major goal of the US sugar lobby was to ensure that such a response would not undermine the extension of the protectionist regime to cover Mexico.

[16] Orden (1996, 380–1) concludes that, although the initial NAFTA signed in 1992 may deserve high marks for agricultural trade liberalization (as granted by Hufbauer and Schott, 1993), the NAFTA that passed into law introduced more trade distortions than trade liberalization in agriculture and accomplished only a small percentage of the goals sought in the Uruguay Round.

agreement to hold bilateral consultations.[17] Most ominously, the willingness of the US government to reopen negotiations and impose additional concessions on Mexico when US interest groups threatened to prevent ratification of NAFTA raises the question of what will happen if similar interest groups lobby for protection when the transition period is expiring in 2009.

NAFTA was widely perceived as evidence of a US shift towards bilateralism as an alternative to multilateralism, represented by the contemporaneous Uruguay Round negotiations, although successive US administrations stressed the complementarity of NAFTA and the Uruguay Round. Western Hemisphere countries were especially attentive to such a shift in US trade policy, and worried about losing their US market to Mexico. The US government tried to forestall any negative fallout by announcing the Enterprise of the Americas initiative in June 1990, shortly after NAFTA negotiations began. Trade and investment agreements were subsequently signed between the USA and most countries in the region.[18]

The process was stimulated by the launch at the Miami 'Summit of the Americas', in December 1994, of the Free Trade Area of the Americas (FTAA), to be completed by 2005. The target of a free trade area from Baffin Island to Tierra del Fuego was accepted, although no agreement was reached at Miami (nor in the FTAA Trade Ministers' meetings in Denver in June 1995 and in Cartagena, Colombia, in March 1996) on how the target was to be achieved. One alternative is gradual expansion of NAFTA, whose ministers began talks with Chile in June 1995. Another, proposed by Brazil, is for the South American countries to construct their own free trade area (SAFTA) which would then merge with NAFTA, and presumably with the CACM and CARICOM.

[17] Although Canada resisted US recontracting in 1993, the relative weight of the USA and Canada is illustrated by the ability of vociferous domestic groups to place environmental issues on the agenda. At the time of the CUSTA negotiations environmental issues were important in Canada, with widespread support for reducing cross-border transmission of acid rain, but the USA successfully side-stepped any serious consideration of environmental matters. In the NAFTA negotiations, even under President Bush, the environment was on the agenda to assuage US domestic groups, with the demands being placed on Mexico (Pearson, 1995, 324–8).

[18] Hufbauer and Schott (1994) review the arguments surrounding a Western Hemisphere free trade agreement prior to the Miami summit.

The competition between these visions has some similarity with the EEC/EFTA debate of the early 1960s, with Chile (rather than Greece) being wooed by both sides.[19]

3. Reactions to European and American Regionalism

The EC92 programme and the extension of CUSTA to incorporate Mexico captured public attention in 1988/9. Countries outside these regional trade arrangements worried about the fragmentation of the global trading system into a small number of regional blocs, especially as EC–US conflicts over agriculture threatened to derail the Uruguay Round with negative consequences for the credibility of the GATT-based trading system. One reaction was the strengthening of other regional trading arrangements, although those involving developing countries were in a different policy environment to the earlier customs unions among developing countries. The new arrangements were presented as components of broader trade liberalization, rather than as attempts to promote import-substituting industrialization over a bigger internal market.

The displacement of inward-looking regionalism by more liberal arrangements is most evident in Latin America. The 1960 Latin American Free Trade Area had failed to liberalize regional trade, and its 1980 successor, the more flexible Latin American Integration Association (LAIA), also had little impact. During the early 1990s, however, subgroups of countries from the region began to negotiate bilateral free trade agreements, aimed at mutual trade liberalization rather than at securing mutual access to a larger protected market. Chile signed agreements with Mexico in 1991 and with Venezuela and Colombia in 1993, and Colombia,

[19] The situation was complicated by domestic and foreign policy considerations. Chilean talks with NAFTA members proceeded smoothly with Mexico and Canada, but the USA lost bargaining credibility when Congress refused to give the administration fast-track negotiating authority (i.e. they reserved the right to review any agreement in detail). The USA also aroused South American suspicions over its emphasis on labour and environmental issues and its willingness to take unilateral measures (e.g. over Argentinian enforcement of intellectual property rights). Meanwhile, there were doubts about whether the SAFTA route was really aimed at hemispheric trade liberalization or at a LAFTA-style protectionist trade bloc dominated by Brazil.

Mexico, and Venezuela signed a trilateral agreement in 1994; other negotiations involved Mexico and the CACM, Venezuela and CARICOM, and Bolivia and Mexico. The Andean Pact members (Bolivia, Colombia, Ecuador, Peru, and Venezuela) agreed to form a free trade area with a common external tariff, which after protracted negotiations over the tariff level came into effect in 1995. The CACM, which had regressed as a regional trading arrangement in the 1980s, was reactivated in the early 1990s, and Panama joined the five original members in 1991. A 'free trade zone' came into effect in 1993, with tariffs reduced to 5–20 per cent on a range of products traded among four CACM members. (Costa Rica and Panama did not participate.)

The most important of the Latin American initiatives in terms of the size of the economies involved is the Southern Common Market (MERCOSUR). A 1991 treaty signed by Argentina, Brazil, Paraguay, and Uruguay called for a common market from January 1995 with free movement of goods, services, labour, and capital. Despite initial disagreements about tariff levels, a common structure was agreed and the Protocol of Ouro Preto, signed by the four presidents in December 1994, allowed the common external tariff to be established on schedule. The CET ranges from 0 to 20 per cent and covers about 85 per cent of all products; the remaining 15 per cent of products are on exception lists with the CET still to be finalized, but with full tariff convergence by 2006. MERCOSUR also established a dispute settlement mechanism modelled on that of CUSTA.[20] In 1996 Chile became an associate member of MERCOSUR, forming a free trade area rather than joining the customs union.[21]

Similar patterns are observable in Africa, the Caribbean, West Asia, and South Asia, but with less practical impact. Renewed

[20] The functioning of the mechanism remains unclear. MERCOSUR's first major dispute, following a 1995 increase in Brazil's tariff on cars from which Argentina was initially not exempted, was settled at the executive level rather than through the formal mechanism. The 1996 agreement on a transitional trade regime up to 1999, when intra-MERCOSUR car trade will be duty-free, contained detailed quantitative restrictions and trade-balancing requirements for automobile producers in Argentina and Brazil.

[21] Chile did not join the customs union because the common external tariff is higher than Chile's tariff. Many items were, however, exempted from the FTA (e.g., wheat and flour were omitted to protect Chilean grain farmers from Argentinian competition).

efforts at economic integration occurred in 1989 among the Maghreb countries (Algeria, Libya, Mauritania, Morocco, and Tunisia), in 1990 among the West African members of ECOWAS and among four of the members of the Central African Economic and Customs Union (Cameroon, Congo, Gabon, and the Central African Republic), and in the 1990s among the old EAC members. The 1991 agreement by CARICOM members to replace national import quotas by a common external tariff, which would be reduced to a 0–20 per cent range by 1998, was intended as an integrative step.[22] In May 1992 trade ministers of the Gulf Cooperation Council members (Bahrain, Kuwait, Oman, Qatar, Saudi Arabia, and the United Arab Emirates) announced the objective of establishing a customs union by the year 2000.[23]

Political developments revitalized some regional arrangements. The Southern African Development Coordination Centre was transformed into the South Africa Development Community (SADC) when South Africa became a member in 1992.[24] In August 1996 the twelve SADC members commited themselves to establishing a free trade area within eight years, as well as signing three other protocols (on energy, water, and drug control) which signalled an intention to strengthen regional co-operation.

The end of the Cold War revived the South Asian Association for Regional Cooperation (SAARC), which had been launched in 1985 by Bangladesh, Bhutan, India, the Maldives, Nepal, Pakistan, and Sri Lanka, and a framework preferential trading agreement

[22] Intra-CARICOM trade accounts for about a tenth of its members' total trade, and internal trade relations are less important than preferential access to their major export markets through the Lomé Convention, the CBERA, and agreements with Canada. (The 1986 CARIBCAN programme extends the old Imperial Preferences by granting duty-free entry to Canada for exports from CARICOM countries and from other Caribbean members of the Commonwealth).

[23] The Iran–Iraq War was the catalyst for the establishment of the Gulf Cooperation Council in 1981. Major concerns have been defence co-operation, co-ordination of oil policies and market access negotiations for petrochemical exports, and, since the 1991 collapse of the Bank of Credit and Commerce International, co-operation in banking supervision. Given the similarity of the economies, which are all heavily specialized in oil, a customs union is unlikely to have any significant impact on trade.

[24] The accession of Mauritius in 1995 brought SADC membership to 12, but economically it is very uneven, with South Africa's GNP almost four times the size of the other countries' combined GNP. The other members are Angola, Botswana, Lesotho, Malawi, Mozambique, Namibia, Swaziland, Tanzania, Zambia, and Zimbabwe.

was signed in 1993. However, the PTA was not ratified until December 1995, and even when implemented will offer only a 10–25 per cent preferential cut in tariffs on a limited range of goods. Trade between the two largest SAARC members has in fact been restricted rather than preferential; Pakistan assented only in 1995, as part of its WTO commitments, to grant MFN treatment to imports from India.

A regional arrangement involving Iran, Pakistan, and Turkey had been reactivated in 1985 as the Economic Cooperation Organization (ECO), but had little momentum until membership expanded to ten countries in 1992 with the accession of Afghanistan, Azerbaijan, Kazakstan, Kyrgyzstan, Tajikistan, Turkmenistan, and Uzbekistan.[25] The three founder members of ECO signed a Protocol on Preferential Tariffs in 1991, by which they agreed to grant each other a 10 per cent preferential tariff reduction on selected commodities. The initial lists of commodities were extremely limited, with few items, some of which were narrowly defined. Five years after the signing of the Protocol, it was unclear if any implementation steps had been taken, and the seven new members were still not involved in the PTA even in principle. The new international environment also lay behind various schemes involving other former CMEA members, which are discussed in the next section.

The striking exception to the proliferation of regional trading arrangements was in East Asia. Despite talks of the division of the world economy into three blocs based on the USA, Europe, and Japan, Japan remains one of the few large trading nations which is not part of a regional trading arrangement. The other significant international traders in this category are also in northeast Asia: South Korea, Taiwan, Hong Kong, and China.

Southeast Asia, by contrast, has a successful regional organization in ASEAN, which has existed since 1967. ASEAN's success, however, does not lie in the promotion of preferential trading arrangements. Attempts to do this in the late 1970s and 1980s failed. ASEAN's success has lain in its role as a regional forum to defuse political tensions, to develop common strategic positions (initially in response to the threat of communism, and then

[25] The 1977 Treaty of Izmir remains the basic document of ECO. Pomfret (1996d) provides more details on ECO.

focused on Vietnamese expansionism during the 1980s), and to co-ordinate negotiations with third countries on economic issues. ASEAN contributed to economic success by promoting political stability in the region, but the driving force behind the exceptional growth of Southeast Asian economies after the mid-1980s was unilateral policy reforms in Indonesia, Malaysia, and Thailand.

In the late 1980s the ASEAN countries reopened the question of a preferential trading arrangement and the ASEAN Free Trade Area (AFTA) was announced in 1992. AFTA involves reduction of tariffs on intra-ASEAN trade in manufactures to below 5 per cent within fifteen years. As in the late 1970s, member governments responded by drawing up long exclusion lists, and AFTA had to be relaunched in October 1993 with a firmer commitment to reducing high tariffs and bringing forward the deadline from 2008 to 2003. (In 1995 the deadline was advanced again to 2000.)[26] In the 1990s, as the political situation changed, ASEAN began to expand its membership, with Vietnam joining in 1995 and Laos, Cambodia, and Burma (Myanmar) preparing for membership.

The most important preferential trading arrangement in the Asia–Pacific region is the Closer Economic Relations (CER) agreement between Australia and New Zealand.[27] The CER replaced a more limited free trade agreement in 1983, when both Australia and New Zealand became committed to substantial economic reform, including dismantling of the highest trade barriers in any OECD countries. The CER is not of much importance beyond the two member countries, but it was interesting as an early example of the new regionalism which went beyond preferential tariff reductions. Unlike the earlier FTA, the CER agreement included a timetable to eliminate all quantitative restrictions on trade between Australia and New Zealand, and they were in fact removed by 1990, five years ahead of plan. The CER covered a wide range of non-tariff barriers, the application of anti-dumping and countervailing duties, subsidies and government procurement, while

[26] Pomfret (1996b) analyses the prospects for AFTA and the forces behind ASEAN enlargement.

[27] The South Pacific Forum, founded in 1971, brings together 12 independent South Pacific territories, with observer status for non-self-governing territories. The members are small island economies, with only Papua New Guinea having a population of over a million, and the Forum's main activity is co-ordinating fishing and transportation policies, disaster relief, and trade and aid negotiations with non-members (especially Australia and New Zealand).

TABLE 6.1 Asia–Pacific Economic Co-operation (APEC) Summits, 1993–1997

Year	Venue
1993	Blake Island (near Seattle), Washington, USA
1994	Bogor, Indonesia
1995	Osaka, Japan
1996	Subic Bay, Philippines
1997	Vancouver, Canada

additional protocols in 1988 and 1992 extended the CER to services and then to harmonization of business law and competition policy (McLean, 1995; Scollay, 1996).

Faced with the threat of regionalism in Europe and the Americas and uncertainty about the Uruguay Round's outcome, most East Asian countries remained committed to multilateralism but concerned about a fall-back position. Two visions of Asian solidarity emerged in 1990. The Malaysian government promoted the idea of an organization encompassing ASEAN and the northeast Asian countries, with the implication that this East Asian Economic Caucus (EAEC) might develop into a preferential trading arangement. The Australian government, in part owing to concern about being left out of the regionalism pattern ('the only kid without a bloc'), espoused a looser organization including countries on both sides of the Pacific. The second vision won, mainly because of the support of Japan and the USA, and the first Asia–Pacific Economic Cooperation (APEC) summit was held in the USA in 1993 (Table 6.1). Despite the high-level attendees at this and subsequent annual summits in Indonesia (1994) and Japan (1995), APEC has remained rather amorphous with its commitment to non-discriminatory 'open regionalism'.

4. The Collapse of the CMEA and the USSR

The end of communist rule in Central Europe in 1989 and the decision of successor governments to abandon central planning foreshadowed the end of the CMEA. Czechoslovakia, Hungary, Poland, and the USSR in particular pushed for CMEA trade to be transacted at world prices with settlement in hard currencies, which effectively made the role of the CMEA as the co-ordinator of trade among non-market economies redundant. CMEA-determined prices and accounting exchange rates continued to apply to some trade during 1990, and even into 1991 on trade between the USSR and some of the poorer CMEA members, but the CMEA was formally disbanded in September 1991.

The contemporary disintegration of Yugoslavia, independence in 1991 of the Baltic Republics, and the 1993 separation of the Czech and Slovak Republics compounded the changes in Central Europe by increasing the number of independent states (although the Czech Republic and Slovakia agreed not to introduce any new barriers on trade between themselves). The only offsetting move was the absorption of the former German Democratic Republic into the Federal Republic of Germany, and hence into the European Union.

The USSR was naturally seen as a single state before 1991. In trade terms, however, the USSR was the CMEA writ large, as Soviet central planners had greater power to enforce specialization patterns (and hence resource misallocation) on the fifteen Soviet republics. This misallocation was exaggerated by a predilection for gigantism and consistent undervaluation of transport costs by the Soviet planners. Production was concentrated in a few large factories, whose location was not necessarily based on economic criteria.[28] Inter-republic trade bore little resemblance to international trade for mutual benefit. After the dissolution of the USSR in December 1991, the breakdown of inter-republic supply channels was extremely disruptive, but at the same time, maintaining past trade flows could only have perpetuated the resource misallocation.

The political changes in the former CMEA and Yugoslavia were an exogenous event, in terms of the evolution of international trade diplomacy during the early 1990s, but they added a large

[28] The sugar refinery, which accounted for 3% of Kyrgyzstan's GDP was an extreme example for the republic concerned (Pomfret, 1995b, 37), but was not atypical of Soviet planners' tendencies towards gigantism and excessive shipments. The refinery's location was intended to promote industrialization in one of the poorest republics. It refined cane sugar from Cuba for shipment throughout the USSR. After 1991 it became uneconomic to ship Cuban sugar via the Black Sea ports and several thousand kilometres of railway, and the refinery was technically unsuited to processing the beet sugar grown in continental Eurasia. The refinery closed down and the trade flows based on it ceased.

number of countries to the global trading system. To varying degrees these countries had traditions of planned trade and had conducted much of their trade within the CMEA, but by 1992 all of the Central and Eastern European and former Soviet states expressed commitment to outward-oriented market-based economic policies. Which way would these countries turn; would they be an added force for multilateralism or would they pursue their own regional trading arrangements?

The trade policy reactions of the economies in transition from central planning contained many proposals for RTAs, driven by a mixture of defensiveness (to preserve established trade flows) and solidarity (to increase bargaining power *vis-à-vis* other countries or RTAs). The most important is the Central European Free Trade Agreement (CEFTA), established in 1992 by the Czech Republic, Hungary, Poland, and Slovakia. Slovenia joined at the start of 1996. Half of CEFTA trade was made tariff-free under the 1994 Protocols of Budapest, and a full free trade area is scheduled for early in the next century.[29] The members of CEFTA have trade agreements with the EU and the rules of origin in these agreements are cumulative for all CEFTA inputs.

The Commonwealth of Independent States (CIS), which by 1994 included twelve of the successor states to the USSR (i.e. all but the three Baltic republics), is not an economic organization. Intra-CIS trade flows remained fairly free as the CIS members generally adopted liberal national trade policies by the mid-1990s, often with exemptions on imports from within the CIS. Some formal agreements on regional trading arrangements were signed, but their impact was unclear. The Russian Federation and Belarus formed a customs union which was joined by Kazakstan in 1995, and extended in scope and joined by Kyrgyzstan in March 1996. Kazakstan, Kyrgyzstan, and Uzbekistan had also agreed in 1994 to form a customs union. Several pairs of CIS members have signed free trade agreements, which appear to be motivated by a desire to keep existing trade flows as unrestriced as possible,

[29] Tariffs on medium-sensitive goods (chemicals, paper, and timber) were lifted in 1996, leaving intra-CEFTA tariffs on some agricultural goods, textiles, steel, electrical equipment, and cars, which are to be phased out by 2002. The original CEFTA countries are often known as the Visegrad Group, following a 1991 summit at Visegrad in Hungary where the leaders of Czechoslovakia, Hungary, and Poland agreed to cooperate in matters of common interest.

without limiting countries' freedom of action in policy towards non-CIS trade.[30]

The end of the Cold War, conventionally identified by the December 1989 Malta Summit between Presidents Bush and Gorbachev and definitive with the disintegration of the USSR in 1991, also had indirect effects on the international trading system. As described in Section 1 of this chapter, it changed the dynamics of European integration for the Central European and Scandinavian countries. The United Nations assumed a more active role as Great Power vetos in the Security Council became less stultifying. Iraq's invasion of Kuwait was met by UN-authorized sanctions as well as a military response. UN-approved sanctions were also used against Serbia and to try to limit the carnage in Bosnia. Only twice before 1990 had UN sanctions been in force—against Rhodesia in 1966–79 and against South Africa in 1977–94—but the 1990 sanctions against Iraq and 1991 sanctions against (former) Yugoslavia were followed by UN sanctions against Somalia, Libya, and Liberia in 1992 and against Haiti and Angola in 1993.

A corollary to the increased use of UN-authorized trade sanctions was the growing controversy over national sanctions. While UN sanctions are mandatory, there is no obligation to pay attention to sanctions introduced by individual nations; indeed, if they are trade sanctions against GATT signatories, then the imposer can be cited for breaking its GATT obligations. In the USA, which uses trade sanctions for economic reasons (as in aggressive unilateralism) and for political reasons, the sanctions' efficacy has been undermined by lack of co-operation from other trading nations. In 1994 the USA lifted its embargo on trade with Vietnam, in part because US exporters were losing market opportunities in the fast-growing and liberalizing Vietnamese economy to rivals such as Australia, the EU countries, and Japan, which had

[30] The actual situation is unclear, but the CIS seems to have operated as a *de facto* FTA in 1993/4 with few constraints on internal trade. The tension since 1994 appears to derive from Russian pressure to formalize the situation and have a common external tariff. Some CIS members accept Russian leadership in determining the CET (e.g. Belarus) or accept the desirability of a customs union but disagree over the CET favoured by Russia (e.g. Uzbekistan), while others reject the supranationality implicit in a customs union (e.g. Turkmenistan). The situation is unstable if a subgroup forms a customs union, because preferential treatment of trade with other CIS countries would probably be WTO-incompatible and would be highly susceptible to trade deflection given the long and porous intra-CIS land borders.

removed their restrictions on trade with Vietnam after the withdrawal of Vietnamese troops from Cambodia in the early 1990s. The USA's other longstanding general embargo, on trade with Cuba, was retained and its supporters tried to discourage non-US firms from taking advantage of the embargo by threatening retaliation against those firms' trade or assets in the USA. Such action, legitimized domestically by the 1996 Helms/Burton Bill, would be illegal under international trade law if taken against a GATT signatory, and it met vociferous opposition from almost all US trading partners. Similar conflicts simmered with respect to China and Myanmar (Burma), against whom many US (and some EU) politicians wanted to use trade sanctions as a lever to promote human rights issues, but were frustrated by lack of support from Asian countries who championed trade as a lever for constructive engagement which would encourage more internationallly acceptable behaviour.

5. The Uruguay Round

The Uruguay Round was the longest of all the GATT rounds of multilateral trade negotiations.[31] In part, this reflected the greater complexity of negotiating non-tariff barriers to trade; the Tokyo Round, the first to address such issues, lasted almost as long. It also reflected the cumbersome bargaining process, which some proponents of bilateralism ascribe to the large and increasing number of GATT signatories—91 in 1986 and 123 in July 1995 (when a further 30 countries had outstanding applications). Numbers alone, however, were not so significant, because many negtiations involved groups of countries. As in previous GATT rounds, agreement between the major trading nations (especially between the USA and the EU) remained the key to a successful end to the Uruguay Round, but a shift occurred, with the developing countries, agricultural exporters (in the Cairns Group), and other medium-sized trading nations becoming more committed negotiators than before.

The main delaying force arose from the EU's intransigence on agriculture and the anomalies of the US negotiating stance, which

[31] Croome (1995) and Preeg (1995) provide historical accounts of the Uruguay Round negotiations.

sometimes started from extreme positions which ultimately were unacceptable to itself. An important question for the present book is whether the EU and USA were distracted during the Uruguay Round by NAFTA and EC92 negotiations. This is difficult to answer, because both sets of negotiators faced serious institutional problems; the EU, although negotiating with one voice, had to ensure prior agreement of twelve nation states each of which wielded a veto, while the US executive branch had negotiating authority, but the final package could be vetoed by Congress. Neither set of negotiators had flexible means of modifying their bargaining positions and being able to guarantee delivery of their promises. An alternative perspective on the influence of regionalism ascribes a positive role to APEC in the Uruguay Round endgame. US focus on APEC in 1993 reassured Western Pacific countries that the USA was not committed to regionalism in the Americas, while the EU leaders were taken aback by the high-level APEC summit attended by the leaders of all major non-European trading nations.

The more active participation by developing countries reflected growing disillusionment with the GSP and more importantly a global shift in trade policy. Disappointment with the outcome of GSP schemes removed developing countries' reluctance to negotiate reductions in MFN tariffs, especially as hopes that the original GSP schemes might be made more attractive were not fulfilled, apart from extra privileges granted to the least developed countries (who were also least able to benefit from export price incentives). The EU's GSP scheme was constrained by the desire to offer a significant preference margin to Lomé Convention partners. All GSP schemes were vulnerable to domestic interests successfully restricting the schemes' scope if imports actually expanded owing to GSP benefits.[32] Moreover, country eligibility

[32] In the USA in 1984 the value of trade from GSP beneficiaries who were denied GSP treatment because of the competitive need criteria exceeded the total value of trade covered by GSP (Annual Report of the President of the United States on the Trade Arrangements Program 1984–5, Washington DC, February 1986, 155–6). The American scheme's product exclusions are also restrictive (e.g. textiles and clothing and leather goods are excluded by law), but no more so than other GSP schemes. Vulnerability to donor country actions was also illustrated during the late 1980s and early 1990s with the growing resort by the USA to s. 301 actions in which the retaliation against unfair trade practices took the form of threatening withdrawal of GSP benefits; the threat was implemented against Thailand (twice) and India.

was being curtailed by the principle of graduation, which was applied first to Portugal and Spain when they became EC members in 1986 and then, by the USA and other donors, to various newly industrializing economies starting in 1989. By 1994 the US GSP scheme had a threshold per capita GNP of $11,389 for graduation which was reduced to $7000 in 1995, cutting out most middle-income countries, but also threatening by further reduction to exclude all but the least developed countries. In sum, GSP offered little to developing countries that achieved even a modicum of export success.

At the same time, the policy orthodoxy was shifting during the 1980s from import-substituting industrialization towards more outward-oriented and market-friendly development strategies. Developing countries became increasingly willing to accept the obligations of GATT membership (in the form of constraints on their ability to implement trade policies which they no longer wanted to adopt) and to seek the rights of members (in the form of legal guarantees of market access); the US pursuit of aggressive unilateralism and increased use of anti-dumping duties by the EU, USA, and Australia in the 1980s underlined the benefits of international rules. GATT membership increased substantially during the 1980s and, for the first time in multilateral trade negotiations, countries from outside the OECD played an active role in the Uruguay Round. Many were simultaneously pursuing regional trade liberalization agreements (see previous sections), but, given the greater importance of US, EU, and Japanese markets, GATT was the principal negotiating forum for many developing countries.

Many of the key negotiating areas in the Uruguay Round were only indirectly related to the issue of discriminatory trade policies. Agriculture and textiles and clothing, which had been allowed to escape from the GATT-based international trade law, were brought back in the fold, albeit with a transition period. New areas such as services, intellectual property rights, and trade-related investment measures were brought into the GATT system for the first time. In addition to usual bargaining matters such as tariff reductions and non-tariff barriers already discussed in the Tokyo Round, these new and contentious issues ensured long negotiations. Successful conclusion of the Uruguay Round ultimately required high-level intervention in the USA and EU after the details of an agreement had been hammered out. At this point, the existence of the EU (in which the EU majority pushed a recalcitrant France into accepting the agricultural terms of the final agreement) and President Clinton's success in pushing NAFTA through Congress (creating a climate favourable to further trade liberalizing legislation) helped to ensure the speedy ratification of the final agreement by the two principal actors. The agreement reached in December 1993 was formally ratified by all GATT signatories at Marrakesh in April 1994.

Successful conclusion of the Uruguay Round was crucial to the regionalism-versus-multilateralism issue in that failure of the Round would have been a major blow to multilateralism and an encouragement to shift trade diplomacy into regional or bilateral channels. The presence of negotiations had itself encouraged the major trading nations to abide more to the spirit of the GATT. The use of VERs declined markedly, which reflected recognition of their negative characteristics, including the systemic threat. Use of anti-dumping duties has been cyclical but does not appear to have an upward trend since the early 1980s, while use of countervailing duties by the USA diminished. Despite much fear of escalating protectionism, the threat appears to have receded in the early 1990s. The steel VERs negotiated by the USA during the 1980s were allowed to lapse in 1992, and several anti-dumping and countervailing duties introduced in their stead were struck down by the US International Trade Commission in July 1993. This withering away of the new protectionism of the 1970s was in stark contrast to the hysteresis introduced by the protectionism of the 1870s.

The establishment of the World Trade Organization (WTO) was symbolic of a new start for world trade law. The developments in the early 1990s created a favourable environment for a stronger multilateral institution to enforce a liberal international trade system based on non-discrimination with the consent of all the major trading nations and an ever-increasing number of other countries. The content of the Uruguay Round in respect to preferential trading arrangements and the prospects for multilateralism under the WTO are the subject of the next chapter.

7

Regionalism and the World Trade Organization

One outcome of the Uruguay Round was the creation of the World Trade Organization (WTO). Creation of a new organization had not been on the original Uruguay Round agenda and was only proposed, as a Canadian initiative, in 1990.[1] When the WTO came into existence at the start of 1995, the practical impact was little more than changing the nameplate on the GATT Secretariat in Geneva. The GATT Articles and amendments remain the basic charter.

Nevertheless, the WTO had some profound implications (Jackson, 1995). Its inclusion in the Final Act of the Uruguay Round highlighted the 'single package' idea, whereby every WTO member accepts (almost) the entire package, in contrast to the Tokyo Round approach of negotiating plurilateral codes to which not all GATT signatories acceded (and which hence were a form of conditional MFN treatment). The WTO also symbolized a new commitment by the GATT contracting parties to more active implementation of world trade law. The WTO has an enhanced mandate for supervision and dispute settlement. Among the major trading nations, the perceived need for a beefed-up body arose primarily in areas other than Article XXIV, but the importance ascribed to this area by the WTO Secretariat is reflected in the title of one of its first publications, *Regionalism and the World Trading System* (WTO, 1995).

This chapter focuses on the three main challenges to the WTO in the context of the regionalism versus multilateralism debate. The first section examines the dispute settlement mechanisms agreed upon in the Uruguay Round and intended to replace the toothless lion image of GATT, which applied to Article XXIV

[1] Preeg (1995, 113–14) describes the WTO's origins. The intellectual input came from US academic trade lawyer John Jackson, but the USA agreed to formation of the WTO only in the final stages of the Uruguay Round negotiations.

more than to any other article. Section 2 deals with the rules on preferential trading arrangements, which remain essentially unchanged; lack of action is particularly apposite to the question of rules of origin. The third section considers the ability of the WTO effectively to cover the new areas in trade negotiations. The final section provides an overview of Part I of the book.

1. The World Trade Organization and Dispute Settlement

Pressures for institutional strengthening of the GATT arose from a widespread belief that GATT enforcement mechanisms were too weak, and from a subsidiary view that, as trade negotiations moved into new areas beyond tariff reduction, a larger secretariat would be needed to deal with these more complex matters.

The view that GATT enforcement mechanisms were too weak was especially prevalent in the USA, where the belief gathered strength that US traders were not playing on a level field. The main targets were Japan and other East Asian countries; evidence that Japan's tariffs and other formal trade barriers were low was taken as proof that other non-formal barriers must be impeding imports. The stimulus for this belief was the emergence and rise of a US trade deficit in the early 1980s; the origins lay in macroeconomic policy, underlining a lesson from the 1930s that macroeconomic imbalances fuel nationalistic trade policies. Other countries, especially mid-sized and smaller trading nations, took up the case for better enforcement mechanisms as they wanted better protection against the unilateral use of VERs, anti-dumping, and countervailing duties by the North American, European, and Australasian countries; these measures were often not against the letter of the GATT, and certainly there were incentives not to initiate a formal complaint (which would get nowhere and would probably lead to reprisals against the complainer), but they usually contravened the spirit of the GATT.

The dispute settlement issue was not centred on discriminatory trade policies, but nor were these policies irrelevant to the US mood. The sense of not being on a level playing field was reinforced by the trade diversion costs of the EC's external trade policies. As mentioned in Section 5.3, the first complaint brought under Article XXIV, in 1982, concerned the preferential treatment of Mediterranean suppliers to the EC, and the injured party was the US citrus fruit industry. Adoption of the panel's report was blocked by the EC and the Mediterranean countries. Failure to make any headway through GATT dispute settlement channels contributed to the US decision to respond with its own preferential trading arrangements. The only two other complaints under Article XXIV were initiated in 1993 by a group of central and South American countries against the EC's preferential treatment of bananas imported from Lomé Convention beneficiaries. The panels again found in favour of the complainants, but the report was blocked.

During the early years of the Uruguay Round negotiations, concerns among other countries were raised by the US adoption of aggressive unilateralism which bypassed GATT dispute settlement procedures. These concerns peaked early in 1989 when Brazil received support from all other GATT members in its opposition to GATT-illegal US tariff retaliation aimed at forcing changes in Brazilian treatment of pharmaceutical patents. When Brazil took its complaint against the US action to GATT, the USA repeatedly blocked the establishment of a GATT panel, which would certainly have found in favour of Brazil, and although the sanctions were withdrawn the threat of reimposition was held over Brazil during the entire Uruguay Round era. US recalcitrance highlighted the prospect that, in the absence of reformed GATT dispute settlement procedures, the USA would take a vigilante approach to international trade law, acting as judge, jury, and enforcer, implementing discriminatory punishment on offenders, and only exempting partners in regional trading arrangements with their own dispute settlement mechanisms.

The WTO dispute settlement procedures limit the blocking option by increasing the automaticity in the system. The establishment of a panel, the adoption of the panel's ruling, and the right to adopt countermeasures if the panel's rulings are not implemented are all made more automatic; the crucial change is that consensus is now needed to halt these proceedings, whereas previously consensus was required before they could move forward. To protect the defendant nation, the new procedures include a right of appeal, but again the outcome is characterized by automaticity; the report of the Appellate Body must be unconditionally accepted within thirty days, unless there is a consensus against its adoption.

2. Clarifying the Rules on Preferential Trade Agreements

The WTO essentially took over the rules established in the GATT articles and amendments. Although there had been discussion during the Uruguay Round negotiations over the need to clarify Article XXIV, as well as the provisions of Part IV and the 1979 Enabling Clause on preferences for developing countries, they remained unchanged. The Final Act of the Uruguay Round did, however, include an Understanding on Article XXIV and an Agreement on Rules of Origin. The General Agreement on Trade in Services established the principle that unconditional MFN treatment should apply to services trade, and Article V provides similar conditions for regional agreements on services trade to those in GATT Article XXIV on goods trade.

As discussed in Chapter 4, all three of the conditions in Article XXIV for a customs union or free trade area are imprecise. The fifty-plus working parties constituted to examine agreements notified under Article XXIV all failed to confirm the GATT consistency of the agreements, but none of the agreements was disapproved. The chairman of the December 1992 session of the contracting parties called for a 'review of the way in which working parties fulfil their remits under Article XXIV, especially to ensure that the results of their efforts are both clear and meaningful' (WTO, 1995, 12). No review was held, and the topic remains on the WTO's agenda.

The Understanding on Article XXIV seeks to clarify several aspects. The comparison of tariff levels before and after the customs union should be a weighted average of tariff rates and duties collected, using applied rates. A reasonable transition period is ten years, apart from exceptional circumstances. Negotiations for compensation of third countries must begin before the common external tariff is implemented. On these and other matters, the Understanding provides guidelines to working parties, but, despite its general call for transparency, the imprecisions of Article XXIV remain.

The Agreement on Rules of Origin is even vaguer. It calls for establishment of harmonized rules of origin to be applied by WTO members in connection with discriminatory trade policies such as preferences for developing countries, anti-dumping and countervailing duties, or other safeguard measures. In the interim, rules of origin should be transparent and procedural rights of exporters should be recognized. The harmonized rules are expected to provide a standard against which rules of origin negotiated in free trade areas may be assessed.

The weakness of the Agreement on Rules of Origin reflects the failure of the Uruguay Round to tackle one of the most contentious elements of recent regional agreements. Rules of origin are not covered in the GATT articles.[2] They only became an issue in 1960, when third countries objected to the EFTA rules of origin both as a practical burden on traders (owing to their highly technical nature) and because they contain the potential for trade diversion if they discourage the import of semi-finished inputs (WTO, 1995, 49). The issue resurfaced in the working party on the EC–EFTA free trade agreement, where examples of highly restrictive rules of origin were identified. The costs could be substantial; Herin (1986) estimates that, on a quarter of EFTA exports to the EC, traders paid the MFN duty rather than meet the rules of origin or do the paperwork necessary to obtain the duty-free access promised in the EC–EFTA free trade agreement. By the 1990s the EU had at least sixteen different sets of rules of origin.

In current practice, at least three tests may be used to determine whether a good qualifies as coming from the country of shipment:

1. if there has been a change of tariff heading;
2. if the value added in that country exceeds a specified percentage of the exported good's value;
3. if specific processing operations have occurred.

The change of tariff heading criterion is superficially attractive; for example, it requires imported steel to be transformed into bicycles rather than to be re-exported as steel. In practice, tariff headings, which were not designed with origin determination in mind, do not correspond to normal definitions of industries or products. If the Harmonized System, the most frequently used tariff schedule, is adopted as the basis for rules of origin, countries still have to select the relevant level of aggregation; in

[2] Marking of the country of origin is mentioned in Art. IX, but as an informational matter. The following discussion of rules of origin is based on Palmeter (1993; 1995) and the more detailed case studies in Vermulst *et al.* (1992).

CUSTA, two-digit categories were used for some goods, four-, six- and eight-digit ones for others.[3] Such discretion makes the criterion non-transparent as well as open to abuse. The second criterion is also open to manipulation as it is sensitive to decisions on how to treat overheads, transport costs, and so forth. The technical amendments to the USA–Canada Autopact contained in CUSTA raised the content requirement from 50 to 70 per cent (see Section 2 below). Exchange rate changes can also make a value added criterion unpredictable. The third approach is inherently discretionary and allows free rein to tailor-made management of trade patterns.

The design of rules of origin in the NAFTA negotiations represented the most blatant tailoring of the details of an agreement to thwart true liberalization of trade. On many items, the CUSTA rules of origin were revised to acccommodate changed circumstances, and according to Palmeter (1995, 193 n.) NAFTA contains over 11,000 separate rules of origin. Such tailor-made rules are the modern counterpart to the tailor-made tariff categories which undermined the MFN principle earlier in the twentieth century, and are clearly against the spirit of the GATT. Failure to address such a blatant challenge to the principles of transparency and of non-discrimination represents a serious challenge to the WTO's credibility with respect to regional trading arrangements.

A more positive outcome has been the establishment of a single Committee on Regional Trading Arrangements. This arose out of discussions over the reporting body for the working party on MERCOSUR: the Committee on Trade and Development (which oversees the Enabling Clause) or the Goods Council (which manages Article XXIV)? With a single committee dealing with all RTAs, there should be some technical spillover and greater consistency in evaluation.

3. The WTO and New Areas

As tariffs have been reduced to low levels in the major trading nations, and increasingly across the world (Table 7.1), other

[3] Palmeter (1995, 193 n.) estimates that CUSTA contains 1498 separate rules of origin.

TABLE 7.1 Average tariffs after the Uruguay Round, selected countries (%)

	Applied rates	Bound rates
EU	2.8	3.2
Japan	2.8	3.7
USA	2.8	3.3
Hong Kong	0.0	0.0
South Korea	7.7	16.4
Argentina	10.3	31.0
Brazil	11.7	29.0
Mexico	10.4	34.1

Note: Tariffs are weighted by 1988 import values.

Source: WTO Integrated Data Base, reported in Finger and Winters (forthcoming, table 2).

TABLE 7.2 Anti-dumping Measures in Force on 31 December 1995, Selected Countries

Country/group	No. of measures
USA	304
EU	172
Canada	94
Australia	88
Turkey	38
New Zealand	25
Brazil	21

Source: WTO Committee on Antidunping Practices, reported in Finger and Winters (forthcoming, table 8).

barriers to global economic efficiency become relatively more important. The 1973–9 Tokyo Round was the first to address non-tariff barriers. The Uruguay Round covered services and considered trade-related investment measures and intellectual property rights for the first time, although it failed to address seriously the rampant use of anti-dumping measures (Table 7.2). Recognition that protectionist trade barriers are but one element of industrial policy lay behind the consideration of subsidies and government procurement in the Tokyo Round, and behind later calls for international agreements on the use of competition (or antitrust) policies.[4] In the 1990s there have been moves to place on the trade agenda issues such as the environment or labour regulations, both of which were included in side-agreements added to NAFTA at the last minute by the USA. This proliferation of issues is one reason for the expansion of the WTO's mandate to initiate studies and of its staff, but it raises the question of whether the WTO is always the best forum for negotiation.

The new areas lend themselves to the revival of conditional MFN treatment. Signatories of the Tokyo Round codes on subsidies and on government procurement were bound to meet the requirements with respect to other signatories, but had no obligation with respect to non-signatories, whether they were GATT contracting parties or not. A logical step was to take negotiation of contentious issues outside GATT and into forums containing the potential signatories. The OECD provides such a forum for the established industrial countries; OECD Codes on Capital Movements and on Current Invisible Operations have the force of treaty obligations for OECD members.[5] On other issues the group of potential signatories may be in a geographical region, and the code could be most effectively negotiated within a regional organization.

Even where the potential applicability of regulations is global, a case can be made for negotiating within a limited forum. A smaller number of countries around the table will speed up negotiations. The resulting agreement can then be tried among these countries, and if it works use will spread until it is global.[6] Such reasoning has led to praise for regional trading arrangements such as the CER, EU, and NAFTA, which have gone beyond

[4] This was advocated by the EC, after it tightened its own harmonization of competition policy in 1990. The EC Commissioner for External Economic Affairs and Competition Policy, Sir Leon Brittan, called in 1992 for GATT rules on competition policy.

[5] The OECD Declaration on International Investment and Multinational Enterprises is a non-binding commitment by members to grant national treatment to other members, i.e. to treat foreign-owned enterprises in their jurisdiction no less favourably than domestically owned enterprises. Acceptance of all Codes and of the Declaration is a condition for OECD membership (as was made clear during the Czech accession negotiations in 1995), so a menu approach to adherence (as is permissible with the GATT/WTO codes) is not possible with the OECD Codes.

[6] A variant of this approach has characterized the early years of the WTO; regular meetings of the Quad (the USA, EU, Japan, and Canada) have provided issue leadership.

GATT to include areas such as competition policy or the environment. Harmonizing different national regulatory systems is challenging enough for Australia and New Zealand, and under present conditions is a non-starter at the global level.

The danger of derogating negotiations in the new areas to regional bodies without WTO supervision is that the drafters of rules will determine their content. The designers of the rules may see themselves altruistically providing the rest of the world with a free ride in observing a laboratory experiment, but the outsiders may be unimpressed if they are later asked to select from a menu of experiments conducted by not-disinterested countries. Investment codes drawn up by the leading home countries of multinational enterprises will differ from foreign investment codes drawn up by groups weighted towards the host countries, and presumably the most appropriate drafting committee would be more balanced.[7]

The competition between global and regional institutions for drafting international rules in the new areas is complicated by the current disarray among the multilateral institutions. Half a century after the establishment of the major international institutions (the United Nations, GATT, the IMF, and the World Bank), the boundaries of their mandates have become less well defined.[8] The new areas of trade negotiations often fall into the grey areas in which the Bretton Woods organizations and various UN agencies have overlapping responsibilities. Bureaucratic imperialism leads institutions to try to increase their responsibilities, while budgetary pressures in the 1990s make most of them less capable

[7] There is a parallel with the manoeuvre by the developing countries to have generalized tariff preferences discussed within a UN forum where they could impose their decision by weight of numbers. The GSP met their aims on paper, but the countries that had been out-manoeuvred were responsible for implementation and they ultimately designed GSP schemes of little practical value. On issues such as child labour, the environment, or drug control, where the high-income countries wish to ensure compliance by poor countries, the only agreements likely to succeed are ones to which the poor countries have voluntarily assented.

[8] Sometimes this is intentional, as institutions' original mandate disappeared but they avoided closure as vested interests (staff, the host country, and other beneficiaries) rallied behind them and they found new mandates. Thus, the IMF survived the end of the fixed exchange rate system and became involved in debt rescheduling and extended loans to developing countries; UNCTAD still exists long after GSP ceased to have any relevance; UNIDO survived the discrediting of import-substituting industrialization.

of expansion. Even if the new areas could be better handled at the global level, institutional competition may prevent negotiations from being located in the most efficient forum.

A major challenge facing the WTO is to establish its authority in new areas of trade-related negotiations. One of its challengers will be regional arrangements such as the CER, EU, or NAFTA. Another challenger will be regional organizations seeking a *raison d'être*, such as APEC, which began drafting an investment code in 1995. Limited membership non-regional organizations such as the OECD are well placed to move quickly on matters of particular interest to their members (whose interests may not be shared by the global community). Finally, other international institutions may seek to set the agenda in their fields (e.g. the specialized UN agencies).

Not all issues should necessarily be seen in terms of competition between international agencies. Some issues are not worth seeking global agreement; e.g. the G7 summits and other meetings aimed at co-ordinating exchange rate movements proved ineffective in the long run. In some issue or sector areas the competent agency is undisputed, e.g. WIPO for intellectual property or ISO for standards or ITU for telecommunications. In other areas the obvious existing agency is mistrusted by leading trading nations, e.g. the ILO on labour standards or UNEP on the environment. This is especially true of UN agencies, where the richer countries fear being outvoted and pushed into undesired outcomes (as with GSP at UNCTAD), and where governance problems can result from politicized appointments (e.g. UNESCO in the 1980s). If the WTO is pressed into taking over issues in the jurisdiction of discredited agencies, then it too is likely to encounter difficulties, because disputes over labour standards, the environment, etc., arise in part because they are controversial areas. In areas where an acceptable agency exists, the likely (and desirable) procedural outcome is that in trade-related matters the WTO will be involved in co-operatiuon with the lead international institution.

In sum, the emergence of new trade-related areas will raise tricky problems for the WTO, both economic and institutional.[9]

[9] This book will not attempt a thorough treatment of 'trade and . . .' issues. In general, even if national legislation affects trade flows, trade policy is unlikely to be the best policy instrument for correcting distortions. Child labour or emission

Although labour standards and the environment received most publicity during the early 1990s (especially in the context of US ratificiation of NAFTA and the Uruguay Round), the most difficult areas are likely to be competition policy and investment. There is no self-evident existing international agency in either of these areas, and yet they can affect trade flows directly. Both competition policy and investment codes have featured prominently in the new regionalism literature of the 1990s as areas where regional bodies can play a positive role in regulatory design.

4. Review of Part I

The first part of this book has traced the history of discriminatory trade policies up to the early years of the WTO. The narrative clearly reveals long swings in the prevalence of GDAs. From a high point of liberal non-discriminatory trade policies in the third quarter of the nineteenth century, world trade became less free and policies more discriminatory until they seriously disrupted world commerce and contributed to depression and war during the 1930s. After a new start with the GATT in 1947, international trade was liberalized and the non-discrimination principle re-established as the cornerstone of the world trading system, but this position was gradually eroded over the following decades until multilateralism appeared to be under serious threat by the late 1980s. This episode, however, had a more positive outcome, as policy-makers sought a co-operative strengthening of the multilateral system, embodied in the creation of the WTO.

The issue of discrimination as a challenge to the global trading system has centred on GDAs aimed at promoting trade with favoured partners. The theoretical analysis in Part II and the empirical evidence reviewed in Part III will focus on such preferential arrangements, emphasizing the magnitude and distribution of benefits and costs, in order to explain why GDAs exist and to determine whether they are desirable. Other discriminatory trade policies will receive less attention, although the analysis of Chapter 8 applies to all GDAs.

standards are labour and environment issues which should be dealt with as such. Lump-sum transfers can be used to ease adjustment or to compensate losers, or other instruments can be found, but trade policy will be far down the list of appropriate instruments.

Discriminatory protectionist measures and sanctions have dynamic significance for the global system because they undermine the legitimacy of the non-discrimination principle. The evolution of VERs during the GATT era is a particularly significant topic because VERs proliferated for short-run reasons (see Chapter 17), but have been successfully rolled back after their adverse systemic consequences became appreciated. The MFA provides an example of proliferating discrimination getting out of control, and this lesson was learned in avoiding a network of footwear VERs or a multi-metal arrangement. The other high-profile VERs, on autos, also provided a systemic threat because the QRs reversed tariff liberalization which had been achieved in GATT rounds. In the WTO, VERs have been proscribed, although anti-dumping and countervailing duties are still permitted.

The story with respect to sanctions in the WTO era is less optimistic. Until the 1990s, sanctions were imposed in breach of GATT obligations, but were of insufficient importance to threaten the system. The end of the Cold War led to an increasing number of UN-authorized sanctions. The driving force behind most of these has been the USA, as the sole superpower. The USA has also been the country most willing to impose its own sanctions on trade with other countries, whether they were GATT signatories or not. In an increasingly integrated world economy, national sanctions are less effective, and US attempts to breach gaps in their sanctions' impact, as with the 1996 Helms–Burton Act, pose a major threat. National sanctions themselves are an aggressive assertion of the priority of national law over GATT/WTO treaty obligations; extra-territorial projection of national sanctions tries to force other countries to join in breaching GATT/WTO obligations.

The controversies over sanctions threaten the GATT system not only because they involve discriminatory trade policies, but also because they challenge the principle of a liberal international economic system in which decisions are made by individuals rather than states. This is related to some of the attempts to introduce new areas into international trade negotiations such as labour standards or other social issues. It is, however, not central to the regionalism versus multilateralism debate as it developed during the 1990s.

Among preferential trading arrangements, regional integration schemes began to dominate the debate in the late 1980s. Regional integration may go far beyond simple preferential trading arrangements, and raise fundamental questions about the basic unit of analysis and the role of distance in economics. These questions will be addressed in Chapter 11.

The remainder of the book will concentrate on explaining the formation and performance of GDAs, but it is worthwhile to draw some preliminary conclusions from the historical narrative. First, history matters. Policy-makers are influenced by the current situation so that trends can gather their own momentum. At the same time, the full effects of GDAs may take years to become apparent, so that causal chains take a long time to work their way through. Thus, the historical patterns include proliferation, hysteresis, and path dependence.

Proliferation has been especially visible in preferential trade policies involving large economies and small partners. The EC's external trade policy involved an ever-increasing number of PTAs as excluded countries sought equal treatment with their rivals (e.g. the Greek association agreement led to Turkey requesting a similar agreement), and this in turn stimulated the USA to establish its own array of PTAs after 1982. A second but less important example of proliferation was the copy-cat customs union proposals which sprouted up in Latin America and Africa during the 1960s, inspired in part by the EC example. These were less important because few were actually implemented, and none lasted long as an effective customs union.

A recent literature (e.g. R. E. Baldwin, 1995) has been concerned with developing models of proliferation, based on the idea that excluded countries will have an incentive to join a FTA or customs union. The stylized facts behind these models are the continuing enlargement of the EU and the potential enlargement of NAFTA. In fact, losses of members have been more common (e.g. the CACM, EAC, and EFTA), so that these domino models of proliferation do not have strong support and will be ignored in the theoretical part of this book.

Second, economics matters too. Inefficient RTAs collapsed and VERs were eventually proscribed, but the effects take time to be felt. The situation is complicated because perceptions also matter. Policy-makers, convinced that GDAs from which their country is excluded have pernicious effects, are often driven to take actions, leading to proliferation or retaliation, rather than waiting to see how the economic effects actually turn out. Perceptions may be widely shared and firmly held, imparting hysteresis to the system in that an increasing number of countries may pursue similar policies, based on a common perception of the economic implications, even if that perception is false. The economic evidence that the perception is false may be slow to accumulate to the point of being convincing, although the prevailing wisdom can be changed by exogenous events; e.g. the breakup of the USSR challenged current thinking on the inevitability of regional integration to create viably scaled (i.e. very large) trading units.

The interplay of economic consequences (and their recognition) with less firmly based perceptions underlies the dynamics of discriminatory trade policies. This is an example of Krueger's life-of-their-own view of trade policy formation; the current set of policies can be understood only in terms of their evolution and people's behaviour at each stage of that evolution, rather than by trying to understand the policies' present optimality or distributive effects. In the long run, this evolution depends also on institutions. The trade liberalization of the 1860s was unstable owing to the absence of any supervisor. Multilateral conferences were unsuccessful in the 1920s and 1930s because they had no authority. GATT was more successful because, despite its toothless appearance, it had the fundamental allegiance of the major trading nations, and a rule-based system provides an anchor aganst changes in fashion. This anchor was crucial in allowing the system to weather the threat from discriminatory measures which grew to alarming proportions during the 1980s (covering over four-fifths of world trade by the early 1990s, according to Fieleke, 1992), and the last GATT round provided trade policymakers with the forum in which they could come up with a cooperative solution to the threat.

PART II

THEORY

Introduction to Part II

From the long history and continuing proliferation of discriminatory trade policies described in Part I, it might be expected that the theoretical analysis of such policies would occupy a prominent position in international trade theory. Quite the opposite: despite the conceptual breakthrough in Jacob Viner's 1950 book, in trade theory textbooks of the following decades one chapter (at most) sufficed on 'customs union theory', and the analysis shed little light on the real-world situation. There remained little consensus on the appropriate measures of the welfare effects of even the most important preferential arrangements (such as the EC/EU), and the conventional explanation of the establish-ment of such arrangements rested on 'non-economic' arguments.

There are some good reasons for the deficiencies. The theory of discriminatory trade policies belongs in the world of second-best, and generalizations are hard to make. The $2 \times 2 \times 2$ neoclassical general equilibrium model of international trade is not applicable, since at least three countries must be involved. Even given these obstacles of outcome and method, however, the literature made disappointing progress, primarily because inappropriate assumptions were overused in order to surmount the methodological problem. In particular, international price changes were often ruled out by assumption, which in turn ensured that analytical attention was focused on the preference donor rather than the recipient and biased the analysis against finding gainers from trade preferences. To the extent that the literature looked beyond the donor, it was to analyse the global welfare effects of preferences; this was obviously a useful goal, but in avoiding the distribution of welfare gains and losses it shed little light on the political economy of GDAs.

The mainstream model is, however, better than its reputation in providing some robust and relevant conclusions. Free trade areas, which are easier to negotiate than customs unions because superficially they impinge less on national policy autonomy, suffer from trade deflection which can make them chronically unstable. The distribution of gains from preferential trading arrangements are fairly clearly in favour of preferred trading partners and against non-participants, with the possibility of tailor-made arrangements ensuring that insiders benefit at the expense of outsiders. Within the mainstream theory there is little scope for expecting the welfare impact on outsiders to be non-negative, although the order of magnitude is an empirical matter.

These conclusions provide a rich starting point for an analysis of the political economy of discriminatory trade policies. Even though it cannot provide unambiguous conclusions about global welfare effects, Vinerian customs union theory does offer a presumption that discriminatory trade policies are inferior to non-discriminatory reduction of trade barriers. This was reflected in the generally sceptical view of discriminatory trade policies held by most international economists in the 1980s.

This scepticism was challenged on several fronts during the late 1980s and 1990s. The most important theoretical refinement was the introduction of imperfect competition into the analysis. The subject matter was broadened by moving beyond an analysis of tariffs and border measures which could be represented by equivalent tariffs to new areas, such as regulatory harmonization or monetary integration, which were captured by the concept of deep integration. The focus also increasingly shifted from discriminatory trade policies to regional integration, in which geographical proximity played a part.

Lloyd (1996, 44) defines economic integration in terms of the law of one price. In a totally integrated world economy, common prices prevail everywhere and utility-maximizing resource allocation is possible. Both shallow and deep regional integration measures should reduce the wedge between world and domestic prices, yet a home market bias remains substantial even between highly integrated economies such as the USA and Canada. The question of what determines the size of Lloyd's wedge and whether it will be reduced by the measures contained in recent regional integration schemes such as EC92 or NAFTA raises basic issues about the economic importance of national boundaries and the location of economic activity, which are poorly understood and hence are a fruitful area for future research.

In Part II mainstream customs union theory will be presented in Chapters 8 and 9. The revisionist literature stimulated since the mid-1980s by EC92 and NAFTA is analysed as the New Regionalism in Chapter 10. The final chapter addresses a number of topics with a geographical dimension; although some of the analysis of issues such as the size or number of trading units and the choice of partners within trading blocs is a-spatial, the role of distance is usually lurking in the background.

8

The Mainstream from Viner to the JCM Proposition

This chapter deals with mainstream customs union theory. The central concepts are Jacob Viner's trade creation and trade diversion. Viner's analysis is important not only for the theory of discriminatory trading arrangments, but also because it led to a better understanding of the general theory of the second best. Movement towards one condition for Pareto optimality, e.g. by reducing tariffs on imports from some sources, may not be welfare-improving when other conditions are not fulfilled, which they necessarily are not when tariffs remain on non-preferred imports.

Analysts of real world situations, however, shy away from the ambiguity of second-best analysis and seek general conclusions.[1] During the 1950s and early 1960s, clarification of the Vinerian concepts led to the proposition that a preferential tariff reduction could never be superior to unilateral non-preferential tariff reduction. From this proposition was drawn the conclusion that preferential trading arrangements could be explained only by non-economic motives. The conclusion, which I will refer to as the Johnson–Cooper–Massell (JCM) proposition, can be supported by either partial equilibrium analysis (Section 3) or general equilibrium analysis (Section 5).

Another strong conclusion, which had a firmer theoretical basis, concerned the instability of pure free trade areas (Section 4). Competition for tariff revenue will tend to drive the external tariffs down to zero, removing the discriminatory intent of free internal trade, unless members agree on a common external trade policy (i.e. form a customs union).

[1] It is noteworthy that, although modern trade theory dates its pedigree back at least as far as Ricardo, modern customs union theory begins in 1950. Ironically, one reason for the failure to identify rigorously the second-best nature of geographically discriminatory trade policies lay in 19th-c. economists being too closely concerned with real-world cases and stating only that half of the analysis which supported their prior position.

1. Some Pre-Vinerian Contributions

The theory of preferential trade policies (or customs union theory) is frequently interpreted as beginning *de novo* with Viner's 1950 book. This is clearly a simplification; most tariff regimes before 1950 had been discriminatory, proposals for customs union had been frequent and some important ones had been implemented, and there had been informed discussion of all this. Yet there had been no resolution of the fundamental dilemma posed to advocates both of free trade and of protection: are preferential tariff reductions better than no tariff reductions, or, alternatively expressed, is protection against some foreign suppliers better than no protection? Neither from a national nor from a global welfare perspective could this be categorically answered. Viner's great contribution was to prove indeterminacy, and, by introducing the concepts of trade creation and trade diversion, to provide tools for identifying conditions under which preferential arrangements are welfare-improving. Nevertheless, there had been important insights before 1950, three of which will now be described.

The controversy that Viner resolved had focused on a preferential tariff's impact on the donor. Some consideration had been given to global considerations, but most contributors took a nationalist viewpoint. Little attention was paid to the impact on the preference recipient, perhaps because it appeared obvious and had been spelled out long ago:

> When a nation binds itself by treaty . . . to exempt the goods of one country from duties to which it subjects those of all others, the country, or at least the merchants and manufacturers of the country, whose commerce is so favoured, must necessarily derive great advantage from the treaty. (Smith, 1776, bk IV, ch. 6)

By emphasizing the gain to the preference recipient, Smith makes an important point about the distribution of gains (both among and within affected countries); the point aroused little controversy, but by the 1960s it appeared to be largely forgotten, or assumed away.

The most controversial word in the above quotation is 'great'. The direction of change seems incontrovertible, but its magnitude is not. In an article foreshadowing Viner, Taussig (1892) showed that the incidence of the costs and benefits from trade preferences depends upon the market share of the recipient. He illustrated this with two examples. Preferences given by the USA to Hawaiian sugar in 1876 scarcely affected American prices (because the Hawaiian market share remained small) but yielded a windfall gain to the Hawaiian producers; i.e. the welfare effect was a transfer from US government revenue to Hawaiian producer surplus. Taussig concluded that 'any remission of duty which does not apply to the total importations, but leaves a considerable amount still coming in under the duty, puts so much money into the pockets of the foreign producer' (Taussig, 1892, 28). His second example concerned the other extreme where the preferred partner provides almost all imports, illustrated by the USA granting preferential treatment to imports of wool from Australia. In this case, if the price elasticity of import supply is high, the primary beneficiaries are domestic consumers. Taussig's examples indicate that the distribution of trade preferences' welfare effects depends upon what happens to prices, i.e. upon whether the exporter is 'large' or 'small'. Taussig's paper is a precursor of Viner's work in so far as it identifies the ambiguous impact of preferential tariffs on the donor (in his examples, the USA), but by considering only the extreme cases he failed to derive any general result.

Along a different track, Torrens (1844) developed an argument for discriminatory trade policies based on the nationally optimum tariff in the presence or absence of other countries' reactions. He opposed unilateral tariff abolition on the ground of negative terms of trade effects and increased vulnerability to other countries' manipulation of the terms of trade, and advocated bilateral negotiation of commercial treaties on a reciprocity basis. Torrens rejected charges that he was opposed to free trade in general; free trade was the ultimate objective, but it could be imposed only upon political dependencies, while independent (large) countries could gain by levying their nationally optimum tariff unless this was made costly by retaliatory tariffs.[2] Torrens's analytical contribution is valuable because he recognized the argument that

[2] 'It is by the enforcement of retaliatory duties throughout the ports of the British empire that free trade is to be conquered' (Torrens, 1844, 67). On p. 102 he calls for 'a British commercial league—a colonial Zollverein' to counter foreign rivals' hostile tariffs. His analysis of commercial policy is contained particularly in letters II, III, and the postscript to letter IX; the clearest statement of policy recommendations is on pp. 47–8. Robbins (1958, ch. 7) provides a modern commentary on Torrens's work.

a country could maximize national welfare by operating as a discriminating monopolist even though the global optimum was free trade, and because he related GDAs to changes in the terms of trade, which occupied centre-stage in his policy discussion—a position which they vacated, with unhappy consequences, in later work.

Several nineteenth-century writers discussed the possibility that a GDA might redirect imports from a lower to a higher-cost source (O'Brien, 1976). McCulloch, in particular, recognised trade diversion as the fundamental economic argument against discriminatory trade policies, and as a claret-drinker he was especially opposed to the Anglo-Portuguese Methuen Treaty which discriminated against French wine exports to England. Nevertheless, these writers failed to anticipate Viner's key insight that, because of trade diversion, the global welfare effects of preferential trading arrangements may be either positive or negative.

During the first third of the twentieth century, economic analysis of GDAs was less prominent. Emphasis was placed upon the trade creation aspects of preferential trading arrangements, although this did not necessarily lead to support for PTAs. Haberler's 1933 text (English edition 1936) was both typical and the most influential. Haberler dismissed the analysis in Viner's 1931 paper as having 'a very limited application' (1936, 386 n.), but this assessment was based upon a complete misunderstanding of the trade diversion aspect of Viner's analysis—revealed in Haberler's conclusion that all participants in a PTA must gain while only third countries whose exports were displaced would suffer.[3] Haberler concluded, apparently on the basis of Taussig's 'very important' 1892 paper, that actual preferential tariff reductions fall between the 'Hawaii' and 'Australia' extreme cases and are therefore a poor substitute for general tariff cuts (equivalent to the 'Australia' case) but better than no tariff cuts (whose resource allocation effects are the same as the 'Hawaii' case). With respect to the form of PTAs, Haberler expressed a strong presumption in favour of customs unions and against weaker arrangements (1936, 390–1), apparently because the latter are more

[3] Failure to appreciate Viner's 1931 contribution was not entirely Haberler's fault. The possibility of trade diversion had been briefly raised in the article (Viner, 1931, 11), and Viner acknowledged (1950, 53) that his mind was still unclear on the issue in the early 1930s.

likely to involve a large and a small country in a 'Hawaii' case of simple revenue transfer; by making the analytically minor distinction between customs unions and other PTAs, he was a major precursor of the attitudes embodied in GATT Article XXIV.[4] Haberler's statement that 'customs unions are always to be welcomed' underlines his failure to see the possibility—let alone the analytical causes—of a welfare-reducing customs union.[5]

During the 1930s, concern shifted towards GDAs formed by increasing trade barriers against non-preferred imports. Since such protectionist measures were likely to be globally harmful, discriminatory trade policies fell into greater academic disrepute. Gordon (1941, 446), for example, took a generally negative attitude, arguing that, even if GDAs were formed by reducing tariffs on members' trade with one another, world trade might not benefit if global imports failed to increase. She even used the term 'diverts trade' in a footnote to this argument, but, like nineteenth-century writers who recognized the trade diversion possibility as a cost of PTAs, she failed to spell out the consequent ambiguity of PTAs' welfare effects.

2. Jacob Viner (1950)

Viner's 1950 book provided a dramatic illustration of the generally second-best nature of GDAs; they may be welfare-increasing or welfare-reducing, depending on the specific features of each case. The distinction between trade creation and trade diversion was crucial for illuminating this point, and paved the way for its rapid acceptance and subsequent generalization (by Lipsey and Lancaster, 1956–7), as well as for critiques of GATT Article XXIV (e.g. Dam, 1963). Clarification of the trade diversion concept was important also because the resource misallocation associated with trade diversion is the fundamental cost of discriminatory trading arrangements which has to be weighed against any benefits from lower tariffs on some imports.

[4] As expressed e.g. by Wilcox (1949); see ch. 4, n. 2.

[5] The problems for customs unions were the 'practically insoluble' difficulties of establishing a common external tariff, dividing customs revenue, etc. (Haberler, 1936, 391), although Haberler acknowledged that the Zollverein had solved these difficulties.

Jacob Viner's seminal contribution is contained in the fourth chapter of *The Customs Union Issue*. Despite this book's title, Viner emphasizes that the customs union is but one of a number of possible preferential trading arrangements whose economic differences are slight (Viner, 1950, 4). The key passage concerns his explanation of the trade-creating and trade-diverting effects of a customs union:

> There will be commodities, however, which one of the members of the customs union will now newly import from the other but which it formerly did not import at all because the price of the protected domestic product was lower than the price at any foreign source plus the duty. This shift in the locus of production as between the two countries is a shift from a high-cost to a lower-cost point . . . There will be other commodities which one of the members of the customs union will now newly import from the other whereas before the customs union it imported them from a third country, because that was the cheapest possible source of supply even after payment of duty. The shift in the locus of production is now not as between the two member countries but as between a low-cost third country and the other, high-cost, member country. (p. 43)

His initial evaluation is:

> From the free-trade point of view, whether a particular customs union is a move in the right or in the wrong direction depends, therefore, so far as the argument has yet been carried, on which of the two types of consequences ensue from that customs union. Where the trade-creating force is predominant, one of the members at least must benefit, both may benefit, the two combined must have a net benefit, and the world at large benefits; but the outside world loses, in the short-run at least . . . Where the trade-diverting effect is predominant, one at least of the member countries is bound to be injured, both may be injured, the two combined will suffer a net injury, and there will be injury to the outside world and to the world at large. (p. 44)

Viner goes on to discuss two other sources of benefits from customs union—scale economies (pp. 45–7) and terms of trade changes (pp. 55–6)—but he plays down the former as unlikely to be substantial and the latter as a welfare transfer involving 'corresponding injury to the outside world'. His prime interest in chapter 4 is in assessing the net impact of a customs union compared with the pre-union situation, and he concludes that confident judgement 'cannot be made for customs unions in general and in the abstract, but must be confined to particular projects' (p. 52). Viner does not explicitly compare customs unions with unilateral commercial policies, although he does advocate the preferability of multilateral non-discriminatory tariff reductions (p. 135).

In a few pages Viner had made the greatest single contribution to the theory of discriminatory trading arrangements. The 'second-best' concept was clearly in the air in 1950; Fleming (1951) was developing the idea in a related area, and Meade (1955a, vi) cites Fleming's article as lying behind his treatment of second-best problems. Nevertheless, Viner's book was the *locus classicus* for most subsequent writers, and his forceful exposition of trade creation and trade diversion had self-evident application to any GDA.

3. Mainstream Customs Union Theory after Viner

Viner's juxtaposition of the trade creation and trade diversion effects of GDAs was an important scientific advance. Unfortunately, however, the branch of economic theory opened up by Viner proved disappointing, partly because of its focus on trade diversion and trade creation. The most powerful apparatus for illustrating these concepts involved assumptions that ruled out many interesting aspects of discrimination among trading partners and which focused exclusively on the situation of the preference donor. After classifying and clarifying the trade creation/ trade diversion aspects of discrimination, the literature centred around the proposition that customs unions were irrational in the standard economic sense.

During the decade following Viner's book, emphasis was largely on clarifying the concepts of trade creation and trade diversion and identifying situations under which each would be more likely. The major theoretical development was to identify a possible welfare-increasing aspect of trade diversion; the lower price in the preference-donor would encourage additional consumption of the imported good, involving increased consumer surplus whether or not the additional imports were from the least-cost supplier.[6] Meade referred to this as 'trade expansion',

[6] The point was made at more or less the same time by Meade (1955b), Gehrels (1956–7), and Lipsey (1957).

and later commentators found the amendment largely semantic (because trade creation could be extended to include all post-preference imports which were not previously imported) without altering Viner's basic evaluation.[7] Meade's 1955 lectures contained the fullest tracing out of trade preferences' effects through the primary impact on trade flows in the preferred goods, the secondary impact on substitutes and complements, and the tertiary impact via any need for a balance of payments adjustment, although his verbal reasoning did not make a lasting impression. Other writers, notably Scitovsky (1956; 1958), focused on the realization of scale economies and increased efficiency arising from greater competition in domestic markets as the major sources of welfare gain from customs union. The domination of trade creation and trade diversion is, however, reflected in Lipsey's influential 1960 survey of the field, which mentions the scale economy, technical efficiency, terms of trade, and growth aspects, but whose analytical core is related to the resource allocation aspects of customs unions.

The year 1960 represented a watershed in customs union theory (as the theory of preferential trading arrangements had come to be known) in that it saw the popularization of the diagram that dominated future textbook presentations of the theory. One problem with Vinerian theory was the lack of rigour of the original exposition, almost all the relevant parts of which have been quoted above. As Meade (1955b, p. 36) pointed out, Viner's analysis is most suitable where demand elasticities are zero and supply elasticities are infinite. Whether Viner made these assumptions is doubtful, and Meade certainly saw any analysis based on them as incomplete, but it became the practice to base customs union theory on infinite supply elasticities of all foreign suppliers.[8] Given this assumption, Fig. 8.1 illustrates trade creation,

[7] This definition was proposed by Johnson (1960a) and endorsed by Corden (1965). The issue returned in a fruitless debate over welfare improvements from trade diversion (Bhagwati, 1971 and 1973; Kirman, 1973), which had to be settled by Johnson (1974). In terms of Fig. 8.1, Johnson defines both CB and GH (and not just the former) as trade creation; this is the definition adopted in the remainder of this book.

[8] Arguments over 'What Viner really said' were continuing a quarter of a century later. Viner (1965) denied making either assumption, although Michaely (1976) shows that Viner neglected demand changes and was inconsistent and ambiguous about whether costs were constant or increasing. See also the Bhagwati (1971 and 1973) and Kirman (1973) debate.

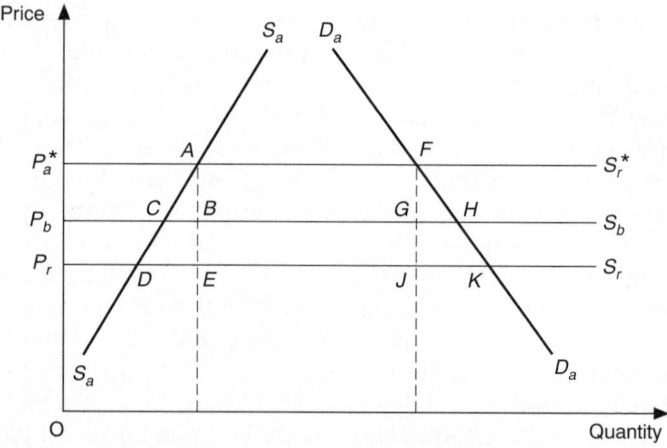

FIG. 8.1 Partial equilibrium analysis of discrimination with a perfectly elastic supply of imports
S_a and D_a are domestic supply and demand curves in A; S_b is the supply of imports from the preferred source B, which is perfectly elastic at a price P_b; S_r is the supply of imports from the rest of the world, and P_r is the world price; S_r^* is the tariff inclusive supply curve, and P_a^* is the pre-preference domestic price in A.

trade diversion, and the primary consumption effect in the simplest manner, with the standard conclusion that the net welfare effect ($ABC + FGH - BEJG$) may be positive or negative.[9]

Figure 8.1 is a splendid heuristic device, but its method runs counter to that of Viner and Meade, its putative fathers. In a long footnote, Viner (1950, 53) criticized previous analyses of customs unions for, among other things, 'applying the standard techniques of partial equilibrium analysis . . . to the tariff problem where its findings are either totally without significance or of totally indeterminable significance'. Meade (1955b), by his emphasis on the secondary and tertiary impacts, also saw tariff

[9] The use of producer and consumer surplus (and the welfare triangles) had already been described by Meade (1955b, 36–43), but he had not drawn the diagram. Corden (1957) developed the diagram for a non-discriminatory tariff. Figure 8.1 appears in Johnson (1960a) and in Humphrey and Ferguson (1960). Whether either article was the source of its popularity is impossible to say, as Lipsey's survey (which used a constant cost example to explain Viner's argument) and Johnson's influential costs of protection article (which popularized Corden's application of the same technique to non-discriminatory trade barriers) appeared in the same year, and it is a short step from them to Fig. 8.1.

preferences as requiring a general equilibrium framework of analysis. Even within the partial equilibrium framework, Humphrey and Ferguson (1960) recognized the restrictiveness of assuming horizontal supply curves from the preference recipient and the rest of the world, but their Model II incorporating increasing costs did not provide any real insights and was largely forgotten.[10]

Both the mainstream theoretical and empirical literature of the next dozen years could be placed within the framework of Fig. 8.1. The net welfare effect of the preferential tariff reduction in the figure can be no better (and will normally be worse) than that of unilaterally eliminating the tariff on a non-preferential basis, i.e. $ADE + FJK$. The implication is that preferential trading arrangements are economically irrational and can be explained only by non-economic motives (Johnson, 1965; Cooper and Massell, 1965). The disappointingly small estimates of the welfare triangles ($ABC + FGH$) for such a major customs union as the European Community led more empirically oriented authors to conclude that scale, technical efficiency, or other considerations were the key ones, but little progress was made in quantifying these so-called dynamic effects.

4. Free Trade Areas and Trade Deflection

An important distinction between analysis of a free trade area and of a customs union arises from the possibility of *trade deflection*. If the external trade barriers differ, then imports from outside the FTA will be deflected through the low-tariff member, wherever their final destination within the FTA. Such trade deflection affects the distribution of benefits since the low-tariff member receives all of the FTA's tariff revenue. Rules of origin could prevent direct trade deflection by banning duty-free transshipment of external goods, but upon closer analysis they turn out to be economically irrelevant if sufficient indirect trade deflection is possible.

The irrelevance of rules of origin for free trade areas was established in the 1960s, when the potential for trade deflection

[10] A similar approach had been used by Johnson (1957; 1958a) in articles that also remained neglected; see Ch. 9 for further developments.

was analysed. In free trade areas, as opposed to customs unions with their common external trade policies, third-country suppliers have an incentive to route their trade through the low-tariff FTA member. If, for example, the Norwegian tariff on a good was lower than the Swedish tariff, then third-country suppliers of the Swedish market would use Norway as the point of entry into EFTA. Rules of origin were intended to ensure that goods entering Sweden duty-free from Norway were truly Norwegian, and not third-country goods trying to evade the Swedish tariff.

As long as the good is also produced in the low-tariff FTA member (Norway in the example), rules of origin cannot affect Swedish output and consumption. The partial equilibrium analysis is presented in Fig. 8.2.[11] The price in Norway (P_N) is equal to the world price (P_w) plus the Norwegian tariff, and free trade with Norway will drive the Swedish price down to the same level (panel (b)). The impact is the same whether foreign goods are trans-shipped to Sweden via Norway or Norwegian supplies are deflected from the home market to the Swedish market, as long as Norwegian output exceeds Sweden's import demand, *ab*, at the intra-FTA price.[12]

With rules of origin, *ab* will be met out of Norwegian output *ob*, so that the Norwegian tariff revenue increases from $bc(P_N - P_w)$ to $ac(P_N - P_w)$. The net welfare effect on Sweden is ambiguous, for reasons familiar from Fig. 8.1. Although the ambiguous welfare impact in the Swedish diagrams looks like the trade diversion in Fig. 8.1, it differs because the ultimate source of added imports is the global low-cost supplier, not the preferred partner. Norway's increased tariff revenue (the shaded area in Fig. 8.2) must exceed the part of Sweden's lost tariff revenue that is not offset

[11] The diagram shows both countries as importers of the good before the FTA. If Norway were an exporter, then its price for the good would be the world price and the FTA's impact on Sweden would be equivalent to that of non-discriminatory tariff elimination.

[12] This analysis assumes no transport costs. With differential transport costs, other welfare outcomes are possible. Suppose Norway's external tariff is zero and Sweden's is 10% and the excess transport costs of shipping third-country goods to Sweden via Norway are equivalent to just under 10% of the world price; with direct trade deflection, Sweden loses tariff revenue but there is no compensatory benefit to others because most of the forgone tariff revenue is dissipated in higher real costs. Rules of origin can be welfare-improving in this setting, which is discussed in Krishna and Krueger (1995, n. 3, with acknowledgment to Will Martin).

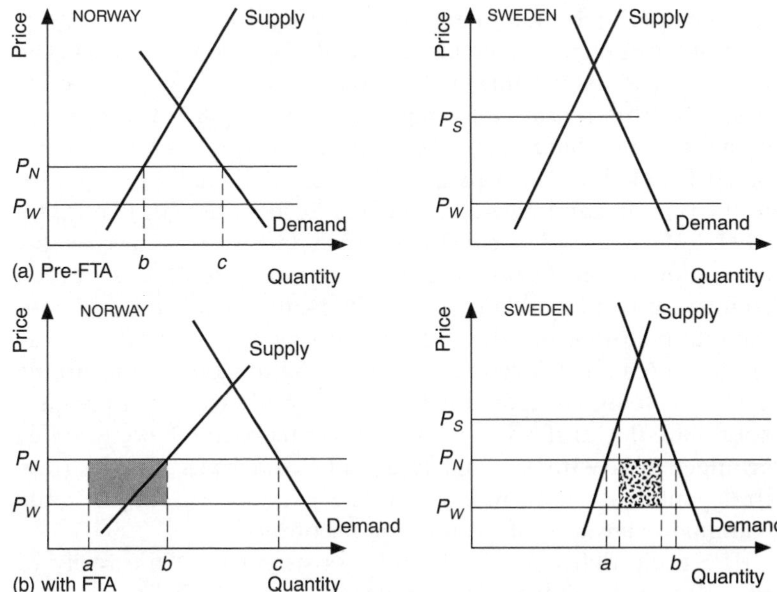

FIG. 8.2 Direct and indirect trade deflection

Before the FTA both countries have tariffs that raise their domestic prices, P_N in Norway and P_S in Sweden, above the world price, P_w. After forming a FTA, imports from Norway will drive the Swedish price down to P_N. Norwegian demand and supply are unchanged, but part of its output (*ab*) is now sold in Sweden and a corresponding quantity is imported from outside the FTA. Norwegian consumers and producers are unaffected, but national welfare is increased by the added tariff revenue ($ab(P_N - P_w)$). Swedish consumers benefit by more than the loss to Swedish producers, but the net welfare effect is ambiguous owing to the disappearance of tariff revenue. The extra tariff revenue received by Norway exceeds the portion of Sweden's lost tariff revenue that is not offset by consumer gains (i.e. the shaded area is larger than the stippled area); the FTA as a whole must benefit from the displacement of high-cost internal suppliers by external imports. There is no trade diversion, so the global welfare effect is positive. By lowering its tariff so that $P_S < P_N$, Sweden could ensure that it enjoys a net welfare gain, but that will initiate a race to the bottom in which the equilibrium external tariffs are zero.

by increased consumer surplus (the stippled area in Fig. 8.2). Since the stippled area is greater than Sweden's maximum possible net welfare loss, the FTA members as a group must gain, which is not necessarily true when a customs union leads to trade diversion. A second difference between the FTA analysis and customs union theory is that Sweden can still change its external tariff unilaterally after the FTA has been formed.

The trade deflection analysis, developed by Shibata (1967), is a potent argument for the instability of true free trade areas. The loss of customs revenue in the high-tariff country will induce it to lower its redundantly high tariff. In Fig. 8.2, Sweden can obtain an unambiguous welfare gain from the FTA by lowering its tariff to below Norway's. The process will continue as a race to the bottom until all FTA-members' tariffs are zero (Vousden, 1990, 234–5).[13] Within a FTA the common internal price is set by the lowest tariff rate; output and consumption levels in each country are independent of which country's tariff establishes the internal price, but the country with the lowest tariff receives all the FTA's tariff revenue. The only way to stop the race to the bottom is to agree upon a common external tariff (and presumably share the tariff revenue). Customs unions are the only stable arrangements with internal free trade, and rules of origin are irrelevant for customs unions because all goods are subject to the common external tariff at the union borders.

The trade deflection analysis is consistent with the rarity of true FTAs (i.e. with no internal trade barriers). Transport costs and the size of within-FTA production at the world price matter, but even if they are not such as to produce full price equalization the tendency to compete for tariff revenue exists unless FTA members collude in setting their external tariffs, which most plausibly involves forming a customs union. Not for nothing was the subject known as 'customs union theory'.

5. The Vanek–Kemp Branch

Figure 8.1 and its progeny (specifically, the Johnson–Cooper–Massell proposition about the non-economic motivation for pref-

[13] Richardson (1995) makes a similar point assuming producer arbitrage rather than consumer arbitrage. In his model all intra-FTA output is sold in the higher-tariff country and the lower-tariff country benefits from increased tariff revenue. Competition among member governments for tariff revenue drives down tariff rates, but not necessarily to zero. Richardson's supporting assumption, that total intra-FTA output is less than demand in either member at any relevant price, and his justifications for ignoring consumer arbitrage (p. 1431 n.) are both less realistic than the assumptions underlying Vousden's consumer arbitrage model. Apart from a few goods (notably cars) whose producers can use after-sales service and warranty restrictions to segment markets, limits on individual consumers' ability for arbitrage are unimportant given the incentives for retailers and other intermediaries to benefit, legitimately, from intra-FTA price differences.

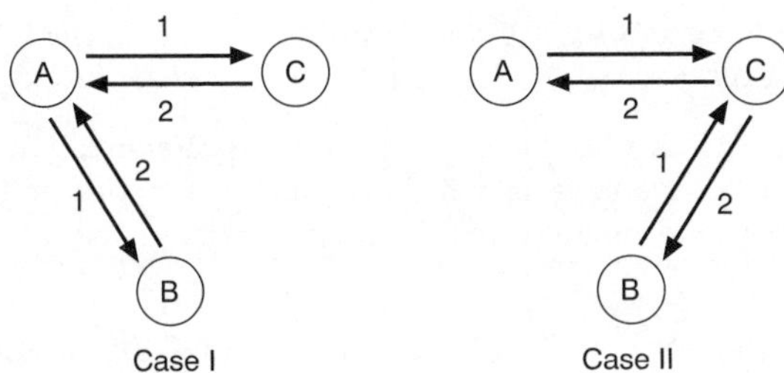

FIG. 8.3 Vanek's approach to customs union theory
1, 2 are goods; A, B, C are countries.

erential trading) dominated the theory of preferential trading arrangements through the 1960s and 1970s, and became the textbook presentation of the subject. There was, however, a substream which developed along its own lines more or less independently of the mainstream literature; its primary source was Vanek's 1965 book.

Vanek uses the neoclassical 2×2 general equilibrium model with production possibility frontiers and community indifference curves, extended to include a third country. The advantage of this approach is to bring prices back to centre-stage, a point emphasized by Vanek (1965, 26):

> perhaps the most important . . . [economic variables] . . . are the terms of trade prevailing within the union, and in world markets after integration.

The drawback of Vanek's approach is that in a two-commodity world pre-union trade patterns can take only two possible forms: either the union members (A and B) trade with one another, or they do not (Fig. 8.3). The second case is almost trivial (unless trade reversal occurs and B starts to export good 2 to A),[14] while the first case will likely have strongly asymmetrical effects.

These effects are explored by Vanek, Negishi (1969), and Kemp (1969). The propositions that emerge are typically second-best:

> The only general conclusion as to the welfare effects of customs unions is that they can be either beneficial or detrimental to the world as a whole. Any more specific statement must contain further qualifications. (Vanek, 1965, 6)

[14] One feature of case II is that A and B in unison can impose an optimum tariff on good 2. This is analysed in Ch. 9.

Kemp derives a stronger conclusion about the impact on A and B individually:

> Strong inferiority aside, the creation of the preferential trading club operates to the advantage of whichever member trades only with the other member, and operates to the disadvantage of the latter. (Kemp, 1969, 31)

However, this holds only if trade with C does not fall sufficiently for A's terms of trade to improve enough for A to gain and B to lose. Kemp also shows that A and B together will normally gain *vis-à-vis* the pre-union situation, in the sense that the loser can be compensated and the gainer can retain a net benefit; but even this is not necessarily true if capital flows exist and B is a net creditor (Kemp, 1969, 49).

The strongest conclusion arises when not only the disadvantaged partner is compensated, but also the rest of the world is compensated by setting the union's common external tariff so that external terms of trade are unchanged. Under these conditions the post-union utility possibility function is consistently superior to the pre-union utility possibility function; i.e., if the welfare of B and C is held constant, then A will be better off after forming a customs union than before it (Vanek, 1965, ch. 7). This elementary proposition was restated in more general form by Kemp and Wan (1976), who went on to ask why we do not observe continuous customs union formation culminating in free trade.[15] They mention difficulties of partner selection, non-economic objectives, and international restrictions on preferential arrangements, but the central point seems to be what they refer to as ignorance and inertia, especially with respect to 'the long list of lump-sum compensatory payments required'.

Thus, the Vanek–Kemp–Wan proposition, which is potentially interesting as an economic justification for preferential trading arrangements, has an esoteric air as an explanation of GDAs in the real world.[16] A further practical problem is that the compensating common external tariff is not necessarily the

[15] Kemp and Wan were partially anticipated by Meade (1955b, 96–8), who held external trade constant by assuming binding quantitative restrictions, and by Ohyama (1972).

[16] Constructing the compensatory common external tariff could also be a huge task, given that the vector of changes in the rest of the world's net exports to the union will have positive- and negative-signed elements, depending upon

welfare-maximizing tariff from the union members' perspective; so, if there is the global consensus for other countries' interests to be respected, why not agree to move directly to universal free trade?

It is easy to see why the Fig. 8.1 literature with its simple exposition and strong (but limited) conclusions remained popular, while at the same time articles kept emerging in the Vanek–Kemp tradition, since this was the only general equilibrium branch of the literature. The two branches of the literature were brought together by Berglas (1979), who used a variant of Vanek's Case I to show that anything A and B could gain by preferential trading could be gained by unilateral tariff reduction. Berglas's conclusion is based on the assumption that world prices do not change; in his model A or C is a large country and the others small, so that the only domestic prices to change are those of B, whose export good's price goes up by the amount of A's tariff and whose import good's price falls by the amount of its own tariff. After A and B form a customs union A will lose tariff revenue, while there is a presumption that B will gain both A's forgone tariff revenue and from its own tariff reduction (depending on unknown income effects). Berglas demonstrates that, if B compensates A for the latter's loss, then all remaining gains to B could be achieved by unilateral non-preferential tariff reduction. Constant terms of trade thus yield the Johnson–Cooper–Massell unilateral tariff reduction proposition, either in a Fig. 8.1 framework or in a Vanek framework.

complementarity and substitutability with items encouraged by intra-union free trade. Grinols (1981) has proposed a compensation scheme and applied it to British accession to the European Community (Grinols, 1984), which to some extent overcomes Kemp and Wan's complexity and ignorance point but which does not resolve the problems caused by lack of respect for other countries' interests.

9

Extending the Model

In contrast to the landmark contributions between 1950 and 1965 by Viner, Meade, Lipsey, Johnson, Mundell, Vanek, and Cooper and Massell, the next fifteen years saw a marked lack of advances in the theory of preferential trading arrangements. Kemp and Berglas developed Vanek's model, the Wonnacotts and Corden cast further light on the relevance of scale economies, and Krauss's 1972 survey attracted some attention (but less than Lipsey's 1960 survey had).[1] In the late 1960s Caves and Johnson (1968, viii) could still refer to the 'large and fast-growing literature' on customs union theory, but during the 1970s disillusionment with this branch of economic theory grew. The cause was not a lack of preferential trading arrangements,[2] but rather the twin conclusions of customs union theory that (a) a preferential tariff reduction could be either better or worse than no tariff cut from the home country's and the world's perspective, and (b) a non-discriminatory tariff reduction will never be inferior to the preferential reduction from these perspectives. Thus, the only generalization that seemed to emerge was that in the absence of domestic distortions a preferential trading arrangement was inexplicable for a welfare-maximizing importing country.

This unhappy state of the art engendered a belief that something must have been omitted from the analysis; customs

[1] Krauss also attracted criticism for *non sequitur* (Michaely, 1976) and for missing the point of one paper and other 'interpretative lapses' (Bhagwati, 1973, 897).

[2] Existing arrangements were extended, e.g. the enlargement of the European Community, the Lomé Convention and the Multifibre Arrangement, and the generalized system of preferences for developing countries (GSP) was implemented. The major studies on GSP were concerned with how restricted the actual schemes were (Murray, 1977), how inferior they were to MFN tariff reductions (R. Baldwin and Murray, 1977), and how the developing countries would do better to participate in multilateral GATT bargaining than to seek preferential treatment (Balassa, 1980). There was little attempt to analyse, or measure, the welfare effects of GSP or to explain why GSP was introduced. (Blackhurst (1972) and McCulloch and Pinera (1977) are the most significant contributions, and neither article received much attention.)

union theory was 'Hamlet without the prince', in the words of P. Wonnacott and R. Wonnacott (1981, 705). Their own candidate for the prince's role is tariffs in the rest of the world, but there were other candidates too. Lipsey (1960) had already suggested possible terms of trade effects, scale economies, improved technical efficiency, and higher growth rates, although they did not attract much interest among economists (in contrast to policy-makers) until the 1980s. Another direction in the search for a missing component was to increase the dimensionality of models.

1. Higher Dimensionality

The theory of preferential trading must diverge from the two-country/two-commodity (2 × 2) trade theory model by introducing a third country, but there is little agreement as to whether more commodities (or countries) are desirable. An analytical framework with more commodities permits complements as well as substitutes, whose significance Meade (1955b) described in his secondary effects, which in turn suggests a need for at least two outside countries to capture the different impact on producers of complements and substitutes (Arndt, 1969). Nevertheless, the *essential* elements of preferential trading could possibly be dealt with in a 3 × 2 model, as Vanek (1965, 13) and Kemp (1969, 21) believed. A series of authors during the 1970s challenged this belief by gaining new insights through 3 × 3 models, but the overall record was clouded by the startling differences in conclusions reached by different authors.

There are four new elements which three-ness permits. First, it can avoid the asymmetry of most two-good models (as in Vanek–Kemp dissimilar economies), although not all 3 × 3 models are symmetrical. The possibility of symmetry was recognized by Vanek (1965, 13), emphasized by Collier (1979), and used by Riezman (1979), but ruled out by assumption by Berglas (1979). Secondly, if a country can have more than one import, then changes in import structures are a possible source of welfare changes (Corden, 1976; Collier, 1979). Thirdly, complementarity relationships can be analysed, as emphasized by Meade and taken up by Berglas (1979), McMillan and McCann (1981), and Ethier and Horn (1984, 213–17), in whose models the degree of substitutability between countries' products becomes a determinant of the welfare changes. Fourthly, the existence of more than one relative price introduces further second-best possibilities owing to the divergences between the ratio of marginal rates of substitution in consumption and marginal rates of transformation (Lipsey, 1970).

Lloyd (1982, 62) concludes that '3 × 3 are the minimum dimensions for models of customs unions'. Yet the outcome of higher-dimension modelling was disappointing because the operation of the last three elements just described depends upon the assumed trade patterns, so that each model (because based on different assumptions) can generate different conclusions: 'every 3 × 3 model is a very special case' (Lloyd, 1982, 62). Thus, despite the advantages of higher dimensionality, such models have had limited influence.

Lloyd (1982) also points out that further analytical benefits could come from introducing intermediate inputs (or service payments on imported capital), which would allow shifts in the transformation surface. Ju and Krishna (1996) have made a start in analysing intermediate inputs (see Section 10.4). Wooton (1988) and Michael (1992) have shown that factor mobility may reduce welfare in a customs union if the external tariffs are not zero or if members' factor tax rates differ. Lloyd (1996, 40–1) argues that this extension of the typical second-best conclusions of customs union theory to a common market is excessively negative; assuming national differences in productivity of factors, the aggregate production in a common market must be greater (or no less) than the sum of member countries' outputs without factor mobility.

Lloyd is making an important distinction between the benefits from free goods movement and free factor movement. Lloyd's proposition implies that members of a customs union can increase their welfare, without harm to non-members, by liberalizing factor flows; some factor-owners' income will fall, but they can be compensated from the increased within-union output, and because there is a pure output gain there is no need to compensate outsiders (as with the Kemp–Wan proposition) to achieve a Pareto-superior outcome. Despite the benevolent conclusion, few preferential trading arrangements turn into genuine common markets with free factor movement. The internal compensations may be difficult to implement, so that potential losers will oppose the move to a common market, but the main obstacles to removing barriers to factor mobility are likely to be non-economic concerns about immigration.

2. Tariffs in the Rest of the World

P. Wonnacott and R. Wonnacott (1981) provide a trenchant criticism of the proposition that, if a preferential trade agreement does not affect the terms of trade, then it does not allow for any mutually beneficial policy opportunities that are not open to each of the member countries separately by unilateral tariff reduction.[3] Their main argument is based on the existence of a tariff in (or net transport costs to) C which opens up a wedge between the price that A receives from its export to C and the price that B pays to import the same good from C. By forming a customs union to divert trade to one another, A and B can trade within the wedge, gaining out of C's forgone tariff revenue. In a two-good world the wedge is formed by B and A facing different tariff-inclusive offer curves from C, and the mutual gain from preferential trading is easily demonstrated. The main caveat to this argument is that in practice the rest of the world (C) is not a single country and part of the burden of tariffs will be borne by domestic consumers in the rest of the world. In such a case Wonnocott and Wonnacott argue that differences in net transport costs will still create a wedge, which explains why geographical neighbours tend to form customs unions. This is not completely satisfactory in so far as, the narrower the wedge becomes, the smaller the welfare gains from trading within it, and because geographically dispersed countries have formed preferential trading arrangements (e.g. the British Commonwealth, the Lomé Convention, Comecon), suggesting that there is something else involved.

The Wonnacotts' analysis is hampered by the self-imposed limitation in their terms of reference. To refute the proposition

[3] This is Berglas's (1979, 329) formulation, which subsumes the earlier Johnson–Cooper–Massell (JCM) proposition. Domestic distortions (including scale economies) are assumed absent.

on its own grounds, they exclude any changes in the terms of trade. Yet this, in combination with the existence of tariffs in the rest of the world, provides a more potent argument for preferential treatment, the point being to reduce the welfare gains to the rest of the world from levying a tariff that improves its terms of trade (as Torrens had argued much earlier). If there are other barriers to equal multilateral trade (e.g. if some currencies are not convertible), then there is also a benefit from discrimination.[4] Indeed, it would be surprising if the move towards Pareto optimality by non-preferential tariff reductions were necessarily welfare-improving in a tariff-ridden world, since the foreign tariffs exclude the first-best outcome. In sum, the Wonnacotts' wedge is sufficient to refute the Johnson–Cooper–Massell (JCM) proposition, but alone it is an unconvincing reason for widespread discrimination.

3. The Terms of Trade

Building higher-dimension models and introducing foreign tariffs into the analysis indicate dissatisfaction with existing theory, but do not get to the heart of the matter. One reason for the lacunae in preferential trading theory is the analytical apparatus of Fig. 8.1, which highlights the trade diversion/trade creation concept by making assumptions that rule out other effects of trade preferences. The horizontal import supply curves exclude price effects or any welfare implications of changes in exports. This is not just a result of the partial equilibrium framework, but rather concerns assumptions about costs and about how prices are set. In the general equilibrium framework of Fig. 9.1, a customs union between two small countries (A and B), with prohibitive external tariff, would bring A and B to point *S*, where B is better off than with non-preferential tariff elimination (point *L*) but A is worse off (than at point *M*); B cannot compensate A

[4] This was generally recognized by postwar policy-makers as a source of conflict with the IMF's position in favour of non-discrimination. If country A had insufficient hard currency to pay for imports from the USA, but could pay for the same imports from a soft-currency country (B) by exports to B, then A, B, and the world would be made better off by A discriminating in favour of imports from B (see s. 5.1).

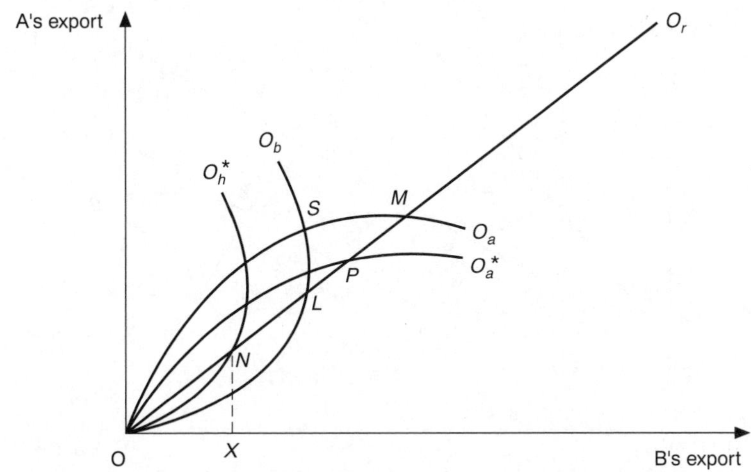

FIG. 9.1 General equilibrium (offer curve) analysis of a customs union involving two small countries

O_a^* and O_b^* are the initial tariff-inclusive offer curves of A and B, O_a and O_b are their tariff-exclusive offer curves. O_r is the rest of the world's offer curve. Initially A trades at point *P* and B at point *N*. Their welfare-maximizing positions, given the world price ratio, are *M* and *L*.

sufficiently, so the welfare optimum is *L* and *M*, i.e. the situation after non-preferential removal of tariffs by A and B.

In the debate over the JCM proposition between the Wonnacotts (1981) and Berglas (1983), both sides agreed to assume no changes in the terms of trade, and this represents the central tradition of the postwar literature. This is, however, an implausible assumption for general analysis of preferential trading arrangements.[5] One symptom of the implausibility of Figs. 8.1 and 9.1 is the stories they tell about the sources of imports (which is after all what discrimination is all about); in Fig. 8.1 all of A's imports come from the rest of the world when there is no discrimination and they all come from B with preferential treatment, while in Fig. 9.1 the source of A's imports and destination of B's exports up to quantity *OX* is indeterminate before the customs union.

[5] The assumption may, of course, be justified and useful in specific cases. Berglas (1979) appears to have in mind an arrangement such as the EC–Israel free trade area, where terms of trade effects may well be minimal (Pomfret, 1978), but this is not a general case.

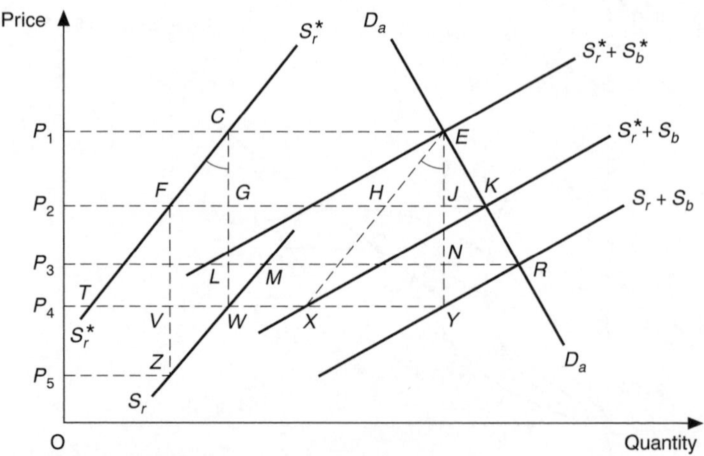

FIG. 9.2 Partial equilibrium analysis of discrimination with upward-sloping supply curves
D_a is A's import demand; S_b is the supply of imports from preferred sources; and S_r is the supply of imports from the rest of the world; S_b^* and S_r^* are the same including A's tariff. Assuming no non-tariff barriers or transport costs and no exchange rate changes, *E*, *K*, and *R* represent demand–supply equilibria with A's tariff, with free access for B's goods, and without A's tariff, and P_1, P_2, and P_3 are the corresponding domestic prices; P_4 is the price received by exporters to A when A's tariff is in place, and P_5 is the price received by non-preferred exporters to A when B receives preferential access.

The all-or-nothing import share stories are tied to the simple treatment of prices.[6]

The introduction of increasing costs is sufficient to create the possibility of both B and the rest of the world exporting to A. This can be analysed within a partial equilibrium framework (Fig. 9.2).[7] With a uniform tariff, A imports *CE* from B and P_1C from the rest of the world. If B is granted duty-free access, its exports to A increase to *FK*, while the rest of the world continues

[6] Vanek allowed the terms of trade to change, although the direction of change can go either way (1965, 30). As mentioned in s. 8.5, however, this branch of the literature failed to reach firm conclusions, until Berglas (1979) introduced assumptions that ruled out international price changes.

[7] Variations of Fig. 9.2 have appeared in the literature several times, apparently independently, without displacing Fig. 8.1 as the norm; e.g. Johnson (1957 and 1958a), Humphrey and Ferguson's model II (1960, 205–10), and Blackhurst (1972). One indication of these papers' limited impact is that an article in a major refereed journal could call B's producer surplus on increased exports an effect 'neglected by previous contributors' (Collier, 1979, 92).

to export P_2F. The welfare gain to B arises from a better price on its previous exports (*GJYW*) plus the producer surplus on its additional exports (*HKX*). The welfare effect for A consists of the triangles ($CGF + EJK$) minus the higher expenditure on goods previously imported and now bought from B (*FJYV*) plus the lower expenditure on remaining imports from the rest of the world (P_4VZP_5), whose net sign is indeterminate. The rest of the world unambiguously loses from the preferential tariff cut (by $P_4VZP_5 + VWZ$), and the global welfare effect may be positive or negative. Thus, Viner's central insight remains, although in slightly different terms, since it is no longer possible to identify high- and low-cost foreign suppliers. The terms of trade effects, however, which from a global perspective must net out, introduce distributional effects on B and in third countries, while B also benefits from the producer-surplus on new exports.[8]

Blackhurst (1972) uses Fig. 9.2 to compare the welfare effects of preferential and non-preferential tariff cuts by A. From a global perspective, the latter's effect is positive and must be at least as big as the welfare effect of a preferential tariff reduction. But from A's perspective this is not necessarily the case, because one positive aspect of a discriminatory tariff cut is lost if the cut is non-preferential, viz. the improvement in A's terms of trade with third countries. The partner, B, is of course better off with the preferential reduction. Thus, the introduction of increasing costs, and hence changes in the terms of trade, qualifies the JCM proposition, since A (and B) may gain more from a preferential than from a non-preferential reduction in A's tariff.

The preceding analysis is partial equilibrium, but it can readily be turned into general equilibrium on the assumptions of low initial tariffs, a small tariff change, and all exports being gross substitutes in world consumption. Now B's terms of trade improve, and the rest of the world's deteriorate. The sum of these changes is equal to the initial change in A's terms of trade, although the final outcome also depends on a budget effect, i.e. how A reacts to its reduced tariff revenues. The terms of trade between A and the rest of the world may end up going either way, but this does

[8] The unambiguous gain to B, the clearest message from Fig. 9.2, recalls the passage from Adam Smith quoted in Ch. 8. If the rest of the world consists of several countries, then some of these clearly may gain, viz. those importing the same good as A (Arndt, 1969).

not affect 'the most important proposition about discriminatory tariff reductions: a tariff reduction in a member country unambiguously improves the terms of trade of the partner country' (Mundell, 1964, 5).

Mutual preferential tariff reductions between A and B can change the partners' terms of trade with the rest of the world in either direction. This is in contrast to a popular view that formation of a customs union will improve the members' terms of trade with the rest of the world, although they can be reconciled under certain conditions.[9] With Mundell's assumptions, some sets of reductions necessarily improve both members' terms of trade with the rest of the world (Mundell, 1964, 7). These sets congregate around the case where the terms of trade between A and B are unchanged, which may be a plausible outcome from a preferential trade arrangement based on roughly reciprocal 'concessions'. Even if A and B do not both improve their terms of trade, mutual preferential tariff reductions will always improve the terms of trade of one of the two countries.

So far I have considered the terms of trade changes likely to result from trade preferences, but it may be that the terms of trade are themselves the objective. Two variations of the optimum tariff argument are relevant to preferential trading. Melvin (1969) has argued that the terms of trade effect will usually reduce A's welfare gain from a preferential tariff reduction because its MFN tariff may be optimal (from a national welfare perspective) and any change will be welfare-reducing. This is not necessarily so. Even if A's tariff is optimal, like any wielder of monopoly power, A could improve its welfare by market segmentation if different partners have different offer curves: the less elastic the partner's offer curve, the higher A's optimum tariff on imports from that source.[10] A second optimum tariff argument is that A

[9] The popular view is usually a variant of the argument by Viner (1950, 55) that formation of a customs union would, *ceteris paribus*, increase the improvement in members' terms of trade resulting from their tariff, because a large economic unit faces a less elastic offer curve. Riezman (1979) sets up a 3×3 model where the terms of trade of A and B improve *vis-à-vis* C but not necessarily *vis-à-vis* one another; in this case mutually profitable customs unions are most likely among countries that trade mainly with non-members.

[10] Caves (1974) analyses within a Vanek–Kemp framework the gains from market segmentation. See also Michaely (1977, 214–16). McCulloch and Pinera (1977) suggest this as a possible motive for GSP schemes (assuming a high elasticity of supply of exports from developing countries).

and B in combination can wield greater market power than either can alone. If A imposes a tariff on goods which its suppliers can also sell to B, then the impact will be to change trade patterns, restricting the improvement in A's terms of trade. If the two similar economies A and B form a union, then they can set a union-welfare-maximizing common external tariff. In this situation 'what country A really desires from country B is an appropriate protective policy against the outside world' (Arndt, 1968, 976).[11]

4. Economies of Scale

The earlier literature on European integration gave scale economies a large role (e.g. Scitovsky, 1956 and 1958; Balassa, 1961), but most writers in the 1960s and 1970s left it out or kept it in the background.[12] To some extent this reflects a wider problem: scale economies can be a source of gains from trade, but can lead to indeterminacy—a problem usually evaded in international trade theory before the late 1970s by assuming that the closed economy conditions for Pareto optimality are met (including perfectly competitive markets). The same assumption could be made in analysing preferential trading arrangements, but, given policy-makers' emphasis on scale economies as a reason for joining a customs union or free trade area, reference was often made to the importance of scale economies (without analysis). The two major analytical contributions in the 1960s and 1970s were those of Corden and the Wonnacotts. Further developments within the framework of imperfect competition trade models are discussed in the next chapter.

Corden (1972) introduced scale economies into the basic theory of GDAs, and found that trade creation and trade diversion

[11] Similar arguments are made by Viner (1950), and by Spraos (1964). Although these are part of the customs union literature (see also Michaely, 1977, 215–16, and Riezman, 1985), cartel behaviour by countries with common interests does not require preferential treatment; OPEC members, for example, try to agree on a common price and to minimize the free-rider problem without forming any economic union or necessarily discriminating among oil purchasers.

[12] One example is Massell (1968), who after discussing non-economic and terms of trade arguments devotes one sentence to scale economies as a third reason for customs unions, saying that these may be the most important! In Lipsey's 1960 survey they are listed as one of the five sources of welfare gain or loss but appear only in the (inconclusive) next-to-last paragraph.

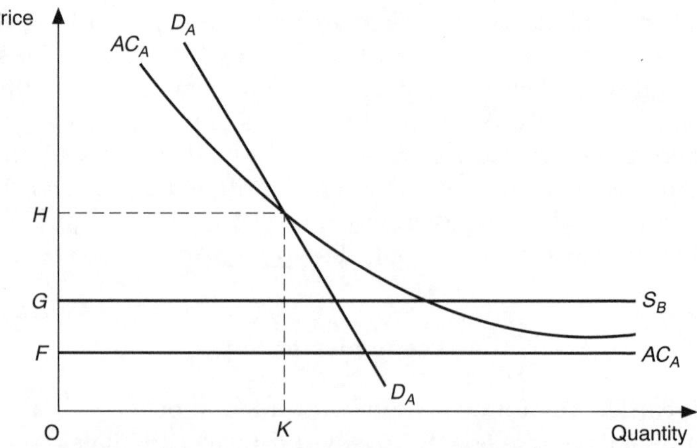

FIG. 9.3 An industry with decreasing costs facing trade barriers
D_A is domestic demand in country A and AC_A is the decreasing average cost curve of the producer in A. Producers in B operate under constant cost conditions with a supply curve S_B at a price of *OG*. *FG* is B's tariff. Assuming average cost pricing, barriers to imports, and no opportunity to segment markets, A's firm will produce *OK* and sell at a price *OH*. Removal of B's tariff permits A's producer to increase output, selling at a price between *OF* and *OG* in B's market.

remained relevant concepts but should be supplemented by two other effects. If preferred imports from B replace A's domestic production, the cost reduction effect of realizing scale economies yields additional gains. If B's exports are replacing goods previously imported by A from a third country (C), there may be trade suppression if B's lower costs and C's higher costs lead to further reduction in C's exports to A and B (even though C may remain the lowest-cost producer). Corden's cost reduction and trade suppression effects leave intact Viner's fundamental insight about the sign of the welfare effect, although they accentuate the gains from trade creation and losses from trade diversion.[13]

R. Wonnacott and P. Wonnacott (1967) provide empirical support for the common presumption that countries gain from joining a free trade area or customs union via access to a wider market. From their studies, the Wonnacotts found most Canadian industries to have cost curves such as that in Fig. 9.3. Removal of

[13] Viner (1950, 45–7) had recognized the former point, and Meade (1955b, 93–4) described the magnification of trade creation and trade diversion with two examples, although neither treated the matter as thoroughly as Corden.

the US tariff would permit expansion of Canadian output on the basis of exports, leading with a fixed exchange rate to higher wages in Canada (or with a flexible exchange rate to improved terms of trade). The Wonnacotts estimated the gain to Canada from a North American free trade area at $10\frac{1}{2}$ per cent of GNP, of which around 4 per cent would come from Canadian tariff cuts and the remainder from the effect just described; i.e., the realization of scale economies is the main source of Canadian gain. This analysis is, however, distinct from all the literature so far discussed because the effects of scale economies do not arise from the home country's preferential tariff reduction. What the analysis does do is to emphasize the gains from freer access to other countries' markets. (In Fig. 9.3 this does not have to be preferential access.) The only sense in which the Wonnacotts' study provides a case for preferential treatment is if reduction in one's own tariff is a critical bargaining counter in persuading other countries to reduce their trade barriers.

5. Technical Efficiency and Growth

Technical inefficiency is not readily explained within standard microeconomic models unless markets are not competitive. Several writers referred to the gains from reducing domestic monopoly power as a possible side-benefit from freer access to preferred imports, as they are with any tariff reduction, but this argument was not formally developed before the integration of imperfect competition models into trade theory in the 1980s. The pro-competitive impact of market integration, addressed especially in the work of Smith and Venables, will be analysed in Section 10.1.

Growth effects independent of the resource allocation effects are also difficult to formalize within standard models. The main practical case is when trade preferences stimulate a relocation of investment from outside to within the preferred area (as seems to have happened in the EC and with other preferential trade agreements, e.g. Pomfret 1982a). This will increase GDP and growth within the PTA, but with an offsetting cost to the rest of the world if it is capital diversion—indeed, the global effect may be negative if the pre-PTA productivity of the investment was higher in a non-preferred location (Kreinin, 1964, 195).

Richard Baldwin (1989; 1992) has analysed situations where market integration promotes new investment, thus shifting the production possibility plane. If a preferential trade arrangement does promote growth in this way, then it opens up the possibility of non-members benefiting.

6. Conclusions

Vinerian customs union theory with competitive markets and horizontal supply curves provides a powerful tool for analysing GDAs, but a blunt instrument for explaining why they are formed. The distinction between trade creation and trade diversion, by emphasizing that a preferential tariff reduction simultaneously reduces one price distortion (between partner goods and domestic goods) but introduces a new one (beteen partner goods and third-country goods), clarified the essential welfare ambiguities of GDAs. At the same time, with constant costs, the normative implication is so glaringly obvious—avoid introducing the second distortion—that the formation of custonms unions is inexplicable.

Extending the model removes this difficulty by highlighting the distribution of welfare gains and losses, and thus opening up to political economy analysis the question of GDA formation. Relaxation of the constant-cost assumption allows international price changes, and distributional effects of GDAs arise such that some participants reap benefits from a discriminatory tariff reduction which could not be obtained from an equal-sized non-preferential tariff reduction. Indeed, Mundell (1964) identified realistic situations where all GDA member countries could improve their terms of trade with the rest of the world, with all participants benefiting in a manner that could not be replicated by MFN tariff reductions, although clearly this is at the expense of countries outside the GDA and is possibly welfare-reducing for the world as a whole. This result can be contrasted to the Kemp–Wan proposition, which predicts customs union formation until all the world is a free trade area; relaxing their unrealistic assumption of no change in external terms of trade still allows predictions of GDA formation, but in an antagonistic manner which is more likely to produce trade wars than global free trade.

The likelihood of GDAs' negative welfare impact on non-members has raised concerns over how to establish guidelines to monitor (and hence avoid or require compensation for) such an outcome. One popular criterion is the level of non-members' trade with the GDA (e.g. McMillan, 1993). An increase in a non-member's trade with members of a newly formed GDA is generally viewed as a sign of the GDA's benevolent impact (captured by measures of positive external trade creation). That may be correct if growth effects of the GDA are significant. As a general guide to protection of non-members' interests, however, focusing on non-negative change in the level of external trade is flawed. If a non-member suffers a deterioration in its terms of trade as a result of formation of a GDA, then no level of balanced trade flows can maintain the non-member's previous utility level. In Fig. 9.4 (adapted from Winters, 1996a), deterioration in the

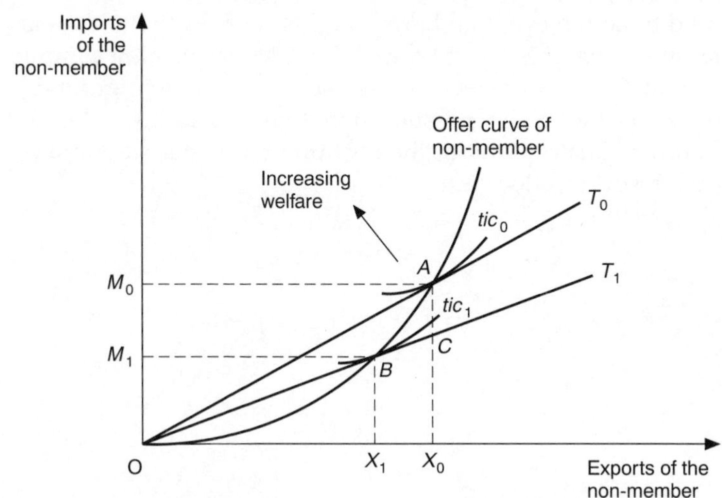

FIG. 9.4 Deteriorating terms of trade of a third country
Assuming that the terms of trade of the third country deteriorate from T_0 to T_1 as a result of a RTA, then the original trade indifference curve tic_0 is unattainable with T_1, and the utility-maximizing trade basket for the non-member country changes from A, importing M_0 and exporting X_0, to B, importing M_1 and exporting X_1. Imposing a requirement that the members of the RTA continue to import the previous amount, X_0, from the non-member shifts the non-member's trade basket from B to C, which is on a lower trade indifference curve than tic_1; i.e. it makes the non-member even worse off.
Source: adapted from Winters (1996a).

non-member's terms of trade must lead to less trade (shift down the offer curve) and lower utility. Requiring that the non-member's exports be maintained at X_0 would only lower the non-member's utilty still further. There is no substitute for the difficult task of identifying terms of trade consequences directly, and non-members cannot be protected by requiring no drop in external trade.

Other modifications to the standard customs union theory described in Chapter 8 make matters more complex. Trade barriers in the rest of the world, higher dimensionality (allowing for substitutes and complements), and international factor flows plunge us further into the world of the second-best. No general rules, such as the WTO tries to lay down, can cover all cases successfully, but in the absence of general rules the distributional effects of GDAs suggest that custom-tailored GDAs benefiting insiders at the cost of outsiders would proliferate. Such a result would be to the eventual harm of all because, although the analysis in this chapter has modified the JCM proposition's implication that GDAs will never be formed on economic grounds, it has not changed the presumption that GDAs are inferior to non-discriminatory trade liberalization from the standpoint of global resource allocation.

10

The New Regionalism

Starting in the mid-1980s, new ideas began to be developed which challenged traditional customs union theory. The main intellectual spur was the 'new trade theory' based on models of imperfect competition. A second influence was the new regional arrangements, especially the EC92 programme and NAFTA, which went beyond preferential tariff reductions. Among the EC members and between Canada and the USA, tariffs were already so low as to have little impact on bilateral trade, so the focus of EC92 and NAFTA was on non-tariff barriers to trade and on national policies perceived to give one country's traders an unfair advantage.

The new regionalism has not been developed as a coherent set of ideas, but there are a number of common themes. The new regionalism downplays the significance of trade diversion in a world in which tariffs have become less important than non-tariff barriers to trade. The new regionalism also draws on the new trade theories which integrated scale economies and imperfect competition into mainstream trade theory. By downplaying the trade diversion costs and emphasizing the scale-based and pro-competitive benefits of integration, the new regionalism has a more positive vision of discriminatory trading arrangements than traditional customs union theory does.

Consideration of non-trade matters is less concrete, but has generally led to conclusions supporting the more favourable assessment of regional trading arrangements. Deeper integration involving institutional integration may be more feasible among neighbouring countries sharing political and economic preferences. In the global context, much of this debate has concerned means rather than ends; given the ultimate goal of liberalization, which is the best route? Are limited negotiations among like-minded or neighbouring countries more likely to make progress than global negotiations within the GATT/WTO framework, and then, having made progress, are they likely to be extended multilaterally?

The impression that regionalism may be theoretically justified was reinforced by a number of papers circulating in 1989/90 by leading economists (Dornbusch, 1990; Summers, 1991; Krugman, 1991c). The arguments by Dornbusch were not particularly strong, centring on practical concerns over the failure of GATT to address US interests, and Krugman's position was ambiguous; Krugman (1991b) is negative towards regionalism in the form of three large blocs (see Section 11.1). Some important contributions, however, cast doubt on the benefits of regionalism, especially in the forms it was taking in the 1990s; analysis of rules of origin, and general considerations of complexity, are discussed in Section 4. The issues raised for the debate over whether regional trading arrangements are stumbling blocks or building blocks on the way to multilateral trade liberalization are raised in the final section.

1. Economies of Scale and Imperfect Competition

The presumption that regional integration will yield benefits from access to a larger internal market is extremely powerful among policy-makers and lay observers, so its recent acceptance by some economists has a receptive audience. There is, however, little empirical support for the proposition. The most salient contrary observation is the absence of any correlation between country size and per capita income.

The rapidly growing literature on international trade and imperfect competition may be briefly mentioned here, because such market structures are often associated with the presence of scale economies. This literature has yielded new arguments to support trade restrictions, either variants of the old infant industry argument or aimed at tapping monopoly rents earned by foreign suppliers. Such theoretical developments are unsurprising since imperfectly competitive markets belong to the world of 'second-best' where free market solutions may be suboptimal and trade barriers welfare-improving; the precise policy recommendation varies from case to case[1] and may in principle include discrim-

[1] The conclusions from imperfect competition models are sensitive to assumptions about the nature of competition (Cournot or Bertrand or other?), the shape of cost curves, and the homogeneity of products and specification of demand curves.

inatory trade barriers. Nevertheless, although one can construct cases of national-welfare-improving discriminatory trade policies (e.g. if imports are purchased from a small number of countries whose exporters earn differential rents), the possibility of such policies being the first-best solution in practical situations is remote.[2] Moreover, a question mark hangs over the practical significance of arguments based on scale economies; despite the blossoming of the new trade theories, identification of actual industries to which they apply has been limited (Pomfret, 1992).

Application of imperfect competition to the analysis of RTAs has largely been in the form of calibrated models, building on the pioneering work of Harris and Cox in North America and Smith and Venables in Europe. Such models are sometimes presented as empirical exercises (and will feature in Part III), but in practice the results depend as much on the assumptions as on the limited data inputs (as is recognized by their designers). They are much more important as contributions to the theoretical debate, helping in the clarification of thinking by highlighting the importance of alternative market structure assumptions.

The Cox–Harris model, following on the Wonnacotts' incorporation of scale economies in their study of Canada–USA free trade (Section 9.4), highlights the importance of scale economies for the magnitude of gains from CUSTA. The advance made by Cox and Harris was to model imperfect competition, a necessary follow-up to the introduction of scale economies, but their work and competing models illustrated that the results were sensitive to the choice of assumptions about firms' pricing behaviour (see Section 13.1). Cox and Harris stimulated a new generation of trade modelling, but their work has little direct relationship to RTAs; although they set their study in the context of what was to become

[2] Greenaway and Milner (1986, 172–88) emphasize this point. The class of justifications for GDAs discussed in this paragraph requires particularly detailed firm-level economic analysis and fine-tuning of policies actually to achieve optimality, and is therefore especially vulnerable to the famous caveat of Johnson:

> The fundamental problem is that, as with all second-best arguments, determination of the conditions under which a second-best policy actually leads to an improvement of social welfare requires detailed theoretical and empirical investigation by a first-best economist. Unfortunately, policy is generally formulated by fourth-best economists and administered by third-best economists; it is therefore very unlikely that a second-best welfare optimum will result from policies based on second-best arguments. (Johnson, 1970, 101)

CUSTA, they are effectively modelling the benefits to Canada from simultaneous unilateral trade liberalization in Canada and its main market, and preferential treatment plays no role.

The family of models due to Smith and Venables makes a more direct contribution to the analysis of RTAs with imperfect competition by distinguishing between market opening and market integration.[3] The Smith–Venables model takes a two-stage approach to the gains from a RTA:

1. Reduced barriers to internal trade lead to lower prices for imports from partner countries and to traditional customs union theory allocative effects.
2. Market integration changes firms' competitive behaviour as they are no longer able to operate in sheltered national markets; reduced market segmentation leads to benefits from more competitive behaviour in imperfectly competitive markets.

In applications to Western European integration (see Section 12.4), the market integration effect turns out to be quantitatively more important; the bigger gain from regional integration comes from more competitive behaviour on the part of firms, rather than from the realization of scale economies or from traditional allocative effects.

The Smith–Venables model makes a major contribution in that it is the first convincing formulation of an effect that has often been discussed in the literature and especially in political debate over integration. Its application has been primarily to the EC92 programme, but it could be applied to any arrangment that reduces firms' ability to segment markets. A key issue is the degree to which such segmentation occurs, and can be reduced by RTAs. Norman (1989), applying a Smith–Venables type model to Norway and Sweden, shows that the degree of market integration varies across industries and across countries. Such an observation is supported by the well-known large cross-country

[3] Venables and Smith (1986) and Smith and Venables (1988) set out the model and calibrate it for 10 EC industries. Smith (1990) appplies a single-industry version to the EC car industry. Gasiorek *et al.* (1991; 1992) provide general equilibrium counterparts to the partial equilibrium model; the first paper focuses on the EC and the second introduces the rest of the world. Haaland and Norman (1992) disaggregate the impact on the rest of the world by modelling the USA, Japan, and EFTA explicitly.

variation of prices for cars and pharmaceuticals within the EC decades after the customs union was established. A practical issue is whether these industries are typical, and whether the market segmentation will be removed by the completion of the internal market or whether it is supported by other features intrinsic to the industries and unaffected by EC92.

Keuschnigg and Kohler (1996) have applied to Austria's EU accession a ten-sector dynamic CGE model with imperfect competition, which stresses variety. The key to the Keuschnigg–Kohler model is the weight given to consumers' love of variety and to the cost-reducing impact of an increased variety of available inputs. These elements introduce multiplier effects, which augment the positive impact of joining a regional trading arrangement. For consumers the fall in trade barriers lowers domestic prices and increases disposable income, leading to higher demand for each differentiated product. Competition for the supernormal profits leads to the entry of new firms. The larger number of firms reduces input costs and hence prices, reinforcing the initial price reduction effect. Investment also plays a role in the Keuschnigg–Kohler model, because the falling prices reduce the cost of capital equipment (changing Tobin's q), leading to increased investment and growth and reinforcing the variety effect on growth. In their empirical work, Keuschnigg and Kohler find much larger gains to Austria from EU accession than do other studies, which is due to model design. As with the Smith–Venables literature, the work of Keuschnigg and Kohler indicates the potential importance of imperfect competition (in this case resulting from the presence of differentiated products), but does not tell us how imporant the variety effects actually are.

2. Non-tariff Barriers

International trade theory conventionally starts from the analysis of tariffs and then compares the effects of quotas and other non-tariff barriers (NTBs) to trade with the tariff benchmark. The general conclusion that non-tariff measures at best will have the negative consequences of a tariff and at worst will be further welfare-reducing underlies the GATT principle that, if countries have trade barriers, they should be in the form of tariffs. This principle is easy to apply to border measures such as import quotas, and harder to apply to NTBs whose trade impact may (or may not) be an unintentional side-effect, e.g. technical or health standards. In this section the focus will be on border measures, making the distinction between cost-increasing measures such as customs formalities (whose reduction is sometimes referred to as 'trade facilitation') and rent-generating quotas.

The ambiguous welfare implications of preferential tariff reductions arise from the trade creation/trade diversion dichotomy. In the simplest partial equilibrium model (Fig. 8.1), welfare gains from trade creation (measured by the two triangles) have to be weighed against the trade diversion loss (the forgone tariff revenue not captured by consumers). Applying the same model to preferential exemption from an NTB, Richard Baldwin (1994, 33) argues that, since there is no tariff revenue with NTBs, the trade diversion area vanishes in the basic diagram; in Fig. 8.1, *AFHC* measures the unambiguous welfare benefit to the importing country A. If the NTB is simply cost-raising, then any reduction in its incidence is welfare-increasing, whether or not the preferred partner is the least-cost supplier.

If the NTB is not purely cost-increasing, then moving from a non-discriminatory NTB to a situation in which some preferred suppliers are exempted from the NTB could still lead to welfare-reducing trade diversion. The key issue is why P_a is above the price P_c, which is the notional price at which the least-cost supplier would sell the good in country A in the absence of the NTB. If rents were being generated before the introduction of the preferential trade policy, then global revenue could be reduced. The maximum attainable rents are equal to *ACJE*, so that the analysis of a non-resource-using NTB is equivalent to that of a tariff $(P_a - P_c)/P_c$; the distributional effects may differ, depending on who receives the rent (importers in A, the government in A, or exporters in C), but the global net welfare consequences are identical. There is an extensive literature on tariff/quota equivalence in a non-discriminatory setting, which highlights the many ways in which equivalence may not hold (with uncertainty, imperfect competition, and so forth). That is relevant here too, and pure equivalence is an extreme (and practically unlikely) case, but so is the pure cost-increasing NTB. In sum, discriminatory reduction of a NTB is more likely to be global-welfare-increasing than is discriminatory tariff reduction, because of the extra source of gain from the reduction of rent-seeking or other unproductive behaviour.

The insight that trade diversion may be less important with NTBs is a useful one, but trade diversion is not as outdated as this section's second paragraph implies. With any but pure cost-increasing NTBs, the welfare implications of preferential treatment are ambiguous. Moreover, identification of cases in which preferential and non-preferential reduction of NTBs may be equivalent distracts attention from the fundamental conclusion of Vinerian customs union theory: that non-discriminatory trade liberalization is superior to discriminatory trade liberalization from a global welfare perspective, and probably from the importing country's perspective. This remains true whether the barriers are tariffs or NTBs, because discriminatory reduction of NTBs may artificially encourage production in other than the potentially least-cost location.

As a corollary to the analysis of preferential reduction in NTBs, a case where trade diversion may be globally beneficial arises when discriminatory NTBs are introduced. The Multifibre Arrangement (and other VERs) benefited importing-country producers at the expense of consumers, and offered the quota rent to the restrained exporters so that they might end up better off than without the export quota. The growth of unrestrained exports, however, undermines VERs by bidding down the price in the importing country to the benefit of consumers, and at the expense of domestic producers (who lose producer susplus) and of the least-cost foreign suppliers (who lose quota rent); the global net welfare effect is ambiguous. The outcome tends to be unstable as the importing country either tries to bring unrestrained suppliers within the VER system (as happened with the MFA) or abandons the VERs because they are not fulfilling their protectionist intention. (Examples can be found in steel, footwear and automobile VERs.) In the latter case governments fear the complexity that arose in the MFA, but more fundamentally they recognize that trade diversion imposes costs, and that non-discriminatory trade is in the importing country's best interest. Thus, trade diversion undermines discriminatory non-tariff barriers and may lead to their elimination, which is globally beneficial.

3. New Areas

A distinctive feature of RTAs in the 1980s and 1990s has been the emphasis placed on non-border measures. In practice, an important reason why issues such as competition policy or investment policies are addressed in countries whose economies are already fairly integrated is that differences in national policies become more significant in giving firms in one country an advantage over firms in another country when trade barriers are low. In principle, however, the arguments about such policies' relationship to international trade are not specifically applicable to RTAs, and most of the arguments in this section apply to non-discriminatory trade. Nevertheless, these new areas relate to discriminatory trade policies and to regionalism in two ways. First, some of them may include instruments for discriminating among trading partners, breaking the non-discrimination principle without contravening international trade law. Second, given the difficulty in reaching international agreement in these areas, regional bodies may be forums for negotiating geographically limited harmonization when global regimes are unattainable.

The situation is more complex when a regional trading arrangement is a prelude to economic or political union. Federal states make a trade-off between the rights of states/provinces to set distinct policies and the benefits from union-wide harmonization. The EU started with its members' independent regulatory regimes and is imposing some degree of harmonization not just for the economic benefits but also to strengthen the union. The inevitable trade-off between federalism and deep integration will be addressed in Section 11.3, but it is important to recognize that acceptance of federalism (or subsidiarity in EU-speak) imposes limits to the extent of desirable deep integaration.[4]

[4] Lawrence (1996) develops the distinction between deep and shallow integration. In its emphasis on institutional integration, the deep integration concept recalls Tinbergen's (1954) idea of positive integration, which he contrasted to the negative integration of removing tariff barriers to intra-union trade (which had dominated EU integration up until the mid-1980s). Lorenz (1990) discusses the relevance to the European integration process of neighbourly co-operation based on shared political and economic values. Yamazawa (1992) emphasizes the importance of investment flows and the need to harmonize rules in order to encourage cross-border business in the Pacific region.

The deep integration issue is often expressed as a concern for 'fair trade'. Thus, environmental or labour standards are brought on to the agenda (mainly by richer countries) if producers in other countries are perceived to be gaining a competitive edge by unrestrained pollution or by neglecting workers' rights. In general, unfair trade practices should not be considered economically harmful by other countries, and have no implication for the other countries' optimal trade policies; trade is determined by comparative advantage, and if environmental or labour standards vary across industries in different countries then that will affect the composition of trade but not the trade balance. Whether the 'spectre of unfairness' (Brittan, 1995, 763) can be ignored or must be addressed is a political rather than an economic matter. Bhagwati (1995) in his debate with Brittan accepts that some labour practices (such as slavery) and social systems (such as *apartheid*) are so morally repugnant to most of the world that trade rights may be revoked (as happened to South Africa despite its GATT membership), but he argues that in most cases there is no need for fair trade demands to be considered in trade negotiations at any level.

The simplest equivalence between a tariff and domestic policies, i.e. a consumption tax plus a subsidy on domestic output of a good, has little relevance to analysis of discrimination in international trade, because the consumption tax is unlikely to be origin-specific,[5] but other domestic policies may have equivalent effects to discriminatory trade policies. Technical requirements have often been tailored to exclude imports from specific sources; simply by making compliance expensive or technically demanding, imports from developing countries might be disadvantaged.

[5] Within the CIS, however, implementation of a value added tax (VAT) has raised problems because most CIS members use the origin principle, levying VAT on all domestic output. When goods are shipped to countries levying VAT on the destination principle (i.e. on domestic sales, including imports, and exempting VAT paid on inputs into exports), double-taxation may therefore occur. Armenia, which follows the destination principle, addresses the problem by exempting imports from inside the CIS from VAT and levying VAT on exports to CIS countries, but this leads to enforcement problems as traders have an incentive to declare all imports as extra-CIS and all exports as destined beyond the CIS, which is difficult for Armenian customs authorities to check because almost all trade passes through Georgia whatever the ultimate destination or origin. There are obvious benefits from harmonizing VAT along the destination principle, but it is easier for fledgling tax authorities to collect VAT at the origin.

Such NTBs fall into the category discussed in the Tokyo Round, where it was agreed that they should not unnecessarily discriminate against imports (even if that principle may be difficult to enforce).

Determination and enforcement of the concept of unnecessary discrimination may be more practicable among members of a regional organization. A major element of the EC92 programme was the intention to reduce the impact of NTBs on intra-EC trade by harmonizing standards or enforcing the principle of mutual recognition of standards. A landmark EC Court ruling was the *Cassis de Dijon* case, in which a German law requiring liqueurs to have a minimum 32 per cent alcohol content was found to have no public health justification and therefore was an illegitimate restraint of trade. Greater publicity surrounded the overturning on the same grounds of the German *Reinheitsgebot*, which set beer purity standards. On the other hand, the European Court upheld Danish legislation requiring beer and soft drinks to be sold in reusable containers, which had been contested by the European Commission as restricting trade in those beverages since EC producers with small sales in Denmark faced unreasonable costs to adapt their packaging to the Danish market; the Court's decision confirmed that environmental considerations could take precedence over the trade-restricting consequences of legislation.

Reducing trade-distorting side effects is hardest of all with respect to policies that have historically been seen as sovereign economic policy areas, such as taxation or labour market or competition policy or policy towards foreign-owned firms, and yet it is precisely into these new areas that trade negotiations began to move in the 1990s (see Section 7.3). The remainder of this section will focus on three of the new areas: foreign investment, competition policy, and monetary integration.

Foreign Investment

Transnational corporations (TNCs) play a major economic role which inevitably links foreign investment with trade, because TNCs choose between servicing a foreign market via exports or via local production, and they choose among alternative global locations for different parts of their global activities. Host countries may welcome foreign investors and offer incentives or they may restrict foreign investment, and once in operation foreign firms may be treated differently from domestic firms. Both host- and home-country governments (and possibly third countries) have an interest in the regulatory regime, but host-country law normally applies—even if the foreign investors' home government may support its interests by *force majeure* or insist that citizens' global activities are accountable under domestic law. International agreements on investment policy will need to reflect all countries' concerns if they are to function well.

At the outset of the Uruguay Round, the USA pushed for broad consideration of investment issues (even proposing a 'GATT for investment'), but backed down in the face of concerted host-country opposition. Thus, establishment and access issues were not addressed. The negotiations concentrated on trade-related investment measures, and the outcome was a restatement of the applicability of GATT rules, which are contravened by some common foreign investment restrictions and incentives. Local content and trade-balancing requirements are inconsistent with GATT Article III, relating to national treatment, and trade and foreign exchange balancing restrictions and domestic sales requirements are inconsistent with Article IX, banning quantitative restrictions (Low and Subramanian, 1995, 416).

More controversial are issues related to the regulatory regime for foreign investment. The right of establishment may be restricted. Typical requirements are for local equity participation or banning direct foreign investment (DFI) from certain activities or sectors. Such restrictions may be simple protectionist devices (e.g. restrictions on domestic operations by foreign-owned airlines), or they may be justified by non-economic arguments (e.g. restrictions on foreign ownership of the media), although the dividing line is fuzzy. Procedures for screening or notification of DFI may be ambiguous and subject to discretionary interpretation by official bodies at various levels of government.

Direct foreign investment includes the transfer of technology, management, marketing, and other skills in a package, which requires some protection of property rights. Thus, the regulatory environment is likely to be more complex than for portfolio investment such as foreign purchase of bonds, which involves a relatively simple monitoring issue of whether interest and principal are repaid on time. Protection (or lack of protection) given to firm-specific assets can create a more (or less) favourable environment for DFI. Foreign-invested ventures may be restricted in their activities (rather than the right to entry) by discriminatory application of taxation polices, labour laws, profit distribution requirements, access to impartial dispute settlement, and so forth. These issues apply disproportionately to foreign investors because they are more likely to employ foreign labour (including foreign specialists on temporary assignments from other locations) and to want to repatriate profits.

Proposed international regulatory codes are based on the principles of transparency, national treatment, and MFN treatment (Pangestu and Bora, 1996). The MFN principle requiring all foreign investors to be treated equally is usually less of an issue than national treatment, but some countries do discriminate by source of the foreign investor (e.g. China's special treatment of investment by overseas compatriots). A problem for devisers of international codes is how to establish a benchmark of openness to DFI, because the concept is multifaceted (i.e. there is nothing comparable to measures of average tariffs or NTB coverage, which for all their weaknesses provide agreed-upon starting points for trade liberalization). Thus, it is difficult to identify more or less restrictive regimes, and to compare the depth of DFI liberalization measures in various countries.

In light of the difficulty of reaching agreement among host countries sensitive to sovereignty infringement and the operational difficulties of devising investment codes, the question arises whether such codes can be better devised by groups of like-minded countries rather than in global forums such as the WTO. Two variants of this argument should be kept distinct. Federal states typically have national investment codes guaranteeing an unrestricted right of establishment and equal treatment for nationals in all states/provinces. In the absence of similar guarantees for foreign investors, the welfare effects are ambiguous in a parallel manner to the effects of tariff preferences, but the practice is acceptable within a nation. Regional arrangements, such as the EU, aspiring to federal status may follow this route, as may RTAs without federal aspirations, such as NAFTA.

The second variant of the argument in favour of regional groupings devising investment codes is that their codes may be tried out and, if found satisfactory, multilateralized within the WTO.

If several RTAs designed differing codes, then regulatory competition could help to sort out the fittest. The advantage of regional experimentation is that a viable investment code will be more difficult to devise than the relatively simple general agreement on tariffs and trade, and the WTO does not have the resources to draft one. The disadvantage, however, derives from the same complexity, in so far as the balancing of interests by like-minded countries may not produce an outcome which satisfactorily reflects the interests of the rest of the world.

The OECD has already devoted resources to devising an investment code, and this illustrates the problem. Developing countries are suspicious of any code designed by the rich countries' club. Similarly, while APEC includes developed and developing countries, it also excludes many countries concerned about DFI both as hosts and as home countries, so that any APEC code would be viewed with suspicion by European and South Asian countries. In sum, if a global investment code is desired, then it should be designed by a global rather than a regional body.

Competition policy

Interest in the interrelationships between trade policy and competition policy was stimulated by the new trade theories which emphasized imperfect competition. With perfectly competitive markets, competition policy is irrelevant. In imperfect competition models a firm may have an edge if it is able to behave noncompetitively in its home market. Moreover, a monopolist, or collusive oligopoly, will maximize profits by charging different prices in markets with differing elasticities of demand. The first consideration does not involve discrimination directly, although it may invoke a discriminatory response by trading partners trying to change the country's policies, while the second one does. In practice, the two become intertwined in the question of whether competition policies should be subject to international rules.

National competition policies are difficult to categorize, because they have many dimensions.[6] Nevertheless, some generalizations can be made (Levinsohn, 1994), and three approaches identified:

[6] Competition policy here refers to regulation of anti-competitive practices such as collusion or abuse of a dominant market position or the creation of such a position through mergers and acquisitions.

1. minimal or no competition policies (e.g. Hong Kong, Taiwan, Denmark, and Italy);
2. competition policy for the domestic market, but no restriction on the behaviour of exporters (e.g. Ireland, Greece, Switzerland, Philippines, Germany, and Japan);
3. competition policy with no distinction between domestic and export markets (e.g. Canada, France, Spain, the Netherlands, Sweden, Belgium, the UK, and the USA).

Within the last two groups, the laxness or rigidity of the law and of its enforcement varies substantially. The EU's competition policy belongs in the third group and thus involves removing the differential treatment of exporters by Ireland, Greece, and Germany and tightening the constraints on anti-competitive behaviour in Denmark, Italy, and probably the UK.[7]

If one country's exporters are unconstrained by competition policy while another country's face tough penalties for anti-competitive behaviour, then the first country's producers may gain higher profits than producers in the second country. This can apply not just on their home market, but also in the foreign market. Figure 10.1 illustrates the point in a two-country world with free trade. In country A, competition policy forces producers to behave competitively (the supply function approximates marginal cost), while in country B producers are unregulated (so they set marginal cost equal to perceived marginal revenue, with the steepness of the perceived *MR* curve positively related to the absence of competition). Free trade ensures that the price (*P*) is the same in both countries. The firm(s) in country B will produce the quantity at which their marginal revenue (derived from D_B, the horizontal sum of their export and domestic demand curves) equals their marginal cost. Since $P > MC_B$, the producers in B are earning supernormal profits on their sales in both markets (the shaded area in Fig. 10.1(b)). In this example, producers in A may feel hard done by because B's producers are earning higher

[7] This is the practice of EU competition policy. The Rome Treaty's Articles 85 and 86 on competition policy require only that competition within the common market not be distorted, with no requirement that EU companies should act or not act in any particular manner outside the EU, unless that behaviour somehow affects intra-EU trade.

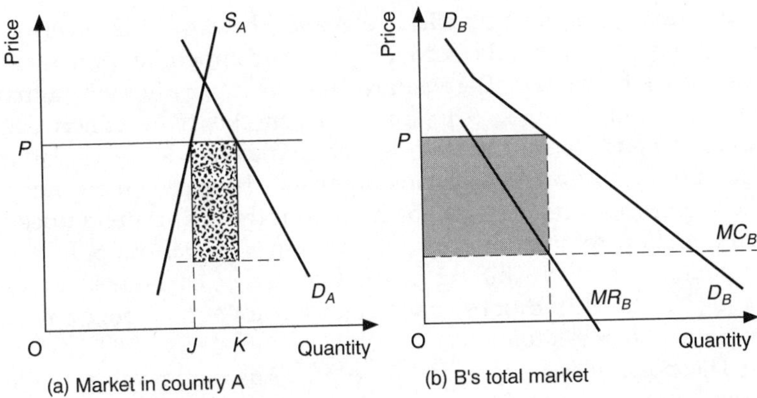

FIG. 10.1 Free trade with imperfect competition in one country
(a) Market in country A
(b) B's total market
The monopolist or cartel in country B faces a demand curve D_B, consisting of domestic demand plus export demand, and will select the output at which $MR_B = MC_B$. Export sales at this price are *JK*, the distance between A's domestic demand and supply curves, and domestic sales in B are the residual horizontal distance between D_B and the vertical axis at price *P*. The shaded area represents the profits of B's producers, of which the stippled area is earned in A.
Source: based on Levinsohn (1994, fig. 1).

profits than they are in their own market (A's producers earn normal profits while B's producers earn supernormal profits on their sales in A, measured by the stippled area), but the producers in A would be harmed by changes in B's competition policy. Producers in both countries would prefer a loosening of the competition policy in A, which would allow *P* to increase and higher profits all round. On the other hand, consumers in both countries would benefit from universal stringent competition policies (i.e. a tightening of the competition policy in B), which would drive *P* down to MC_B; net benefits are maximized by harmonizing both countries' policies on the model of country A. This example illustrates the common interests of producers, and in the opposite direction of consumers, in both countries, and the optimality of competition policies which preclude monopolistic behaviour.

The situation is more complex when collusion in a protected domestic market is permitted and it allows firms to become exporters.[8] This is of practical relevance, because it is precisely the point underlying the second group of competition policies in the above taxonomy. The welfare analysis for the home country is ambiguous (Basevi, 1970), but clearly, in the trade-off between producer and consumer interests that normally underlies competition policy, the interests of consumers may be given little weight. Foreign producers may also be harmed if the artificially induced competition reduces their profits. Within a global duopoly, the potential for profit-shifting at the expense of consumers exists under certain conditions, and lack of competition policy may facilitate such a situation.

The possibilities sketched in the previous paragraph provide some, not very conclusive, support for retaliatory measures to open up the market in which collusive behaviour is permitted —to create a level playing field for other countries' firms. Such reasoning appears to underlie US policies to open up imperfectly competitive markets in South Korea and Japan by discriminatory trade policy action. In the Fig. 10.1 environment, such action if successful would benefit consumers in both countries, but would hurt country A's firms. In more plausible settings of oligopoly in both countries, the outcome is more complex, depending on the type of behaviour and other industry-specific parameters.[9]

Anti-dumping (AD) duties represent a GATT-authorized reaction to anti-competitive behaviour. The principal argument in favour of AD duties is that they prevent predatory pricing behaviour. They may also be supported by cross-subsidies from home market monopoly profits. Competition policy could outlaw the former behaviour and eliminate the latter practice. Thus, international competition policy could be a substitutue for AD actions, which would be an improvement because AD policies

[8] The argument for domestic market protection to cover fixed costs and hence make exports profitable is popular with policy-makers and easy to illustrate (Basevi, 1970; Pomfret, 1975; Krugman, 1984), although the case does not depend upon the presence of scale economies (Bhagwati, 1988).

[9] Oligopoly is more plausible in the sense that action in the aggrieved country is more likely if the industry is imperfectly competitive and opportunities for rent-shifting are possible only with imperfect competition in both countries. Whether such conditions are common is an empirical question, and even when they do exist retaliatory trade policies may shoot the aggrieved nation in the foot. (For example, Baldwin and Krugman's (1988) simulation study of 16K RAM chips found that, although free trade and no collusion was optimal, given a restricted Japanese market, US retaliation reduced US as well as global welfare.)

in practice are anti-competitive, as well as deviations from the non-discrimination principle.

The global optimum here is likely to involve co-ordinated reasonably stringent competition policies. The 'reasonably' has to be inserted because there will always be a possible trade-off between technical efficiency and allocative efficiency in industries with large economies of scale. An obstacle to reaching the optimum arises from cross-country differences in opinion about the weight to be given to such offsetting considerations; for example, the UK's relatively lax competition policy reflects a longstanding official belief in the technical benefits from consolidation. Individual countries with lax competition policy, or in the group that exempts exporters, may be unwilling to be among the first movers to a global policy, because they believe that their competition policy gives their firms an edge in world markets. Both of these obstacles will be reinforced by industry lobbyists, since more stringent competition policies benefit consumers at the expense of producers. Industry lobbies might also capture trade policy and instigate measures targeted against specific countries in order to force market opening.

With no restrictions on collusive behaviour by exporters, they will set prices in different markets to equalize marginal revenues. With competitive world markets the prices will be the same, the 'world price', but if the colluding exporters have market power in world markets then they will charge higher prices in countries with less elastic demand curves. In theory this is a reason for discriminatory trade practices, although it is difficult to identify cases. Even in highly concentrated industries like large civilian jet aircraft, such price discrimination is not observed.[10] Differentiated products like books, compact discs, or computer software may provide examples, although the market segmentation necessary to support price discrimination can be undermined by international mail order companies. Military equipment is another possible example, although many international arms sales are

[10] Even this apparent duopoly or triopoly may be competitive because the durability of the product means that producers have to compete with the large stock of existing planes. Discrimination among purchasers is also complicated by the existence of large leasing companies, who buy on their own account and lease to airline companies which may include the ones who could be price-discriminated against by the manufacturer.

governed by other motives besides profit maximization and markets are quite competitive for simple means of destruction.

Although the connection between imperfect competition and discriminatory behaviour in international trade is tenuous, there are arguments for harmonization of competition policies in order to increase global welfare and reduce sources of international tension.[11] Such harmonization may be easier to achieve in a regional setting than in global negotiations, and it may be necessary to ensure a level playing field among producers within a common market.

Early US antitrust experience provides some evidence of a link between economic integration and the need for harmonized competition policies. In the two decades following the 1890 Sherman Act, state antitrust policy was more important than federal antitrust policy; the situation was sustained by an 1895 Supreme Court decision that a merger of Pennsylvanian sugar refiners was a state matter, because it involved manufacturing rather than commerce. State laws varied and were weaker or absent in the more industrialized states. In industries where gains from merging existed and location mattered little, producers would concentrate in states with lax antitrust policies. This unleashed a race to the bottom as states dropped antitrust measures. The process was accelerated by the emergence of holding companies, which provided shells for mergers (including mergers of out-of-state firms) and within which collusion could occur freely. New Jersey led the way in selling charters to pay off state debt, followed by Delaware, Nevada, and West Virginia. This development undermined not only states' policy independence with respect to mergers, but also federal restrictions on price-fixing, and the only practical solution to maintaining an effective competition policy within the US economic union was to turn all aspects over to the federal government. After 1912, Supreme Court decisions reflected

[11] The increasing importance of transnational businesses adds technical arguments for harmonization to reduce jurisdictional complexities. A merger between two transnational corporations may need approval by several competition authorities, who might impose contradictory conditions, and in some cases even when that hurdle has been overcome private actions can be launched to prevent the merger. Co-ordinated competition policies would reduce compliance costs by increasing transparency and reducing uncertainty, and should also avoid undesirable regulatory arbitraging and ensure that only one set of conditions needs to be met.

this imperative, and state antitrust laws have been completely superceded by federal policy.

A similar process is happening within the EU, where a competition policy envisaged in Articles 85 and 86 of the Treaty of Rome has been given more scope since 1990 (and the precedence of EU law over national law in this area has been established since the Costa/Enel case), and is intended to happen within the CER. If such regional steps are towards more stringent policies, then they will be welfare-increasing, although they will not necessarily reduce tensions between the countries with a harmonized competition policy and other countries with laxer or more stringent competition policies.

Where RTAs have no ultimate goal of economic union, and do not involve societies as similar as Australia and New Zealand, then a common competition policy may not be worth aiming for. Hoekman and Mavroidis (1994) have argued that, if the goal is to improve the contestability of national markets, pursuing more effective application of GATT/WTO rules and closing loopholes might be a more productive approach. Such an incremental approach may be politically difficult because exceptions and loopholes are exploited for a reasoon, but if that is unattainable then devising and enforcing an international competition policy will be even less feasible.

Monetary integration

The theory of currency areas has developed separately from that of regional trading arrangements, and during the second half of the twentieth century regional agreements rarely mentioned monetary integration. Such separation was not always the case; the pre-1950s European customs unions between San Marino and Italy, Monaco and France, and Luxemburg and Belgium (but not Benelux) involved currency union, and the European Payments Union was a regional arrangement which can be viewed as part of the process of Western European economic integration. After the establishment of currency convertibility for trade transactions, however, monetary impediments to regional economic integration in Europe were ignored. The Rome Treaty makes no mention of monetary integration.

The theory of optimal currency areas developed by Mundell (1961) and McKinnon (1963) emphasized macroeconomic considerations. A national currency allows a government to pursue independent macroeconomic policies, but this power is limited if factors can flow readily across the national borders or if the economy is so open that all economic agents accurately predict the consequences of exchange rate changes. Thus, breaks in desirable currency areas correspond to breaks in factor mobility and in openness. These conclusions help to explain the common correspondence between national borders and currency areas, but, apart from a suspicion that the size of optimal currency areas might be increasing with global economic integration, optimal currency area theory had little operational content.

Discussion of monetary integration was off the agenda during most of the 1960s, when fixed exchange rates were the rule and monetary obstacles to trade seemed less important than tariffs and other non-tariff barriers. The situation changed after the major realignment of the exchange rate between the French franc and the German mark in 1969, and with the report of the Werner Commission on EC monetary union. The 1970 Werner Report proposed a three-stage process leading to monetary integration by 1980, beginning with a period during which the EC currencies' bilateral exchange rates would be fixed within a narrow band which could move within the wider band established with non-EC currencies (notably the US dollar); the system was initially known as the Snake in the Tunnel, although with the shift to generalized floating the Snake soon escaped from the tunnel.

The Snake's history was a troubled one. The UK, in anticipation of its forthcoming full EC membership, joined the Snake at its inception in 1992, but then left within six weeks. The Italian lire also made a quick exit. The French franc left the Snake, then returned and exited again in 1976, by which time the Snake's participants consisted only of Germany and smaller countries which chose to peg their currencies to the mark. The reason for the exits was straightforward; governments wished to pursue independent monetary policies, and could not do this with a fixed exchange rate. The fact that it was the larger EC members that exited could be explained by the greater openness of smaller economies such as the Benelux countries or Denmark, or by the higher transactions costs of a floating exchange rate for a smaller economy with less efficient forward markets for its currency.

Almost immediately after the effective death of the Snake in 1976, top-level efforts to revive the monetary integration process were initiated by the German chancellor, Helmut Schmidt, the French president, Giscard d'Estaing, and the EC Commission president, Roy Jenkins, who put together arrangements for a European Monetary System (EMS). The exchange rate mechanism (ERM) was practically identical to that of the Snake, although it was dressed up with innovations such as the replacement of the EC's unit of account by a European currency unit (the ecu) and formal divergence indicators requiring action by governments whose currency was reaching prescribed limits against the ecu as well as bilateral exchange rate limits. The EMS began in 1979 with eight members. (The UK did not participate.) During the early 1980s there were several realignments within the ERM, but after 1986 these practically ceased, and with the accession of Spain in 1989 and the UK in 1990 the EMS covered all EC members except Greece and Portugal by the early 1990s.

Why were the EC leaders so anxious to re-establish a fixed exchange rate system after the collapse of the Snake? With floating exchange rates, agricultural prices in a common currency unit will change in national currency units; consumers in countries with depreciating currencies face higher food prices and farmers in countries with appreciating currencies receive lower prices.[12] Under pressure from the disaffected groups, the common market will be difficult to maintain. The solution adopted by the EC as a temporary expedient after the 1969 FF/DM realignment, and formalized in a 1971 EC Regulation, was to introduce green exchange rates to limit fluctuations in domestic agricultural prices and to use monetary compensation amounts (MCAs, i.e. taxes and rebates based on the difference between green rates and market exchange rates) to equalize the incentives to sell in all EC markets. The unilaterally determined green rates proliferated during the 1970s (sometimes with different rates for different products), making the system more administratively complex. The bias, whereby green rates involving subsidies from the EC budget

[12] The argument is developed more fully in Pomfret (1991). Basevi and Grassi (1993) take a similar position in relating the 1992 EMS crisis to the EU's common agricultural policy.

tended to persist whereas those involving taxes were phased out quickly, led to escalating costs; the MCA system absorbed 2.2 billion ecus in 1977, or 11 per cent of the agricultural budget (itself three-quarters of total EC expenditures). Farm price variations were large (e.g. in 1978 about 40 per cent higher on average in Germany than in the UK), so there was no common price for consumers, and rampant smuggling by producers required increased border patrols—both highly visible contradictions in a common market. After exchange rates were stabilized within the EMS some MCAs remained, but they became much less significant (accounting for 144 million ecus of EC spending in 1986).

The EMS was intended to put EC economic integration back on track. For France, saving the Common Agricultural Policy, from which France was the biggest national beneficiary, provided a specific economic benefit from the EMS. In Germany and Italy, central bankers opposed EMS membership because of its monetary policy implications, but were overruled by their political leaders who saw the EMS as a major Community initiative. In Britain, where political leaders of both major parties were less Community-minded, the reservations about lost monetary sovereignty carried the day.

The EMS has evolved over its lifespan. After the frequent and general realignments of its first four years, realignments became rarer after March 1983 and often involved a single currency. Although long-term exchange rates were not stabilized after the establishment of the EMS, the short-term variability of bilateral EMS exchange rates did fall significantly (Ungerer *et al.*, 1986, 17–21; Artis and Taylor, 1988); this improved the functioning of the CAP and of the internal market in general. Changes in operating procedures (e.g. the 1987 Nyborg agreement) gave the EMS central bankers deeper pockets to defend the fixed rates against speculation. By the end of the 1980s, most EMS members had accepted the logic of permanently fixed exchange rates or a common currency as a prerequisite for the smooth running of the common market and for the survival of the Common Agricultural Policy. The array of forces in the 1990–1 debate over monetary union was remarkably similar to that in the original EMS debate, with the UK opposed and central bankers elsewhere (especially in the Bundesbank) sceptical but overruled by the political leadership.

The 1991 Maastricht Treaty formally committed the EC members to monetary integration. A timetable was established for making bilateral exchange rates increasingly inflexible, in the runup to their replacement by a single currency before the end of the decade. Guidelines were also established for inflation rates, budget deficits, and debt levels which would need to be achieved if a country was to be able to adopt the single currency. The process was disrupted by the September 1992 crisis, when the British government addressed massive speculation against the pound first by raising interest rates and then by withdrawing from the ERM and letting the pound float. Italy and Spain also withdrew from the ERM or established wider exchange rate bands, which nullified the concept of fixed exchange rates.

In sum, free trade in a product whose price is regulated by buffer stock arrangements at a negotiated common price is difficult to maintain in the face of daily exchange rate fluctuations. On the other hand, the record of fixed but adjustable exchange rates is spotty; speculators tend to face a one-way bet when a currency comes under pressure, and the speculative capital flows can become self-fulfilling when capital markets are well developed and short-term capital flows unrestricted. Capital controls are undesirable because they lead to a misallocation of capital. For a regional integration scheme such as the EU, which aims for free movement of factors as well as goods in the long term, capital controls are especially undesirable (and were finally phased out in the early 1990s). The economic logic of eventual monetary union is powerful.

Even in the absence of regulated markets such as those covered by the CAP, closer economic integration underlines the transactions costs of separate currencies. These are difficult to estimate (although the Cecchini Report tried), because larger transactions are efficient, but the petty inconvenience costs for millions of travellers are hard to measure.

The differing histories of the Snake and the EMS have a parallel in the early 1970s debate between Corden and Ingram over European monetary integration. Corden (1972) argued that monetary integration was not workable because countries would be unwilling to bear the losses arising from 'enforced departures from internal balance', while Ingram (1973) pointed out that this view is 'antipathetic to the evolutionary trend toward economic integration'. Corden identified the short-run difficulties and correctly predicted the Snake's instability, while Ingram pinpointed the crucial long-run consideration. Ingram's prescient view captured the secret of the EMS's success:

> Economic integration leads logically toward fixed rates, monetary union and ultimately a common currency. Advocacy of flexible exchange rates within the European Community is essentially an expression of opposition to economic integration. (Ingram, 1973, 3)

The eight original EMS countries shared this view and were committed to economic integration, while the British remained ambivalent.

A common currency area can hinder trade if the monetary policy is inflationary. This consideration was ignored in optimum currency area theory, but it should have been familiar from historical experiences such as that of the Austro-Hungarian successor states after 1918 (Dornbusch, 1992). If the seigniorage from monetary emission accrues to one country, but the costs of inflation are spread over other countries in the common currency area, then there is an incentive bias towards inflationary monetary policies. In 1919 the Austrian government faced this situation, and other users of the crown were forced to adopt their own national currencies if they wished to re-establish monetary stability in their territory.

The experience of the successor states to the Soviet Union has some parallels. After the dissolution of the USSR in December 1991, many foreign advisers recommended retaining the ruble as a common currency; the advice fitted with the conclusions of optimum currency area theory, and aimed to minimize the disruption of trade within the region. In practice, the ruble zone was a disaster because each member's central bank could create ruble credits, which fuelled hyperinflation. The Russian central bank had a monopoly on printing ruble banknotes, but banknote shortages led to several ruble zone members printing parallel currencies to supplement the means of cash payment. As the means of exchange proliferated and distinctions were made between ruble credits issued by different central banks, the situation became chaotic as well as inflationary. Meanwhile, as the ruble zone members transformed their economies from central planning to market-based systems, price reform continued at differing paces, opening up arbitrage opportunities, which tended to dominate new trade within the ruble zone in 1992–3. As in Central Europe in 1919, the countries most committed to establishing macroeconomic stability were first to introduce their national currencies (the Baltic states), but other countries established national currencies in order to run more expansionary monetary policies (Ukraine, Georgia, Azerbaijan). The remaining countries stayed in the ruble zone, in part attracted by the carrots of cheap credit and primary products offered by Russia, but as Russian export prices approached world prices these incentives diminished. The ruble zone finally disintegrated in November 1993, when all of the members of the Commonwealth of Independent States (CIS) apart from Tajikistan introduced national currencies.

Whether maintenance of the ruble zone helped or hindered intra-regional trade during the twenty-four months after the end of the USSR is an open question. At least initially, the large, quasi-barter transactions in products such as oil, natural gas, and cotton dominated intra-CIS trade, but as these transactions were shifted on to a world price basis the failure of the monetary systen to encourage new trade based on comparative advantage became more apparent. By the mid-1990s trade among those CIS countries that had established reasonably stable convertible currencies with low trade barriers was on a much firmer basis than it had been in the 1992–3 ruble zone.

In sum, the relationship between monetary integration and regional economic integration is non-monotonic. At the levels of preferential trading arrangements discussed in this book, monetary union is relatively unimportant. As long as there is a reasonable degree of exchange rate stability and absence of exchange controls, other restrictions to intra-regional trade are more important than the transactions costs arising from separate currencies. On the other hand, establishing an economic union with common policies and a high degree of factor mobility appears to cause tensions with the existence of multiple currencies.[13] The CAP price support schemes illustrate the difficulty

[13] Exchange rate volatility does not appear to disrupt trade, although it does exacerbate trade tensions as import-competing activities in countries with appreciating currencies seek higher trade barriers. Such a reaction is difficult to accommodate within a GDA in which internal trade barriers are limited by agreement, although some large French companies called for measures against UK and

of implementing one specific common economic policy, but the fluctuating national currencies problem could inhibit any common policies where agreement has been reached on contributions and the distribution of costs and benefits on the basis of pre-existing exchange rates. The EU, at the border between a common market and an economic union in the 1990s, is clearly experiencing such tensions, but monetary issues do not appear important to other GDAs.

4. Rules of Origin

Rules of origin received little attention from economists before the 1990s. While it was recognized that rules of origin were necessary to define eligiblity for preferential tariffs, they did not appear to pose any significant theoretical challenges. In one-way preferential arrangements, the rules of origin might be drafted in a restrictive manner in order to limit access and reduce competitive pressure on producers in the importing country, but that was a straightforward non-tariff barrier (similar to customs valuation or tariff classification NTBs).[14] In discriminatory arrangments with internal free trade among members, rules of origin to prevent trade deflection will normally be ineffective owing to the substitution of extra-FTA products for domestic products in the low-tariff country's consumption (Section 8.4).

Rules of origin were brought back on the agenda in the 1990s, mainly as a result of their prominent role in the NAFTA negotiations (Krueger, 1993 and 1995; Lloyd, 1993; Krishna and Krueger, 1995). The connection to the topics in the previous

Italian imports after the depreciation of the pound and the lire in 1992. Eichengreen (1993) argues that avoiding competitive pressures arising from 'capricious' devaluations, and their poitical consequences, is the main benefit from European monetary union.

[14] This appears to have been the main purpose of the Lomé Convention rules of origin, even though they resembled the NAFTA rules in permitting potentially trade-diverting cumulative content (i.e. inputs from other ACP countries or from the EC could be counted). The Lomé Convention rules were in part designed to prevent the ACP countries from developing exports to the EC of items covered by the Multifibre Arrangement (from which they were exempt); when the rules of origin were insufficient to prevent clothing exports, EC members threatened to resort to the safeguard clause unless the ACP country voluntarily restrained its exports—as, for example, the UK did against knitwear imports from Mauritius in the late 1970s (Grilli, 1993, 167; McQueen, 1982).

section is that rules of origin are an element in the increased complexity of regional trading arrangements, which have gone beyond the simple preferential tariff arrangements analysed in Chapters 8 and 9 to encompass the management of regional trade. In contrast to advocates of the new regionalism as a desirable way of bringing new issues into international trade agreements, Krueger and other analysts of rules of origin see them as examples of pernicious complexity aimed to pervert trade patterns, rather than as a step towards freer international trade.

The new-style rules of origin apply to goods with intermediate inputs and require that a certain proportion of the good's content must originate within the RTA. They have been justified, e.g. in EFTA and the CER, in order to deal with the intermediate good problem (Lloyd, 1993, 701); by locating in the low-tariff country and paying less duty on imported inputs, a firm can gain an advantage over competitors located elsewhere in the RTA. This is an extension of the old rules of origin argument, and trade deflection should make the origin rules redundant. There is, however, popular sentiment against such assembly operations, captured in the epithet 'screwdriver plant'. Such issues have arisen with respect to foreign investment within RTAs,[15] but the novelty of the NAFTA rules of origin was that they could apply to existing producers within the RTA whose goods would be ineligible for duty-free treatment on intra-NAFTA trade.

Intermediate inputs add another element of ambiguity to the analysis in Chapters 8 and 9. In Fig. 8.2 a FTA cannot be welfare-reducing: it can only lead to trade creation, because, owing to trade deflection, imports from non-members cannot be reduced so there is no possibility of trade being diverted from the least-cost producer to higher-cost internal producers. The presence of intermediate inputs complicates this conclusion, as envisaged by Lloyd (1982, ch. 9.1) and analysed by Ju and Krishna (1996).

Ju and Krishna analyse a FTA between two small countries, A and B, each of which produces a final good x and its input z,

[15] The issue had arisen in the EC in 1988 when Nissan first began shipping UK-assembled cars to other EC countries. France and Italy refused to accord free market access to these cars unless they had a minimum 80% EC content. France and Italy eventually backed down on the inclusion of transplants in VER ceilings on Japanese car sales in the EC, although disagreement remained over enforcement of EC local content requirements in other areas (e.g. television programming).

both of which they import from the rest of the world in return for a numeraire consumption good. Suppose that tariffs are such that A's tariff on the final good is higher than B's ($t_x^A > t_x^B$) and that A's tariff on the intermediate good is lower than B's ($t_z^A < t_z^B$). Price equalization within the FTA will reduce the price of x in A, so that A benefits from trade creation, but the reduced output of x in A will lead to reduced demand for z; the latter is the derived demand effect. In B there will be no impact on the price of x, but the fall in the price of the intermediate good will shift the supply curve of x-producers; this is the input price effect. The two additional consequences of the FTA, the derived demand and input price effects, introduce the possibility of negative net welfare impact. Nevertheless, if the tariff cuts on x and z are equal then net welfare increases, and this is the presumed sign of the welfare effect in most plausible cases. Only if the relative price of the good with the lower tariff falls, and certain (fairly extreme) elasticity conditions hold, will the FTA be welfare-reducing. This is a classic second-best situation, but prima facie the standard conclusion that, assuming lump-sum transfers among members are possible, a FTA cannot be net welfare-reducing seems to hold in all reasonably plausible circumstances.

In sum, the existence of intermediate inputs is a further source of second-best ambiguities, but is unlikely to reverse the conclusions of traditional CU/FTA theory. The rules of origin ostensibly introduced to deal with the intermediate good problem are themselves a more direct source of new assessments. First, within CUSTA, and especially NAFTA, rules of origin were designed to determine which goods produced within the area qualified for CUSTA/NAFTA treatment; i.e. rules of origin were methods of ensuring that NAFTA did not cover all of North American trade. Secondly, the rules of origin induced behavioural change by encouraging firms within NAFTA to alter their input structure in a trade-diverting manner.

The design of rules of origin is discretionary. Principles, such as equalizing the marginal benefit from trade creation and the marginal disadvantages of trade and production deflection (Balassa, 1961, 71–2) are not operational. A 50 per cent content requirement (as in the CER) is arbitrary, and any modifications in the percentage may be good or bad. Moreover, it makes a difference whether content requirements are set in price or cost terms, but it is impossible to draw unambiguous conclusions about their relative desirability. Worst of all, more stringent content requirements may or may not reduce welfare (Krishna and Krueger, 1995).[16]

In general, rules of origin act as a tax on the use of inputs from outside the RTA. Thus, if a producer is close to the content margin, there is an incentive to replace external suppliers by within-RTA suppliers. Since the existing suppliers are presumably the least-cost ones, the change in input source is trade-diverting. In the plausible case of a Mexican textile manufacturer replacing yarn imported from Asia by US yarn in order to gain free access to the US market for its output, both the US yarn-maker and the Mexican textile-maker benefit. US textile consumers will also benefit from lower prices. The cost of trade diversion is the forgone tariff revenue on the yarn previously imported by Mexico and on any external textile imports into the USA displaced by Mexican textiles. The net welfare effect on Mexico and the USA individually is ambiguous (since either or both may suffer from uncompensated loss of tariff revenue), while the rest of the world loses.

The distributional effects are crucial in this type of example. The rules of origin, which are essentially a tax on inputs from outside the RTA, must have negative net welfare effects on the RTA and on the world (absent any imperfect competition or optimal tariff argument for the tax), but some producer groups within the RTA will benefit. The lack of guidelines for the design of rules of origin and the lack of transparency in their functioning make rules of origin powerful instruments of protection. The domestic industries can assist in the design of the rules, because they are familiar with the technical characteristics of the product, and this is likely to bias the design to these firms' benefit.

The opportunities for implementing content rules of origin are practically limitless. Although they may seem more applicable

[16] Clearly, rules that are so stringent as to be prohibitive (e.g. requiring x% content when more than $(1 - x)$% of inputs are only obtainable elsewhere) makes the product concerned ineligible for preferential treatment; whether that is a good or a bad thing is ambiguous for standard second-best reasons. For political economy reasons, however, exclusion might be expected to occur when it would lead to trade creation at the expense of internal producers rather than when it leads to trade diversion (i.e. the potential for selective exclusion is likely to have negative net welfare effects).

to manufactures, even agricultural products whose nationality would appear readily defined by where they are grown could be enmeshed in a web of content rules. Thus, if content requirements are set high enough, they could provide an incentive to purchase pesticides (and the inputs with which the pesticides are made?) from within the RTA. The possibilities for excluding individual items from the RTA's scope are almost infinite and for encouraging trade diversion, immense.

5. Conclusions

Mainstream customs union theorists generally saw GDAs as second-best, both in the technical sense of having ambiguous welfare effects and in the popular sense of inferior. Welfare generalizations about whether they were or were not improvements over the *status quo* are impossible, but preferential tariff reduction is inferior to multilateral trade liberalization from the global perspective, because it can induce trade diversion. Furthermore, bilateral or regional trade negotiations might distract policy-makers' attention from the goal of multilateral trade liberalization. Such reasoning is compatible with the spirit of GATT, and certainly with the ideas of those founders of the post-1945 trading system who were reacting against the discriminatory excesses of trade policies in the 1930s. It also underlay US trade policy in the 1950s and 1960s. When US policy began to shift in the early 1980s, bilateralism was initially defended on national rather than cosmopolitan terms.

At the end of the 1980s, however, a number of prominent US economists began to advocate regional trading arrangements not only on the basis of national welfare benefits, but also as stepping stones to multilateral trade liberalization. Among the most influential was Larry Summers, soon to become a senior economic policymaker under President Clinton, who claimed that:

> economists should maintain a strong, but rebuttable, presumption in favour of all lateral reductions in trade barriers, whether they be multi, uni, bi, tri or plurilateral. Global liberalisation may be best, but regional liberalisation is very likely to be good. (Summers, 1991)

He based this claim on four propositions:

1. RTAs are likely to have trade-creating effects which exceed their trade-diverting effects.
2. Even trade-diverting RTAs are likely to increase welfare.
3. RTAs are likely to have beneficial non-trade effects.
4. Reasonable RTAs are as likely to accelerate global liberalization as to slow it down.

The first point draws on the idea of natural trading blocs (discussed in Section 11.2), but is essentially an empirical issue (to be addressed in Part III); in itself, it reasserts the standard conclusion that preferential trading arrangements may (or may not) be welfare-improving. The second point is in part a rerun of the Bhagwati–Kirman debate settled by Johnson (1974), discussed in Section 8.3, and in part based upon an (unsupported) empirical observation that, 'while trade diversion is unlikely to involve large efficiency costs, trade creation is much more likely to involve real efficiency gains'. The third point refers to the increased competitive forces (as, for example, in the integrated markets model discussed in the first section of this chapter) and the 'new areas' discussed in Section 3 of this chapter. The final point concerns the growing unwieldiness of a GATT/WTO with over a hundred separate negotiating parties and the likelihood that a small number of trading blocs could conduct intra-bloc negotiations more efficaciously.

The argument over whether RTAs are building blocks or stumbling blocks on the road to multilateral trade liberalization became highly topical during the 1990s with the contemporaneous completion of NAFTA and Uruguay Round negotiations. It is an important component in the more positive attitude towards discriminatory trading arrangements embodied in the new regionalism. The brief review above of Summers' arguments underlines, however, that the building blocks-versus-stumbling blocks debate cannot be evaluated without first examining the empirical evidence on GDAs' effects and second analysing the political economy of RTAs.[17] Krueger's concern about content rules of origin, for

[17] The building block-versus-stumbling block terminology is due to Bhagwati (1991, 77). Bhagwati and Panagariya (1996) distinguish between trade creation and trade diversion as a static guide to a GDA's desirability and between building block and stumbling block as a dynamic guide to the desirability of GDAs. Winters (1996b) reviews the extensive theoretical literature on the building blocks-versus-stumbling blocks issue, emphasizing the various models' fragility with

example, is largely based on their political economy, since she fears that their opaqueness and discretionary nature make them attractive vehicles for protectionist and bureaucratic interests to pursue their goals to the detriment of national welfare.

A complication raised by several of the issues covered in this chapter is an appeal to fairness which reflects popular sentiment but is difficult to accommodate in economic theory. The desire that other countries' regulations should not set domestic firms at a competitive disadvantage in international trade is vacuous, given that comparative advantage is what matters in international trade; there is no reason why different societies should not have differing regulations on the environment and so forth which will affect output and consumption patterns (and hence trade), and such taste differences are one reason for having separate jurisdictions (Section 11.3). Similarly, the appeal to assemblers to use domestic components often enjoys popular sympathy, even though there is no more reason to promote autarchy in intermediate goods than in goods and services as a whole. To a large extent, the 'fairness' dimension has contributed to a politicization of debates over RTAs, which in previous decades were often treated as technical matters of weighing more narrowly defined costs and benefits.

Deep integration is viewed by some as an essential component of a liberal world economy and by others as an unacceptable infringement of national sovereignty. Neither extreme position is tenable. Many regulatory or other NTBs have an effect equivalent to that of discriminatory tariffs, and enforceable international agreements (whether regional or global) are justifiable to ensure that the spirit of the non-discrimination principle is not abused. On the other hand, many NTBs have other legitimate purposes which may dominate any trade implications, and thus should not be subject to international control. Any preference diversity among nations, or among parts of a federal state, ensures that full harmonization must be welfare-reducing. In sum, the correct question concerns not the desirability or otherwise of deep integration, but rather the extent of desirable harmonization.

respect to parameter values and their implausibility as representations of the real world owing to symmetry or simple asymmetry assumptions. The fundamental problem with this literature is that models to support either case are easy to construct but difficult to confront with empirical tests, because there is only one international trading system and it evolves slowly.

11

Numbers and Geography

Mainstream international trade theory takes the country as its basic unit, and treats each nation as a point in space. Size matters only in the distinction between small (i.e. facing infinitely elastic demand for exports or supply of imports) and non-small countries, and geography is ignored. These conventions were challenged by Paul Krugman (1991a), who argued that international economists should pay attention to the geographical location of economic activity. Krugman (1991b) also introduced a new dimension into the theory of preferential trading arrangements by raising the question of the optimal number of trading units.

Krugman's model of the number of trading units is analysed in the first section of this chapter. The analysis leads on to two related issues, which are discussed in Sections 2 and 3. First, units are not randomly formed and geography, among other things, matters. In the regional trading bloc context this opens up the possibility that some regional arrangements (e.g. those among neighbours) may be more likely to form or be more beneficial than others. Secondly, the size of units is not determined solely by trade policy considerations, and a debate has developed over the optimal size of economic units. This has some connection with the new regionalism discussed in the previous chapter, in so far as it presumes the existence of some economies of scale, but it is distinct in that the source of scale economies is external to the firm and hence they have different economic implications. The optimum size argument also contains important non-economic elements relevant to the creation of regional arrangements and relates to the deep integration issues discussed in the previous chapter.

The fourth section of this chapter takes up Krugman's main point about geography and trade. Economic activity concentrates in certain locations, which do not necessarily correspond with national boundaries or the limits of regional trading blocs. The significance of sub-regional economic zones raises the distinction between regionalism and regionalization (Chapter 1) as well as the question of whether regionalization might promote regionalism.

1. The Optimal Number of Trading Units

Mainstream customs union theory followed the conventions of trade theory by taking the country as its basic unit of analysis and not questioning how many countries there are in the world; the analysis concerned a customs union among an arbitrary number of nations, existing in a world of many other nations. Common recourse to the small-country assumption reflected the presumption that, although analysis might focus on three representative countries, application would be in a multi-country atomistic setting. Exceptions to this (in Chapter 9) involved fairly standard adaptation of optimum tariff analysis to cases where the resulting union had market power in the world economy.

Such assumptions made sense in the world of the 1950s. They would have been less applicable before the nineteenth century, when nation states were not synonymous with internal free trade. During the century before 1950, however, the distinction between domestic and foreign trade became clear and the number of major trading units remained fairly constant, while the minor changes in number showed no relationship between number of units and global trends towards or away from free trade.[1] The assumptions made less sense in the 1980s and 1990s as a larger number of Western European nations subsumed their international trade policies to the European Union and as hemispheric trading blocs came on the trade policy menu. Meanwhile, in Eastern Europe and Central Asia new units with independent trade policies were being created out of former members of the defunct Comecon.

Krugman (1991b; 1993) provided the first rigorous analysis of the optimal number of units. In his model, a large number of small geographical units, which he calls provinces, each produce a distinct good. The world is organized into a number (B) of blocs with internal free trade and a tariff on imports from outside the bloc. In order to analyse the relationship between the number

[1] The amalgamation of trading units in Canada and Australia was associated with higher trade barriers on external trade, while the dissolution of larger trading units such as the Austro-Hungarian Empire was also associated with higher trade barriers.

of blocs and world welfare, Krugman imposes two symmetry assumptions:

1. All goods enter symmetrically into demand with a constant elasticity of substitution, σ, between any pair of goods.
2. All trading blocs are of equal size.

He also assumes that tariffs are set non-cooperatively to maximize bloc welfare. These are strong simplifying assumptions, but they make the problem tractable and yield some important insights. World welfare depends upon the value of σ and the number of blocs. Solving numerically for a 'reasonable' range of parameter values ($2 < \sigma < 10$), Krugman found that world welfare was minimized when $B = 3$.

Krugman's result initiated virulent debate, especially as the world was perceived by some observers to be heading towards a three-bloc system. That reaction was, however, misdirected. It is easy to deride Krugman's model as failing to fit reality. For one thing, the tariff values in the three-bloc solution are very high; in the real world countries do not act non-cooperatively in setting tariffs to maximize national welfare.[2] More important is to recognize Krugman's model as an abstraction which highlights forces influencing the optimum number of trading units.

World welfare is maximized with free trade, which exists either when $B = 1$, i.e. when free trade is imposed by agreement, or when B is large, i.e. when all countries are small and adopt free trade as their optimum trade policy. What happens to global welfare in between those extremes? As B increases from 1 to 2, half of world trade is within blocs, but the other half is subject to tariffs which reduce welfare. Moving from 2 to 3 blocs reduces the amount of intra-bloc free trade to one-third, although the optimum tariff of each bloc will be smaller than in the two-bloc case. As B becomes larger two opposing forces are at work: the optimum tariff becomes smaller, increasing global welfare, but the amount of free trade within blocs diminishes, reducing world welfare.

[2] More empirically grounded models also find that optimum tariff levels are well above actual tariffs for the largest trading units; e.g. in Whalley's (1985) model the optimum tariffs for the USA and EC are over 100%. The benefits of co-operation have been recognized at least since the Smoot–Hawley tariff (and the ensuing retaliation).

Krugman (1993) points out that the major cost to the world of having a small number of blocs is not so much the level of the tariffs, but the large amount of trade diversion. With more trading units the internal market in each is smaller, but the welfare loss from moving to a smaller internal market is outweighed by the gain in reduced trade diversion when the world trading system becomes more atomized. This is the opposite of popular arguments for larger blocs, which focus on the benefits of larger internal markets, but Krugman's analysis is quite consistent with the presumption from Vinerian customs union theory. If small countries form a PTA, then the trade diversion cost to them is likely to be high, but the reduction in world welfare is minor. On the other hand, if a group of countries accounting for a large share of world economic activity form a PTA, then the trade diversion cost to them is likely to be small but its impact on non-members substantial. The most important contribution of Krugman's model is to highlight the potential trade diversion costs of the division of the world economy into a small number of blocs. His assumptions may not be realistic, but by their simplicity they do provide a useful baseline case for comparing the global costs and benefits of bloc enlargement.

Srinivasan (1993) dismisses Krugman's contribution as being 'uncomfortably close to being "theory without relevance"' because it relies on the strong-symmetry assumptions. Suppose there are two homogeneous goods and the world consists of two types of province, one with a comparative advantage in good 1 and the other with a comparative advantage in good 2. Global welfare will be maximized in an integrated world economy without trade barriers (Krugman, 1995a). If all of the first type of provinces become members of one trading bloc and all of the second type become members of another bloc, then barriers to intra-bloc trade will reduce world welfare. In an alternative two-bloc world, however, each bloc could consist of half of the type 1 provinces and half of the type 2 provinces, with no negative effect on global welfare because the integrated economy can be reproduced within each bloc. Thus, the number of blocs matters less than their composition.

Srinivasan's point does not undermine Krugman's contribution, but rather is a reminder that in the second-best world of GDAs anything can happen. The idea that blocs could be miniature replicas of the global economy is just as unrealistic as the idea that all blocs will be symmetrical, but it does highlight a consideration in evaluating the creation of blocs. The next section discusses the literature on those membership characteristics that are likely to make blocs more or less harmful.

2. Your Bloc or Mine? The Economics of Partner Selection

Following Viner's (1950) contribution, a number of articles tried to establish conditions under which customs unions would be more or less likely to be benefical. This literature (reviewed in Lipsey, 1960, and Johnson, 1962) had little impact because the conclusions were too tentative and were subject to qualification. In the 1990s, however, the question was revived and popularized around the concept of 'natural trading partners', among whom a preferential trading arrangement is likely to be welfare-enhancing.

The 'natural trading partners' hypothesis was introduced by Wonnacott and Lutz (1989), who emphasized two points:

1. Are the prospective members already major trading partners? If so, the FTA will be reinforcing natural trading patterns, not artificially diverting them.
2. Are the prospective members close geographically? Groupings of distant nations may be economically inefficient because of the high transportation costs.

They also considered other criteria for partner selection based on complementarity versus competitiveness and on relative level of development, but found these 'much more difficult to evaluate'. The concept of 'natural trading partners' was subsequently popularized by Krugman and Summers at the Federal Reserve Bank of Kansas City Symposium (Federal Reserve Bank . . . 1991) as justifying a presumption that regional arrangements will be welfare-enhancing.

A large volume of intra-regional trade reduces the scope for trade diversion, in the sense that there is less extra-regional trade to be diverted, but it is not a useful guide to actual trade diversion. Key variables in determining the balance between trade diversion and trade creation are the cross-price elasticities of demand between goods from different sources. Neither a high volume of trade nor proximity guarantees that the partner's goods are closer substitutes to domestic goods than they are to non-members' goods.[3]

Lipsey (1960, 507–8) made the point with a little example. Suppose a country imports only eggs from one partner and only shoes from the rest of the world, and is self-sufficent in all other goods. A customs union with the egg-supplier brings the price ratio of eggs to all commodities other than shoes to its correct level (i.e. equal to the real rate of transformation) but distorts the relative price of eggs to shoes. This is likely to be welfare-enhancing because the loss from the distorted eggs : shoe price ratio is likely to be minor compared with the gain from having the correct egg : bacon, egg : cheese, etc., price ratios. Now reverse the example and suppose that the country produces only shoes and imports all goods other than eggs and shoes from the rest of the world. Now a customs union with the egg-supplier is likely to be welfare-reducing because the benefits from establishing the correct shoe : eggs price ratio are likely to be outweighed by the costs from distorting the price ratio between eggs and all other commodities. As Lipsey stresses, the size of imports from the partner is *per se* unimportant to the conclusion.

This can readily be applied to specific cases of contiguous countries. Within NAFTA, for example, trade creation is relatively more likely to result from a reduction of US tariffs on imports from Canada, whose goods are close substitutes to US goods, and trade diversion is relatively more likely to result from reduction of US tariffs on imports from Mexico, whose goods are close substitutes to non-NAFTA countries' goods. Neither proximity nor volume of trade is itself a good guide to this outcome.

[3] Kreinin and Plummer (1994) propose a measure of the similarity between a country's commodity structure of trade (measured by its revealed comparative advantage) with the world as a whole and with its proposed partners. If the two structures are similar, then they argue that a PTA will not distort the country's trade and hence is likely to be welfare-enhancing. This is an unsatisfactory guide to the PTA's welfare effects. Consider the East Asian groupings used in Kreinin and Plummer's empirical exercise; although the structure of Indonesia's exports to East Asia is similar to the structure of Indonesia's global exports, a PTA could still lead to trade diversion as Japan replaces imports from India by imports from Indonesia and as Indonesia replaces imports from the USA by imports from Japan. The key variables are the cross-elasticities, which may be high between Indian and Indonesian goods and between Japanese and US goods.

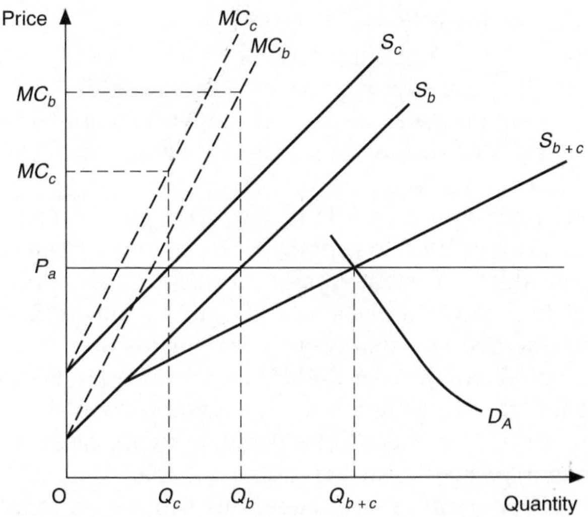

FIG. 11.1 Trading partners with different transport costs
With a non-discriminatory tariff, country A imports Q_{b+c} and the price paid to suppliers is P_a. Supply conditions in countries B and C are identical, apart from the fact that C's exports to A involve higher transport costs. Thus, A's pre-FTA imports from B are greater than imports from C; i.e. $Q_b > Q_c$. MC_b and MC_c indicate the marginal cost of obtaining imports from B and C respectively. At pre-FTA trade levels $MC_c < MC_b$; if additional supplies are to be encouraged by discriminatory trade measures, they should favour imports from C.

Source: adapted from Bhagwati and Panagariya (1996).

The transport cost argument can be traced back to the P. Wonnacott and R. Wonnacott (1981) model discussed in the previous chapter, where the argument was assessed as being of little practical importance. It is easy to imagine cases of PTAs among distant partners which would be less harmful than PTAs among contiguous countries; for example, following the logic of the previous paragraph, a USA–Mexico FTA is likely to be more harmful than a USA–Switzerland FTA. Bhagwati and Panagariya (1996) have developed a neat counter-argument which goes beyond agnosticism to show how a PTA with a distant partner is superior to a PTA with a neighbour.

Figure 11.1 illustrates the situation where the importing country A imposes a non-discriminatory tariff, and of the two supplying countries C faces higher transport costs than B. Since C's supply price exceeds B's, imports are larger from the closer country ($Q_b > Q_c$). Now, if A introduces a preferential tariff in favour of B, it will be distorting trade in favour of the partner with the higher marginal cost of supplying A's market ($MC_b > MC_a$). The 'natural trading partner' is precisely the wrong one with which to form a PTA on static welfare grounds; the country with the higher elasticity of supply, C, should be the one facing the lower tax on its products.

Although the volume-of-trade and transport-cost arguments are frequently conflated to support PTAs among neighbours, they are only weakly consistent. Gravity models usually find a positive correlation between distance and trade volume *ceteris paribus*, but the relationship is often weak and depends upon the data set (see Section 5 below). Dhar and Panagariya (1994), for example, estimate the gravity equation for twenty-two countries and find the common-border effect to be negative in six cases. Bhagwati and Panagariya (1996) further point out that the positive contiguity coefficients in gravity equations sometimes reflect intra-regional trade, which is a result of existing PTAs, and hence provides little guide to the 'natural' trade flows in a distortion-free world.

In sum, both variants of the 'natural trading partners' argument have weak theoretical underpinnings. Moreover, the two criteria may yield inconsistent indications of who the national partners are. The general conclusion remains that it is difficult to find any simple rule of thumb to identify good rather than bad partners for PTAs.

3. The Optimum Size of Nations

The discussion so far in this chapter has ignored any scale effects. The basic units, Krugman's provinces, can be infinitely small. Yet, in popular discussion the most common arguments for regional integration centre on the advantages of size. In this section I will distinguish between scale economies in production and other scale economies relevant to the determination of jurisdictional boundaries, and then analyse the latter.

A salient stylized fact of the world economy is the lack of correlation between country size and welfare. A scatter diagram with population on one axis and per capita income on the other yields no discernible pattern; there are large and small poor nations, and large and small rich nations. As long as a country participates in the global economy, there appears to be no disadvantage in having a small home base. A few models of integration assume that large countries enjoy lower costs, but their testable hypotheses are not supported by the facts.[4] The argument in favour of being part of a larger nation or trading bloc in order to realize scale economies in production is more plausible in the context of a protectionist trade policy *vis-à-vis* non-members, but the overwhelming weight of evidence is that the costs of external protection outweigh any scale-induced benefits (see Section 14.1).

The world is not, however, composed of micro-nations. Being in a larger unit has its advantages. Defence against outside aggressors is one advantage, given the economies of scale in the provision of military services. Most public goods have some fixed costs, such that tiny jurisdictions may have difficulty in their provision, although the threshold beyond which the average costs become constant appears to be small for most public goods other than defence.[5]

Big countries can also provide insurance against localizd misfortune. When California was hit by flooding in 1995 it received compensation from the US government. International aid for similar disasters is typically less generous. More permanent problems can be met by people moving from depressed to booming areas within the country, which is usually easier than migrating internationally.

The disadvantage of larger units lies in the co-ordination costs. Reaching decisions on the provision of public goods and avoiding large-scale free-riding is easier when the unit contains people with shared values (Buchanan and Tullock, 1962; Olson, 1982). Redistribution of tax revenue is also easier with a sense of shared identity. Indeed, the more heterogeneous the population is, the harder it will be to reach agreement on any tax and public

[4] In the model of Casella (1995), for example, the gains from enlarging a trade bloc should go disproportionately to smaller members, because enlargement diminishes the importance of domestic market size. Casella found, however, that empirical evidence from the 1986 EC enlargement is mixed, as the UK and France lost market share but Italy and Germany gained market share relative to the small EC members (Belgium, Denmark, Ireland, and the Netherlands); the null hypothesis that size is irrelevant cannot be rejected.

[5] Thus, units as small as Singapore or Kuwait or Hong Kong are capable of supplying public goods efficiently, but the last two proved incapable of independent resistance to take-over by powerful neighbours.

spending decisions. In a democracy, the majority may be able to enforce its preferences, but that will increase the temptation for the minority to secede. An authoritarian regime may impose a set of values, but it will incur enforcement costs if significant parts of the population do not share its values.

The optimum size of a nation is that at which the marginal costs of extra size equal the marginal benefits. This economic formulation clearly gives considerable weight to non-economic considerations, which determine the degree of shared values.[6]

Actual size may differ from optimum size. Changing political, social, and economic institutions is costly, and creation or dismemberment of nation states is infrequent. Thus, the international system has considerable hysteresis, with many cases of the actual size of nations being an accident of history. Changes in size tend to occur discretely at particular moments in history: 1919 in Central Europe, 1947 in South Asia, the late 1950s and early 1960s in Africa, 1989–93 in Eastern Europe and the former USSR. The stimulus for change has often been exogenous, but the outcome is influenced by the optimality considerations.

The optimum size can change over time. Schachmurove and Spiegel (1995) give the example of Israeli kibbutzim. In early years membership was homogeneous and many activities were communal, but the growing heterogeneity of members led to a decentralization of dining, children's sleeping arrangements, and so forth. At the nation state level, the weight given to provision of defence against an outside threat may change; the major motive behind Canadian Confederation and the accession of British Columbia in 1867 and 1871 was to resist absorption in the USA, but by the 1990s the military threat had long since receded and that motive for Canadian unity was weaker. At the regional organization level, the original and current composition of ASEAN has been determined by changing perceptions of the common outside threat (from international communism in the 1960s to Vietnamese expansionism in the 1980s to Chinese expansionism in the 1990s).

The optimum size may be modified by institutional innovations. Democracy may lead to more smaller countries as minorities

[6] Alesina and Spolaore (1995) make a similar argument, with some differences of emphasis.

seek to evade the tyranny of the majority. The authoritarian federalism of Tito's Yugoslavia successfully prevented a Balkan War for over three decades, despite the obvious pressures for disintegration into the constituent republics. Other federations, such as the USA or Germany, have balanced the benefits of size in some areas and of decentralization in others, reducing the prob-lem of co-ordination when preferences within the nation are more heterogeneous than preferences within provinces. International or regional organizations can add to this flexibility.[7]

How does this relate to recent debates over regionalism? Changes in the second half of the twentieth century are pulling in opposite directions, towards larger and smaller units. Innovations in mass destruction, transport, and communications have contributed to an awareness of the need for the provision of some public goods on a supranational scale.[8] Meeting such needs inevitably undermines existing national states, and encourages decentralization as the benefits of being in the nation are reduced. Rising incomes contributing to more heterogeneous preferences may add to this decentralizing pressure. One response is a fragmentation of redundant nations, which happened especially in the fluid situation of Eastern Europe after 1989. Another response is institutional innovation to create different levels of governance to handle different tasks. This is the EU model; the nation state remains the most powerful level of government in Western Europe with greatest legitimacy, but some powers have been derogated to the Union, while several member states have allowed devolution of other powers to regions within the nation. The process was retrospectively accepted in the early 1990s by the EU as the principle of subsidiarity; decisions should be devolved to as close to the grass-roots level as is possible, given the nature of the problem.

Recognition of the desirability of differing levels of government, as in EU subsidiarity or in federalism, has important implications for the analysis of deep integration. Harmonization and positive integration tend to be treated in the new regionalism literature

[7] R. Cooper (1976) discusses 'optimal areas of jurisdiction' in terms of scale economies, externalities, and the provision of stabilization policies.

[8] The precursors of this were the Universal Postal Union and other international agreements in the late 19th c., but the need for institutions in which to negotiate, monitor, and enforce agreements became more pressing in the 20th c.

as *per se* desirable. Measures of the costs of non-Europe (as in the Cecchini Report) or of non-Canada (reported in Trebilcock and Schwanen, 1995) are large, and are given as gross costs. Yet, if subnational governments provide through idiosyncratic regulations a lifestyle which their residents value, then harmonization imposes a cost. The benefits from peculiarity are more difficult to measure than the costs of forgone trade because they are likely to be psychic rather than pecuniary, which is why they are achieved in the political rather than the economic arena. Nevertheless, as soon as any benefits of subsidiarity or federalism based on differences in preferences are admitted, then harmonization and positive integration must involve a trade-off; full integration cannot be desirable, and the issue is how deep to go.[9]

4. Sub-regional Economic Zones

Krugman (1991a) reintroduced geographical considerations into economists' work on international economic development. He pointed out that concentration of industrial activity as in the North American rust-belt or the Western European industrial heartland reflects agglomeration effects, and that they do not respect national borders. Trade policy can affect the locational pattern, but the interconnections are complex.

The growth of Canadian industry in southern Ontario is often ascribed to trade barriers which encouraged US investors (or Canadian imitators of US plant) to locate behind the tariff wall. Many Canadian commentators have feared that free trade with the USA would lead to an exodus of Canadian industry to US locations (see Appendix). On the other hand, US concerns about free trade with Mexico included fears of US firms hopping across the border to take advantage of lower-cost Mexican labour once trade barriers were lifted and it became easy to integrate US and Mexican production activities. Both are plausible arguments, but with opposite implications for the relationship between trade barriers and the location of activity.

Krugman and Venables (1990) have developed a model to illustrate some of the competing pressures when a high-wage economy

[9] Breton (1995) provides a brief but forceful statement of the inevitability of the trade-off between federalism and economic integration.

forms a customs union with a low-wage economy (based on the stylized facts of the EC enlargement in the 1980s). Internal free trade might lead to deindustrialization of the periphery as industry concentrates at the core of the customs union in order to be close to the market. On the other hand, there are opposite pressures to seek the lower production costs in the periphery. The outcome is ambiguous and the relationship between location and trade barriers is not monotonic.

The locational issue became a major research topic in East Asia in the 1990s with the emergence of sub-regional economic zones (SRZs). An SRZ crosses national borders, but does not necessarily cover the entire national economies of the countries involved. The paradigm for an SRZ is the Sijori region, covering Singapore, Johor in Malaysia, and the Riau Province of Indonesia. The Pearl River Delta, covering Hong Kong, Macau, and part of Guangdong Province of China, is sometimes seen as an SRZ too. The main feature of these SRZs is their spontaneous emergence. They are market-driven with a clear economic basis in the differences in factor endowments of the constituent parts. Trade liberalization (in Indonesia for Sijori and in China for the Pearl River Delta) was a prerequisite for realization of the gains from specialization within the SRZ, but they were not the result of regional initiatives (Pomfret, 1996a; Toh and Low, 1993).

In the mid-1990s some Asian political leaders were promoting SRZs as an attractive form of regional development. Malaysia in particular was the driving force behind the Northern Triangle and the East ASEAN Growth Area. Neither of these would-be SRZs, however, have shown the dynamism of the regions centred on Singapore and Hong Kong. The project sponsored by the United Nations Development Programme to stimulate regional integration in the Tumen River area, where China, Korea, and Russia meet, has also had little impact (Pomfret, 1996c, 130–42).

In the Preface to a collection of studies sponsored by the Asian Development Bank, the Bank's president described these growth triangles as 'a unique Asian solution to the operational problems of regional co-operation among countries at different stages of economic development and with different social and economic systems' (Thant *et al.*, 1994, xi). There is, however, nothing intrinsically Asian about the Pearl River Delta and Sijori triangles, which resemble the metropolitan spillover and cross-border specialization involving, for example, Tijuana and San Diego or El Paso and Ciudad Juarez.[10]

The SRZ concept highlights the distinction between regionalism and regionalization (Chapter 1). The Asian SRZs have been market-driven and reflect the tendency towards agglomeration in economic activity. Such agglomeration effects can be strong enough to overcome the barriers associated with national boundaries, and their impact will be strengthened by the reduction of trade barriers. They do not, however, have to do intrinsically with preferential tariff reduction. Within a customs union there will be counteracting centrifugal and centripetal forces whose net effect will depend on specific circumstances.

5. Does Distance Matter?

The theory dealt with in this part of the book has undergone subtle name changes during the second half of the twentieth century. Following Viner (1950), it was referred to as 'customs union theory', and the trade deflection analysis indicated that this was an appropriate characterization of all arrangements aimed at internal free trade. During the 1980s broader names were used, reflecting the spread of discriminatory trade practices such as VERs in response to growing protectionist pressures during the 1970s. In the 1990s economists' attention returned to arrangements with internal free trade, but now under the name of 'regional trading arrangements' or 'regional integration'. The emphasis on regional integration (as in the titles of the 1993 volumes edited by Anderson and Blackhurst and by de Melo and Panagariya) partly reflects the growth in importance of the new areas analysed in the previous chapter, but it also reflects a focus on geographical proximity as a characteristic of the trade arrangements being analysed.

[10] Hanson (1996) found a statistically significant relationship between 1975–89 manufactured export growth in six Mexican cities bordering the USA (Tijuana, Mexicali, Matamoros, Ciudad Juarez, Nuevo Laredo, and Reynosa) and growth in their US counterparts (San Diego, Imperial, Brownsville, El Paso, Laredo, and McAllen); a 10% increase in export manufacturing in the Mexican town was associated with a 2.4–4.9% increase in manufacturing employment in its US counterpart. Since this export growth was based on liberalization of US import restrictions, Hanson expects the process to accelerate after the implementation of NAFTA.

Is distance an important consideration in economic transactions, and if so why? Amelung (1990), Petri (1993) and Lorenz (1995) have emphasized the role of transaction costs in recent regionalization of world trade. This is paradoxical in so far as transport and communication costs have been in decline over the last two centuries. Krugman (1995c) argues that the post-1945 boom in international trade has had little to do with technical innovations and much to do with trade policy changes. Drysdale and Garnaut (1993), broadening the concept of transaction costs, see regionalization as a means to reduce 'objective and subjective resistances to trade', in which they include considerations like investment codes, rule harmonization, and so forth. The subjective resistances to trade include the general perception that closer markets are easier for suppliers to deal with.

Despite low transport costs and the rather vague alternative theoretical justifications for considering distance important, distance is still a strong explicator of the volume of bilateral trade flows, even though it is largely ignored in trade theory (Leamer and Levinsohn, 1995). In the gravity model of trade flows developed by Linnemann (1966), trade between two countries i and j depends upon the size of the two economies, measured by total output (Y), and the distance between them (d):

$$\text{Trade }(i,j) = f(Y_i, Y_j, d).$$

The specification is usually in logarithms and the Y variables may be decomposed into per capita output and population. There are measurement issues associated with both sets of independent variables; should Y be measured at market prices or in purchasing power parity prices, and what points should be used to measure distance between geographically large countries? Nevertheless, the gravity model does produce estimates of bilateral trade flows which satisfy usual statistical significance criteria.[11]

The gravity model has been applied to the empirical evaluation of GDAs by adding a dummy variable for the presence of

[11] J. Anderson (1979) and Bergstrand (1985; 1989) provide some theoretical justifications for the gravity equation. Thursby and Thursby (1987), C. Hamilton and Winters (1992), Oguledo and Macphee (1994), and Hellvin (1994, 35) are some of the many studies finding a negative relationship between distance and bilateral trade volumes.

a preferential trading arrangement between *i* and *j*. The problem with this procedure is that the GDA dummy picks up all residual effects not explained by relative size and distance. Wei and Frankel (1995) try to decontaminate the residual by including separate variables for a common language and for shared borders, both of which turn out to be significant. Bayoumi and Eichengreen (1995) work with first differences rather than levels for the trade and *Y* variables, so that their results will not be contaminated by heterogeneity across countries that is constant over time. These are both plausible procedures, but the difficulty in assessing the results of the studies is that they are strongly contradictory on some points, and yield implausible findings on others. Both studies examine the second enlargment of the EU (to include Greece, Portugal, and Spain); Bayoumi and Eichengreen (1995, 23) find 'no evidence of trade diversion', while Wei and Frankel (1995, 16) find 'massive trade diversion due to membership expansion'. Among the implausible results is the finding that Iceland's accesion to EFTA in 1970 was associated with a 24 per cent drop in EFTA's imports from non-members (Wei and Frankel, 1995, 16). There are clearly shortcomings in using this residual approach to assessing the impact of GDAs on trade flows, which may be ascribed to omitted variables (e.g. the trade policies of third countries or multilateral trade liberalization) or may cast doubt on the gravity equation itself.

The importance of the distance variable has been stressed on the basis of even simpler specifications. Leamer and Levinsohn (1995, 1385) plot a scatter diagram of West German trade in 1985, which shows a strong negative correlation between distance and Germany's bilateral trade divided by the partner's GDP. Casual observation suggests that Leamer's sample is bifurcated, with the purported correlation holding for trading partners within 4000 miles of Germany, but a more random scatter for more distant trading partners. Leamer's German result can be replicated in a similar diagram for 1993, but carrying out the exercise for China and Japan produces a poorer fit with some outliers; Hong Kong and Taiwan lie well above the regression line for China, while some Southeast Asian countries are above the Japanese regression line. These admittedly casual observations suggest that distance in itself is not decisive, but some degree of proximity does matter.

Firms tend to supply local markets initially and then gradually broaden their horizons; at any stage in this expansion, firms seem likely to distinguish between a home market in which they are actively competing and distant markets which they supply more passively by offering their product at a certain price. As with the agglomeration effects analysed in the previous section, the market effect contrasts with the trade patterns predicted by neoclassical trade theory, which are independent of distance. The market effects, however, are more complex. The concept of 'home' and 'distant' markets applies within national economies (e.g. a New York firm is more likely to sell its goods in New Jersey than in Texas) and may cross national borders. (For example, New England or Michigan firms may view Ontario as more a part of their home market than Texas, and yet consider California more a part of their home market than equidistant parts of Mexico.) Similarities of language, culture, and tastes play a role, although they are difficult to measure precisely and may be correlated with economic variables such as income. The difference between European and non-European patterns in Leamer's German exercise or the strong connections between the economies of China, Hong Kong, and Taiwan are examples of a distance variable also picking up shared culture. The relative weights of home and distant markets will vary across industries; many of the labour-intensive industries of the high-performing Asian economies have been oriented almost exclusively to distant export markets from the start, while other activities, such as some prepared foods or traded services, tend to be highly localized.

The distinction between home and distant markets seems to be multilevelled, with the national market representing one stage and a wider regional market a second stage. McCallum (1995) has shown that for Canadians the domestic market precedence is very strong, despite the linguistic and cultural similarities of adjacent markets in the USA. Using provincial data from the 1988 input–output table, he estimated a gravity equation for Canadian provinces and US states and found that intra-provincial trade was twenty times larger than predicted on the basis of incomes and distance. Ontario, for example, in trading with the west coast exported more than three times as much to British Columbia as it did to California, whose population is ten times that of BC and where per capita income is also higher. Thus, although CUSTA and NAFTA may stimulate US–Canadian trade, there is still a long way to go before all subjective resistances to international trade between the USA and Canada have been overcome.[12]

Although McCallum's work provides strong evidence of home market bias, it offers no insight into why that bias is so strong. Trefler (1995) simply writes such a bias into preference functions, but that does not help understanding and seems implausible as an explanation of the Canadian results (or for other countries in view of the typically poor response to 'buy national' campaigns). This unanswered question is central to understanding the extent to which deep integration measures will turn intra-regional trade into something more like domestic trade.

6. Conclusions

This chapter deals with fuzzy issues, ranging from abstract theories of the optimum number of trading blocs or optimal size of the state, which are far removed from the real world, to the literature on sub-regional economic zones and gravity equations, which is driven by observation of the real world and is largely atheoretical. The unifying theme of the chapter is an attempt to determine the basic unit in analysing the world economy and the role that geography plays. In neoclassical trade theory the nation state is the unit of analysis, but it is conceived as a point, and the distance between points is irrelevant to the explanation of trade patterns or to the gains from trdae. The new trade theory of the 1980s modified this analysis by introducing scale economies and imperfect competition, but it did not change the geographic aspects of the analytical framework.

The significance of the nation state for economic analysis has been challenged by the increasingly federal nature of the EU, and to a lesser extent by the changing national boundaries of Eastern Europe and the former USSR. The old argument in favour of

[12] Helliwell (1996) has confirmed McCallum's findings with data from 1988–94. Wei (1996) finds a similar home bias for OECD countries, although the bias has declined slowly but steadily between 1982 and 1994. Wei's study is pioneering but also more problematic than the Canadian studies because he has to construct a domestic trade counterpart (which he calls the goods part of GDP) to the available trade data rather than observing internal trade directly.

focusing on the nation state was the break in regulatory regimes, factor mobility, and goods mobility which national frontiers represent. With falling trade barriers, more efficient international capital markets, and lower transport costs, goods and factors are increasingly mobile, and with increased globalization regulatory peculiarities often become anachronistic and are reduced. Thus, man-made breaks in the spatial dimensions of economic transactions are less, and geographical considerations become more significant.

How does geography matter? Urbanization is an obvious feature of the modern world, implying that agglomeration economies are powerful. These occur mainly within the nation state, but the SRZs centred on Singapore and Hong Kong indicate that their impact can cross national frontiers. More amorphously, there are the horizon effects analyzed in the previous section of this chapter, which suggest that most suppliers do not have a global vision but do see their market as spreading out from their home base (but not necessarily coterminous with their country). Transport costs do not seem to be a critical consideration, apart from a few specific cases (notably land-locked countries such as Armenia or Chad); and, especially for long-distance trade, unit costs per additional kilometre are effectively zero (which is convenient, because this theoretical part of the book has almost totally ignored transport costs by assumption).

PART III

EMPIRICAL EVIDENCE

Introduction to Part III

Measurement is important because the theoretical results are ambiguous. Therefore we need to have some idea of the relative magnitude of the various effects, and what these magnitudes depend upon.

The various empirical methods have their strengths and weaknesses. If these shortcomings are recognized, we can draw some general conclusions, especially if various methods consistently lead to similar conclusions.

The main distinction in the empirical literature is between *ex ante* and *ex post* estimates. In principle it should not matter whether the work is done before or after the GDA comes into operation: what is required is a trade model which can predict the level of exports and imports with and without the GDA. A major problem with both *ex ante* and *ex post* studies is our lack of empirical knowledge of σ, the elasticity of substitution between goods from different sources.

Partial equilibrium *ex ante* models (based on Fig. 8.1) have relatively simple data requirements, i.e. knowledge of actual trade flows and of demand and supply elasticities (some of which may be assumed to be infinite). They cannot, however, deal with general equilibrium effects via factor markets or the exchange rate or with the dynamic effects on factor accumulation and technical efficiency. General equilibrium *ex ante* models can avoid these drawbacks, but are limited by the simple structure and aggregation levels which are needed for tractability. The data requirements are also greater, and applied general equilibrium models almost all resort to the Armington assumption that σ is the same for all pairs of import suppliers (and often assume $\sigma = 2$). Computable general equilibrium models can highlight potential effects ignored by partial equilibrium models, but it is often hard to trace why a particular CGE model yields a specific result or to test the model against independent data; without transparency or independent testing it is difficult to decide which CGE models deserve most serious consideration.

The simplest *ex post* method is to use trade shares to make before/after comparisons. This can provide a very rough guide, but assuming that all changes in shares are due to the GDA being examined is often implausible. A more sophisticated counterfactual can be obtained from running regressions with a dummy for the GDA, although these can be only as good as the specification and data, and usually assume that the impact of a GDA on trade is instantaneous. The gravity model is the most frequently used approach to establishing the counterfactual, but the theoretical foundations of this class of trade models are unclear. None of these approaches to *ex post* measurement provides a guide to the welfare consequences of trade policies.

These methods all deal with the direct trade effects of GDAs. Some empirical workers have tried to incorporate wider aspects of GDAs (shifting supply curves, scale economies, etc.), although the lack of a firm theoretical basis has not produced a strong corpus of empirical literature. Even in the most studied cases (the EU and GSP), research on the economic consequences has mainly been limited to estimating the effects on trade. More sophisticated studies aim to make at least the distinction between trade creation and trade diversion, but without focusing on prices they cannot capture the welfare effects; if welfare effects are referred to, it is typically in the form of assuming trade creation to be good and trade diversion bad. As a rule of thumb this is valid, but in practice empirical work on both the EU and GSP has understated the importance of trade diversion. In consequence, since both of these GDAs involve positive discrimination, the empirical literature has tended to be favourable towards GDAs as welfare-improving over the status quo and not so inferior to the first-best policy of free trade.

The survey in this third part makes no claim to being exhaustive. There is a huge literature, from the descriptive institutional to the abstractly analytical, on a large variety of discriminatory trade arrangements, and without background knowledge of each arrangement it is difficult to assess all the studies. Priority will be given to studies using analytical techniques (rather than pure description, opinion surveys, etc.), although I shall argue that all of these are fundamentally flawed by lack of knowledge about plausible values for σ, the elasticity of substitution between imports from different sources. To be sure, knowing σ for all pairs of import suppliers is a huge requirement, but we do not in fact have good estimates of σ for *any* pair of import suppliers to any importing nation, and, when evaluating arrangements that discriminate among trading partners, σ is a crucial parameter without whose knowledge the trade effects of GDAs can be only roughly guessed.

Despite these weaknesses, the empirical work is rooted in reality and a recurring finding is that GDAs can have an economic impact, which provides a starting point for explaining their proliferation. Trade patterns have been affected by GDAs, sometimes dramatically so (as in various Imperial Preference schemes, the CMEA, or for EFTA in the 1960s). Less direct impact on capital flows or technical efficiency is also evident in some cases, but this evidence is weaker than that for trade effects. Evidence on the welfare effects of GDAs is difficult to assess, but the optimistic assessments are often based on blueprints for GDAs, while studies taking into account the restrictions contained in the GDAs as actually implemented have less positive conclusions.

12

Western European Integration

The customs union among the six original members of the European Community is undoubtedly the most studied preferential trading arrangement. It is a difficult case because the customs union was introduced over several years and involved 'large' trading partners. By its volume, and perhaps through its difficulty, the EC literature illustrates the major methodological issues that have arisen in empirical work on GDAs. For the same reasons, however, the EC literature does not yield strong conclusions with a firm basis.

The European Free Trade Association is less important in the world economy than the EU, but empirical work on EFTA has yielded some strong results. The EFTA countries, apart from Britain, which exited from EFTA at the end of 1972, have had asymmetrical trade patterns; a high share of their trade is with the EU, but they are of little importance in the trade of any EU member. Thus, EFTA sheds light on the impact of preferential trading arrangements on excluded but concerned countries.

The enlargements of the EC are examined in Section 3. They also involve problems in identifying the counterfactual situation. The 1973 enlargement coincided with a period of instability in the world economy. The enlargement of the 1980s involved long transition periods, e.g. up to a decade for Spanish fruit and vegetables to gain full access to other EC markets. Nevertheless, the economic consequences, at least in terms of the impact on allocative efficiency, are fairly consistent. As a price for expanding the European Union, existing and new members have accepted probably negative net welfare effects (mainly because of the spreading impact of the CAP), which have in part been passed on to non-members. This is not true for applicants whose agricultural policies were even more restrictive than the CAP, e.g. Finland, Norway, and Switzerland; in the last two, however, membership was rejected by voters.

Section 4 reviews the literature on the EC's 1992 programme. One distinguishing feature of this debate was the publication of a weighty set of *ex ante* studies sponsored by the European Commission. Subsequent independent studies almost all found much smaller effects than those claimed by the 'official' estimates, but, because the EC92 programme involved NTBs and regulatory integration, which are difficult to quantify, there is considerable scope for disagreement over estimated effects.

1. The EC Customs Union

In one of the earliest empirical studies of regional integration, Johnson (1958b) used partial equilibrium models in the spirit of Fig. 8.1 to estimate the gains to Britain from membership in a European free trade area. This approach provided welfare estimates for the UK, but could not separate trade creation from trade diversion. To estimate trade diversion, it is necessary either to drop the simplifying assumption of perfectly elastic supply or to assume non-homogeneous goods with finite substitution elasticities between different suppliers. Both solutions involve large additional data requirements. Verdoorn (1960) adopted the second approach in a study of the Benelux customs union, and, following a suggestion by Johnson (1964, 23–4), Krause (1968, 49–53) used the 'Dutch' model to estimate the loss to non-members from the EC's customs union. In both of these studies the value of σ, the elasticity of substitution, was assumed to be 2.[1]

With respect to the central trade issue of European integration, i.e. the impact of the EC customs union, the *ex ante* approach has not been popular. The data requirements described in the previous paragraph are one reason for this. A second reason was the publicity given to the dynamic effects—even Verdoorn (1960, 298) refers to the promotional impact of a customs union treaty, while Scitovsky (1958) and Balassa (1961) concentrated on parameter shifts arising from West European integration. Methods based on pre-EC parameter values would clearly understate the

[1] The differentiated products model is spelled out more fully by Janssen (1961). In his 1964 review article, Johnson clearly believed trade diversion to be a substantial cost to the USA from the EC customs union (implying high values of σ), but he made no comment on the $\sigma = 2$ assumption. He also pointed out the drawbacks of assuming supply elasticities of infinity and of ignoring general equilibrium aspects, as both Verdoorn's and Krause's estimates did. Krause did conduct sensitivity analyses for various σ values (1968, 250–2), but made no attempt to assess their plausibility.

EC's impact if the dynamic effects were significant. A third reason for the paucity of *ex ante* studies was the lack of operational general equilibrium models; for a customs union among four fairly open trading units, having large shares of their trade with one another and significant world market shares, a partial equilibrium approach with 'small' country price assumptions was unattractive. Thus, despite the early work of Johnson, Verdoorn, and Krause, the dominant approach to estimating the trade effects of the EC customs union has been *ex post*.

Ex post methods face the fundamental problem of determining trade flows in the absence of the customs union, i.e. they also require a trade model. This requirement may be hidden by a few sweeping assumptions, but all this does is to substitute a simple implicit model for an explicit one. At first sight *ex post* estimation has more available data, i.e. both from before and after the GDA, not just from before it; but, since the true comparison is between with and without the GDA, estimates always involve comparing one actual situation with one hypothetical situation. The crudest *ex post* analysis, by making a simple before and after comparison, is valid only if no other contemporaneous changes affected trade flows. In the case of the EC customs union, which was not completed until over a decade after the Rome Treaty (and this was a decade of global trade liberalization and expansion),[2] simple before/after comparisons are clearly inappropriate.

The earliest *ex post* analyses of the EC customs union used simple trade share measures to identify an impact (e.g. Krause, 1963; Verdoorn and Meyer zu Schlochtern, 1964). The assumption that market shares would have been unchanged in the EC's absence is a strong one, and the simple shares approach cannot identify trade creation and trade diversion. Truman (1969) and Prewo (1974) make the most sophisticated shares analyses; by taking shares in apparent consumption, Truman could separate trade creation from trade diversion, while Prewo extended the analysis into an input–output framework. An alternative approach to specifying the hypothetical no-EC situation is to use a control

[2] Implementation of the customs union did not begin immediately after the signing of the Rome Treaty, but economic agents seem to have anticipated the intra-EC trade liberalization and Aitken (1973) found its impact in the annual data as early as 1958. The process of removing tariffs on internal trade among the Six and establishing the common external tariff was completed by July 1968.

group of non-members to represent the Six's experience without the customs union; for example, Kreinin (1972) used the USA and UK as controls, while Williamson and Bottrill (1971) and Verdoorn and Schwartz (1972) used the rest of the world. Balassa (1967; 1975) simulated EC import growth in the absence of the customs union by assuming constant gross income elasticities, which is a neat way of allowing for differing demand conditions but neglects the supply side. Others (e.g. Aitken, 1973; Verdoorn and Schwarts, 1972) have used a gravity model. The weakness of all of these *ex post* methods is that the trade effects of the customs union are calculated as a residual, so it is difficult to evaluate how good the simplifying assumptions are and how much non-EC-related trade effects are picked up in the residual.

The empirical literature on the EC has been surveyed by Verdoorn and van Bochove (1972), Balassa (1975, 79–118), Mayes (1978), and Robson (1984, 192–203). Several of these commentators are critical of the *ex post* methods, but the last three surveys all draw comfort from the similarity of the estimated trade effects which emerge under a range of differing assumptions. For example, Robson concludes that:

> Although there must be a wide range of uncertainty, collectively the available evidence does suggest certain general conclusions and perhaps also enables the relative order of magnitude to be established with reasonable confidence. (Robson, 1984, 200)

The general conclusions are twofold. First,

> for manufactured products (to which most of the studies are limited) the trade created was considerable and far outweighed trade diverted ... Secondly, several of the studies suggest that the formation of the EEC has resulted in a good deal of external trade creation. From both points of view it may be concluded that the effects of the EEC have been favourable to allocative efficiency at a global level. (Robson, 1984, 200)

This positive assessment is shared by the other surveys and in individual studies.[3]

There are reasons for doubting both of Robson's general conclusions. Although most of the trade creation estimates do bunch

[3] e.g. Kreinin (1972, 918) concludes that, whatever the precise magnitude of the dynamic and external trade creation effects, 'the static estimates themselves leave little doubt that the establishment of the EEC was on balance favorable to world efficiency'.

within a range of $8–$11 billion a year on a 1967–70 base, there are variations; e.g. those of Prewo (1974) are ten times higher than those of Resnick and Truman (1974).[4] Thus, the 'considerable' trade creation is not firmly established, and whether it 'far outweighed' trade diversion depends crucially upon what happened in agricultural trade. The EC's Common Agricultural Policy was explicitly designed to keep the least productive EC farmer in business; i.e. trade creation is ruled out. On the other hand, there has been substantial trade diversion as EC products have replaced extra-EC imports, although there are no firm estimates. So far as the external trade creation is concerned, Robson's assessment rests entirely on the estimates of Prewo and Truman—all the other estimates indicate a negative impact on non-members. If the logic of emphasizing the bunched estimates of trade creation is to be pursued, then the conclusion about external trade creation cannot be maintained. In sum, it is not obvious from a consensus of the empirical studies whether the volume of trade created outweighed that of trade diverted, whether there was any external trade creation by which non-members benefited from the increased EC market size, or whether the customs union among the original EC members improved global allocative efficiency.

The only attempt to go beyond the trade effects and estimate the EC's impact on allocative efficiency, or 'welfare effects', is a rough calculation by Balassa (1975, 115).[5] Balassa assumed an average EC tariff rate of 12 per cent on manufactured products and used his own trade creation estimates of $11.4 billion for 1970 to calculate an annual welfare gain of $0.7 billion (i.e. one-half of 11.4 multiplied by 0.12), or 0.15 per cent of Community GNP. Against this he estimated trade diversion in agricultural products to be $1.3–$1.75 billion, which with an average tariff of

[4] The three surveys understate this variance by not giving all estimates in their summary tables or, in the case of Mayes, using a scatter diagram dominated by many observations from a single study. Nevertheless, even in Robson's table 12.5, the trade created in manufactures varies from $2.5 billion to $18.0 billion.

[5] Scitovsky (1958, 64–7) refers to earlier calculations by Verdoorn which also yielded small welfare effects (less than 0.05% of the Six's GNP). Given the height of pre-EC tariffs, any reasonable import demand elasticities are bound to give small estimated welfare effects when the standard welfare triangles formula is used. One reason for the unpopularity of this model in the EC context seems to be the *a priori* belief that the EC must have had a bigger allocative effect than a fraction of 1% of gross Community product. Scitovsky calls Verdoorn's estimates 'ridiculously small' (1958, 67).

47 per cent implied an annual welfare loss of $0.3–$0.4 billion. Thus, Balassa's estimates of the net welfare effect of the EC customs union are equal to less than 0.1 per cent of the members' GNP. These are, of course, rough estimates and they may be underestimates, e.g. because the welfare cost of trade diversion depends upon the difference between the external and internal least-cost suppliers' prices, which may be less than half the tariff.

Balassa's figure is more likely to overestimate the static welfare gains from the EC customs union, especially as it evolved after the 1960s (Pomfret, 1986e). First, although the tariff equivalent of the product-specific import barriers under the Common Agricultural Policy varies from year to year, there was an upward trend during the 1970s and early 1980s. (For example, Eurostat data quoted by Moore (1985, 77) give tariff equivalents on the major grains of 100 per cent, on sugar 200 per cent, and on butter over 500 per cent). Secondly, the EC trade regime became more protective on certain manufactured products after the early 1970s; in particular, textile and clothing restrictions under the Multifibre Arrangement and voluntary export restraints on cars and steel involved trade diversion as, for example, Italian clothing or French automobiles replaced Asian imports in British and German markets. Both the application of the CAP to new members and the MFA involved trade destruction as well as trade diversion.

In sum, the static welfare gains from the EC customs union, measured by the standard 'Corden triangles' approach, are very small and, if my points about the underestimation of trade diversion and the trade destruction in the 1970s and 1980s are accepted, may well be negative.

Balassa's calculated static welfare effects of the EC customs union are something of a hybrid. The trade effects are estimated by an *ex post* method and then plugged back into the standard partial equilibrium international trade model, which was rejected as the basis for making estimates of the trade effects because it ignored dynamic and general equilibrium aspects. How important are these aspects? Balassa (1961), Scitovsky (1958), and others have argued that they are likely to be the main source of economic gain from the EC customs union. There has, however, been little systematic work on the magnitude of the scale economy, *X*-efficiency, or induced factor flow effects of the original EC customs union.

On scale economies, the most ambitious empirical work before the mid-1980s is contained in two studies by Owen. His econometric analysis of bilateral trade flows among France, Germany, and Italy found that net exports of manufactured goods in 1964 were 'partially explained by the differing extents to which industries exploited plant economies' (Owen, 1976, 156). This has frequently been quoted as evidence that scale economies played a part in the growth of intra-EC trade, but Owen himself admits that the explanatory power of his best-fit equation is not high, which he explains by the observation that 'in most industries scale economies are quite modest'.[6] Owen (1983) provides microeconomic evidence of scale economies in three sectors of the EC economy: cars, trucks, and white goods (i.e. household durables such as refrigerators). He extrapolated from these sectors to estimate that, if similar scale economies existed in three-quarters of European industry, then the trade creation estimates for the EC customs union should be \$40–\$96 billion rather than the \$8–\$11 billion found in studies ignoring scale economies. Caves (1985), however, has raised two critical objections to this exercise. First, while Owen demonstrates the existence of scale economies, he does not establish a causal link to trade liberalization. Secondly, Owen's three sectors are unlikely to be typical because (a) realization of scale economies was contemporaneous with sector-specific technical change, and (b) the technical opportunities for scale economies are likely to be greater, and the product differentiation limitations on their exploitation smaller, than in other sectors. In sum, the available evidence shows that increased scale economies were realized in some EC sectors after the establishment of the customs union, but gives little indication of a causal relationship or of the magnitude of any allocative efficiency gains.

The effect of the EC customs union in reducing *X*-inefficiency through increased competition is often emphasized in political debate, but is very difficult to pin down in practice. Scitovsky

[6] Owen reports 32 equations with differing independent variables, and it is unclear which he regards as the best fit. Of the equations containing his preferred plant economies variable and no firm-size variable (which introduces multicollinearity), only one has an R^2 over 0.2, and in that case the plant economy variable is not significant at the 10% level. In all 32 equations none has an R^2, apparently unadjusted, greater than 0.4, and Owen's modesty about the results seems fully justified.

(1958, ch. 3) discussed the 'soft' competition in many West European national markets, and Pelkmans's (1984) survey of progress towards market integration suggested that the broad picture may not have changed much, at least prior to the launch of the 1992 programme. The cold gale of competition expected by many observers often proved to be no more than a gentle breeze. Either by using non-tariff barriers (e.g. standards or government procurement practices) or by agreement among oligopolists, national markets remained segmented for many industrial goods and *X*-efficiency is unlikely to have increased much under these conditions. Jacquemin and Sapir (1991) conclude that EC firms' price–cost mark-ups are constrained by imports from outside the EC but not by intra-EC competition. There is even less incentive for reducing *X*-efficiency in agriculture, and in some member states the Common Agricultural Policy may permit greater inefficiency than did the pre-EC national policies.

The role of the EC customs union in attracting foreign investment has been controversial. The incentive to locate within the EC in order to supply the whole customs union is clearly greater than the earlier incentive to locate within a member state to avoid only the national tariff and supply only the national market. Early empirical studies were, however, inconclusive in establishing a response to this incentive. Scaperlanda and Balough (1983), using superior output and tariff discrimination variables and a longer time series than earlier studies, found a statistically significant relationship between intra-EC trade liberalization and direct investment there by American corporations.[7] The rightward shift in the aggregate supply curve should raise material welfare in the EC, but it may hurt non-members and lower global welfare if the capital is diverted from its world-output-maximizing location.[8]

The EC has been concerned about the spatial effects of policies on the distribution of economic activity and income within Western Europe. Molle (1990) has marshalled evidence that regional

[7] De Melo *et al.* (1993, 185–6) in a cross-country regression exercise also found a positive effect of the EEC on investment in 1960–72, although they found no evidence of a direct impact on economic growth.

[8] Kreinin (1964, 195) sees investment diversion as the main unfavourable impact on the USA from the EC customs union, although he offers no empirical support for this position.

disparities have been reduced since the formation of the customs union.[9] The relative causal importance of freer internal trade, redistributive polices such as the EC's social and regional funds, and other forces is unclear. The explicit redistributive mechanisms became important tools for maintaining political solidarity among member states in the 1980s and 1990s. In 1980 11 per cent of the EC's budget was spent on structural, regional, and social policies; by 1994 this share had increased to around 30 per cent. The size of the transfers is small compared with relevant EU macroeconomic aggregates so that their impact is unlikely to have been large for the EU as a whole, but transfers have been important for the four poorest members, Greece, Ireland, Portugal, and Spain—for Portugal, EU transfers amounted to 3.5 per cent of GNP in the early 1990s.

Distributional effects between the EC and the rest of the world are more controversial. Although it is widely agreed that the EC customs union has involved terms of trade effects, there are few estimates of their magnitude. Verdoorn predicted a terms of trade gain for the original EC members over six times as large as the static welfare gains from the customs union (quoted by Scitovsky, 1958, 66), although Scitovsky pointed out this would still not be a large magnitude. Petith (1977), using a model in which each country produces a composite product (based on Mundell, 1964), estimated the value of terms of trade improvements to be between 0.3 and 1.0 per cent of the Six's GNP. Such a model necessarily makes strong simplifying assumptions and the precise estimates are sensitive to the elasticities used, but the results are suggestive of substantial welfare transfers from non-members.[10]

More specifically, Sampson and Snape (1980) have illustrated how the EC's variable levies on agricultural products lower world prices and enable the EC to capture both the economic rent from

[9] Ben-David (1993) presents evidence of strong convergence of national per capita incomes among the original six EC members since the early 1950s, but does not find convergence among the EFTA countries or for the three countries joining the EC in 1973.

[10] Verdoon's estimated static welfare gains were less than 0.05% of GNP (see fn. 5 above), so his 'six times' guess is at the bottom end of Petith's estimated range. Whether this is large or small is a judgement call, but I disagree with Scitovsky; even 0.3% of EC, GNP would be a substantial transfer from non-members (e.g. that share is about the same as total official development aid from EU members).

their own trade restrictions and the agricultural subsidies by their foreign food suppliers; they claim that in 1976 'a significant portion' of the $1.6 billion variable levy revenue on wheat, barley, and maize was a transfer from agricultural exporting countries to the EC. Again, the precise numbers are uncertain, but Sampson and Snape's postulated welfare transfers on just three agricultural products are in the same range as Balassa's estimated static welfare gains on all manufactured products.

A final question concerns the impact of the EC on global trade negotiations. Hufbauer ('An Overview' in Hufbauer, 1990) and Lawrence (1991) have argued that formation of the EC was a catalyst to the great multilateral trade liberalization of the 1960s; the USA was moved to the negotiating table by concerns over the trade diversion impact of an EC with high external tariffs, while the Six were better able to negotiate as a coherent group with liberal goals than if they had retained individual bargaining positions. This argument is really difficult to assess because the conjuncture of the long boom and the prospect of GATT negotiations after the re-establishment of currency convertibility in Western Europe represented a unique setting for which the counterfactual of separate national negotiating positions is hard to establish.

Winters (1993a; 1994) has expressed scepticism about the EC's positive impact on multilateral trade negotiations, especially since the 1960s. He emphasizes the obsession with intra-trade as a guide to integration, and aspects of internal bargaining. During the 1960s and early 1970s the share of intra-trade in the Six's total trade increased, and the EC was self-confident in its external trade policy. When the share of intra-trade in the EC's trade in manufactures began a steady decline in the late 1970s, however, this was interpreted as being due to lack of competitiveness, which was addressed by introducing contingent protection in the form of anti-dumping and countervailing duties.[11] The intra-share of EC agricultural trade has grown more continuously as a result of

[11] Winters argues that the AD and CVD actions by sheltering EC producers led to their falling further behind the technological standards of competitors in North America or Asia, increasing resistance to trade liberalization still further. Sapir (1993, 231–2) strongly disagrees with Winters's conclusions and argues that the EC has been a force for global trade liberalization, a point also made in Sapir (1992). The interchange highlights the difficulty of judging between two opposite interpretations on this issue.

the CAP, but with obvious costs to external agricultural exporters. Winters argues that two aspects of EC internal bargaining, universalism and the restaurant bill problem,[12] have exaggerated the EC's negative stance on agriculture in multilateral trade negotiations. If a few EC members find themselves outnumbered on a general policy issue, such as opposition to extension of CAP coverage, it is easier to lobby for inclusion of items of special interest to them than to fight a losing battle on principle. Moreover, because the costs of CAP support programmes are paid out of the EC's general budget but the benefits go to farmers of specific commodities, there is a free-rider incentive for a single member to lobby for extension of benefits on items that its farmers produce knowing that the costs will be shared among the EC membership.

Has the EC been a 'good thing'? The answer goes well beyond economics, but economists should at least be able to assess the customs union's impact on material well-being. The presumption has been of a beneficial effect, but the situation is not so clear-cut and depends critically on the hypothetical no-EC situation. If liberalization of international trade in manufactures had proceeded at the same pace (or, conceivably, even faster) within the GATT in the absence of an EC, then the welfare gains from the customs union are likely to be small. Meanwhile, even if the hypothetical national agricultural policies were as restrictive as the Common Agricultural Policy (which is difficult to believe for all EC members), the negative welfare effects of CAP-induced trade diversion would still be substantial. There is no empirical evidence that additional scale economies or *X*-efficiency gains resulted from the customs union. Landau (1995), based on cross-country regressions with Summers–Heston 1950–90 data for seventeen OECD countries, concludes from an insignificant EC dummy that the EC made no significant contribution to EC members' economic growth. There is some evidence that the EC benefited from additional direct foreign investment and especially from terms of trade gains, but both of these involve redistribution

[12] The restaurant bill problem arises when a group of diners agree to share the bill equally, thus giving each diner an incentive to order expensive dishes. Whether that is in fact the outcome depends upon whom you dine with; some people observe norms which prevent them from being gluttons just because they are not paying the full cost of their dishes.

rather than net gains to the world. In sum, the EC customs union seems to have involved small (and perhaps even negative) static welfare gains, possible but unproven dynamic benefits, and a welfare transfer from non-members.

2. The European Free Trade Association

Establishment of the European Free Trade Association was followed by reorientation of EFTA members' trade away from the EC Six during the 1960s; this reversed itself after 1972 when EFTA and the EC formed a free trade area in manufactured goods. The empirical studies have used *ex post* shares analysis (Price, 1982) or a gravity model (Aitken, 1973), i.e. rather simple specifications, but the results seem robust enough about the direction of change. The changes in shares were stronger with respect to EFTA exports than with respect to EFTA imports, reflecting the relative height of the EC's common external tariff on manufactures and the average EFTA tariff on these goods (7.4 per cent and 4.7 per cent respectively in 1972; EFTA, 1980, 47).

How much of these changes was due to EFTA and how much trade diversion the EFTA members would have experienced from the EC customs union in the absence of EFTA is conjectural. Price (1982) concludes that countries outside Western Europe did not suffer from trade diversion due to EFTA. This fits expectations; because of the large share of EFTA and EC members in EFTA countries' trade in manufactures, the combined impact of EFTA and the EFTA-EC free trade area is likely to be overwhelmingly trade creation. In view of the low MFN tariffs on manufactured goods the net welfare gain is unlikely to be large, but, because the EFTA agreements do not cover agriculture, it should be positive.

EFTA members appear to have shared in the positive impact of Western European integration on investment flows during the 1960s and early 1970s (de Melo *et al.*, 1993, 185–6). On the other hand, as EC integration deepened during the late 1980s, the EFTA countries suffered from some investment diversion (Winters, 1993b, 111).

Much of the academic debate about the impact of EC92 on EFTA focused on the pro-competitive effect of being in an integrated market. Norman (1989) applied the Smith–Venables model to EFTA and the EC and concluded, primarily on the basis of case studies of the automobile and pharmaceutical industries, that Norway and Sweden would lose from being outside the more integrated markets created by EC92 and would gain from being inside those markets if they became members. Haaland (1990) reviews the *ex ante* studies of the impact of EC92 on Norway and Sweden and of the gains from EC membership.

3. EC Enlargement

The three EC enlargement episodes must be seen as extension of the existing regional trade arrangement rather than as formation of a new customs union. Although accession is preceded by negotiations, the existing EC members make no compromise on the application of its fundamental policies as they stand at the time. The applicant must accept the *acquis communautaire*, and the bargaining is over specifics of implementation (such as the transition period in adopting various elements of the *acquis* and the new member's political representation). As the *acquis* expands over time, most notably with the completion of the EC92 programme, the task of accession becomes more strenuous.

In the 1973 enlargement the UK sought access to EC markets for industrial goods (and a place at the decision-making table), while accepting the costs of adopting the CAP; Denmark and Ireland were concerned about the trade diversion costs to them from British CAP membership if they remained outside the EC. These expectations are born out by *ex ante* and *ex post* studies. Trade diversion in agricultural goods dominates estimates of the welfare effects of British membership in the EC. In constrast to the small but positive static welfare effects calculated by Johnson (1958b), all estimates in the 1970s were of negative static welfare effects for Britain.[13] The quantity of trade creation in manufactured

[13] Robson (1984, 206) surveys these estimates. The negative effect is *before* allowing for official transfers, which were also negative. The period after UK accession provided an example of the political use of transfers to assist cohesion; Prime Minister Thatcher achieved considerable publicity for reducing the British budget contribution, assuaging domestic concerns about the cost of EC membership, even though the transfers represented a small cost relative to the loss of consumer surplus resulting from the CAP.

goods turns out to be substantial, but makes little contribution to British welfare because the price change is small. Miller and Spencer (1977) estimate a 50 per cent increase in imports of EC manufactured goods, yet the value of this, the principal benefit to the UK in their analysis, comes to 0.17 per cent of British income.[14] This gain is dwarfed by the loss resulting from the Common Agricultural Policy, with an estimated net welfare loss from EC membership of 1.8 per cent of national income (Miller and Spencer, 1977, 91).[15] The international distributional effects seem to have been that the six original EC members gained and non-members, particularly agricultural exporters, lost.

The second enlargement involved three Mediterranean countries (Greece in 1981 and Portugal and Spain in 1986) which had recently experienced non-democratic governments. The EC's goals included cementing the political and economic reforms undertaken by the post-dictatorship governments. A smaller economy liberalizing its trade with a large economy can expect to reap most of the gains from increased trade, but Greece, Portugal, and Spain each suffered from trade diversion owing to the restrictive nature of the CAP. Plummer has estimated trade diversion in each case, which amounted to less than 1 per cent of total trade but was heavily concentrated in a few agricultural commodities.[16] The EU also suffered from trade diversion, concentrated in a few agricultural and manufactured goods. The accession process was

[14] Winters (1984, 114), on the basis of econometric analysis of British manufactured imports, also concluded 'that accession has led to substantial trade creation' of at least £6 bn per annum by 1979. In his survey of *ex post* studies of UK–EC trade in manufactures, Winters (1987) calculates the static welfare gains from accession to have been roughly £5 per capita.

[15] Grinols (1984), using a Vanek–Kemp general equilibrium framework, also estimated large net welfare losses for the UK, but some of this is due to a simple counterfactual which ascribes all non-oil terms of trade changes to EC membership and thus picks up large 'costs of membership' after the 1973–4 commodity boom and the 1976 sterling devaluation. Although individual models and results are open to criticism, there seems a firm consensus as to the negative economic impact on Britain.

[16] Plummer (1991a) uses control groups to estimate the *ex post* impact of Greek accession, and finds net trade diversion concentrated in agricultural imports for the EC and in manufactured imports for Greece. Plummer (1991b) estimates import demand functions to make *ex ante* calculations of the impact of Portuguese and Spanish accession; the trade diversion is heavily concentrated in both of the new members' grain imports and Spanish tobacco imports (because Spain had to increase its tobacco duties to the EC level) and in the existing members' sugar and cereals imports.

smoothed by the promise of financial transfers, as well as of market access for exports of special importance to the new members.

The special regimes for individual goods appear to have been tailored to favour trade diversion rather than trade creation. Thus, non-member Mediterranean suppliers of agricultural goods expected to lose market share (Pomfret, 1981), while existing EC suppliers were sheltered by a ten-year transition period for free entry of some Spanish fruit and vegetables. Increased internal EC competition in textiles, clothing, and footwear markets arising from the comparative advantage of the new members in labour-intensive activities led to tighter restrictions on external suppliers of such goods (see e.g. Winters, 1993a, 213, on footwear).

Winters's (1992b) work on footwear is one of the most careful sectoral studies of the impact of preferential trading arrangements. He uses a calibrated model, but in running scenarios he is sensitive to the economic characteristics of the industry. Winters calculates that the accession of Greece, Spain, and Portugal to the EC led to both trade creation and trade diversion in footwear, with benefits to consumers throughout the EC and to producers in the new members, but with costs to producers in the nine existing EC members and in non-members. The net welfare effect of enlargement on the EC9 is positive.

Despite the net welfare gains, the distribution of losses led France and Italy (the two EC9 countries for which footwear accounted for over 1 per cent of industrial employment), to react in 1988 by imposing bilateral quotas and negotiating VERs with Taiwan and South Korea. The French and Italian quantitative restrictions reduced EC welfare; consumers lost and producers gained—not just in the protected national markets, but throughout the EC owing to the changed competitive conditions. In 1990 the bilateral quotas were replaced by an EC-wide quota, which was roughly as restrictive as the bilaterals but led to a redistribution of the costs of protection; EC consumers outside France and Italy suffered, while EC producers (apart from French producers) benefited from the EC-wide protection. Replacing national by EC-wide quotas led to a slight decline in total welfare of the EC12 and an increase in the quota rents going to Taiwan and South Korea.

Winters's results illustrate one of the fears of opponents of regionalism; if a RTA yields economic benefits through trade creation, then insider producers may try to offset the rise in internal competition by seeking protection against outsiders. The reaction of the French and Italian shoemakers to the EC enlargement of the 1980s was to lobby their national governments for protection from the main external suppliers, and they were successful despite the EC climate in which national trade policies were supposed to be a thing of the past. The distributional impact of subsequently making the trade barrier EC-wide is industry-specific, but Winters's result that Italian producers, the biggest EC exporters of footwear, gain most is plausible. Most striking of all, however, is the manner in which an initial change, which benefits consumers and yields a net welfare gain to the EC, is turned into a situation in which almost all producers benefit and consumers lose; footwear consumers in the EC9 end up worse off than before the accession to the EC of three low-cost footwear suppliers!

Generalizations are, however, difficult. Spanish accession increased the internal lobby for protection of the toy industry. Initial support from the other major EU producing country, Germany, was subsequently withdrawn and restrictions on toy imports dropped (Newton and Tse, 1996). One difference between the toy and shoe cases is that the least-cost toy producer, China, appears to possess a large comparative advantage over the German and Spanish producers, so that the cost of increasing the EU's external trade barriers would be high.

The 1995 enlargement reflected the concerns of EFTA countries about the trade and investment diversion costs of EC92, as well as the changed political situation in which neutrality was no longer a relevant consideration. The conventional view has been that the trade effects of the 1995 enlargement would be small because EFTA had already formed a free trade area with the EU since 1972. Replacement of a FTA by a CU removes the need for rules of origin, which reduces paperwork. The reduction in real trade costs has been estimated at between 1.4 and 5 per cent of the transactions values, with most studies using a midpoint guesstimate of 2.5 per cent (e.g. Keuschnigg and Kohler, 1996; various papers by Haaland and Norman). Finland may have benefited from liberalization of agriculture and services when they adopted the *acquis*, and Austria had slightly more restrictive external trade policies before joining the EU. Sweden had more liberal agricultural and trade policies; for example, Sweden had unilaterally withdrawn from the MFA in 1988, but after 1995 was forced to observe the EU-wide textile and clothing quotas. As relatively rich EU members, all the 1995 newcomers made net budget contributions, so that the net welfare effect could be negative (as it had been for the UK). Flam (1995) provides a fairly standard set of estimates for the economic consequences that are least difficult to quantify (i.e. budget transfers, CAP and trade policy effects), showing positive but small net welfare gains; 0.86 per cent of GDP for Finland, 0.22 per cent for Sweden, and 0.08 per cent for Austria. Ironically, Flam's highest estimated gains are 0.94 per cent of GDP for Norway, whose voters rejected EU membership.

The most innovative empirical work on the 1995 enlargement has incorporated imperfect competition and dynamic effects. The work of Norman and Haaland, based on the Smith–Venables model of market segmentation, has found the pro-competitive benefits of being inside the integrated EU markets to be positive and significant for Norway and Sweden (see the previous section). Kueschnigg and Kohler (1996) have applied their variety-based model (see Section 10.2) to Austrian accession and estimated a net welfare gain equal to 1.24 per cent of GDP (i.e. much higher than Flam's negligible 0.08 per cent). As with all CGE modelling, it is difficult to assess the numerical results; the Smith–Venables and Keuschnigg–Kohler models highlight potential pro-competitive gains from integration, but still await evidence of how important these channels actually are in the European context.

Ex ante studies of the prospective fourth EU enlargement to include the formerly centrally planned economies of Central and Eastern Europe indicate welfare benefits for existing and new members (Faini and Portes, 1995). Even in sensitive sectors such as steel and textiles, the adjustment costs may be less than is feared in the EU because of the possibilities for intra-industry specialization. Although much of the resistance to Eastern enlargement is coming from southern EU members, the main impact is likely to be felt by unskilled industrial workers and farmers in northern Europe. These empirical results are not inconsistent with the political bases for resistance to enlargement (see Section 5.3) in so far as the trade effects appear to be relatively small and are therefore swamped by the budgetary impact of admitting poor agricultural countries to the EU as currently organized.

German economic and monetary union (GEMU) in 1990 also involved EC enlargement, although it is usually seen as a special case. GEMU is interesting as the most dramatic example of regional economic integration in the late twentieth century, with little prior negotiation or planning and a very rapid transition period. Moreover, GEMU involved very deep integration with the goal of creating a single nation state. The adjustment costs were asymmetric because the former German Democratic Republic (the East) accepted the economic, political, and legal system of the German Federal Republic (formerly the West). The main adjustment costs for the West were the financial transfers and labour market effects resulting from unrestricted internal migration; the latter were minimized by the choice of currency conversion rate plus the high degree of common wage and social security policies in East and West after unification. Overvaluation of the Ostmark meant that adjustment was through unemployment of Eastern workers (who would be encouraged not to migrate by the generous social security benefits), rather than by internal migration driving down the wage level in the West.

Was GEMU a good thing? Although the East had to bear severe adjustment costs, the rapid transition and substantial aid left citizens of the former German Democratic Republic best placed among all former CMEA residents in terms of future economic prosperity. For the West, labour market and housing market disruption were minimized, but the financing burden led to higher interest rates and slower growth than would otherwise have occurred in the first half of the 1990s.

4. Completing the Internal Market (EC92 and the EEA)

A unique feature of the empirical work on the effects of the EC92 programme was the pre-emptive publication of a detailed study which provided 'official estimates'. The sixteen volumes of research reports summarized in the Commission of the European Communities (1988) and popularized in the report by Cecchini *et al.* (1988) set the terms of the debate. In particular, the Commission's estimates found substantial net welfare gains from a set of measures which, in terms of mainstream customs union theory, might have been expected to have minimal benefits, given that formal barriers on internal trade were already low and that the two most distorted sectors in the EC (agriculture and coal) were excluded from the programme.

The welfare effects estimated by the Commission have four components. The resource allocation benefits from reduced internal trade barriers are indeed small, even allowing for the liberalization of public procurement decisions which remain a major source of national preference (Tsoukalis, 1993, 82); all told, they come to less than 5 per cent of the welfare gains. Of roughly equal importance are the three other components:

1. elimination of internal cost-increasing restrictions such as excessive regulations, fragmented standards, and border controls;
2. greater competition arising from the integration of segmented imperfectly competitive markets;
3. scale economies.

The overall net welfare effects are estimated to be about 180 billion ecu, or 6 per cent of the EC's GDP. An interesting aspect of these estimates is that the last two components are reminiscent of the dynamic effects claimed for the initial EC customs union, and for which little empirical evidence could be found. They are also the elements of the Commission's estimates which have been most criticized.

The pure scale effects of EC92 are based on the Commission's report by Schwalbach. The consensus among outside commentators, however, is that little scope remained in the EC for realizing internal scale economies. Caballero and Lyons (1990; 1991), studying manufacturing industries in Belgium, France, Germany, and the UK, found evidence of scale economies internal to the firm in only five cases out of the fifty-two two-digit categories studied: agricultural and industrial machinery in Germany, rubber and plastics in Belgium and in the UK, mineral products in Belgium, and 'other manufacturing' in the UK. Caballero and Lyons (1990, 824) conclude that 'opportunities for unexploited increasing returns in manufacturing are much less widespread than the Commission's (1988) analysis concludes'. Geroski (1989) also argues that, in introducing imperfect competition, the Commission had put too much stress on scale economies and too little on the benefits from increased diversity of available product varieties.

The modelling of imperfect competition by the Commission is based on the Smith–Venables approach described in Section 10.1. The welfare gains, which arise mainly from market integration, are quantified by extrapolating the estimates from the ten industries covered by Smith and Venables to the whole economy. The extrapolation process may be biased, because some of the studied sectors (pharmaceuticals and autos) lie at one extreme end of the segmentation spectrum, or because the translation from a set of partial equilibrium estimates to a macro estimate may be flawed. Most importantly, however, this procedure places a heavy burden on a model which should be considered an aid to thinking about the competitive impact of EC92 rather than an accurate estimating tool, and which is only one of a wide range of imperfect competition models, each yielding different results, which could be conceptualized. To present 'official' estimates based on such a model is unconvincing.

Peck (1989) has attacked the Commission for being over-optimistic in its assumptions and selective in its use of the detailed studies. His own 'back of the envelope' estimate of gain from EC92 comes to around 2 per cent of EC GDP, which is non-trivial even if much smaller than the 'official' estimates. Haaland and Norman (1992), using a computable general eqiuilibrium model with Smith–Venables assumptions, calculate a real income gain from EC integration equal to 1.9 per cent of expenditure on manufactures, which is equivalent to less than 0.25 per cent of EC GDP; this omits benefits outside manufacturing, but is well below the range of 2.5 to 6.5 per cent of EC GDP suggested as plausible by the Cecchini Report and illustrates the model sensitivity of assumptions based on calibrated models. On the other hand, Richard Baldwin (1989; 1992), drawing on the new growth theories of the late 1980s, argues that the benefits of EC92 are underestimated, because the improved investment environment will have positive growth effects via external economies of scale and induced innovation.

The arguments are difficult to resolve because the two most controversial components of the Commission's estimates are the ones for which there is least agreement about estimation methods. If, however, the resource allocation and scale effects are agreed to be small, then a positive impact for EC92 rests heavily on these internal cost reduction and improved competition benefits.

Klepper (1992), in his study of the pharmaceutical industry, concludes that market integration may reduce prices (as in Smith–Venables), but it may lead to higher prices (the outcome which he seems to consider more plausible); the welfare effects are ambiguous, unsurprisingly, given the second-best nature of the outcome even with an integrated pharmaceutical market. Baldwin's positive growth effect via increased R&D is also contradicted by Ulph's (1991) study of technology policy in the EC, which concludes that R&D will be reduced by the EC92 programme.

In sum, empirical work on the EC92 programme has led to some innovative approaches, especially the work of Smith and Venables on market integration and of Baldwin on the dynamic effects. The overall impact of the empirical literature is, however, reminiscent of the assessment of the original customs union. The resource allocation benefits from reducing restrictions on internal trade in manufactures are positive but small, while the 'dynamic' benefits from increased efficiency arising from greater competition and from accelerated growth are claimed by some observers to be more substantial but remain difficult to measure.

5. Conclusions

The welfare effects of the formation of the EC customs union are rather small, typically positive for the customs union in manufactures but possibly negative when 'sensitive' items (agriculture, coal, steel, textiles, and clothing) are included. Some of the poorly measured effects involve welfare gains which may be substantial, but the empirical support for such conclusions is weak. Many observers dismiss the empirical findings because the small estimated effects of the EC are judged to show the inadequacy of the methods, but that stands the purpose of empirical work on its head (Winters, 1993a).

The most critical issue in assessing the EC/EU's economic impact is the counterfactual. If, in the absence of the EC, trade liberalization within GATT had proceeded as quickly, then the outcome is likely to have been similar, as all MFN tariffs would have been low and the added impact of duty-free internal intra-European trade would be small; indeed, the no-EC outcome would have been superior because there would be no CAP. If, on the other hand, a less integrated Western Europe had been associated with more limited liberalization within GATT, then both Western Europe and the rest of the world would have been worse off. That issue is, however, one that is more open to speculation than to serious empirical study.

Empirical work on Western European integration casts more light on the issues of trade patterns and of perceptions. The EC/EFTA split in the 1960s clearly affected intra-European trade patterns, although the welfare consequences were less dramatic. Formation of the EU–EFTA free trade area in manufactures in 1972 reversed the changes in trade patterns that had occurred during the previous decade and undid the trade diversion which the EFTA countries had suffered from. Perceptions that EFTA countries would suffer from being outside the completed EU market (or at least from being away from the negotiating table which set standards and policies for the European Economic Area) led to investment diversion from EFTA to EU locations and underpinned the 1995 EU enlargement. Neither the shifting trade patterns nor the investment diversion have been shown to involve substantial welfare losses, but perceptions of injury are significant for policy-makers involved in international commercial diplomacy.

The various EC enlargement episodes contain several examples of regional integration having negative welfare effects. New members have accepted the distortions of the EC's agriculture and other policies such as the MFA in order to be part of the club. Where possible, the new and old members have passed on part of the costs to non-members, most clearly with respect to some agricultural products and footwear.

13

North America

Empirical work on North American regional trade arrangements has passed through two stages. Until the second half of the 1980s, it consisted of studies by Canadian academics of a hypothetical USA–Canada free trade area. This literature was distinguished less by its results than by the pioneering approaches to scale economies and imperfect competition, two elements that were largely neglected in the contemporary literature on European integration. Then, starting in the second half of the 1980s, when CUSTA became a reality, more empirical work was done in the USA and the quantity grew rapidly in the early 1990s as NAFTA was being negotiated. The NAFTA literature was much more results-driven as the political debate heightened in 1992–3. It also brought in new areas of study, notably the employment and environmental effects, which had received little attention in the literature on the EC.

1. Free Trade between Canada and the USA

The trade effects of a USA–Canada free trade area are easily analysed with the customs union theory of Chapter 8. Because Canadian imports come overwhelmingly from the USA, preferential reduction of Canadian tariffs is unlikely to lead to much trade diversion and the trade creation benefits could be substantial. Given that the Canadian economy is less than one-tenth the size of the US economy, the benefits from preferential access to US markets will accrue to Canada and could also be substantial. It is a classic case of free trade between a large and a small country, from which the benefits go mainly to the small country with little impact on the large economy.[1] Canadian reluctance to sign

[1] In terms of the dichotomy made by Taussig (see S. 8.1), Canada was in the fortunate position of being 'Hawaii' as an exporter and facing 'Australia' as an importer.

free trade agreements with the USA in the first half of the twentieth century was due not to an expected net loss of economic welfare, but to a combination of non-economic reasons and sectoral interests (see Appendix).

In an early study using the partial equilibrium model described in Section 9.4, R. Wonnacott and P. Wonnacott (1967) estimated the gain to Canada from free trade with the USA at 10.5 per cent of Canadian GNP, of which about 4 per cent was due to eliminating Canadian tariffs and over 6 per cent to the removal of US tariffs. These are much higher than the trade benefits estimated for the EC customs union, and the Wonnacotts argued that much of the gain to Canada arose from newly realized scale economies (see also P. Wonnacott and R. Wonnacott, 1982).

Harris continued the innovative treatment of scale economies, by embedding them in a general equilibrium model. His initial exercise concerned estimation of the gains to Canada from eliminating its own tariff and from multilateral tariff elimination (Harris, 1984a; 1984b); given the dominant role of the USA as a trading partner, the estimates will approximate the gains to Canada from free trade with the USA. The estimated welfare gain to Canada is equal to 8.6 per cent of GNP, which is within the same ballpark as the Wonnacotts' estimate. A large proportion of the gain to Canada in Harris's model comes from rationalization; i.e. average production runs increase by 40 per cent (reducing average fixed costs by around 20 per cent) and this force is strong enough to promote increased employment in the more competitive manufacturing sectors (Cox and Harris, 1985)—contrary to the simple view that Canadian industry would shrink in the face of international competition.

The model developed by Harris and Cox goes beyond the Wonnacotts' model not only by being a general equilibrium model, but also by incorporating the imperfect competition which is likely to be associated with scale economies. The trade-off is that Harris is forced to make simplifying assumptions about both the structure of the economy and the behaviour of imperfectly competitive firms. Several critics (e.g. Deardorff and Wooton in Srinivasan and Whalley, 1986, 311–21, and Markusen in Whalley and Hill, 1985, 157–70) believed that Harris overstated the potential scale economies and that his results relied on implausible pricing behaviour. Harris considered two pricing rules, a mark-up over marginal cost and a focal price based on the world price plus tariff; in his estimates he used a weighted average of mark-up and focal pricing, which was not necessarily profit-maximizing or based on reasonable assumptions about rivals' behaviour. Whether the assumptions are plausible or not is difficult to assess, but subsequent exercises showed that the results are sensitive to modifications in the model.

The Canadian Department of Finance (1988) ran a modified version of the Harris model and found a net gain equal to about 2.5 per cent of Canadian GNP, a much smaller welfare effect than Harris's 8.6 per cent. Wigle (1988) did some more substantial retooling, adopting a different calibration procedure and modelling the rest of the world more carefully, as well as assuming either mark-up or focal pricing rather than a weighted average of the two. He estimates a small Canadian net welfare loss, equal to about 0.1 per cent of GNP. These three sets of estimates, all based on the same type of model, represent a huge range, from the substantially positive to the mildly negative!

Brown and Stern have used the Michigan world trade model to assess the importance of competing assumptions in computable general equilibrium models, taking a USA–Canada free trade area as the case study.[2] Brown and Stern (1987) assume perfectly competitive markets and national product differentiation (the Armington assumption). Such a structure produces strong terms of trade effects and little opportunity for increased welfare arising from rationalization. Bilateral tariff elimination by the USA and Canada increases global welfare, but the distribution is uneven: a net welfare loss for Canada (–0.3 per cent of GNP), a net welfare gain to the USA (0.3 per cent of GNP), and a loss to the rest of the world. The key to Canada's welfare loss and the US welfare gain is Canada's higher pre-FTA tariff.[3]

Brown and Stern (1989a) compare estimates from the Michigan model under three different market assumptions:

[2] The importance of the choice of assumpions, especially about market structure, in general equilibrium models is also discussed in Markusen and Venables (1988) and Norman (1990).

[3] A feature of world trade models with a limited number of 'countries' is that the terms of trade effects become significant and optimal tariffs are much higher than in national partial equilibrium models, where terms of trade effects are often assumed to be zero. Neither extreme is fully convincing, but it is difficult to make plausible estimates of world price changes.

TABLE 13.1 Welfare Effects of a USA–Canada FTA under Alternative Assumptions (US$m)

	Armington	Harris–Cox	Smith–Venables
USA	+781	+476	–1175
Canada	–29	+2304	–1389
Rest of world	–145	–116	–240

Source: Brown and Stern (1989a, 232).

1. perfectly competitive markets with products differentiated by nationality (the Armington assumption);
2. monopolistic competition with products differentiated by firm (Harris–Cox);
3. market segmentation (Smith–Venables).

The estimates using the second and third assumptions vary substantially from the net welfare loss to Canada in Brown and Stern (1987), using the first assumption (Table 13.1). With product differentiation by firm, the trade effects are larger; the welfare effects on the USA and the rest of the world are similar—signed but slightly smaller than with national product differentiation —but the welfare impact on Canada switches from negative to positive (equal to 1.2 per cent of GNP). The market segmentation assumption produces larger trade effects, but negative net welfare effects for the USA, Canada, and the rest of the world. The authors disown this last result (Brown and Stern, 1989a, 233), which casts some doubt on the excessive reliance on the Smith–Venables model to estimate the effects of European integration in the 1980s and 1990s.

Brown and Stern (1989b) adopts their best-guess market structure out of the above three options for each sector. This exercise produces an estimated net welfare gain to Canada of 1.1 per cent of GNP, with a small terms of trade loss. Given the prior expectations set out at the start of this section and the higher tariff in Canada, these results seem reasonable, but in view of the high assumption-sensitivity of this class of model that conclusion is based more on prior beliefs than on confidence in the results of the empirical exercise.

During the mid-1980s a number of groups produced macroeconometric estimates of the effects of Canada–USA free trade.

Some of these are reported by the Canadian Ministry of Finance (1988, 32) and in Brown and Stern (1989b, table 4.2). The estimated gain in Canadian real income bunches between 2.5 and 3.3 per cent of GNP, which is similar to the model-based estimate of the Canadian Ministry of Finance (1988).

2. NAFTA

Following the initiation of negotiations with Mexico in 1990, a huge polemical, descriptive, and empirical literature developed. A feature of this literature was the use of a range of general equilibrium models, clearly building on the work of Harris and Cox and Brown and Stern on Canada–USA free trade, and in contrast to the more limited range of models applied to European integration. The introduction to François and Shiells (1994) contains a discussion of why applied general equilibrium studies achieved such prominence in debates over the impact of NAFTA. These debates focused almost exclusively on the impacts of free trade between the USA and Mexico, since Canada–Mexico trade flows were not expected to change much and the effects of Canada–USA free trade area had already occurred through CUSTA.

A USA–Mexico free trade area involves a large and a small economy—Mexico's GDP in the early 1990s was less than 4 per cent of US GDP—so we would expect the economic impact on the USA to be small. The *ex ante* studies of the early 1990s confirmed this, and also found small direct economic effects on Mexico. Lustig *et al.* (1992, 2) explain the small impact by the low levels of tariffs and quantitative restrictions on USA–Mexico trade during the early 1990s, and by the slow phasing out of remaining non-tariff barriers under NAFTA. The main potential for a stronger positive impact is if investment in Mexico is stimulated by NAFTA, leading to faster economic growth.

Brown (1992) surveys the general equilibrium models applied to NAFTA.[4] The models confirm the expectation that all three

[4] A flavour of the general equilibrium models applied to NAFTA is given by the symposium in the January 1992 issue of *The World Economy*, which includes papers by Brown, Deardorff, and Stern and by Cox and Harris using aggregate models, by Sobarzo modelling the Mexican economy, by Trela and Whalley on textiles and steel, and by Hunter, Markusen, and Rutherford on automobiles. Kehoe and Kehoe (1995) also provide an accessible introduction, with contributions by many of the same authors.

NAFTA signatories will benefit and that the gains will be greatest for Mexico and trivial for Canada. As empirical exercises, these are not very satisfying because of the big range of welfare outcomes (from net gains of less than 1 per cent of Mexican GDP up to 10 per cent), which are assumption-dependent. This is a familiar story from the previous chapter and from Part II. Constant-returns-to-scale models produce less dramatic effects than imperfect-competition models with economies of scale, and dynamic elements increase the calculated welfare effects still further. There is, however, no basis for determining which assumptions are most plausible for producing good estimates of NAFTA's impact.

Much of the US debate over NAFTA focused on the potential job losses arising from competition from cheaper Mexican labour. In this context, a set of estimates of the employment effects by Hufbauer and Schott (1993) had a major political impact, because they calculated that NAFTA would create 170,000 new jobs in the USA. Hufbauer and Schott's estimate is based on the assumption that NAFTA will encourage net US investment in Mexico, which will have a corresponding Mexican trade deficit. The difference between the US trade surplus with and without NAFTA divided by the value added per trade-related worker gives the estimated net job creation, 170,000.

This is a shaky calculation and an even poorer justification for NAFTA. The estimate is based on what is essentially a guess about capital flows, and on a crude demand-driven view of US output. In practice, US macroeconomic policy-makers are likely to lean against any effects of NAFTA on aggregate demand, so that the employment-via-demand effects of NAFTA are going to be small (Krugman, 1995b). The key point is that preferential trading arrangements, like any trade policies, may affect the distribution of jobs, but aggregate employment depends on macroeconomic and labour market policies, not on trade policy.

Prestowitz *et al.* (1991) used a similar technique to produce diametrically opposed employment effects. In their exercise, the inital capital inflows into Mexico generate exports which turn the bilateral trade flows into a US trade deficit by the late 1990s. Now, a similar division of the projected trade balance by value added per trade-related worker shows NAFTA to be destroying 900,000 US jobs. Applied general equilibrium models produce far more modest effects on both US and Mexican labour markets, apart from the impact of lower maize prices on Mexican agricultural labour (see below).

Economists were also drawn into the political debate over the environmental consequences of NAFTA. The fear of environmentalists was that environmentally unfriendly industries would escape US restrictions by relocating south of the border. Grossman and Krueger (1993) consider the impact of NAFTA via increased scale of production, changed output composition, and changed production techniques and conclude that NAFTA is likely to improve Mexico's environmental quality. Pastor (1992) makes a similar point and generalizes it to labour standards and other social issues; demand for environmental, workplace, and other social legislation increases with income, so that, if NAFTA has a positive impact on Mexican income, then it will also lead to improved standards in these areas of US concern.

The investment effects of NAFTA appear to offer the largest potential economic gains to Mexico. Increased capital formation is expected because Mexican real interest rates will be brought down to US levels and because foreign investors will be attracted to Mexico by the greater credibility given to the liberalization process. Neither of these arguments is fully convincing. Real interest rate differentials continue to exist in the EU, and are unlikely to be wiped out within NAFTA, where investors may continue to demand a risk premium from Mexico for whatever reason. NAFTA-induced foreign investment inflows are more plausible, but quantification is difficult.

Aggregative *ex ante* studies of NAFTA contributed usefully to the political debate, mainly by countering alarmist claims about disastrous consequences for the USA, but they add little to our knowledge of the effects of GDAs. The most plausible studies came out with unsurprising results of small consequences for the already fairly open and much larger US economy and potentially larger benefits for Mexico, which were difficult to disentangle from the benefits of ongoing unilateral trade liberalization. Given the complexity of the final agreement, sectoral studies are likely to provide more original and relevant insights into NAFTA's actual impact.

Lopez de Silanes *et al.* (1994) model the North American automobile industry as imperfect competition among transnational corporations.[5] The structure allows the rules of origin to be analysed. They conclude that the NAFTA content rules will operate to the benefit of the Big Three US car makers and US component makers, at the expense of non-US firms (including those with manufacturing operations in North America) and overseas components suppliers. This study supports the conclusion that the US car makers were successful in designing (and having incorporated in NAFTA) rules of origin tailored to favour US-owned producers rather than to encourage use of inputs made in North America. Such a tailor-made agreement benefits shareholders in the US car makers, but creates new distortions which almost certainly reduce North American welfare.

For Mexico, the most important sectoral effect of NAFTA is on maize farming. About half of Mexico's arable land is cultivated in maize, involving almost four-fifths of Mexican farmers, of whom over 90 per cent had less than 5 hectares planted; in sum, most maize farmers are small-scale producers, living in poverty. Maize is also the basic staple. As part of Mexico's economic liberalization since the late 1980s, support for maize farmers and subsidies for tortilla consumption have been reduced, but the producer subsidy equivalent in 1991 was still 44 per cent of the value of production.[6] NAFTA will further reduce the farmgate price of maize, and Mexican commentators' claims ranged up to assertions that 15 million people in agriculture would be displaced. CGE modellers (e.g. Levy and van Wijnbergen, 1992) predicted about three-quarters of a million displaced farmers, which is still a large adjustment burden, i.e. some 15 per cent of the economically active population in agriculture. Based on detailed farm survey data, de Janvry *et al.* (1995) reach a more optimistic conclusion about NAFTA's impact on maize producers: about half of Mexican maize producers are subsistence farmers who will be unaffected by price changes, while the remainder will have opportunities to modernize their maize production or diversify

[5] Markusen *et al.* (1995) also report on this project. Mexican car buyers will benefit if consumer arbitrage is feasible, and this would be the main source of gain to Mexico. A feature of the 1965 Canada–USA Autopact was that producers were allowed to trade duty-free but consumers were not, so that producers achieved efficiency gains but consumers failed to benefit from a single market. The extent to which this feature carried over into CUSTA and NAFTA is unclear.

[6] Calculations by the Economic Research Service of the US Department of Agriculture, quoted in de Janvry *et al.* (1995, 1350).

into non-traditional field crops or fruit and vegetables where new opportunities will be created by NAFTA.

3. Impact on Third Countries

A free trade area between Mexico and the USA and Canada could be expected to have little impact on the rest of the world for the same reasons that the other trade effects of NAFTA were expected to be small. This presumption is supported by the applied general equilibrium models discussed in the previous section. As with the intra-NAFTA trade effects, the major reservation to this statement concerns the behaviour of investment, which may be driven by perceptions and be diverted from non-NAFTA locations to within NAFTA.

Several studies have estimated the effects of NAFTA on specific non-members or regions. Kreinin and Plummer (1992) use a simple technique to measure the adverse effects of NAFTA on Asian exports; their estimated effects are small despite the technique's upward bias (Pomfret, 1993).[7] Hufbauer and Schott (1994, 252) also argue that the trade diversion estimates of Kreinin and Plummer (1992) and Safadi and Yeats (1993) are overestimates because they use MFN tariff rates whereas many Mexican products, especially in the critical apparel sector, already entered the USA at preferential tariff rates pre-NAFTA. Erzan and Yeats (1992) estimate that about $28 million in US imports from other Latin American countries will be displaced by Mexican goods as a result of NAFTA. Leamer *et al.* (1995) are less certain about the impact on Central America, mainly because of unpredictability about the relative attractiveneess to foreign investors of Mexico and Central American locations, but the trade effects of NAFTA on Central America are likely to be small and in some scenarios even positive.

The aggregative estimation techniques used in all of these studies may, however, be inappropriate if the detailed content of

[7] Hufbauer and Schott (1994, 163) estimate that extending NAFTA into a Western Hemisphere Free Trade Area would affect only 2.6% of East Asian (China, Hong Kong, Japan, South Korean, and Taiwan) exports to the USA; corresponding trade diversion effects on Western Europe (EU, EFTA, and Turkey) and South Asia (CER, ASEAN, and SAARC) are estimated at 3.5% and 2.8% of their exports to the USA.

NAFTA was structured to avoid trade creation and promote trade diversion (see Sections 6.2 and 10.4 above). The importation by the USA of frozen orange juice concentrate from Mexico instead of Brazil was the most frequently mentioned example of trade diversion; although the static trade effects are small, Brazilian orange growers could suffer more seriously if NAFTA stimulates new investment in the Mexican citrus sector.[8] Other niche exporters may be seriously affected; e.g. Whalley (1993) reports that Nicaraguan rock lobster sales suffered from trade diversion as a result of CUSTA.

4. Conclusions

The empirical literature on North American regional integration has followed different paths from that on Western Europe, with a greater emphasis on CGE models from the start and with a focus on new issues such as labour markets and the environment. Nevertheless, some common results emerge, and two recurring themes are worth emphasizing.

Empirical studies of NAFTA suggest fairly limited trade and welfare effects. The wide range of reported results has, however, allowed proponents and opponents of NAFTA to quote outliers in support of their position. Shoddy empirical work, especially on employment consequences, has also been enlisted to justify prior positions. Both of these practices undermine the credibility of empirical economic studies; as with the EU literature, a root cause of the problem is an unwillingness to admit that well publicized and controversial regional integration schemes may have small net welfare effects.

Most of the literature on North America has studied the impact of a North American FTA, rather than the actual NAFTA. Studies that have attempted to model the actual terms produce less positive net welfare effects, although they do identify beneficiaries (e.g. the US automobile companies). This is comparable to the evolution of empirical work on the EC, which initially ignored

[8] Primo Braga (1992, 223) reports 'static' estimates of a 0.5% decline in US concentrated orange juice imports from the rest of the world, but a doubling in Mexican output growth would seriously divert trade, reducing Brazilian output by 4.5% and her on-tree revenues by 14.4% in 2000.

agriculture and other senstitive sectors, with adverse trade diversion effects. In NAFTA the degree of detailed market engineering is greater than in the EU, especially through the use of rules of origin, which consequently makes it more difficult to model deviations from a pure FTA without detailed microeconomic studies. Nevertheless, the expectation is that the negative effects on third countries described in Section 13.3 may be just the tip of the iceberg.

14

Other Free Trade Areas and Customs Unions

Other regional trading arrangments have been less important than those covered in the previous chapters. Moreover, empirical studies indicate effects that are broadly in line *mutatis mutandis* with those of the RTAs already discussed.

The many regional trading arrangements among developing countries in the 1960s and 1970s were often designed to promote industrialization through trade diversion. Recognition of the costs of trade diversion, however, quickly led to second thoughts about their implementation. Trade creation, which would hurt domestic industries, was also unwelcome. Thus, these RTAs tended to have short lives or to be characterized by dissent, unless they were watered down to have little impact on trade flows. The new wave of RTAs among developing countries in the 1990s differs in that most of the particpants are now pursuing outward-oriented rather than inward-oriented development strategies. It is too early to provide empirical evidence on the new RTAs, but they too can be expected to have minor economic impact because liberal trade policies leave little scope for discrimination among trading partners.

Trading arrangements among the centrally planned economies were clearly discriminatory, but their analysis does not fit easily into this book because of the non-market allocation mechanism and extreme barriers to external trade. Compared with total autarchy, Comecon must have been trade-creating and hence welfare-improving, but compared with any reasonable counterfactual based on even-limited participation in the global economy, Comecon was probably trade-diverting. The more developed Eastern European countries suffered from some trade disruption with the disintegration of Comecon in the early 1990s, but beyond the short-run adjustment costs the reorientation of trade flows was welfare-improving because it undid trade diversion.

The outcome is harder to evaluate for the poorer Soviet republics and Mongolia, where trade disruption and loss of transfers contributed to huge drops in GDP during the first half of the 1990s, even though in the long run they should benefit from pursuing more liberal non-discriminatory trade policies.

1. FTAs and CUs among Developing Countries

Customs unions among developing countries have often been based upon a type of infant industry argument. The aim is to promote import-substituting industrialization, but the fear is that national markets alone would be too small. In this context trade diversion does not seem a cost to the union,[1] and the key empirical question is the extent to which scale economies can be realized within the union. Several studies indicated the existence of unrealized scale economies in Latin America (e.g. Carnoy, 1970 and 1972).

Pearson and Ingram's (1980) study of the effect on seven industries of economic integration between Ghana and the Ivory Coast is the most detailed empirical treatment of this case for customs union. Based on firm-level data, they forecast post-integration specialization by Ghana in two and by the Ivory Coast in five of the industries, and estimate welfare gains of 33 per cent of gross output at world prices for Ghana and 22 per cent for the Ivory Coast; about two-fifths of these gains come from trade creation, one-fifth from Corden's cost reduction effect, and two-fifths from 'production effects' (i.e. the gain from selling to the partner goods whose social benefits exceed private benefits). There are no trade diversion or trade suppression effects because both countries supply their home market for all seven goods before integration.

Although the existence of unrealized scale economies suggests that customs unions among developing countries may achieve their goal, the practice has been littered with failures. One problem

[1] If the sole aim is to replace imports from outside the union by production within the union, then trade diversion is a benefit. This is the Johnson–Cooper–Massell explanation of why customs unions are formed. In theory it does not necessarily require the existence of scale economies, but in practice these have been a central concern of policy-makers.

is that the scale economies may not be realized even within the customs union. Willmore (1978) provides evidence from the Central American Common Market of firms pursuing oligopolistic market sharing, which leads to inefficient cross-hauling rather than the realization of technical scale economies.[2] A more serious problem is that the benefits of import-substituting industrialization are unlikely to be spread equally across the customs union although the resource misallocation costs are; i.e. trade diversion does matter.[3]

Historical accounts of the Central American Common Market and of the East African Community agree that, whatever the immediate stimulus for departure, Honduras was dissatisfied with the CACM and Tanzania and Uganda with the EAC for this fundamental reason. In both cases redistributive mechanisms had been conceived to forestall such grievances, but the failure of these schemes to work smoothly is well documented (Cohen Otrantes, 1972; Hazlewood, 1979). CARIFTA had a similar experience, as the growth of intra-regional trade in the late 1960s and early 1970s was seen by the smaller poorer members to be disproportionately benefiting the more developed members (Barbados, Guyana, Jamaica, and Trinidad and Tobago), but the redistributive

[2] Although the existing tyre plant in Guatemala utilized only two-thirds of its 300,000 tyres per annum capacity behind a common external tariff of over 100%, a second plant was built in Costa Rica with a 100,000 tyres per annum capacity. Both plants supplied the entire CACM (e.g. the Guatemala–Costa Rica tyre trade flourished and was 80% intra-industry trade in the early 1970s), emphasizing product differentiation by brand name rather than specialization by size or variety. Such cross-hauling raised average costs, but this could be absorbed be setting prices as high as the market would bear (while Honduras, outside the CACM, had considerably lower tyre prices). According to Willmore, this 'miniature replica' effect (to use a term popularized by Eastman and Stykolt in the context of Canadian protectionism) is also characteristic of the CACM textiles industry.

[3] Even without trade diversion, distributional conflicts may arise. In Pearson and Ingram's study, although the absolute value of the welfare gains is the same for Ghana and for the Ivory Coast, the authors point to political difficulties facing integration because of the differing sources of gain. The Ivory Coast's gain comes two-thirds from the 'production effects' and one-fifth from cost reductions, but the Ghanaian gains are overwhelmingly from trade creation and from a transfer from Ivorian food buyers—presumably, producers in the five Ghanaian industries to be phased out will be unhappy (and the government may not see the loss of these industries as too favourable a bargain for the expansion of food and footwear industries), and the Ivory Coast government may be unhappy about redistributing food buyer's income to foreign food producers. In fact, the hypothetical Ghana–Ivory Coast economic integration scheme never left Pearson and Ingram's drawing board.

mechanisms envisioned in the replacement of CARIFTA by CARICOM in 1973 were ineffective. The CACM is especially striking in that it was extremely successful in boosting intra-regional trade, which rose from 7.8 per cent of members' exports in 1961 to 24.2 per cent in 1968, but the two poorest members, Nicaragua and Honduras, were dissatisfied with the distribution of benefits. Edwards and Savastano (1989, 196–7) emphasize the relative success of the CACM, including the maintenance of fairly free intra-regional trade during the 1970s, to the relative weakness of lobbies created by ISI policies.

Similar difficulties accompanied schemes to promote ASEAN-wide import-substituting industrialization after 1977. Despite early assignment of one Asean Industrial Project to each member state and Japanese financial aid for the programme, the first project did not come on-stream until 1984, by which time Singapore had effectively dropped out of the programme and Thailand's position was anomalous.[4] Attempts to establish complementary production within sectors began with automobile components, but this scheme was torpedoed in the mid-1980s by Malaysia's decision to proceed with its own integrated automobile industry.

ASEAN members also signed a preferential trading agreement in 1977, but this too had little impact. Despite the many announced preferential tariff cuts, these affected only a small share of intra-ASEAN trade and, not surprisingly, all empirical studies find that the preferential tariffs had minimal impact on trade flows (Imada, 1993, 4–8). Indeed, intra-ASEAN trade as a percentage of members' total trade was lower in 1989 than it had been in 1970 (Ariff and Tan, 1992, 254). While the projects described in the previous paragraph failed because countries were unwilling to bear costs of trade diversion, the preferential trading arrangement was stymied by resistance to trade creation; any domestic producer powerful enough to have tariff protection was able to avoid preferential reductions in the tariff on its output.

[4] Indonesia wanted modifications in Singapore's original AIP (a diesel engine factory) because part of its output range would compete with an Indonesian plant, but limiting the output range would make the Singapore factory unprofitable. Singapore eventually found a new AIP, but one very much smaller than the other AIPs. After a long gestation period, the Thai AIP was dropped and a national plant competing with Indonesia's AIP was announced. Both sets of decisions reflect an unwillingness to buy the high-cost output of other countries' AIPs.

Quantitative estimates of the effects of GDAs among developing countries are most firmly based for the CACM,[5] and even here there is little agreement. W. T. Wilford (1970), using the Balassa method, found rather more trade creation than in the EC, but revisions of his figures based on more appropriate dating and income elasticities reduce estimated trade creation below the low EC level (Nugent, 1974, 44–50), and found trade diversion to be more important (Willmore, 1976). Cline and Delgado (1978) also estimated low trade creation effects and larger trade diversion effects, but the net welfare impact of these was so small as to be 'irrelevant'. In their study the total welfare gain from the CACM is substantial (3–4 per cent of members' combined GDP), but this derives almost entirely from a foreign exchange effect and from induced investment.[6] According to Cline and Delgado, all members gained, but Honduras benefited least; with respect to Honduran secession from the CACM, their conclusion implies that, even if a customs union benefits all members (*vis-à-vis* the no-union alternative), imbalance in the sharing of the gains can cause dissatisfaction; alternatively, if Cline and Delgado's estimates are uniformly too high, then Honduras is the country most likely to have lost from CACM membership. Whatever the specific

[5] Cline and Delgado (1978, 6) list intra-trade as a percentage of total exports of economic groupings involving developing countries between 1960 and 1974; the CACM's ratio of 26% is well ahead of second-place EAC's 14%, while other Latin American and African groupings have below 10%. In Nugent's econometric study of 38 developing countries' exports, a CACM dummy is positive and significantly different from zero while a LAFTA dummy is not (Nugent, 1974, 50–60). The more descriptive literature supports the impression that GDAs among developing countries, apart from the CACM and EAC, had little economic impact during the 1960s and 1970s. The EAC's impact is difficult to measure because it represented the final stages in the slow disintegration of the colonial common market involving Kenya, Uganda, and Tanganyika.

[6] The foreign exchange effect consists of the net foreign exchange saving by CACM members multiplied by the difference between official and shadow prices of foreign exchange (estimated at 25%). The investment impact is based upon a survey in which the sample firms report some CACM-induced investment; Cline extrapolates to find total induced investment, and the welfare gain consists of the net social benefits from the extra labour employed and from the additional domestic investment. Both of these non-traditional customs union effects involve a structuralist view of economic development with rigid foreign exchange and capital constraints, captured by non-variable shadow exchange rates and factor prices. As with Comecon, lack of opportunity cost pricing makes the measurement of welfare gains from the CACM difficult, but assuming fixed premia on foreign exchange inflows and on factor employment is dubious when the magnitudes turn out to be large.

interpretation, the practical experience in the CACM, as in other integration schemes involving developing countries, has been of distributional conflicts outrunning either the desire of the main beneficiaries for change or the members' capacity to administer redistributive measures.

A major reason for the paucity of quantitative studies on the effects of the many GDAs agreed upon among developing countries in the 1960s and 1970s is the poor implementation record. Many of the paper GDAs described in Section 5.4 were scarcely implemented, because when it came down to specific tariff reductions few developing countries were willing to expose their sheltered industries to competition, even from other developing countries. Nor were they enthusiastic about buying the products of their partners' sheltered industries. Thus, in a climate of import-substituting industrialization, the theoretical case for regional integration was easy to make but practical implementation proved uninviting.

The new wave of regional trading arrangements among developing countries in the 1990s differed fundamentally from the earlier GDAs in that it was part of a general liberalization of trade and other economic policies. Some of the earlier problems recurred; for example, launching the ASEAN free trade area (AFTA) was delayed by selective exclusion of goods, and early conflicts in MERCOSUR concerned protected leading industrial sectors such as cars.[7] Nevertheless, the new generation of regional arrangements has better implementation prospects, but if MFN tariffs are also substantially reduced then the preference margins will be slim and economic impact is unlikely to be large. The general point is that, if a country is serious about reducing its trade barriers, then it may as well import from the global, rather than the regional, least-cost supplier.

There is, at the time of writing, no solid empirical evidence to support or reject this hypothesis of limited impact. Studies of AFTA essentially project studies of the earlier ASEAN preferential trading arrangement or assume little effect, owing to the similarity of most ASEAN economies (Imada, 1993; Pomfret,

[7] The phenomenon of minimal coverage was even more pronounced in the preferential tariff schedules submitted by ECO members. On their lists of products for which a 10% tariff reduction would apply to intra-ECO trade, Pakistan and Iran each included a mere 16 narrowly defined items (Pomfret, 1996d).

1996b). MERCOSUR is even harder to assess, as it began later and had little precedent. Paraguay suffered some economic losses because it used to benefit from smuggling across its neighbours' borders and because its own tariffs have actually been increased to bring them in line with its MERCOSUR partners (Connolly *et al.*, 1995). On the other hand, there are anecdotal reports of increased specialization, especially by transnational corporations operating in several MERCOSUR countries. Other RTAs such as ECO, SAARC, and SADC have scarcely been implemented, and as yet have insufficient credibility to have generated any anticipatory investment or specialization.

2. Comecon

Comecon had a more dramatic impact on its members' trade patterns. Comecon's initial impact was trade-destroying. Although the USSR's economy was already extremely closed by the late 1930s, the eastern European countries' economies had been open and their trade westward-oriented before the 1940s. After the formation of Comecon, the eastern European members were able to obtain only a fraction of their prewar imports from Comecon partners and were practically excluded from non-Comecon import sources (Holzman, 1985). The consequences of Comecon as a GDA are difficult to assess, because comparative advantage is difficult to identify and the counterfactual situation hard to specify. Whatever the net welfare effects, Comecon has been the subject of muted but bitter controversy about the distribution of benefits and costs. Administered pricing, barter arrangements, non-convertibility, etc., are the source of these complications.

The customs union approach has been championed by Holzman (1962; 1976; 1985) and Bergson (1980), who emphasize the predominance of trade diversion and trade destruction and the lack of trade creation. Early estimates of trade diversion and trade creation tended to be impressionistic and conflicting; Holzman (1976, 73) believes that post-1949 trade flows must reflect trade diversion of an 'extraordinary magnitude', while Pelzman (1977), using a gravity model, finds net trade creation among Comecon members during the 1960s. Later studies (Brada and Mendez, 1985; Havrylyshyn and Pritchett, 1991; Wang and Winters, 1991) are more consistent in finding that Comecon had a substantial impact on trade patterns and predicting a 50–75 per cent drop in intra-regional trade as a result of the demise of Comecon. The actual drop in intra-regional trade was smaller than this, which is striking in light of the accompanying income losses which should have accentuated the fall (Brada, 1993); but whatever its magnitude, the reduction in intra-regional trade should be welfare-improving if Comecon trade represented trade diversion.

The bilateral bargaining aspect of Comecon is highlighted by Marrese (1986), although the political nature of the bargain hypothesized by Marrese and Vanous (1983) has been criticized by Brada (1985) and Desai (1986). Proposals during the 1950s and early 1960s for supranational planning within Comecon were strongly opposed by Romania and Bulgaria, the less industrialized members, which disliked being assigned roles of specializing in primary products. After that, distributional conflicts focused on intra-Comecon pricing policies and the countries that benefited from them; Robson (1984, 144–7) and Holzman (1985) provide introductions to this literature.

The Soviet Union itself was a planned regional trading arrangement which operated as an extreme version of Comecon, because the national central planners had greater powers to enforce specialization patterns. Planners often located production of a commodity in a few huge plants, whose location was not based on economic criteria, and which led to excessive shipment over long distances. After the dissolution of the USSR in December 1991, these specialization patterns collapsed and trade disruption was undoubtedly costly. On the other hand, maintaining or restoring intra-CIS trade could perpetuate resource misallocation because many of these production links make no sense at appropriate prices. The situation is complicated by substantial explicit and implicit transfers which occurred within the USSR (and incorporated the Mongolian People's Republic, often referred to as the sixteenth republic after the imposition of central planning in the late 1940s) and whose magnitude (and even direction) is a source of ongoing political dispute. On balance, the intra-USSR transfers probably benefited the poorer Asian republics, which lost doubly from the disruption of trade and cessation of transfers in 1991–4, although like the poorer members of Comecon they complained about the role assigned to them in the intra-USSR specialization (Pomfret, 1995b; 1995c).

15

Trade Preferences for Developing Countries

Non-reciprocal tariff preferences given by developed to developing countries are the most studied discriminatory trade policies after Western European and North American integration. The wide range of developing countries and of preferential trading arrangements has led to a variety of specific outcomes, but the individual studies do yield some generalizations.

The methods used are similar to those described in Chapter 12, although *ex ante* methods have been relatively more popular than in the EC context because small country assumptions are more plausible. For example, in estimating total trade creation resulting from GSP, it is reasonable to assume a perfectly elastic supply of imports to the donor so that the crucial parameter is the import demand elasticity; while in estimating export expansion of a single GSP beneficiary, it is usually plausible to assume a perfectly elastic demand by the donor so that the crucial parameter is the beneficiary's export supply elasticity. In both of these cases terms of trade changes are excluded by assumption, and the data requirements are not too onerous. Estimating trade diversion is more difficult because it requires knowledge either of export supply elasticities of beneficiaries and non-beneficiaries or of elasticities of substitution between imports from beneficiaries and non-beneficiaries.

1. Gross Trade Effects

The poorest countries in Africa have manufacturing sectors whose price responsiveness is close to zero, which explains why manufactured exports to the EC under the Lomé Convention have not been dynamic. Agarwal *et al.* (1985, 1) refer to 'the meagre trade effects of tariff concessions', and *ex post* analysis based on market shares supports this general assessment.[1] Within this broader picture, however, textile, clothing, and footwear exports have been more dynamic and the Lomé beneficiaries increased their share of the EC market, although over 90 per cent of these exports in 1982 came from Mauritius, Ivory Coast, and Madagascar (Agarwal *et al.*, 1985, 20–2). Moss and Ravenhill conclude from their analysis that 'trade preferences in the contemporary international economic system will have only a marginal impact in the short-term on the exports of developing countries' (1983, 149), but this ignores both the generally 'worst-case' nature of sub-Saharan Africa and the Lomé exceptions whose exports are price-responsive.

All studies of the GSP find positive trade effects, i.e. beneficiaries' exports increased. The contrast to the Lomé studies reflects that some GSP beneficiaries have price-responsive manufacturing sectors. A variety of methods have been used: Clague (1971; 1972), Robert Baldwin and Murray (1977); Murray (1980), and Karsenty and Laird (1987) adopt variants of the *ex ante* Dutch model, Davenport (1986) uses the Blackhurst model for a subset of GSP beneficiaries, MacPhee (1984) applies *ex post* shares analysis, Sapir (1981) a gravity model, and Brown (1987) a computable general equilibrium model. The most detailed of these estimates (Karsenty and Laird, 1987) found a GSP impact on trade flows in the early 1980s of $6.5 billion, i.e. a 2.3 per cent increase in the donors' imports from GSP beneficiaries, and for nineteen of the beneficiaries exports to GSP donors were increased by over 10 per cent as a result of GSP. When beneficiaries are identified separately, a handful of exporters accounts for a large part of GSP-induced export expansion; for example, in Karsenty and Laird's study Hong Kong, South Korea, and Taiwan account for $2.9 billion or 45 per cent of the total, even though their participation in some GSP schemes was restricted.

The conclusion that tariff preferences can stimulate developing countries' export growth *if* domestic conditions are favourable also emerges from case studies of the EC's Mediterranean

[1] Both Agarwal *et al.* and Moss and Ravenhill make simple before-and-after comparisons, but the overall picture is so clearly one of no (or negative) change in market shares that it would scarcely be worth doing more sophisticated analyses. The Moss–Ravenhill analysis is described more fully in Moss (1982) and in their 1982 article, which concludes that 'the impact of the Convention on the trading relationship appears to be negligible' (Moss and Ravenhill, 1992, 853).

agreements.[2] All these agreements offer free access for manufactured exports to the EC, but the outcomes have varied considerably. *Ex post* shares analysis and anecdotal evidence both point to a strong Greek response to the 1961 agreement, whereas the Turkish agreement of 1963 had no observable impact on trade flows until Turkey's adoption of a more outward-oriented development strategy in 1980. In North Africa EC association agreements led to an energetic positive export response from Tunisia, a much more sluggish response from Morocco, and negligible reaction by Algeria, reflecting differing degrees of outward orientation in development strategy and of bureaucratic constraints on business activity in general and on exporters and foreign investors in particular. Among the smaller countries, Maltese exports grew rapidly during the 1970s, led by foreign investors attracted by free access to the EC, while exports from Cyprus, Lebanon, and Portugal were more erratic. Among the larger countries, Spanish manufactured exports to the EC grew faster than those of Egypt. In all of these comparisons export supply conditions, i.e. domestic variables in the beneficiary country, were the crucial determinants of export success or failure, but in the successful cases trade preferences contributed to the degree of success.

The clearest evidence that trade preferences can stimulate developing countries' export growth comes from microeconomic studies. The impact of the EC's Mediterranean agreements is clearly visible in the textiles and clothing trade, where effective rates of protection are high and non-tariff barriers of increasing severity were introduced by the EC after the mid-1970s (Pomfret, 1982b). Among the Lomé Convention signatories, the undoubted beneficiaries include a handful of small banana producing Caribbean countries, who have higher costs than mainland Latin American producers but have guaranteed access to EU markets. The vegetable oils and citrus studies by Clark (1985) and by Gaines *et al.* (1981) referred to below also indicate the impact of trade preferences. Badgett (1978) shows that preferential access to the USA between 1900 and 1940 encouraged the processing of several raw materials within the Philippines, and Davenport (1986,

[2] The empirical evidence on these agreements is assessed in Pomfret (1986a, ch. 4).

110–28) provides microeconomic evidence for 10 items that the EC's GSP scheme encouraged the rise of some infant industries (e.g. umbrellas from Malaysia and Macau, micro-circuits from El Salvador and radios from Brazil).

2. Trade Creation, Trade Diversion, and Welfare Effects

In contrast to the foregoing studies of the gross trade effects on the developing country, there have been few attempts to measure trade creation and trade diversion due to trade preferences for developing countries. This emphasis follows from the primary concern about the beneficiary's welfare, and less interest in the welfare of the donor or of other developed countries which might suffer from trade diversion. There is, however, a debate about whether developing countries would do better with MFN tariff cuts than with GSP treatment and some country-specific concerns about trade diversion aspects of the EC's Mediterranean policy.

The most-cited GSP study is by Robert Baldwin and Tracy Murray (1977). They resolve the need for elasticity of substitution (σ) values by assuming that the cross-price elasticity between imports from preferred and non-preferred sources is equal to the cross-price elasticity between imports and the donor's domestically produced goods.[3] The value of σ is thereby implicity related to more readily available donor-country parameters (Pomfret, 1986b), and trade diversion can easily be estimated. Baldwin and Murray estimate trade diversion from the main GSP schemes to be much smaller than trade creation. This is, however, a consequence of their assumptions, which undervalue σ; at the margin we would expect beneficiary and non-beneficiary goods to be fairly close substitutes because newly industrializing economies lie on both sides of this divide.[4] Other studies using similar *ex*

[3] Thus, for a given price change, $\Delta V/V = \Delta M_n/M_n$ where V is domestic output and M_n imports from non-beneficiaries. They also assume no consumption effects, so trade creation (TC) is ΔV. Trade diversion (TD) is ΔM_n which, from the two assumptions, is equal to $TC\ (M_n/V)$. Because the ratio M_n/V tends to be well below unity, Baldwin and Murray's assumptions normally guarantee TC much greater than TD.

[4] The argument is presented in more detail in Pomfret (1986c). It seems likely that, say, Korean and Taiwanese goods were seen as close substitutes by EC

ante methods but assuming σ values of around 2 have larger trade diversion estimates than Baldwin and Murray (Clark, 1985; Karsenty and Laird, 1987). Clague (1972) showed that such estimates are highly sensitive to the assumed value of σ, and he avoured a higher value of 6.16, derived from relationships among US parameters and justified by the standardized nature of developing country manufactured exports. It is difficult to choose between these alternative σ values, but Baldwin and Murray are outliers. All that can reasonably be concluded is that the GSP schemes involve some trade diversion.[5]

In Brown's (1987) application of CGE methods to GSP, both the size and the sign of the welfare effects are sensitive to changes in σ, although her central case estimates support my view that trade diversion exceeded trade creation. Her CGE approach also suggests some indirect effects of GSP unforeseen by partial equilibrium methods; for example, graduation of Hong Kong and Singapore from the US scheme is estimated to have little impact on American welfare and mainly to benefit the UK (via lower price for imports from Hong Kong and Singapore).

There is little evidence about trade diversion resulting from the Lomé Convention, which is not surprising in view of the small trade effects in total, although it is worth recalling that pressure for the GSP partly reflected non-African developing countries' fears of losing markets because of EC tariff preferences to African countries. On a few commodities the Lomé Convention is highly discriminatory, although this works to protect the interests of previously preferred colonial suppliers. In bananas, for example, Lomé led to little trade diversion compared with the previous situation, especially as the EC members without preferred colonial

importers and Greek and Yugoslav goods were similarly viewed by American importers. In practice, we have no good estimates of the elasticities of substitution. Chen (1994, 145) estimates that the elasticity of substitution between Taiwanese and South Korean exports to the USA in the early 1980s was 2.55 in the short run and 4.54 in the long run, but he points out that these values were changing substantially over time; e.g. during the 1980s South Korea became a less close competitior of Taiwan but Thailand and China became closer competitors of Taiwan.

[5] This is supported by the *ex post* studies of MacPhee (1984) and Sapir and Lundberg (1984). Davenport (1986), using a Blackhurst *ex ante* model (Fig. 9.2), found that for ASEAN countries the EC's GSP scheme led to more trade diversion than trade creation, but all the aggregate magnitudes are small.

suppliers kept liberal banana import regimes (see Section 6.1), but the EU's banana policy involves extensive trade diversion compared with a free trade counterfactual.

Ex ante estimates for the Caribbean Basin Initiative indicate small trade effects (equal to less than 1 per cent of the beneficiaries' exports), but disagree about their division between trade creation and trade diversion. Sawyer and Sprinkle (1984), using the Baldwin–Murray assumption, estimate trade creation of $102 million and trade diversion of $7 million,[6] while Feinberg and Newfarmer (1984) estimate trade creation at $23 million and trade diversion between $40 and $80 million based on boundary assumptions of $\sigma = 1$ and $\sigma = 3$. In view of my earlier criticism of the Baldwin–Murray assumption, I should place more trust in the higher trade diversion figures, and, given the subsequent product exclusions in response to domestic US pressure groups, trade creation under the actual tariff preferences would be less than these early estimates projected.[7]

Trade diversion resulting from the EC's Mediterranean trade preferences is almost certainly greater than that under the GSP or Lomé or the Caribbean Basin Initiative. Non-Mediterranean industrializing countries compete directly with the major beneficiaries of EC tariff preferences (Greece, Spain, Israel, and, on a smaller scale, Tunisia and Malta). Anecdotal evidence suggests that Hong Kong, South Korea, and Taiwan are their main competitors in supplying standardized manufactures to the EC, but unfortunately there has been no systematic study of this trade diversion. Such studies have been undertaken only when the affected non-members have sufficient influence to raise a political issue. Thus, complaints from Florida have highlighted the trade diversion in citrus products, and Gaines *et al.* (1981) have shown that this has been substantial and extends to other external suppliers beside the USA. Concern about the negative impact of EC enlargement to include Greece, Portugal, and Spain on

[6] Applying similar methods to the USA–Israel free trade area, they estimate an $11 m increase in US imports ($9 m trade creation and $2 m trade diversion) and a $178 m increase in US exports ($127 m trade creation and $51 m trade diversion), which are small relative to US macroeconomic aggregates but represent significant changes in Israeli trade flows (Sawyer and Sprinkle, 1986).

[7] Specific examples of exclusions are given in the next section. Clark and Zarrilli (1994) provide an overview of non-tariff restrictions on US imports from CBERA countries.

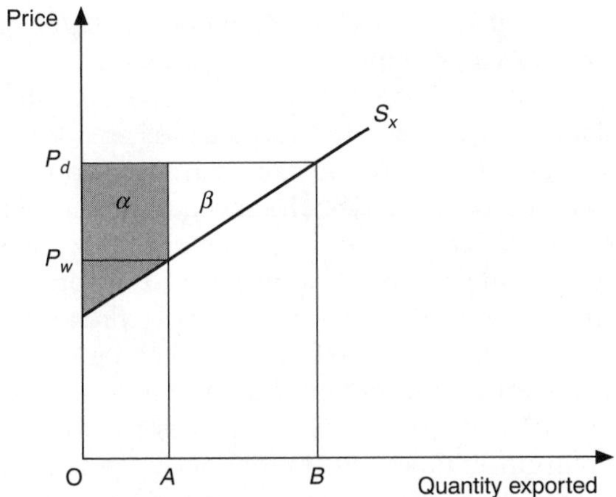

FIG. 15.1 Trade preferences for a small country
S_x is the preference recipient's export supply curve, P_w is the export price received without the trade preference, and P_d is the price received with the trade preference.

Mediterranean non-members has led to a number of studies showing that, while Turkey would be the most affected by Greek accesssion, Morocco, Tunisia, Cyprus, and Israel would be the most affected by Spanish membership.[8] These examples of trade diversion may involve substantial welfare losses because they concern primarily agricultural goods whose EC prices are well above world prices.

The welfare effects of trade preferences for developing countries have seldom been explicitly estimated. With respect to GSP, a reason for this gap is that trade creation estimates are mainly based upon Fig. 8.1, assuming that supply from developing country beneficiaries is perfectly elastic. Within this model, all welfare gains go to the donor countries' consumers. This is implausible in view of the small market share of developing countries in many of the manufactured goods which they export, and for an individual beneficiary a more appropriate partial equilibrium framework is Fig. 15.1. Here all the benefits accrue to

[8] See Tovias (1979) and Taylor (1980). A useful tool has been the Finger–Kreinin similarity index, which provides a rough ranking of relative impact; see Pomfret (1981), Kellman and Schroder (1983), and Donges *et al.* (1982). The wide range of values taken by this index implies substantial variation in σ across different pairs of suppliers to the EC, which casts doubt on the simple assumption used in many

the preference-recipient in two components: α (equal to existing exports covered by GSP multiplied by the size of the preference margin) represents a transfer of tariff revenue from the donor to the beneficiary, and β is the producer surplus on additional GSP-induced exports.[9] The figure indicates why tariff preferences are so popular among beneficiaries: the revenue transfer takes place without any need for change in economic policy or structure, and, if the government chooses to impose an export tax equal to the preference margin, α can become simply financial aid without strings. The gains from GSP are likely to be small for most beneficiaries because the preference margins are not large,[10] and because their export supply elasticities are low. Where the preference margin is more substantial and export supply more elastic, however, the welfare gains from facing preferential tariffs can be significant; for example, the value to Israel of free access to EC markets for manufactured exports under the 1975 Free Trade Area agreement has been estimated at almost 1 per cent of domestic consumption (Pomfret, 1978, 532).

3. Conclusions

Although the term 'developing countries' covers a wide range of economies, and although trade preferences for developing countries have taken various forms, empirical work on this type of

estimates of GDAs' trade effects that $\sigma = 2$ for all country pairs. Sawyer (1984) has used the Baldwin–Murray model to estimate the trade diversion loss suffered by the USA as a result of Spanish EC membership, but the figures are not large and are upward-biased (Pomfret, 1985b). Plummer's (1991a; 1991b) estimates for Greece, Portugal, and Spain suggest aggregate trade diversion from the EC's second enlargement, with grain exporters the most affected third-country producers.

9 Figure 15.1 is discussed in Blackhurst (1971). This analysis assumes competitive markets. Where donor-beneficiary trade is dominated by a small number of donor-based trading companies, they, rather than the developing country exporters, may absorb area α. Kreinin (1973) found some evidence of such behaviour by French importers *vis-à-vis* francophone African beneficiaries of EC tariff preferences.

10 In most GSP schemes (except for those of the USA and some EFTA members) GSP tariff rates have not been zero, so the margin is less than the full MFN tariff rate, and goods with high effective rates of protection (e.g. textiles and clothing) are typically not covered. Quantitative ceilings on GSP imports cut out some of β and perhaps of α too, and, by turning the benefits into a windfall gain for the first to the customs shed, they may increase the bargaining power of traders relative to developing country producers (see fn. 9).

arrangement yields two common-sense general conclusions. First, trade preferences can have an impact on developing countries' exports. Of course, the preference margin, product coverage and any other restrictions will affect the size of this impact, as will the beneficiaries' export supply elasticity. For at least two decades, development economists have been recognizing that response to export incentives is not limited to industrialized and newly industrializing countries, and the evidence in this section for countries as disparate as Tunisia, Mauritius, and the Philippines shows that trade preferences are no different from other export incentives in this respect.[11] Secondly, whether trade preferences affect the volume of a developing country's exports or not, they yield welfare gains to the beneficiary, which can be undisruptive in the sense of not requiring economic and social change. Admittedly, the number of empirical estimates of these gains is limited, but the qualitative result follows from the small-country character of most developing countries and the unambiguous welfare implications of freer trade between a large and a small country.

More debatable than the possible impact on trade flows or the beneficiary's welfare gain is the desirability of trade preferences for developing countries when non-beneficiaries' interests are taken into account. The empirical contribution to this debate is trade diversion estimates. Lack of trade diversion arising from the Lomé Convention should assuage other developing countries' fears of losing EC markets.[12] On the other hand, Florida citrus producers clearly lost EC markets to Mediterranean oranges as a result of trade preferences, which led to US–EC disputes over compensation and played a significant role in the shift in US attitudes towards introducing its own discriminatory trade policies.

[11] This view of economic behaviour in developing countries has become so widely accepted that the evidence on trade preferences' impact should be no surprise, but politicians and political scientists often ascribe extreme values of potency or impotency to tariff preferences. The unfounded hyperbole surrounding the launch of the Lomé Convention or the Caribbean Basin Initiative represents one extreme; the other is reflected in the quote from Moss and Ravenhill in the first section of this chapter or on the disparaging assessment of the EC's Mediterranean preferences by Tsoukalis (1977, 435–6).

[12] In the case of bananas, however, the lack of trade diversion relative to the pre-Lomé situation is too narrow a basis for assessment. A non-discriminatory EU policy would allow lower-cost non-traditional suppliers to increase their exports to the EU, benefiting EU consumers as well as the new exporters.

With respect to the GSP, the debate has focused on whether the beneficiaries would benefit more from cuts in the donors' MFN tariffs than from GSP. In a crucial respect this is an incomplete question, because first of all the MFN tariff cuts to be compared with GSP must be specified; if all GSP tariff rates were made MFN, then the beneficiaries would be worse off by the amount of their trade diversion gains under GSP, but better off to the extent that ceilings ceased to apply. The more far-reaching the MFN cuts were, the more likely it was that developing countries could gain by throwing their weight behind GATT/WTO negotiations. The outcome is a matter of bargaining strategy and strength, which economists are poorly equipped to assess; but the more trade diversion results from current GSP schemes, the more the developing countries risk to lose by swapping GSP for MFN tariff reductions. Baldwin and Murray conclude that developing countries would be four times better off with MFN tariff cuts, but this is because their method yields low trade diversion estimates and because their comparison is with MFN liberalization which goes far beyond current GSP schemes. Higher estimates of trade diversion tilt the comparison more in favour of GSP, although Karsenty and Laird still find that MFN cuts without GSP-type ceilings would be better for developing countries. Ahmad (1978) concludes in favour of GSP because he believes that trade diversion is greater and that MFN liberalization would be restricted. This debate remained unresolved because of our poor trade diversion estimates and lack of agreed point of comparison. Of course, the presence of *any* trade diversion—and all empirical studies of GSP do find some—implies that GSP is inferior to equal MFN tariff liberalization in terms of global resource misallocation.

Even more important in determining LDCs' attitudes towards one-way preferences has been the widespread tendency towards preference limitation. This has characterized the GSP, where the USA has responded to increased trade by lowering competitive need and graduation trigger points. The USA also backed up its shift to aggressive unilateralism in the second half of the 1980s by withdrawing GSP privileges from Thailand and India; this was a more attractive form of retaliation against other countries' perceived unfair trade practices than raising bound tariffs, precisely because it was not GATT-illegal. The EU too has excluded from

GSP treatment specific categories of imports from certain countries; this appears to be more discretionary than the US practice, with no criteria other than increased import competition (e.g. the January 1996 exclusions applied to a variety of categories of goods from China, Libya, Chile, Brazil, Saudi Arabia, South Korea, Hong Kong, Brunei, and Singapore). Thus, the comparison between GSP and MFN tariffs is deficient if it neglects the greater possibility of a whittling away of access under one-way GSP schemes than under GATT/WTO-negotiated MFN obligations.[13]

The problem of preference limitation has also arisen for beneficiaries of the Lomé Convention and the Caribbean Basin Economic Recovery Act.[14] As described earlier, the Lomé trade provisions have become so meaningless, and so hemmed in by threat of safeguard actions if they do have any trade-creating impact, that the Lomé Convention is now viewed mainly as an aid arrangement. CBERA beneficiaries soon suffered from unilateral restrictions on access to the US market for exports that had begun to grow quickly in response to the tariff preferences; for example, a 1986 countervailing duty action against cut flower imports from Costa Rica led to imposition of a 46 per cent tariff, and (also in 1986) the US banned imports of ethanol made from EC wine. Most important of all was the reduction in US sugar import quotas accompanying increases in domestic price supports in the 1980s. The CBERA partners were not sheltered from this unilateral measure and did not receive preferential shares of the quotas, so that exemption from US sugar duties of $0.006 per pound was a meaningless clause in the Act; sugar exports from the Caribbean partners dropped from a 1975–81 annual

[13] According to UNCTAD's 1994 GSP Review, only 68% of the EU's dutiable imports from developing countries qualified for GSP treatment and only 33% (i.e. less than half of those eligible) actually took them up; corresponding figures for the USA were 36% and 18%, and for Japan, 35% and 16%.

[14] Another example of the restrictiveness of donor-designed trade agreements was provided by the EU's treatment of the Central European countries in 1991/2. Although the EU promptly dismantled many quantitative restrictions on imports from the economies in transition, there was no immediate change with respect to sensitive items (iron and steel, textiles and clothing, and food and agriculture products), which accounted for more than 40% of Polish and Czechoslovak exports and 60% of Hungarian exports to the EU, and on which restrictions were to be dismantled slowly. Sereghová (1995, 257) argues that lack of market access during the early 1990s led to the unnecessary collapse of many enterprises which could have survived had EU markets been open to them.

average of 1.7 million tons to 442,200 tons in 1989. Pastor (1995, 69) reports US government estimates that the CBERA created 136,000 manufacturing jobs in the Caribbean between 1983 and 1989, while the cut in sugar quotas cost CBERA countries 400,000 jobs (and $1.8 billion in forgone revenue) over the same period. When CBERA renewal legislation was drafted in 1989, it initially extended coverage and offered guarantees against unilateral US measures (e.g. by fixing the sugar quotas at their 1989 level), but all of these provisions were eliminated as the legislation passed through Congress (Fishlow and Haggard, 1992, 22).

Empirical evidence sheds light on why the LDCs lost interest in GSP and other one-way preferential arrangements in the 1980s and 1990s. Most important of all was the acceptance of donor stinginess (apart from a few specific beneficiaries such as EU banana suppliers); the design of one-way schemes was influenced by domestic interests in the importing country who resisted possible trade creation, and even when increased imports had not been anticipated the preference donors showed little compunction in amending the schemes to close the doors. The contrast between forced acceptance of increases in GSP tariffs and the weight of pressure against any increases in bound MFN tariffs was highlighted in the US super and special 301 cases of the late 1980s (see Section 17.1), but it was also evident from many other examples. By the late 1980s, an increasing number of developing countries were willing to throw their weight behind the Uruguay Round.

16

Global Issues

In order to analyse the relationship between regional trading arrangements and world trade patterns, a few studies have applied the *ex post* and *ex ante* methods described in previous chapters at a global level. Analysis based on changes in world trade shares is suggestive, but it is difficult to establish the causal connection between increasing or decreasing regionalization of world trade and policy-induced regionalism. *Ex ante* methods can capture such causality, but models of the world economy inevitably involve major simplifying assumptions so that their specific results are easily challenged.

1. Has Regionalism led to Regionalization of World Trade?

The simple question of whether regionalism is waxing or waning is difficult to answer. A count of regional trading arrangements does not resolve the matter because many are paper projects only, while even those that have an impact are of differing significance. Some observers (e.g. Snape, 1996) cite the increased number of RTAs reported to GATT in the first half of the 1990s as evidence of a surge of regionalism, but these were dominated by RTAs among former Comecon members and between EU or EFTA countries and Eastern European countries; i.e. they resulted from a realignment of RTAs rather than net additions. This episode could plausibly be considered one of economic disintegration as the number of trading units expanded with the dissolution of Yugoslavia, the USSR, and Czechoslovakia, rather than an upsurge of regionalism.

This raises the additional issue of which RTAs are important? CUSTA was more important than NAFTA in that USA–Canada bilateral trade flows were much larger than CUSTA–Mexico trade flows, but the distortionary impact of NAFTA is likely to be larger owing to the bigger differences between the CUSTA and

Mexican economies. The Caribbean Basin Initiative led to a GDA that was of minimal importance to global trade flows, but of major significance in signalling a crucial shift in US trade policy from its previous commitment to non-discrimination.

A more tractable question is whether world trade is becoming more or less regionalized. This can be a preliminary to then asking whether the regionalization is due to regionalism in trade policies.

Measurement of regionalization is not straightforward. The obvious criteria are trade shares, but simple trade shares suffer from the *ceteris paribus* problem and from the adding-up constraint.

An example of the *ceteris paribus* problem is the rapid growth of intra-East Asian trade in recent decades. This is due in part to the rapid growth in the region which has made these countries' markets more important, so that ascribing all of the increased intra-regional trade to discriminatory policies is obviously false (Frankel, 1993). This market-size effect can be separated out by using a trade intensity index, TI_{ij}, which measures the intensity of country i's exports to country j by normalizing the share of exports to j in i's total exports by j's share in global imports (Drysdale and Garnaut, 1982):

$$TI_{ij} = (X_{ij}/X_i)/[M_j/(M_w - M_i)],$$

where X and M refer to exports and imports, and the subscripts i and j refer to countries and w to the world. (M_i is subtracted from total world imports, because country i cannot export to itself.) The trade intensity index is a rather crude measure—it does not, for example, allow for the varying commodity composition of countries' trade; but further adjustments to the index risk obscuring what is happening.

Anderson and Norheim (1993) is the most through study of long-term regionalization.[1] Their main tool is the trade intensity index. They find that regionalization has increased since the 1940s,

[1] A related exercise is reported in Norheim *et al.* (1993). A further difficulty in such exercises lies in defining regions. Defining Europe as a region would indicate the 1939–45 war as a major disruption in intra-regional trade and 1989 as an important event in restoring intra-European trade flows, whereas defining Western Europe and Eastern Europe as separate regions would produce regionalization measures suggesting greater significance to the EC and the CMEA.

and ascribe this especially to the end of imperial trade preferences which had artificially stimulated inter-regional trade during the nineteenth century and the first half of the twentieth century. The same point was made less systematically in Part I of this book and by Kleiman (1976).

The central result of Anderson and Norheim illustrates the second difficulty of trade share analysis. Many observers of world trade have pointed to the increased regionalization of Western European trade in the second half of the twentieth century and have ascribed it to the discriminatory trade policies pursued by the EC/EU. Anderson and Norheim, however, emphasize the declining share of imperial trade following the decolonization in the two decades after 1945, which has as a necessary counterpart the increase in other trade shares because all shares must add up to 100 per cent. Whether the changing geographical patterns of trade of the former imperial powers in the second half of the twentieth century reflects a declining share of former colonies or an increasing share of European neighbours is akin to asking whether a glass is half full or half empty. Separating out the policy-based causes of these long-term shifts in trade patterns is difficult.

2. General Equilibrium Models of World Trade

John Whalley's construction in the early 1980s of computable general equilibrium (CGE) models covering the major world trading areas was an innovative approach to modelling world trade patterns. The CGE models have the advantage of incorporating crucial microeconomic linkages, which in particular permits them to capture the terms of trade effects of alternative policies. To make computation manageable, however, aggregation and simplifying assumptions are required; specifically, Whalley's model utilizes the Armington assumption, i.e. products from differing countries are qualitatively different.

Whalley (1985) estimates the effects of unilateral tariff reductions, multilateral trade liberalization, and various GDAs among seven major trading areas. In all of these exercises terms of trade effects dominate, so that unilateral tariff reduction is seldom beneficial for the country making the changes. Multilateral liberalization leads to small global gains, and the implication is that GATT is beneficial not so much for its potential to reap further gains but rather because it deters countries from imposing optimum tariffs which would be well above present levels. With respect to GDAs, Vinerian trade creation and trade diversion effects are far less important than terms of trade effects.

Whalley's conclusions about GDAs focus on their distributional impact:

> geographically discriminating protection that leaves average protection levels much the same seems to have small effects on the protecting region, with the largest effects detrimental to the region discriminated against and to the advantage of the region favoured by discrimination. (1985, 215)

Accepting this conclusion implies that the whole theoretical development of customs union theory around Fig. 8.1 had little practical significance! Whalley's results are sensitive to his choice of parameter values, and with respect to GDAs the parameter σ is critical. With respect to a US–EC free trade area, for example, replacing the central case value for σ in the neighbourhood of unity by values of 3 or 5 increases the terms of trade changes and gains to the participants 'sharply', while increasing the negative impact on the rest of the world and changing the global welfare effect from positive to negative.[2] In general, the greater the elasticity of substitution between goods from different national sources, the sharper the distributional conflicts and the more likely are negative global welfare consequences of GDAs.

How plausible are Whalley's conclusions, which conflict with the more common emphasis by economists on mutually benefiting gains from international trade? To a large extent the conflict is inherent in the design of CGE models, which involve aggregation levels which are the antithesis of the small open economy with competitive markets. By working at an aggregation level involving very broad sectors, Whalley's models cannot capture gains from within-sector specialization (Parmenter, 1986). The aggregation level also biases upwards the terms of trade effects; with only seven trading units, all are likely to have market power, whereas disaggregation to more trading units would bring more

[2] The sensitivity analysis is reported in Bob Hamilton and John Whalley (1985).

competition into the model and reduce the terms of trade benefits from tariffs.

Whalley's book provides an antidote to the partial equilibrium nature of most empirical work on GDAs. Its only real predecessors are the papers by Petith (1977) and by Miller and Spencer (1977) on the EC. Like them, Whalley finds a major role for price changes. Although the biases inherent in current-vintage CGE models generally lead to an overstatement of terms of trade changes and an underestimation of Vinerian resource allocation effects of GDAs, these models provide a counterweight to methods which can only capture the latter and assume away the former. Whalley's work also emphasizes once again the central role of σ: as his central case he assumes a fairly low value, which, even if appropriate for broadly defined trading units, would not be for individual trading nations.[3] In a multi-country extension plausible σ values would often be higher and the global resource misallocation and distributional conflicts even greater than in Whalley's exercises.

3. Conclusions

The defining feature of GDAs is that they favour one trading partner over another. Thus, the central parameter for empirical studies is the elasticity of substitution between imports from different sources, σ. Lack of knowledge about plausible σ values plagues all empirical work on GDAs, and deprives all *ex ante* estimates of claims to precision. On the other hand, *ex post* methods are inevitably dogged by the need to create a convincing counterfactual situation. Despite these problems, the large body of empirical literature on GDAs does yield some fairly robust conclusions.

[3] The value of σ can also be expected to vary according to the commodity aggregation level and from product to product (Srinivasan and Whalley, 1986, 332). The Armington assumption with a single σ value is a source of discontent among CGE modellers, but they continue to use it because it avoids the unrealistic specialization levels which otherwise tend to characterize solvable models (Srinivasan and Whalley, 1986, 7). One empirical problem is the existence of documented cases where relative price changes were nowhere near sufficient to account for market share changes if σ had been in the normally assumed 1 to 3 change; e.g. Petri calculates that the 1960–80 substitution of Japanese for US steel would require $\sigma = 32$ to fit with reported price data (Srinivasan and Whalley, 1986, 227).

First and foremost, GDAs can have an impact on trade flows. There is no necessary impact; for example, a preferred trading partner's export supply may be perfectly inelastic for one reason or another, but there are many cases in the contemporary world of preferential margins being sufficient to elicit a response. Relative prices do matter in international trade, although price responsiveness varies.

The immediate beneficiaries of GDAs are exporters receiving trade preferences, and their competitors are the losers. The magnitude of the positive welfare effects tends to be small, unless the patchy evidence on scale economies is widely applicable. There is a widespread belief that the negative welfare effects are even smaller, although I have argued that the EC's agricultural policy and the GSP involve more trade diversion than is generally believed. If the larger role for trade diversion is accepted, then the losers are non-participants in the GDA and the population at large within the GDA (as taxpayers and consumers), while import-competing producers in GDA member states are shielded from trade creation.

More controversial are the general equilibrium effects of GDAs on world prices. Many studies assume these to be zero, while a few models find terms of trade changes to be the principal effect of GDAs involving large trading nations.

Although well designed *ex ante* and *ex post* studies of a particular discriminatory trading arrangement should yield similar results, anticipatory and after-the-event estimates differ systematically. Anticipatory studies usually assume a pure arrangement (i.e. a customs union or free trade area with unrestricted internal trade or an unrestricted set of one-way preferences), while later studies can be adjusted for all the details of a GDA as actually applied. The pattern is for later studies to find a smaller ratio of trade creation to trade diversion and usually to find smaller trade effects in general. The trade diversion bias of implementation is apparent in the CAP and in NAFTA.[4] The effect limitation bias is present in most one-way preferences, including GSP, and in most regional integration schemes among developing countries.

[4] On the EC the most dramatic contrast is between the positive welfare effects of Britain's participation in a European free trade arrangement estimated by Johnson (1958b) and the substantial negative estimates of the welfare effects of the UK's accession to the EU in 1973 reported in S. 12.3.

PART IV

POLITICAL ECONOMY

Introduction to Part IV

The first part of this book raised the question of why, despite the strong GATT statement in favour of non-discrimination, discriminatory trade policies have flourished since 1947 and the trend away from non-discrimination accelerated in the 1980s to the point where the multilateral trading system based on non-discriminatory trade policies was seriously threatened. The theoretical and empirical analysis in Parts II and III heighten the paradox and suggest a solution: discriminatory trade policies are against the global interest, but they lead to a variety of economic consequences, which may be beneficial to the participants. In Part IV, the political economy of discriminatory trading arrangements is examined first from the national perspective and then from the global perspective.

Chapter 17 recapitulates the reasons why discriminatory trade policies may be adopted. The economic arguments derive mainly from the existence of gainers and losers, and from the political economy of trade policy formation in which potential gainers may have disproportionate weight because they invest in greater lobbying effort or because institutions work in their favour. Thus, the institutional framework and perceptions of gains and losses matter as well as the actual consequences of alternative trade policies. Other non-economic factors may play a role if policy-makers use trade policy in support of strategic goals such as creating influence spheres or promoting political integration. Chapter 17 also provides some examples of how political economy considerations may lead to the adoption of policies involving net national welfare loss (illustrated by VERs), how perceptions are shaped by other countries' policies (illustrated by the interaction of EU and US preferential trading arrangements with other countries), and how arrangements between large countries and small countries are asymmetrical, with the small country seeking economic benefits and the large country political benefits (illustrated by GSP).

Chapter 18 turns to systemic consequences of the proliferation of discriminatory trade policies. The only historical episode is the deterioration of the global trading system which culminated in the 1930s. A similar process seemed to be in train by the late 1980s, and a major question is how (or whether) the negative outcome of the 1930s was averted. The simple economic explanation, that trade breakdown is a negative-sum game and thus will be avoided, is inadequate in light of the 1930s' experience. What is necessary is to identify the differences in global environment in the late twentieth century which allowed the major trading nations to step back and seek a co-operative outcome by strengthening the GATT trade regime based on non-discrimination.

17

Why do Discriminatory Trading Arrangements Exist?

In this chapter, I will analyse why geographically discriminatory trading arrangements exist, first by examining their immediate consequences to find proximate explanations and in Section 2 by trying to situate discriminatory trade policies into endogenous tariff theory; the former approach yields a taxonomy of actual discriminatory arrangements, while the latter goes deeper in explaining why they occur when they do and why they take the form they do.

1. Four Sets of Explanations for the Existence of Discriminatory Trade Policies

Proximate explanations for the existence of discriminatory trade policies can be divided into four categories. First, most reasons for non-discriminatory trade barriers can also apply to discriminatory trade policies. Secondly, the gains to exporters provide a reason for seeking preferential access to markets, perhaps by reciprocal exchange of tariff preferences. Thirdly, discriminatory treatment of a trading partner can be used as a bargaining lever to obtain changes in the partner's trade policies. Fourthly, discriminatory trade policies may be used to further foreign policy objectives.

Extension of general arguments for trade barriers

The main arguments used to support non-discriminatory trade barriers can be adapted to explain discriminatory trade policies; indeed, two of these arguments are even stronger when discrimination is possible. A large country can exploit its monopsony power by using import restrictions to improve its terms of trade;

the 'optimum tariff' (i.e. the tariff level that maximizes the importing country's net gains) is inversely related to the elasticity of import supply. If the large country can isolate import suppliers from one another, setting discriminatory tariffs according to differences in their supply elasticities will increase the importing country's net gains above those from the uniform optimum tariff —just as a discriminating monopolist can obtain higher profits than a single-price monopolist. McCulloch and Pinera (1977) have suggested the discriminatory monopsonist argument as a partial explanation of GSP, assuming that donors' supply of imports from developing countries is more elastic than from industrialized countries. The validity of this assumption is debatable, but in any event the small GSP trade effects reported in Chapter 15 make it unlikely that terms of trade changes in favour of GSP donors could have been significant.[1] More substantial terms of trade changes for the importing countries have been associated with EC policies (especially towards agricultural imports), but I will argue below that there were more important motivations for EC formation. In sum, it is widely believed that the optimum tariff argument has not laid behind postwar trade barriers, and it seems even less likely to explain discriminatory trade policies.

The revenue motive for imposing tariffs may also be strengthened by the possibility of geographical discrimination, although this motive too seems of little practical relevance. If administrative costs depend upon length of borders and gross revenue upon GNP, then under some geographical configurations a customs union of contiguous states could increase members' net tariff revenues. For smaller German states with dispersed territories this may have been a motive for joining the Zollverein (Dumke, 1976).[2] With economic development, however, capacity to administer non-trade taxes improves and the drawbacks of trade taxes (with respect to resource misallocation, equity, etc.) become more apparent, so that the share of trade taxes in total revenue decreases until it is quite small for more developed

[1] Some pre-1919 colonial trading arrangements may fit the McCulloch–Pinera hypothesis better than GSP, but I know of no empirical work in this vein.

[2] Exemption from transit duties was also a motive for some smaller states to join the Zollverein and for the Transvaal and the Orange Free State to join the South African Customs Union. Transit duties have, however, disappeared in the 20th c. (Viner, 1950, 62–5).

countries (Greenaway, 1984). Thus, we would expect the revenue motive to now be of little relevance to customs unions involving developed economies, although it may retain importance for mini-states forming customs unions with large neighbours (e.g. San Marino or Monaco).[3] More surprisingly, the revenue motive seems to have been unimportant in customs unions among developing countries,[4] perhaps because the declining share of trade taxes in government revenue continued apace; in El Salvador, for example, import taxes' share of total government revenue rose slightly during the 1950s (from 36 to 41 per cent) but fell substantially (to 19 per cent in 1974) after CACM membership (Wilford and Wilford, 1978, 508).

In practice, the main motivation for trade barriers has been to protect import-competing sectors of the domestic economy. Discriminatory trade barriers provide protection from imports from a specific source, but their effectiveness from the domestic producer's perspective depends upon who is the next most competitive supplier—the domestic producers or producers in another foreign country. When trade diversion is the main consequence, trade barriers must be extended to cover all potentially significant foreign suppliers if they are to achieve their protectionary goal. Textiles and clothing provide an example of expanding coverage; trade barriers were extended from Japan to all low-wage producers, from cotton to other fibres, and from textiles to clothing in order to plug gaps in effective protection left by each discriminatory measure (see Chapter 5). Similar trade diversion was observed during the 1977–81 orderly marketing arrangements imposed by the USA on footwear imports from Taiwan and South

[3] Smuggling is an added complication. The immediate impetus for Monaco's customs union with France was French desire to forestall smuggling (Viner, 1950, 83–4). As long as the EU retains internal trade barriers the administrative savings from customs union are small, but intra-EU smuggling provides an incentive for members to move further towards internal free trade; Norton (1986) provides a case study of smuggling across the Irish border induced by the CAP.

[4] The Syria–Lebanon customs union and some customs unions, among British African colonies before their independence are possible exceptions to this generalization. Loss of tariff revenue may be a (minor) reason for newly independent nations' scepticism about the various African preferential trading schemes, and fiscal compensation figured prominently in West African blueprints (Robson, 1983). Attempts to turn SADC into a customs union are frustrated by disagreement over the common external tariff and the distribution of tariff revenue; the revenue is crucial for small land-locked SADC members such as Lesotho.

Korea (C. Pearson, 1983), although in this case the trade barriers were removed rather than expanded. Where substitution possibilities are small, discriminatory trade barriers can provide more substantial protection for domestic producers; the post-1981 voluntary restraints on Japanese automobile exports to the USA are a good example (European car exporters failed to increase their American market share significantly, and US car-makers enjoyed some prosperous years), but even in this case, where new entry is costly and risky, alternative foreign suppliers (e.g. South Korea) eventually began to replace some of the barred Japanese imports in the US market. In sum, if a trade barrier is truly discriminatory, then its protective effect is limited.

There are two related reasons why, despite their shortcomings as protectionist measures, discriminatory trade policies may be used to protect domestic producers. The GATT provided for a co-operative system of multilateral trade liberalization, in contrast to the prewar situation where the only external check on high national tariffs was fear of retaliation. If a country raised its bound MFN tariffs or introduced import quotas, it would both contravene GATT and risk retaliation. A bilaterally negotiated trading arrangement was a way of sidestepping GATT obligations without incurring an open breach, since the countries most likely to object to a trade barrier are the ones whose exports are harmed and without a formal complaint there would be no GATT investigation. Acquiescence of a targeted exporter is obtained because by voluntarily restraining exports the country can realize a quota rent, which at least partially compensates for lost export volume and which leaves the exporting country better off than with an equal-sized quota administered by the importing country.[5] Discriminatory trade policies reduce the risk of retaliation both because of the compensation effect via quota rents and because

[5] The magnitude and distribution of the quota rents will depend upon demand and supply elasticities in the importing country, the competitive position of third-country suppliers, the size of the quota, and the institutional arrangement for issuing export permits. Although the magnitude is usually difficult to observe, evidence from Hong Kong (where the market for export licences is open) and from studies of the Japanese auto VERs suggests that it can be substantial. The willingness of Japan to continue observing VERs on auto exports to the USA and VCR exports to the EC even after the importing countries ceased to request restraint confirms that there are benefits to being invited to adopt monopolistic pricing policies.

they can be selectively used against small or weak countries. None of these advantages, however, removes the drawback (from the protectionist perspective) that imports from other sources may replace the voluntarily restrained imports and leave domestic producers exposed to competition in the long run.

The infant industry argument can be extended to justify protection within a supranational grouping; if national-level support of infant industries is limited by the size of the market, then a customs union among like-minded industrializing nations could overcome the obstacle. This philosophy has underlain many integration efforts in Latin America and Africa, although with little success (Chapter 5 and Section 14.1). Trade barriers are not the best means of encouraging a new industry, and when several nations are involved disputes about industrial location are inevitable. More durable have been customs unions that increased the protected market of already politically powerful producers and where debate over the location of economic activity was precluded (e.g. the incorporation of the Prairie provinces in the Canadian customs union, and of Tankanyika into a 1920s customs union with Kenya and Uganda), although other motives were also relevant in these cases. Similarly, the political influence of French and German farmers helps to explain their governments' support for including agriculture in Western European economic integration, while the food-importing European countries were attracted to a free trade area excluding agriculture.

The new trade theories of the 1980s based on imperfect competition also provide justifications for discriminatory trade policies, which could increase national or even global welfare. With monopolistic competition, measures to increase the market share of domestic firms could yield benefits through increased scale economies, although the presumption is that free trade will be beneficial because it will increase the number of varieties available in the national market as well as maximizing global welfare. In oligopoly models the policy implications depend upon the specific assumptions, although the most influential models have been based on duopoly in which case trade policies cannot be discriminatory. (They either affect the one foreign firm or they do not.)

Finally, national security reasons may justify the favoured treatment of suppliers of strategic products or the extension of trade barriers to include in the customs area like-minded nations whose reliability in time of crisis is undoubted. German bilateral agreements during the 1930s and British Imperial Preference were in part based on such considerations (Chapter 3), although they merge imperceptibly into the more general political arguments considered below.

Discriminatory trade policies necessarily involve manipulation of trade barriers, and thus it is no surprise that general arguments for trade barriers can be applied to discriminatory trade policies. In two cases the general argument may be strengthened by discriminatory implementation (i.e. the optimum tariff and revenue arguments), but the practical relevance of these cases is minimal. There is also a theoretical basis for modifying the infant industry argument to explain discriminatory trade arrangements among developing countries,[6] but, despite providing the intellectual foundations for a number of integration schemes, this case too is of limited relevance to explain the increasing share of world trade affected by discriminatory trade policies. In contrast, the most important motive for postwar trade barriers (i.e. protection of specific domestic producers) cannot be modified logically to explain recourse to discriminatory rather than non-discriminatory trade policies, but for institutional reasons the industrialized countries have increasingly resorted to discriminatory trade policies in order to protect domestic industries.

The gains to exporters

The clearest economic motive for discriminatory trade arrangements lies in the gain to the recipient of favoured treatment. In standard customs union theory (as in Fig. 8.1) this source of gain is ruled out by assuming constant costs on the part of the exporting nation, but more generally (as in Fig. 9.2) the favoured exporter is the only unambiguous gainer—as Adam Smith pointed out two centuries ago.

In cases of one-way trade preferences, the favoured exporting nations have often pressed for the original arrangement, and invariably support the arrangement's continuing existence

[6] This was essentially the argument used by Johnson and by Cooper and Massell to resolve the paradox between the JCM proposition and the existence of discriminatory trade policies.

under almost any terms. The reason for this acquiescence lies in the non-negative economic gain which involves no necessary domestic redistribution (cf. Fig. 15.1). The magnitude of the gain may be small, and the terms of one-way preferences are often outside the beneficiaries' control, but there is no economic reason for refusing this type of gain. Thus, the beneficiaries of GSP, the Lomé Convention, etc., actively sought preferential treatment, and, although they complain about the terms (and changes in the terms to their disadvantage), they end up going along with the donor's conditions.[7]

If the preferential treatment is reciprocal, then all partners will be favoured exporters of some products, and will enjoy gains from increased exports. If the initial (internal) terms of trade remain unchanged, then the partners will enjoy improved terms of trade with the rest of the world. That this was a conscious aim of the EC is doubtful but, if Petith's results are any guide, it was an economic benefit to the Six which could have contributed to the Community's success. More generally, analysis of the empirical evidence (in Chapter 12) suggests that the economic success of the European Community can be ascribed not to a favourable balance between trade creation and trade diversion, but rather to the shifting of some economic costs to non-members so that the Six enjoyed net benefits.

The exporting motive becomes more complex in the presence of footloose transnational corporations (TNCs), which engage in global scanning to identify the best location for each activity. As mentioned in Part III, several cases of small countries with preferential access to large markets have resulted in capital inflows by TNCs using the small country as an export platform. This has been a motive in, for example, Maltese and Tunisian PTAs with the EU and the Caribbean countries PTAs with the USA and Canada. In NAFTA, there is evidence that TNCs from the more developed members designed the agreement so that they would be especially favoured (via rules of origin) in the less developed partner; in this case Mexico might gain from capital inflows but by less than if the nationality of the foreign investors were unrestricted, and US and Canadian TNCs would reap additional benefits.

[7] The behaviour of Hungary and Bulgaria towards Germany during the 1930s followed a similar pattern.

Bargaining motives

Bargaining motives for discriminating among trading partners are related to arguments in the previous two subsections. If tariff levels are not contingent on other countries' tariffs, then a country has an incentive to levy nationally optimal tariffs. This was the essence of the French and Spanish case during the interwar period for withholding MFN treatment from the USA until American tariff levels were reduced. A country's bargaining strength depends upon its own optimum tariff rate; the larger the optimum tariff, the more willing trading partners should be to bargain in order to keep the tariff below its optimum level. Readiness to bargain also follows from the benefits of gaining market access for exports; if preferential access is offered (or discriminatory restriction of access is threatened), the incentive to bargain should be even stronger. The obvious generalization is that bargaining is more likely to succeed when pursued by a large country offering special treatment, positive or negative, to a small country.

The pre-GATT commercial history recounted in Chapters 2 and 3 offers little support for the efficacy of bilateral bargaining methods. On the one hand, the 1930s provide several examples of successful bargaining threats, e.g. by the UK against the smaller northern European countries. On the other hand, the conditional MFN clause that characterized US commercial treaties up to the First World War used the threat of non-MFN treatment (or the offer of MFN treatment) to extract concessions from America's trading partners, but in practice the conditional MFN clause led to frequent controversies and in the early twentieth century the USA received poorer market access than many rivals; the conditional MFN clause was then dropped in favour of a non-discriminatory trade policy. Between the wars France twice tried to adopt a conditional MFN strategy (in the 1920s and the mid-1930s), but on both occasions abandoned the approach as it failed to yield any advantages for French exports.

The bargaining approach was to some extent incorporated in GATT procedures, especially in the 1950s and 1960s when negotiated tariff reductions were made on the basis of reciprocal bargains with the principal supplier of a good. Since MFN tariff reductions are passed on to all GATT signatories, the effect is on the whole non-discriminatory, although there is some evidence that the outcome has not been totally non-discriminatory. Developing countries were not active participants in GATT rounds before the 1980s, and consequently liberalization of trade in goods of special interest to them was weak. Similarly, US tariffs are higher when weighted by imports from Japan, a latecomer to GATT, than when weighted by imports from Canada, a GATT founder member who already had two trade agreements with the USA from the 1930s (Lavergne, 1983). Later GATT rounds continued to involve bargaining, but bilateral commodity-by-commodity negotiations were abandoned in favour of more multilateral negotiations on general tariff-cutting formulae or on non-tariff measures.

Actual cases of bargaining motives being relevant to postwar discriminatory trade arrangements are difficult to identify. The EFTA was a response to the formation of the EC, which had imposed some trade diversion costs on non-members; EFTA in turn imposed similar (although small) costs on EC members. If this was a bargaining ploy, it was successful, in so far as all EFTA members gained free access to EC markets for manufactured goods after 1972, but it is unbelievable that the first EC enlargement and agreement on the EC–EFTA free trade area represented EC submission to EFTA's bargaining strength. Israel's 1975 free trade agreement with the EC might also be seen as putting pressure on the USA to sign a similar agreement in order to avoid loss of Israeli markets by American exports competing with EC goods; but again, it is inconceivable that the American decision to negotiate a USA–Israel free trade agreement was in response to such pressure. The bargaining element was a component of Canadian advocates' case for a USA–Canada free trade area, since the larger part of Canadian benefits would come from access to American markets; unilateral Canadian tariff elimination was presumably less attractive because it would give away a potential bargaining chip for US agreement to reduce duties on Canadian goods. The last is the most plausible case of bargaining motives playing a part, although the real issues concerned non-tariff measures which both parties wanted to address. While a logical case can be made for using discriminatory trade policies as bargaining levers, the bargaining motive has not been the driving force behind actual postwar discriminatory trade policies.

Advocacy of discriminatory trade measures as a bargaining chip became popular in the USA during the early 1980s, when the widening trade deficit was blamed by some legislators on the unfair trading practices of specific countries (notably Japan). The 1980s revival of the bargaining argument for discriminatory trade policies in the USA was concerned with means rather than ends. Discriminatory trade measures aimed at opening up other countries' markets would be temporary; if they became permanent then the policy would have failed, although it might be captured by domestic interests that benefited from the measures.

Can the goal of universal trade liberalization be better achieved by bilateral confrontation or by multilateral GATT negotiations? The answer to this question is not self-evident, nor is it readily analysed with economists' tools; economists simply do not have good theories of negotiating strategies among a small number of agents. Cline (1982), in analysing the US debates, drew up a taxonomy of outcomes, but the crucial and unknown variable is the probability of each outcome.

Bayard and Elliott (1994), znalysing the effectiveness of US section 301 actions between 1975 and 1994, conclude that US negotiating objectives were at least partially achieved in 35 of the 72 cases studied and that the success rate climbed after the adoption of aggressive unilateralism in 1985. Success is judged in terms of opening markets for US exports rather than in terms of contribution to global trade liberalization, although these are presumed to be correlated. (Bayard and Elliott claimed that the outcomes, some $4–$5 billion in extra US exports, contained little trade diversion.) Their measure may underestimate success because some goals were achieved by the threat of action without needing an actual 301 case, let alone actual retaliation. On the other hand, it may overestimate success, if the goals would have been achieved even in the absence of US action. The 1980s were a good decade in which to pursue market-opening threats because an increasing number of countries were recognizing the merits of unilateral trade liberalization and deregulation; it is always easier to push on an open door than to break down a locked door. Moreover, many of the successes were achieved with countries especially amenable to US pressure, which were likely to try to appease the USA on trade-related matters for essentially non-trade-related reasons (e.g. Japan, South Korea, and Taiwan).

Aggressive unilateralism was much less successful when it was applied to less clientist partners (such as the EU) or touched on issues where there was little domestic support in the target country for the US position (such as intellectual property rights, and especially the issue of pharmaceutical patents in poor countries).

The high point of US aggressive unilateralism was 1985–9. The US executive gained political victories (in market-opening commitments from Japan, South Korea, and Taiwan) for domestic consumption. In fact, implementation of these agreements in the early 1990s fell short of US expectations, although all three East Asian countries eventually liberalized their markets for domestic reasons. Pursuance of aggressive unilateralism began to lag after the bad experience of the Brazilian pharmaceutical case, where the USA imposed retaliatory tariffs and experienced universal opprobium within GATT; the threat is always greater than the execution, and the credibility of a policy like aggressive unilateralism derives partly from shock value which cannot be recreated in the near future. The USA was also given pause by the banking component of the EC92 programme, which looked in 1988–9 as though it might include reciprocity; if so, US banks could be excluded from the single European market because EC banks did not receive equally unrestricted access to US markets, where there were legal restraints on universal banking (i.e. on banks dealing in securities) and on interstate banking. This prospect was averted by the EC restating its commitment to national treatment rather than reciprocity as the appropriate criterion for market access (i.e. foreign firms should be treated as well as domestic firms), but the close scrape alerted US policy-makers to the dangers of 'reciprocity' as a slogan to force open other markets considered less open than the USA. By the late 1980s, the bilateralism debate over means became subsumed by the regionalism debate, and will be taken up in the discussion in the next chapter of whether regional arrangements are building blocks for multilateral trade liberalization or stumbling blocks.

Although the historical examples are suggestive rather than conclusive, the absence of the bargaining motive as an explanation of actual postwar discriminatory trade policies seems soundly based. There is little evidence that bilateral bargaining would have succeeded better than GATT negotiations as a route to global trade liberalization or that it would have much success in extracting better market access from trading partners—if anything, pre-1939 experience suggests the opposite. Whether this assessment applies equally to more complex new areas of trade negotiation will be taken up in the next chapter.

Political motives

The two unambiguous consequences of discriminatory trade policies are the changed trade patterns, and the gains to favoured exporters and losses to countries discriminated against. Both of these consequences offer scope to politically motivated discrimination.

Economists pay little attention to the source of imports or destination of exports, but if the flag follows trade (i.e. if political allegiance is positively correlated with the strength of trade links) then geographical trade patterns have political significance. Formation of the EC was a politically motivated move towards West European union, which the customs union's impact on trade patterns would reinforce. Earlier, the Zollverein had preceded German political unification, and customs union among American and Australian states and Canadian provinces reinforced those federations' political cohesion. Comecon and various African economic integration schemes also included the strengthening of political ties among their goals, although this stopped short of political union.

For a large country granting preferential tariff treatment to a small country's exports the economic cost is likely to be minimal relative to magnitudes such as GNP, but for the preference recipient the economic benefits are unambiguous and possibly large relative to GNP and thus are difficult to refuse. Although there are no economic benefits to the large country, this type of arrangement offers a low-cost method of achieving political goals. Viner summarized pre-1950 large country/small country preferential trading arrangements in these terms:

> Of the more serious movements which involved a great power and a small country or a number of small countries, it appears to have been the case without exception for the great power that political objectives were the important ones . . .

while, for the small countries in such arrangements,

only the economic consequences as a rule were regarded as attractive, while the political aspects were thought of as involving risks which might have to be accepted for the sake of the economic benefits with which they were unfortunately associated. (Viner, 1950, 91–2)

The large country's political objectives vary (e.g. desire to avoid political isolation among developing countries played a part in Swedish and American acceptance of GSP), but most commonly they involve spheres of influence. The EC's preferential trading arrangements with African and Mediterranean countries strengthen those countries' traditional political links with Western Europe, and the 1982 US initiative towards Caribbean countries was in similar vein.[8] In these cases trade policy is foreign policy; because tariff preferences offer attractive economic benefits to a small trading partner and then strengthen its trade links to the donor, they are a low-cost influence-strengthening tool for a large country.

Whether or not trade preferences will be used as a foreign policy tool depends upon the relative efficacy of this and other tools. The EC has used commercial policy, and trade preferences in particular, for political purposes, because the Community had foreign policy pretensions but did not have other instruments at the Community level. The United States, at least up to the 1970s, had more effective foreign policy instruments and thus eschewed the use of trade preferences, which might alienate non-preferred friendly nations and would threaten the MFN foundations of the GATT trading system. Only when traditional foreign policy tools were being questioned after various débâcles in the 1970s, and the benefits of observing the MFN principle were being discounted in congressional debates over other countries' trading practices in the early 1980s, did the USA abandon principled opposition to discriminatory trade policies and use preferential tariffs as a foreign policy tool.

Negative discrimination, or sanctions, can equally be used as a foreign policy tool. Sanctions are most likely to succeed in achieving their political goal when they are imposed by a large country (or a group of countries) on a small target country, but even then there have been conspicuous failures (e.g. the USSR

[8] As was German policy towards eastern Europe during the 1930s—and the EU's policy towards the same region in the 1990s.

against Albania, and the USA against Cuba in 1960–1). One limitation, which also applies to the positive discrimination described in the previous two paragraphs, is that trade-related costs and benefits are seldom sufficient to change a well entrenched government or its fundamental policies. A further reason for sanctions' mixed record is the incentive for free-riders to take advantage of the artificially favourable terms of trade with the boycotted country, so that even globally agreed sanctions are evaded.[9] Evasion brings its own costs in addition to the cost of forgone trade, which is why sanctions provide some incentive for change and can achieve limited political goals. There is a parallel with the bargaining motive (indeed, discriminatory trade policies for bargaining purposes and sanctions for limited goals merge in many instances); economic sanctions may work, but they often fail, and when they do succeed the payoff is limited.

2. The Political Economy of Discriminatory Trade Policies

The four sets of explanations just discussed can each explain the existence of discriminatory trade policies, but they are not equally important in practice. The first two sets focus on the distribution of economic costs and benefits, and their practical importance will depend upon the relative power of gainers and losers in the trade policy process. The outcome of these domestic policy struggles will have to be weighed against the foreign policy considerations involved in the last two sets of explanations. The interplay of these forces has been analysed in the public choice literature with respect to MFN tariffs (sometimes referred to as endogenous tariff theory) and with respect to some discriminatory trade barriers (e.g. voluntary export restraint agreements), but has not been studied in the context of discriminatory trade policies in general.

[9] Preferential trade arrangements also offer incentives for evasion (e.g. by false labelling or by routing exports via a preferred country, a non-beneficiary's products may receive the preferential tariff rate). However, since policing is done by the importing country and the preferred countries have an incentive to co-operate with them (for fear of losing their preferred status if they are caught as accomplices in evasion), it is easier to stop this type of smuggling than it is to stop sanctions-busting.

The dominant focus of endogenous tariff theory has been on the role of pressure groups—a focus with a long US tradition (e.g. Schattschneider's (1935) classic account of the 1929–30 tariff) and a ready appeal to economists' view of economic agents driven by short-term self-interest. Econometric studies during the 1970s sought to explain tariff structure in terms of industry variables capturing the returns to producers from tariff protection and their ability to organize successful lobbying of policy-makers. The empirical studies were able to relate tariff structure to these variables, but it became increasingly clear that pressure group activity was not the whole story. The public choice literature on MFN tariffs then developed in three new directions.

The point of departure for Robert Baldwin's (1985) study of US trade policy formation is the belief that, while the short-term self-interest model can go far, it is insufficient if it is not placed within the relevant institutional setting. He discusses in detail the relevant US institutions and their relative importance. Congress, where pressure group politics have freest rein, transferred tariff-making power to the Executive in 1934 and continued to accept this position until the 1970s, when it attempted to regain control, both directly and via closer oversight, of the International Trade Commission. Thus, protectionist pressure groups' influence was strong before 1934 and revived in the 1970s, but during the 1940s, 1950s, and 1960s a more nationally balanced view of US tariff policy prevailed.

Cross-country variations in trade policy depend on the institutional framework of trade policy formation as well as on the sectional economic interests involved.[10] The EU is an interesting case because the responsiveness to pressure groups was at first rather low (for example, the common external tariff and Kennedy Round tariff reductions were set by general rules with few specific exemptions except for agriculture),[11] but, as industry organizations were able to lobby national governments and learned to co-operate at the Community level to lobby the EC Commission,

[10] Kindleberger (1951) used such a framework for his classic study of European tariff policies in the last quarter of the 19th c. Goldstein (1993) emphasizes the role of ideas in influencing trade policy choices, and of institutions in fossilizing the impact of past ideas.

[11] The studies by Cheh (1974) and Riedel (1977) on Kennedy Round tariff cuts show that during the 1960s vested interests had less impact on inter-industry variations in tariff changes in the EC than in the USA.

pressure group politics became increasingly important. The institutional format, whereby the Commission makes administrative decisions subject to control by the Council of Ministers, played a role in this transformation, because the natural representatives of consumers' interests (i.e. members of the European Parliament) have little or no influence in EC trade policy.[12]

Lavergne (1983) also argues that pressure group variables are not enough to explain US tariff structure, and he supplements them with variables concerning American trading partners. This is a major departure from the previous mainstream, which considered only US domestic variable to be significant determinants of the US tariff structure (e.g. Finger *et al.*, 1982). Historically, however, many observers saw the US retreat from high tariffs in the mid-1930s as at least in part induced by the adverse foreign reaction to the Hawley–Smoot tariff, and the US adoption in 1934 of a negotiated rather than a unilateral approach to trade policy made foreign considerations an explicit influence on US tariffs. Helleiner (1977) has also tried to explain the positive correlation between tariff levels and unskilled labour intensity in industrialized countries' tariff structures in terms of developing countries' non-participation in GATT negotiations, i.e. by foreign considerations. In Lavergne's econometric work, developing country dummy variables were not significant (and the force of Helleiner's argument with respect to tariffs has been weakened by GSP),[13] but Japanese and Canadian dummies did have the expected positive and negative signs (i.e. US tariffs tend to be

[12] The same point is made by Hine (1985, 270) and Patterson (1983). On EC trade policy formulation see also Waelbroeck (1984). Winters (1994) argues that the power of the Council with one representative from each EU member leads to the restaurant bill problem; rather than fighting against other members' requests to provide protection for industries of special importance in their national economies, each member will include its own protectionist measures since the costs of protection are spread across the whole EU.

[13] Balassa and Balassa (1984) argue that GSP only partially offsets the tendency of US, EC, and Japanese tariffs to be higher on imports of special interest to developing countries, because many relevant items (especially among textiles and clothing and footwear) are excluded from the GSP schemes. Their figures (e.g. on p. 181) are, however, more convincing for the USA than for the EC or Japan, and this country-specific pattern is supported by UNCTAD calculations. UNCTAD (1987, 19) estimated 1983 trade-weighted average applied tariffs against the world at 3.4% for the USA, 2.5% for the EC, and 3.1% for Japan, while the average applied tariffs against imports from developing countries were 3.6%, 2.1%, and 2.3%, respectively.

higher on goods of greater weight in imports from Japan and lower on goods of greater weight in imports from Canada).

The third new direction has been to introduce the government, or more specifically the bureaucracy, as an actor in its own right. This has some similarity to Baldwin's approach, but Baldwin continues to view the politicians as intermediaries (the President for the public will, members of Congress for their constituents). Writers like Messerlin (1981), however, emphasize the welfare functions of bureaucrats, whose goals may be quite different from those of politicians and tend to be biased in favour of protecting domestic producers. Where bureaucrats' offices are industry-specific, they are likely to be 'captured' by their industry[14] and, apart from this, they will favour measures to increase or maintain their industry's size in order to increase or maintain their own prestige. More generally, bureaucrats are likely to prefer discretion over rules, since the former enhances their own power. The most recent development in this branch of the literature is Anne Krueger's work on complexity, discussed in Section 10.4.

The pressure group framework, supplemented by institutional and foreign considerations and by bureaucratic influences, helps to explain why discriminatory trade policies take the form they do. Because of the limited number of cases, my approach will be to study individual policies, rather than to attempt cross-sectional analysis. Before turning to the case studies, one weakness of the endogenous tariff theory literature should be emphasized: while empirical tests have been fairly successful in explaining the inter-industry structure of trade barriers, they have been far less successful in explaining the changing level of trade barriers over time; in particular, they have failed to account for system-wide shifts such as the tremendous postwar liberalization of international trade. This issue, and the question of where the international trading system is headed, will be taken up in the next chapter.

The political economy of VERs

Voluntary export restraints provide a clear-cut illustration of the political economy of trade barriers. Although as protectionist

[14] The 'capture' theory was developed in context of domestic regulatory boards by Stigler (1974), but applies equally to import regulation.

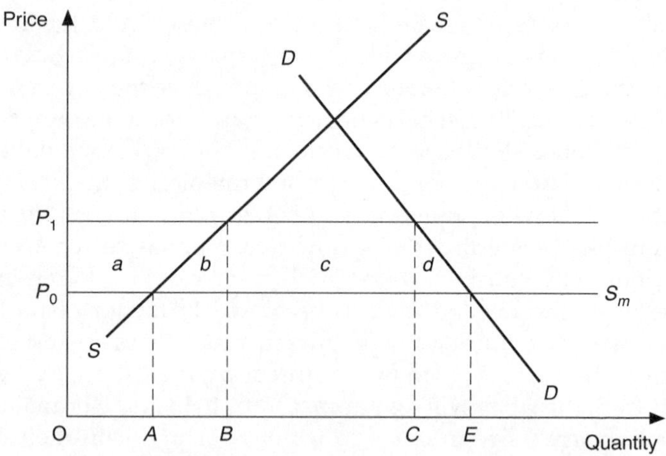

FIG. 17.1 Partial equilibrium analysis of VER imposed on all imports
S and D are domestic supply and demand curves in the importing country, and S_m is the pre-VER supply of imports.

measures they have shortcomings relative to non-discriminatory trade barriers, VERs have been used as a method of protection which will not incur either protests within GATT or retaliation, because the exporting country is compensated via a quota rent. Thus, the existence of these globally harmful trade barriers arises from their benefits to import-competing producers and to foreign suppliers, both of whom have an influence on the policy decision, while the losers from VERs are consumers in the importing country whose voice is rarely heard.

Figure 17.1 provides a simple partial equilibrium illustration of the distributional effects of VERs. With free trade, a single exporting country supplies all imports, *AE* units, at price P_0. After introduction of a VER set at *BC* units, the price increases to P_1. The higher price and greater output (from *OA* to *OB*) increase the domestic industry's producer surplus (by area *a*). The foreign suppliers now sell fewer units at a higher price; they may be better off or worse off than with unrestricted trade. They are, however, clearly better off than if an import quota of *BC* units (or the equivalent tariff, $P_1 - P_0$) were imposed, because then the quota rent or tariff revenue (area *c*) would accrue to the government or to import-licence-holders in the importing country; with a VER the quota rent accrues to holders of export licences allocated in

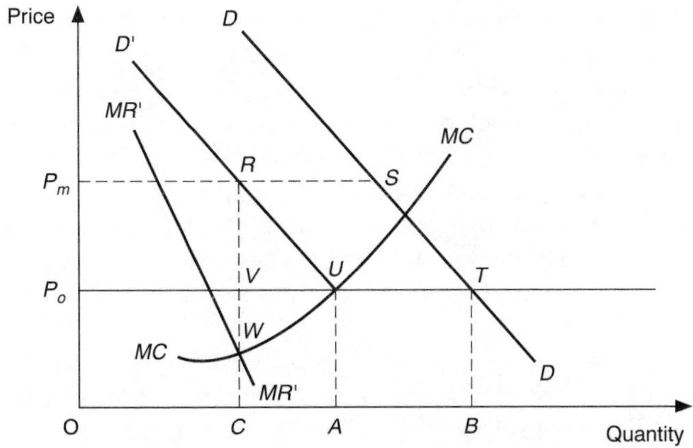

FIG. 17.2 A VER in the presence of domestic monopoly
With a domestic demand curve *DD*, a marginal cost curve *MC*, and unrestricted imports at price P_0, the domestic monopolist will produce *OA* and domestic consumption will be *OB*. If imports are restricted to *AB* by a VER, the monopolist's demand curve is *D'UTD* and he will sell *OC* at price P_m. Compared with the unrestricted imports situation, the foreign suppliers gain RSTU in quota rent, consumer surplus is reduced by P_0P_mST, and the monopolist gains $P_0P_mRV - UVW$; with equal weights, the global welfare loss is equal to area *RUW*.

the exporting country. Consumers in the importing country suffer a loss of consumer surplus (area $a + b + c + d$), and if each unit of consumer surplus, producer surplus, and rent were weighted equally there would be a net welfare loss from the VER (equal to $b + d$). Introduction of a VER, therefore, implicitly places more weight on the domestic and foreign producers' welfare.

The community of interests between domestic and foreign firms may be strengthened further if the number of firms in the importing country is small. In the limiting case of a single domestic firm, quantitative limits on imports will allow the monopolist to charge a higher price than it would under either free trade (Fig. 17.2) or an equivalent tariff, and the exporting firms will receive a larger quota rent than with an atomistic import-competing industry. Generally, in concentrated industries VERs not only protect domestic firms from unrestricted imports, but also provide government approval for market-sharing decisions which permit the domestic firms to act as price-leaders. Under these conditions VERs are even more harmful to consumers, but the monopolistic pricing yields additional benefits to producers (including the foreign suppliers). Thus, concentrated industries will prefer quota to tariff protection and will have an extra incentive to seek import quotas or VERs, as well as being better able than atomistic industries to co-ordinate lobbying activities in order to achieve the desired policy outcome (Pomfret, 1989; Rosendorff, 1996). Market structure could also produce situations where an exporting country would be better off with a VER than with unrestricted trade, and thus would have an incentive to initiate truly voluntary restraints (Harris, 1985). In practice, this does not seem to happen, perhaps because an exporter-initiated VER might be viewed by the importing country as a restrictive practice harmful to consumers. Once the importing country has taken the initiative and requested a VER, however, the exporters may obligingly continue voluntarily to restrain exports even when the request has been withdrawn, e.g. Japanese auto exports to the USA after 1985 and VCR exports to the EC after 1984.

In other cases, e.g. where the domestic market is competitive or demand is more price-elastic, there is less community of interest between domestic and foreign firms. The latter would prefer not to restrain exports if the quota rents are insufficient to compensate for the benefits on forgone exports, but will accept VERs for fear of the alternative. Nevertheless, the quota rents may still be substantial; C. Hamilton (1986) estimates the 1982 quota rent from Hong Kong clothing VERs at over 10 per cent of the industry's value added.[15] So, although Hong Kong clothing exports have been hard-hit by MFA agreements, there is an incentive to keep playing the game. Such large quota rents are likely to be associated with big VER-caused increments in producer surplus for the importing country's industry, so it is no surprise that they are happy with these measures.

In sum, politically influential domestic industries under competition from imports have gained protection in the form of

[15] In 1984 US dollars, $218 million in 1982 and $507 million in 1983, i.e. 0.7% and 1.7% of the colony's GNP in these two years. The tariff equivalent of the VERs varies over time, but as the US dollar appreciated in value the tariff equivalent of VERs on Hong Kong clothing exports to the USA rose to 140% in late 1983; in 1982 the tariff equivalents of VER plus tariff centred around the still high rates of 33% in the EC and 56% in the USA (Hamilton, 1986, 343). The survey of earlier estimates of MFA-induced price increases in Keesing and Wolf (1980) also contains examples of prices 40%–50% higher than without MFA restrictions.

VERs, which forestall negative foreign reactions by compensating exporters via a quota rent. Consumers, the main losers, seldom oppose VERs, because usually the impact on any individual consumer is small. Also, VERs are frequently negotiated by government officials without public debate and may not even be known about by consumers. (They are even difficult for economists at international agencies to monitor.[16]) Only in exceptional cases of highly publicized VERs on big-ticket items (e.g. the 1981–5 VERs on Japanese auto exports to the USA) is there much consumer response.

Figures 17.1 and 17.2 do not, of course, tell the whole story; like Fig. 8.1, they leave out a key aspect of discriminatory trade polices, substitution between different sources of imports. If alternative supplies at a price close to the pre-VER price are offered, then the main consequence of the VER will be a shift in the national origin of imports, whose effects can be analysed with a model like Fig. 9.2. In order to maintain protection from imports, the domestic industry must work to bring the new suppliers within the VER framework, although their success in doing so has been mixed; for example, the first cotton textile VERs were over time transformed into the MFA, and OECD steel trade became cartelized around fixed market shares, but the US government allowed the 1977–81 VERs on footwear exports from Taiwan and South Korea to lapse rather than request VERs from the rapidly increasing number of substitute suppliers. In practice, the main constraint on VER proliferation has been the emergence of substitute import sources—although this is a double-edged constraint in that it may induce further spread of VERs rather than their abandonment.

Discriminatory trade policies of the EC and the USA

The key actors in the postwar erosion of the non-discriminatory trading system are the two leading trading units, the European

[16] The American shift from bilaterally determined orderly marketing arrangements to VERs in the late 1970s had the substantive point that VERs required no legal authority, because they are introduced by a foreign country, and therefore need not be published in the Federal Register (Murray *et al.*, 1978, 626). The EC maintained a similar position in not publicizing VERs because they were introduced by the exporting country.

Union and the USA. Their use of discriminatory trade policies will be analysed in this section. The next section will consider discriminatory arrangements involving developing countries, whose significance for the international trading system is less.

The European Community was founded for political reasons, but economic integration was given the key functional role. This marriage worked well because the customs union led to a rough balance of internal economic gains, and the long boom of the 1960s made distributional inequities harder to perceive and easier to bear. Free trade in manufactured goods led to trade creation; in a full employment context displaced workers could readily find alternative employment, and the increased division of labour contributed in a small way to higher material welfare. Establishment of the internal market for agricultural goods was more difficult because farm interests were strong pressure groups, supported by national agricultural ministries; the Common Agricultural Policy (CAP) was designed to avoid disruption of EC farmers by trade creation, and the costs were borne by the less influential EC consumers and taxpayers and by farmers in non-member countries. The CAP was the first, and largest, postwar example of a discriminatory trading arrangement which is globally welfare-reducing, and welfare-reducing even for the participating countries, but which came into being because of the political power of sectional interests. Since then, the development of the EC's trade-policy-making framework and increased adjustment costs since the mid-1970s for import-threatened producers have led to a further adoption of protectionist measures which had similar welfare-reducing effects to the CAP, with similar distribution of benefits and costs among EC producers and consumers and non-member suppliers.

Whether the EC itself was a major setback for the non-discrimination principle in international trade is debatable. If it is a step towards confederation along American, Australian, or Canadian lines, then these other countries can scarcely object. If it is a discriminatory trading arrangement aimed at realizing economic gains to members at the expense of outsiders, then it is less palatable. The real criticisms of the EC's role involve not its own status but its trade policy behaviour, first in adopting the protectionist practices described in the previous paragraph, and secondly in using trade policy as a foreign policy tool.

The EC turned to tariff preferences as a foreign policy tool because it had limited access to other foreign policy instruments. Early policy decisions were crucial, both as precedent setters and because tariff preferences tend to generate their own momentum for proliferation. The decision to include preferential treatment for colonies and franc zone members in the Rome Treaty (Chapter 5) was not taken without debate among the Six, but France prevailed over German and Dutch support for a global rather than a regional policy towards developing countries.[17] The other big initial step towards a discriminatory external trade policy, the 1961 Athens Accord, was less internally contentious; Greek association at a time of bloc competition with EFTA was a foreign policy coup for the EC, and the association agreement could be justified under GATT in so far as it contained a timetable for full EC membership within twenty-two years. Greek association discriminated against Turkish trade with the EC and, when Turkey applied for a similar agreement, the EC felt constrained not to alienate Turkey.

By 1967, when events in Greece and the Middle East stimulated the EC's sense of the geographical importance of the Mediterranean Basin, the Community was already experienced in the use of trade preferences.[18] Special terms for Spanish and Israeli exports to the EC were balanced by similar offers to Arab countries, until preferential trade agreements with the EC covered

[17] A full explanation of EC external trade policies would need to account for this French victory. It would seem to have little to do with important economic interests, and perhaps the strongest factor was that for the Germans and Dutch this issue involved no important interests of any kind, and certainly none worth arguing over. The French position was that colonial preferences were a *sine qua non* for her signature on the Rome Treaty. At the time, special treatment for about 20 African countries and colonies may have seemed of no great importance compared with the main terms of the Treaty.

[18] The Greek and Turkish precedents were also important in allaying EC concerns about GATT compatibility. Both of these association agreements had been presented under Art. XXIV; GATT working parties had reported inconclusively, and the agreements were given neither formal approval nor rejection within GATT. The later EC–Mediterranean preferential trade agreements were also justified by Art. XXIV and, although they were all much further than the Greek agreement from satisfying the Art. XXIV conditions, the EC could expect the same GATT outcome. The American decision to base the CBERA's GATT-compatibility on the Enabling Clause footnote (Ch. 5) reflected dissatisfaction with EC abuses of Art. XXIV, but in practice the differing legal bases made little difference to the operation of these preferential trading arrangements.

almost every country in the region. Meanwhile, when the UK applied for EC membership, the influence sphere approach dictated offering preferences similar to those enjoyed by French and Belgian ex-colonies to the British ex-colonies in Africa, and in order to deflect charges of neo-colonialism the offer was extended to the handful of independent sub-Saharan African developing countries. In sum, preferential trading arrangements had a tendency to proliferate as each agreement created newly disadvantaged trading partners, some of whom the EC had no wish to alienate, so that it offered further tariff preferences which created new discrimination (or irritated past beneficiaries by eroding the value of existing tariff preferences).

Proliferation of the EC's preferential trading arrangements was helped (or rather, not hindered) by the absence of a strong executive which could reconsider the trend as it came into obvious conflict with GATT principles. Apart from a break during the mid-1960s when the Commission was forced to take few foreign policy initiatives, external trade policy (especially when it doesn't directly affect other OECD countries) has largely been made in Brussels. Community officials dealing with external relations had little to offer their clients besides trade preferences, and as we have seen such offers are always attractive to small trading nations.

Apart from the limited success of economic tools in achieving political goals, the EU's policy has become more and more difficult to administer. Each partner's desire for adequate preference margins needs to be taken into account. Reduction of the EU common external tariff on manufactures after successive GATT rounds has left the EU with little room for manoeuvre there, and the phasing out of the MFA after the Uruguay Round will reduce the opportunities for preferential allocation of textile and clothing import quotas. At the same time, the impact of the CAP (and strong protectionist pressure within the EU with respect to other sensitive sectors such as coal and steel) has left a slowly increasing import total to be allocated between non-preferred, preferred, and more preferred trading partners; the balancing act is being achieved in part by detailed changes in rules and coverage, which increase bureaucratic discretion. Ironically, the complexity and haggling, which the 1919 US Tariff Commission saw as a major reason for adopting simple trade policy rules, may be contributing to the attractiveness of a bilaterally based EC trade policy, because the location of policymaking in the highly bureaucratic world of the Commission puts it in the hands of people favouring discretion over rules.

The United States remained for the most part aloof from using discriminatory trading arrangements as a foreign policy tool before the 1980s. The only substantial exceptions were US refusal of MFN treatment for imports from Communist countries and other economic sanctions against ideologically unacceptable governments, although the latter were often short-lived unless they were against a small trading partner or involved military-related goods. (For example, the grain embargo against the USSR after the Afghanistan invasion was abandoned under pressure from US grain exporters.) By the 1980s, however, America's traditional foreign policy instruments were seen as becoming increasingly ineffective (culminating in events in Iran), while at the same time the EC was perceived to be using a low-cost instrument to create influence spheres in Africa and the Mediterranean. Thus, the USA adopted preferential trading arrangements as a means of strengthening links with friendly nations in the Caribbean and Israel.

The new US policy encountered problems similar to those of the EC's preferential tariff policies, but with some variation owing to the different institutional setting. The CBERA and the USA–Israel free trade agreement required congressional approval, and in Congress every adversely affected domestic industry (i.e. all who would suffer from trade creation) succeeded in gaining exceptions to the proposed across-the-board free access for Caribbean and Israeli exports to the USA. The economic impact of these arrangements was then restricted mainly to revenue transfer and trade diversion; the transfer of tariff revenue on existing exports to the USA could equally be described as foreign aid, while the trade diversion effect has negative resource allocation consequences for the USA and for third countries. Even with trade creation excluded, the trade preferences still hold attractions for the beneficiaries (and thus may fulfil some US foreign policy purposes), so all participating countries have reasons for continuing with the preferential trading arrangements despite their adverse effects on global resource allocation.

Discriminatory trading arrangements involving developing countries

Discriminatory trading arrangements involving developing countries have been especially problematic and more unstable because, in both regional integration schemes and the GSP, trade diversion has been encouraged and global resource misallocation is probable. At least before the 1990s, preferential trading arrangements among developing countries were usually based on an extended infant industry argument, which implies that no desire for trade creation and vested interests in the member countries will act to prevent any trade creation from arising. If the new infant industries are not spread evenly, then some members will enjoy the desired benefits disproportionately while the cost of resource misallocation will be more equally spread. Compensation mechanisms could deal with the problem, but they inevitably lead to disputes over the degree of compensation, and, given the small economic size of the participants, there is little chance of shifting the costs to non-members. Thus, the record of customs unions and free trade areas among developing countries has been one of failure, with the arrangement being either ineffective or short-lived.

GSP was demanded by the developing countries, which expected unequivocal economic gains, and was agreed to by the developed countries as a low-cost off-budget development assistance programme.[19] Individual GSP schemes contain product exclusions, ceilings, etc., because donors are willing to bear the costs of trade diversion but not the costs of trade creation, which fall on domestic interest groups who were strong enough to obtain tariff protection in the past. From a practical perspective, the developing countries may have been smart to push for trade-related assistance in the form of preferential rather than MFN tariff cuts by the developed nations; the latter would have aroused powerful domestic opposition, as well as involving greater adjustment costs in the importing countries. The losers from GSP are consumers in the donor countries and producers in newly industrializing nations excluded from GSP schemes, neither of which have much impact on donor-country trade policies—unlike domestic producers in labour-intensive branches of industry.

[19] The budget constraint is particularly strong for the EU, whose Community resources are limited and the greater part of which is committed to agricultural price support.

The relative influence of gainers and losers in relevant policy-making arenas is more favourable to the continued existence of GSP than to that of regional integration schemes among developing countries. This should not be interpreted as a seal of approval; the welfare of donor-country consumers and third-country producers should count; and, even if dominant weight is placed on GSP beneficiaries' gains, the welfare transfer could be achieved more efficiently (from the global perspective) by multilateral aid, leaving non-discriminatory trade policies to govern the international division of labour. An extreme case of inefficient trade as aid is the EU banana policy, described in Section 6.1.

In general, the allocative inefficiency aspect of trade preferences for developing countries is limited, because the schemes themselves have limited scope. Although there is often no strong opposition to GSP, there is also no influential positive lobby. GSP schemes, and in practice Lomé and the CBERA too, are donor-determined, so that any potential challenge to domestic producers is excluded, however small. Thus, these schemes have longevity, but little practical impact.

3. Concluding Remarks

No discriminatory trade policies are motivated by the desire to improve global resource allocation, and most such policies can be explained by the interplay of interest groups and a balancing of political with economic benefits and costs. As with all trade policies, GDAs create gainers and losers; in the absence of compensation, potential gainers will support a policy and potential losers will oppose it. The distributional aspects are more important with respect to GDAs than with respect to non-discriminatory trade policies, because extra layers of relative opaqueness are present.

The clearest beneficiaries from a GDA are preferred exporters. In a reciprocal arrangement, such as a FTA or customs union, some producers in all participants may benefit, while part of the cost is shifted to suppliers outside the GDA who lose market share. The largest costs are usually borne by domestic residents, who as consumers are prevented from buying imported goods from the cheapest supplier, and as taxpayers lose the tariff revenue forgone. As with other trade barriers, individual consumers/taxpayers will be affected to a fairly small extent and are unlikely to expend their political influence (i.e. the ballot) on this issue, so that their interests will not affect the policy decision. Moreover, with a discriminatory trade policy voters are less likely to be aware of the costs.[20] Even in egregious cases such as the EU's banana policy, it is difficult to imagine a chagrined European shopper at the supermarket fruit stand fuming over the high price of bananas compared with what they would cost if non-ACP bananas were freely admitted.

The complexity and non-transparency, which help neutralize consumer reactions, add to GDAs' attractivenees for bureaucrats. Administrative discretion increases public officials' influence, as well as shielding them from public scrutiny. It may also translate into pecuniary benefits through opportunites for corruption or, more commonly in the high-income countries, by public officials moving to private-sector jobs where their specialized knowledge of regulations is valuable.

Political leaders also seem especially vulnerable to the charm or fear of discriminatory trade policies. When producers lobby for preferential trading arrangements, or for parity with other countries' special access provisions, or for retaliation against a preferential arrangement benefiting competitors, political leaders are often responsive because the required action fits with common ideas of promoting or defending the national interest. Politicians used to the zero-sum games of elections and power struggles relate readily to arguments about winning and losing market share, and are often less comfortable with arguments about distortions which reduce the gains from trade. On the other hand, they are often cavalier about the tariff revenue loss from schemes such as GSP because it is a small part of the total government budget, even though it may represent a large part of the net welfare loss. The discriminatory trade policies of the larger trading

[20] An exception was the 1981 US auto VER, which significantly increased the price of a big-ticket item. Consumers of luxury products, although less numerous, may be more influential than consumers of mass-produced items. The European Commission dropped a proposal to ban unpasteurized cheese. More surprisingly, a similar ban proposed by the Canadian government in 1996, which would have favoured domestic cheese producers by outlawing the sale of French camembert and brie or Italian parmesan, was jettisoned after cheese-lovers raised a stink.

nations often have a political motivation, in part because the policy-makers are bureaucrats and politicians who are predisposed to putting greater weight on political benefits than on widely spread economic costs. The concern of policy-makers with trade patterns and with bilateral trade balances is in stark contrast to economists' lack of concern with these matters.

A common pattern is for political leaders to make grandiose joint declarations of regional integration schemes or other GDAs, which are subsequently whittled away or never implemented. Often this reflects a political rather than an economic priority among political leaders. It also reflects a tendency of leaders to think in the abstract of their role in promoting exports, but when international agreements come to be ratified import-competing groups have greater clout than potential exporters. There is also ongoing unfamiliarity with the costs of distortions and ignorance of the costs of trade diversion for the importing country.

The question of whether the political economy of trade liberalization will be improved by shifting trade policy formation to a supranational authority is unresolved. Some, mainly US, observers argue that distancing trade policy from Congress where vested interests play a powerful role will lead to trade polices being more in the national interest, i.e. to less protection. This appears to have happened in Western Europe in the late 1950s and 1960s; the EC's tariff structure was less a result of pressure group politics than was the US tariff structure. As producer lobbies learned how to deal with Brussels, however, the new institutional structure became more conducive to opaque and distortionary trade policies; the EC bureaucracy went along with policy innovations which increased their power and influence (such as the MFA, more discretionary use of VERs, and anti-dumping and countervailing duties), while the weak European Parliament provided little oversight on behalf of the public interest. A similar learning process appears to have occurred in North America, where CUSTA contained some illiberal innovations, which blossomed in the anti-competitive rules of origin for autos and apparel in NAFTA.

Grossman and Helpman (1995) argue that FTA formation is a two-stage process in which domestic interests determine whether two countries want to form a FTA and then the two national governments bargain over the terms. In spirit, this is similar to the approach taken in this chapter, but I have downplayed the international bargaining because few GDAs are agreements hammered out between equals. Apart from the obviously one-sided arrangements, the RTAs among developing countries (which most closely approximate the Grossman–Helpman model with two equal-sized small economies) have been ineffective and the RTAs among more developed countries (EU/EFTA, CUSTA and the CER) are more idiosyncratic.

18

Consequences for the International Trading System

The central concern of this book is the paradox between the spread of discriminatory trading arrangements during the GATT era and the negative attitude of both economic theory and international trade law towards such policies. The previous chapter applied a pressure group model, adapted to allow for institutional and foreign policy considerations as well as bureaucrats' preference for discretionary policies, to the analysis of gainers and losers from GDAs and was able to explain the evolution of the major postwar discriminatory trade policies. One weakness of the 'public choice' approach is its failure to explain the clearly apparent long-term trends in international trade policies. In this chapter I shall examine these system-wide shifts, and then ask where the system is heading and whether this is a desirable direction.

1. The Tendency of GDAs to Proliferate

The previous chapter set out reasons why countries might enter into GDAs. These arguments were developed in a static context, but in reality there appears to be a strong dynamic element in the evolution of discriminatory trade policies.

Several authors (e.g. Richard Baldwin, 1995) have pointed out that the costs of being excluded from a regional trading arrangement increase as the number of members grows. Thus, as the EU expanded and EFTA shrank the attractiveness of remaining in EFTA diminished. This argument also underlies Krugman's model, which predicts increasing regionalism until the world is divided into three blocs (see Section 11.1). Empirical estimates of the costs of GDAs to non-members suggest that the costs are rarely very large, but the perception is usually negative and the reaction is that something should be done. The gap between outsiders' exaggerated perceptions of negative effects and insiders' disappointment with the actual benefits from GDAs was a recurring theme in Part I of this book.

Discriminatory trading arrangements spread by example. The Rome Treaty and the economic success of EC members during the late 1950s and the 1960s provided an impetus for integration schemes in Latin America and Africa, as well as leading directly to EFTA's formation. Moreover, GDAs often create economic pressures for imitation. The EC's preferential trade agreements with individual Mediterranean countries harmed other Mediterranean countries which exported similar goods to EC markets, and at the same time the agreement provided the blueprint for the disfavoured country's remedy. The Yaoundé Convention gave an incentive for developing countries not associated with the EC to seek a generalized system of tariff preferences in order to reverse the discriminatory treatment which they faced in EC markets. The USA, seeing the EC utilizing a low-cost foreign policy tool whose use the USA had renounced, eventually decided to offer preferential tariffs for political purposes. Thus, whether by a demonstration effect or to protect legitimate interests or out of misplaced envy, GDAs have a general tendency to proliferate.

The types of GDA that proliferate are apparent from the historical account in Part I. Despite heightened interest in regional trading arrangements during the 1990s, proliferation of FTAs and customs unions does not pose a major systemic threat. Against the arguments for bloc creation advanced by Baldwin and Krugman, the distributional and resource misallocation effects appear to be more influential in practice, and FTAs or CUs rarely last. The exceptions are the France-Monaco type convenience arrangements that have existed since before GATT and are of no global significance, and economic integration schemes as preludes to confederation (represented in the second half of the twentieth century by the EU). The introduction of NAFTA, AFTA, MERCOSUR, and the CER may contradict this conclusion, but whether any of these are significant preferential trading arrangements is yet to be proved.

The more serious proliferation threat comes from preferential trading arrangements between a large country and smaller clients. Individually such PTAs may be of minor significance, but collectively they undermine the non-discrimination principle. The threat is more serious because the small country enjoys unalloyed economic benefits even if the scope of the scheme is unilaterally restricted by the large country, while the large country sees unquantifiable (and hence difficult-to-challenge) political benefits for which it is willing to pay small economic costs. Such arrangements proliferate because they face no checks and they tend to take the hub-and-spoke form which is least economically justifiable.[1]

2. The Role of History

Endogenous tariff theory has focused on domestic variables to explain inter-industry variations in trade barriers, and it fails to explain global events like the move to free trade which culminated in the 1860s or the swing back to protectionism which ended in the 1930s. Among economists, only Charles Kindleberger has written influentially on the latter issue. His survey of the mid-nineteenth-century free trade movement emphasized nation-specific developments, but he also assigned some role to Britain's moral leadership. In other work Kindleberger ascribes the economic breakdown of the interwar years to a lack of leadership associated with a change at the top of the international economic hierarchy; the USA was not ready to lead, while the UK was no longer able to. American willingness to assume a leadership role changed during the 1930s and 1940s, and lay behind the creation of a postwar international economic order based on non-discrimination.

Kindleberger's approach is close to the hegemony concept used by some political scientists, although he has doubts about the concept's fuzziness. The difficulty with this approach is that generalizations tend to be based upon two periods of hegemonic dominance, the 1860s and 1960s, which were associated with exceptionally free international trade. The two cases do, however, differ. In the first period Britain adopted free trade policies, but did not actively work towards converting other European countries to free trade (e.g. by withholding access to British markets); if others followed the British lead, it was for their own reasons. In the mid-twentieth century, American trade liberalization

[1] R. Wonnacott (1996) provides a good review of the added misallocation and administrative costs associated with hub-and-spoke arrangements.

contained no commitment to free trade, but the USA designed a body of trade law in which non-discriminatory trade policies were an obligation, and refusal to sign the GATT left open the prospect of being denied access to the American market.

The hegemonic leadership theory is inadequate as a monocausal explanation of trade policy trends,[2] but it does bring out the point that the policies of the leading economic power(s) do play a role in creating the milieu within which other countries' trade policies are determined. The British move to almost total free trade (and therefore non-discrimination) had ripple effects across western Europe in the third quarter of the nineteenth century; it was reinforced by national reasons for trade liberalization, which were relatively strong in Prussia and weak in France. The liberalization movement in the large continental European countries was, however, reversed by the inflow of cheap grain from North America and Ukraine, which accelerated in the 1870s. Thereafter, British prestige and faithfulness to free trade principles were never sufficient to reverse the protectionist tide, although when Britain abandoned free trade in 1931 this was a signal for a new wave of protectionism, and British conversion to bilateral bargaining during the 1930s encouraged others to adopt such policies. In the postwar period, although the USA favoured liberal non-discriminatory trade policies and surely influenced other countries' policies in the same direction, this was not sufficient to forestall the EC's adoption of a restrictive agricultural policy and predilection for offering preferential tariffs. Even accepting these limitations on American influence, the Caribbean Basin and USA–Israel arrangements, by providing a clear signal that the USA was ceasing to lead the non-discrimination cause, gave an added push to the disintegration of the international trading system based on non-discrimination.

[2] McKeown (1983) has questioned the theory's applications to the 19th c. on three grounds: (1) Britain was neither willing nor able to influence other European countries' trade policies; (2) the free trade leader in Europe during the first half of the century was Prussia rather than Britain; and (3) important trading nations (notably the USA and Russia) remained outside the liberalization movement. As an alternative explanation of long-term tariff policy changes, he proposes national and international business cycles via the mechanism of reduced tariff revenues during depressions encouraging tariff increases. This would not seem to be applicable to the major trading nations in the 20th c., whose reliance on trade taxes for government revenue is small. Keohane (1984) provides a more general critique of the hegemonic leadership theory.

Bhagwati (1993) views the postwar trading system as having passed through two waves of regionalism. In the 1950s and 1960s, many customs unions and free trade areas were formed, with the goal of promoting intra-regional trade and not necessarily with any commitment to global trade liberalization. In the late 1980s and the 1990s, the second wave involved regional integration rather than regional trading arrangements, and in most cases with the stated goal of contributing to global trade liberalization. The two waves were not as distinct as Bhagwati implies; the EC clearly played a linking role, as will be emphasized below. Nevertheless, Bhagwati does highlight important differences, which reflect the differing environment in which policy-makers operated. In the early postwar era memories of the 1930s depression were vivid and the USSR was viewed as a success in war and peace. By the 1980s the high-performing Asian economies had demonstrated the benefits of participating in the international division of labour, the USSR was in terminal decline, and the advantages of market-friendly policies were widely accepted.

The many RTAs of the 1950s and 1960s were spurred by the EC's example, but they also reflected the prevailing belief in import-substituting industrialization as the most desirable development strategy. The theoretical arguments for such RTAs are valid so long as participants are willing to accept the resource misallocation costs of promoting globally uncompetitive industries, or if the industries eventually become competitive (and the discounted net social benefits are positive). In practice, none of the RTAs in Africa or Latin America lasted, because the less industrialized members were unwilling to bear the costs in terms of expensive or low-quality imports from their partners in order that the partners could industrialize further. The EC was the exception, partly because for most non-agricultural products it adopted liberal rather than protectionist external trade policies, and partly because members found it politically preferable to tolerate some trade diversion costs rather than challenge the European integration process.

The EC lasted, and its external trade policies provided the link between Bhagwati's two waves. Chapter 6 and Sections 5.5 and 17.2 have already dwelt on the US shift away from being the defender of the non-discrimination principle to adopting its own discriminatory trade policies. The first US arrangements (the

CBERA and the USA–Israel FTA) were old-style RTAs focusing on border measures, but CUSTA and NAFTA became examples of the new regionalism involving areas beyond the traditional trade policy concerns of tariffs and quotas. Similarly, the CER and EC92 were portrayeed as regional integration measures rather than simple RTAs. Moreover, sponsors of all of these regional integration schemes claimed that they were stepping stones towards global trade liberalization.

That the integration schemes of the 1990s differ from those of the 1950s and 1960s is incontrovertible, but whether they are any less exclusive and any more in the global interest is debatable. The late 1980s and early 1990s represented a watershed; widely held fears of the global trading system's disintegration into a handful of blocs contrasted with the promise of multilateral trade liberalization through the Uruguay Round. The next two sections will look at the two sides: first the growth of discrimination, and then the resilience of the unconditional MFN principle. Section 5 will then address the question of whether the regional integration arrangements of the 1980s and 1990s should be viewed as stepping stones or stumbling blocks on the road to global trade liberalization.

3. The Growth of Discriminatory Trade Policies

The existence and growth of discriminatory trade policies in recent decades is easy to document. There are, however, two sets of reactions to their extent and significance for the world economy. One, the apocalyptic view, sees the world economy disintegrating into regional trading blocs. The other, the indifferent view, shows no concern about existing discriminatory trade policies (because they either have little economic impact or yield net benefits because trade creation exceeds trade diversion) and seeks to justify new discriminatory trade policies as minor deviations from the MFN principle.

Will the international trading system disintegrate into regional blocs?

Many postwar observers have seen signs of the world economy's disintegration into a set of regional trading blocs. The roots of this idea go back before the Second World War, and it received striking treatment in George Orwell's *1984*. Its postwar popularity was boosted by discriminatory trading arrangements like the Sterling Area, OEEC group discrimination, Comecon, and the European Community. Current forms of the argument usually identify three regional blocs: the Americas, Europe and Africa, and Japan and the Western Pacific.

The argument has a certain plausibility. Large powers do seek to create spheres of influence, and small countries have a strong economic incentive to accept preferential access to a large country's market. Preferential tariffs are, however, a weak reed with which to build spheres of influence. Their impact may be large enough to attract clients' attention and to strengthen economic ties, but is unlikely to be sufficiently large to be, by itself, a critical consideration in their political alignment.[3] In the post-colonial era, the bloc argument does not receive strong empirical support.

Thorbecke (1960) was an early advocate of the regionalization hypothesis. Using intra-regional trade shares as his guide, he found that 'Trade regionalization . . . was to become the predominant characteristic of the pattern of world commerce after 1945' (p. 200) and that 'The UK took the lead in what became the era of "economic regionalism"' (p. 201). With hindsight, however, many of Thorbecke's findings about the postwar situation can be seen to capture transitory phenomena of reconstruction rather than features that would be permanent; the results were, after all, based on less than a decade's observations. The UK's prominence in Thorbecke's case for regionalization was based on bulk purchase agreements of the late 1940s and, most of all, on the Sterling Area, which was on the verge of breakup as he was writing.

Updating Thorbecke's study requires a new set of blocs as the Sterling Area is no longer relevant. Kihl and Lutz (1985) tried to identify regional bloc membership by the objective criteria of assigning countries to blocs on the basis of their largest export market. They list five blocs, of which the Western Hemisphere, Western Europe and Africa, Japan and the Asia–Pacific Basin, and Comecon are plausible groupings, but unfortunately the

[3] The low MFN tariffs of recent decades limit the size of preference margins, so that, apart from a few small ex-colonies, changes in preferential trading arrangements encourage marginal rather than drastic reorientation of trade patterns.

largest bloc turns out to be the 'Variable partners' (i.e. countries whose principal market changes over the ten-year period of study) and the 'Other' group. Other writers have avoided this problem by *ad hoc* allocation procedures, but Kihl and Lutz, by seeking explicit criteria, highlighted the difficulty in making the regional bloc hypothesis operational.

Two fundamental difficulties prevent rigorous assignment of countries to regional trading blocs: (1) receiving preferential treatment from one major trading nation does not preclude preferential treatment by another; and (2) bloc allegiance is not necessarily for ever. Israel and several Caribbean countries receive preferential access to both EC and US markets, while some Pacific islands participate in both Lomé and SPARTECA; there is every incentive for a small country to be a multi-bloc member. The most dramatic postwar bloc switches have been by Cuba in the early 1960s and by Egypt in the early 1970s, although in Egypt's case it is more apparent which bloc it left than which it joined. Other bloc changes may have occurred (e.g. by Albania, in Indo-China and in Africa, and by Indonesia), but it is easier to identify these in terms of East–West or Sino–Soviet political divisions than in terms of regional trading blocs. Finally, on any reasonable criteria, there are several nations, some important or potentially important on the world trade scene, whose bloc allegiance has been uncertain for some time; these include former Yugoslavia, India, and China (and contain almost half of the world's population!).

Some regionalization of world trade is inevitable (nearby markets are usually more familiar and, *ceteris paribus*, trade flows will minimize transport costs), but the establishment of regional trading blocs was less pronounced in the 1980s than in the late 1940s. The EC had created a network of privileged trading partners with African and Mediterranean countries receiving the best treatment, and the EC's goal has been to increase influence in this region. Similarly, the Western Hemisphere countries all (except for Cuba) had strong trade links with the USA before NAFTA, but these were not exclusive arrangements. Asia is very difficult to divide into blocs; in Kihl and Lutz's study the only important Asia–Pacific members of the Japanese bloc are Thailand and Australia, but their trade flows can be explained in simple comparative advantage terms.

In contrast to the bloc hypothesis, inter-regional trade appears to have flourished despite the proliferation of GDAs.[4] One reason for this is the postwar reduction in transport and information costs, which enables entrepreneurs to consider a wider range of national markets for buying imports and selling exports. A second reason, most pronounced since the early 1970s, is the rise and fall of new markets (e.g. in the Middle East) and the large fluctuations in exchange rates, which have often swamped preferential tariff margins in determining the relative attractiveness of different markets. The clearest example was the shift in countries' share of exports going to the USA during the first half of the 1980s, which is evident in almost every region of the world (Table 18.1); the US dollar's rise relative to the yen or the ecu provided a price incentive which dominated GDAs as an explanation of changes in trade patterns during this period.[5]

In sum, fears of the world economy's disintegration into regional trading blocs are misplaced. Apart from the East–West division, early postwar evidence of such a tendency was picking up transitory rather than permanent phenomena; and, although some regionalization of world trade is normal, this is neither growing nor a salient feature of the present world economy. Since the 1950s it has been operationally difficult to assign countries to trading blocs, long-term alignments have tended to be incomplete and reversible, and many countries have developed the flexibility to make short- or medium-term trade pattern shifts in response to price or other incentives regardless of PTA ties.

. . . or will the GATT/WTO system die of neglect?

Dramatic scenarios of the breakdown of the GATT-based international trading system are not supported by the facts. There was

[4] The share of inter-regional trade in world trade declined in the second half of the 20th c. because of the breakup of European-based empires (S. 16.1), but the scope for inter-regional responses to new circumstances probably increased. Röpke's distinction between actual and virtual multilateralism (S. 3.4) is relevant; during the GATT era the latent possibility of switching to multilateral exchange was widely guaranteed.

[5] Excepting countries with exports concentrated in dollar-denominated primary products, the generalization applies to EC and EFTA members, most Asian (including ASEAN members) and larger Latin American countries, and to Canada, but is not apparent in African, Comecon, or Australian exports.

TABLE 18.1 Share of Exports going to the USA, Selected Countries, 1978–1984 (%)

	1978	1979	1980	1981	1982	1983	1984
West Germany	7.1	6.6	6.1	6.6	6.6	7.6	9.6
France	5.6	4.9	4.4	5.5	5.7	6.3	8.1
UK	9.5	9.5	9.5	12.4	13.5	14.1	14.5
Italy	7.1	6.5	5.3	6.8	7.1	7.7	10.9
Netherlands	3.3	2.8	2.5	3.2	3.2	4.2	5.0
Austria	3.0	2.5	2.2	2.6	2.9	3.0	4.1
Portugal	7.1	6.0	5.7	5.2	6.2	6.1	8.8
Sweden	6.3	6.0	5.4	6.1	7.1	8.9	11.4
Spain	9.3	7.0	5.3	6.7	6.4	7.3	9.6
Pakistan	6.3	5.8	5.3	7.1	7.1	6.3	10.1
Japan	25.8	25.8	24.4	25.6	26.4	29.5	35.6
South Korea	32.1	29.2	26.4	26.7	28.6	33.9	36.0
Hong Kong	30.3	27.4	26.1	27.8	28.9	32.3	33.2
Macao	22.8	23.2	19.6	21.0	23.4	26.6	30.4
Philippines	34.3	30.2	27.5	30.9	31.6	36.0	38.0
Thailand	11.0	11.2	12.7	12.9	12.8	15.0	17.2
Singapore	16.0	13.8	12.7	13.2	12.6	18.1	20.1
Brazil	22.7	19.3	17.4	17.7	20.5	25.9	28.5
Chile	13.8	10.2	10.0	14.4	21.6	28.2	26.0
Canada	70.3	68.0	63.1	65.9	67.8	72.7	75.5

Source: UN, *1984 International Trade Statistics*, vol. I.

no trend towards the disintegration of the multilateral system into three or four regional blocs. Another early fear, that developing countries would not play by GATT rules, also proved not to be a serious threat to the system. During the 1950s and 1960s many developing countries were attracted to discriminatory trade policies (as well as illiberal import policies) and refused to become GATT signatories, but during the 1970s and 1980s the discriminatory arrangements turned out to be of little economic significance, trade policies were liberalized, and most developing countries joined GATT.

The danger facing the GATT system was not dramatic breakdown, but gradual atrophy. The previous chapter gave examples of discriminatory trading arrangements which yield benefits to participants at the cost of third countries. Such policies are precisely what GATT was intended to prevent, but countries found means of bypassing GATT's intentions. The weak enforcement procedures of GATT did little to hinder evasion, but the crucial point was that the real requirement for long-term observance of international trade laws is their acceptance by the nations being regulated. The danger sign for GATT in the 1980s lay in the diminishing number of important trading nations that accepted its principles as applying to their own trade policies.

The EC had fewest scruples about contravening the MFN principle. Although the EC's customs union was arguably GATT-consistent, external trade policy embraced discrimination from the beginning. Other major trading nations have also disregarded the MFN principle, but at least before the 1980s these deviations were regarded as special cases rather than as the basis for external trade policy (e.g. US trade policy towards communist countries, the USA–Canada Autopact, the Australia–New Zealand free trade area, and the North–South problems addressed by GSP, and the Cotton Textile Arrangements).

The EC's behaviour and the accumulation of 'special cases' led Patterson to characterize the international trading system in 1965 as 'caught up in a headlong flight toward a massive recrudescence of discrimination' (1966, 356). He exaggerated the immediacy of the problem, in so far as the USA retained a principled opposition to discriminatory trade policies and other non-EC countries followed this lead, albeit with some deviations (e.g. discriminatory NTBs against labour-intensive imports, and new intra-European GDAs). Nevertheless, Patterson was right on fundamentals—each new discriminatory trade policy weakened the international system based on non-discrimination by eroding the share of world trade carried out under MFN conditions, by increasing conflicts among beneficiaries of complex preferential systems, by encouraging dissatisfaction in countries sticking to non-discriminatory policies (because other countries were seen as stealing a march on them), and by undermining the legitimacy of GATT. This systemic retrogression towards a situation reminiscent of the 1930s is what Patterson foresaw and, although it progressed less dramatically than he predicted, the world economy had moved further in that direction by the 1980s and the danger signs were becoming stronger.

The shift in US trade policy during the early 1980s was an important step. The American ability to influence other countries' trade policies by example is second to none, and, although this power may be less than is suggested by hegemonic theories, US policy has been the main bulwark against the spread of discriminatory trade policies since the late 1930s. Symptomatic of the erosion of the MFN principle's standing was the cavalier manner in which US officials talked of exploring new trade policy paths in the early 1980s; even after the CBERA and USA–Israel free trade area had been finalized, they were referred to as 'tentative tests' of a new approach.[6] The language could not be in starker contrast to Cordell Hull's zeal for a non-discriminatory trade regime, nor did it inspire confidence that the significance for the international trading system of the policy shift was appreciated.

The most immediate spillover from the US policy shift was to Canada. Popular expressions among Canada's policy-makers and their advisers during the early 1980s were that Canada should seek means of 'supplementing its multilateral options' and should 'show a balanced multilateral/bilateral approach to our trade policies'—as if the two approaches were not mutually inconsistent.[7] Bilateralism in the Canadian context was usually shorthand for a PTA with the United States, which could be viewed as primarily a North American concern, but to ignore the systemic implications of setting the world's largest bilateral international trade flow on a non-MFN basis was absurd.

Other countries could act as spokesnations for GATT Article I, but none carried anything near the influence exerted earlier by the USA. Japan, South Korea, and Taiwan have remained committed to non-discrimination and also are among the major

[6] Weintraub (1986, 359) has described the American public reaction to the CBERA: 'There was practically no commentary in the US press or by scholars of US trade that this departure from past practice might have important repercussions for the MFN principle. Hardly anyone seemed to notice; or if they noticed, to care very much.' After the Israel agreement commentaries on the implications for the MFN principle appeared in a *New York Times* article by Jagdish Bhagwati and in a *Challenge* article entitled 'The Quiet Shift in US Trade Policy', but there was no evidence of second thoughts in Washington.

[7] The quotations are from the *Collected Research Studies* for the Royal Commission on the Economic Union and Development Prospects for Canada, vol. 10, 131–2. Weintraub (1984) suggested that it would not take much to make a USA–Canada free trade area cover substantially all trade and hence satisfy GATT Art. XXIV, but the same point was seldom made in Canada precisely because Canadians do not want full economic (or political) integration with the USA. The Appendix discusses this bilateral relationship in greater depth.

losers from other countries' discriminatory trade policies, but their ability to provide leadership in support of GATT/WTO principles is limited by the question-marks over the restrictiveness of their own trade barriers (reminiscent of US impotence in stemming increased discrimination during the 1930s) and for South Korea and Taiwan by their special political situations.[8] In the GATT debate on the CBERA it was left to the Swiss delegate to raise the fundamental issues of principle (e.g. that the CBERA was overtly discriminatory even against GATT members within the Caribbean region, such as Nicaragua), but this bore about as much weight as Czech opposition to the ECSC thirty years earlier.

Academic writing contributed indirectly to the retreat from a non-discriminatory international trading system by failing to sound any alarms. Many individual GDAs have, rightly, been dismissed as unimportant in their effect on trade patterns, but such dismissals ignore the psychological effects of frequent contraventions of GATT principles. The most publicized empirical work on the EC and on GSP found trade creation to be dominant, implying that these major GDAs were welfare-improving; the authors set out their assumptions and caveats, and in Chapters 12 and 14 I have argued that trade diversion was likely to have been much larger than originally thought, but meanwhile perceptions were formed and US government departments continued to use Baldwin–Murray formulae to crank out biased predictions of future GDAs' effects. Even a critic of Baldwin and Murray's GSP study argued that, despite global resource misallocation resulting from trade diversion, GSP is desirable because it benefits developing countries:

> It would be incongruous indeed if in the midst of prolonged rhetoric on the 'new international economic order' a relatively minor concession involving only 3 per cent of trade in manufactures could not be accommodated. (Ahmad, 1978, 264)[9]

[8] Taiwan is not a WTO member, and its accession has been delayed by its being linked to China's controversial application.

[9] Ahmad, at the time a consultant to UNCTAD, further muddied the waters by stating that 'Preferences for developing countries under specified conditions are complementary, and not contradictory, to the principle of non-discrimination in trade' (1978, 264). His point is that GSP offsets other inequalities in international trade, but this opens up a Pandora's Box of limitless justifications for GDAs.

But it is precisely these small percentages that cumulated to the situation in which a majority of world trade was conducted under non-MFN conditions (Table 5.3). Moreover, given the propensity of GDAs to proliferate, any exception to the MFN principle may spawn further exceptions (as, for example, did the associated overseas territories provision of the Rome Treaty and the 1961 Athens Accord), which is why the common reaction of indifference towards the US agreements with minor trading partners was misplaced. Economic theory strongly implies the undesirability of discriminatory trade policies from a cosmopolitan welfare perspective, but economists' intellectual front against such policies has been much less solid or vociferous than the comparable front against the level of trade barriers.

4. Why is the MFN Principle so Resilient?

The fears reviewed in the previous section were given a boost by the EC92 programme and NAFTA, but by the mid-1990s they appeared far less threatening. The ineffectiveness of moves towards regionalism in Asia and the recognition that the EU was not establishing a Fortress Europe assuaged fears of a world of three trading blocs. The growing acceptance among developing countries of the merits of liberal trade policies (and dissatisfaction with the operation of GSP schemes) led more and more countries to join GATT and to accept GATT principles—a process that was augmented by the abandonment of central planning by many countries after 1989. The conclusion of the Uruguay Round and establishment of the WTO were the capstones of the triumph of multilateralism in the first half of the 1990s.

Why has the non-discrimination principle been so resilient in the face of recurring and strong challenges? Four countervailing forces can be set against the general tendency towards proliferation of GDAs. Other things being equal, a country will prefer to purchase its imports from the cheapest source. This desire was a major force for dismantling West European group discrimination during the 1950s. Other things are, however, often not equal and policy-makers may consider the trade diversion costs of discrimination a small price to pay for gaining preferential access to another country's markets (and if terms of trade effects are favourable there may be net economic gains for both countries) or for achieving a foreign policy goal. Moreover, whatever the national costs and benefits, producers who benefit from discriminatory trade barriers may have more influence over public policy than do the consumers/taxpayers who are denied the possibility of purchasing imports from the cheapest source.

A second countervailing force is fear of retaliation by countries that are discriminated against. There are many examples of this force at work, perhaps most clearly in restraining France from its intended ditching of the unconditional MFN clause during the interwar period, and countries have come to recognize the mutual damage that trade wars can cause. Nevertheless, countries have become adept at defusing the possibility of retaliation by bending rather than breaking MFN pledges, e.g. by tariff specialization or customs valuation procedures before the 1940s, by VERs in the 1970s and 1980s, and by other non-transparent measures such as rules of origin in the 1990s. Fear of retaliation is especially weak in restraining the largest trading units; the EU and USA have little to fear from small countries' retaliation, and both giants can count on the other's reluctance to start a major trade war over a minor departure from the MFN principle.

As GDAs proliferate, countries' trade policies become more complex, increasing administration and enforcement costs and opening up greater possibilities for dissatisfaction and international tension. Administrative costs are, however, no great deterrent, and the industrialized countries' bureaucracies can comfortably handle very complex GDAs. (For example, the EU's several thousand bilateral agreements within the MFA came under no threat of demise from administrative overload, and US policymakers happily took on the task of enforcing the detailed regulations embodied in NAFTA.) The enforcement costs of checking origin declarations are unambiguous but not unbearable. Balancing preferred trading partners' conflicting interests is more difficult, but even within the EU's complex hierarchy of preferred partners, balancing foreign interests (together with domestic interests affected by trade policy) is not beyond policymakers' capabilities—or, at least, the policy-makers don't think it is: despite frequent predictions that the EU's 'pyramid of privilege' will collapse under its own weight, there is no sign in Brussels of impending doom or repentance about the EU's network of preferential trade agreements.

Under normal conditions these three countervailing forces are inadequate to stem the general tendency towards proliferation of GDAs. Thus, the pattern, since the establishment of national customs units and efficient bureaucracies in the second half of the nineteenth century, has been for increasing discrimination in international trade policies. The major break in this pattern occurred during the 1940s, and it was a dramatic one. The 1930s revealed to all participants in the world trading system the economic and political costs of wholesale abandonment of the MFN principle, and the architects of GATT recognized that international agreement to outlaw discriminatory trade policies was the only way to prevent repetition of this systematic collapse. The idea was well-expressed by a senior GATT official in a 1956 speech:

> discrimination in any form is likely to lead to more discrimination, and . . . in the long run all countries will suffer from the inevitable distortion of trade patterns which will arise out of discrimination, even though they may be the temporary beneficiaries. However, because there are undoubted benefits that can be obtained in the short run from reciprocal discrimination, the only way to prevent a country or a pair of countries from making the move that will set off this chain reaction is to obtain the simultaneous pledge of the largest possible number of trading countries that they will not discriminate against each other.[10]

Although the hegemonic power played the leading role in putting together this international agreement, it is important to remember that *all* major trading nations among the United Nations agreed about the centrality of the non-discrimination principle to a desirable postwar international economic order.[11]

[10] Lecture by John W. Evans, Director of Commercial Policy at GATT, at the Johns Hopkins University Bologna Center on 20 February 1956; quoted in Curzon (1965, 68).

[11] Patterson (1966, 13–14) identifies four points of view on postwar trading rules: (1) the USA, Canada, Belgium, the Netherlands, and the Scandinavian countries wanted commitments to non-discriminatory multilateralism; (2) the USSR saw bilateralism as the logical approach; (3) Latin American, Middle Eastern, and Asian countries were preoccupied with economic development and were unwilling to commit themselves to trade rules; (4) Britain and France saw non-discrimination as the long-term goal but wanted flexibility to deal with postwar reconstruction. This taxonomy, however, masks the fact that the pro-non-discrimination groups (1 and 4) included all the major trading nations; the USSR had withdrawn into autarchy, and the independent developing countries were minor actors on the international stage.

As memories of the 1930s systemic collapse became more distant, the commitment to this principle became weaker, and the trend towards more discriminatory trade policies was set in motion once again. A second major break appears to have occurred in the mid-1990s, when the spectre of regionalism encouraged a reaffirmation of the non-discrimination principle. This was easier than in the 1930s because the commitment to liberal trade policies was much stronger, and discriminatory trade policies have less scope when trade barriers are low. It was also easier in the 1990s because there was less incentive to use trade policies to cement spheres of influence in the post-Cold War decade than there was in a world heading for war.

The general point is that non-discriminatory trade policies are superior (the JCM principle), but that this is more obvious to policy-makers in the long run. The disadvantages of discriminatory trade policies become more apparent in the long run as trade diversion costs are recognized, and as perceptions of benefits to insiders (and of costs to outsiders) usually turn out to have been exaggerated. At this point, there is pressure for reversion to observance of the MFN principle, unless political motives for discrimination dominate. Thus, even in the 1930s, some countries were trying to return to MFN treatment and multilateral trade, while the countries committed to discrimination were increasingly withdrawing from the world trading system.

5. Are Regional Arrangements Building Blocks or Stumbling Blocks?

Discriminatory trade policies have typically been viewed as an indisputable challenge to a liberal world trading system. This was especially true for policy-makers who experienced the 1930s, most of whom saw the growth of bilateralism as one of the adverse developments of that decade. Top priority was given to unconditional MFN treatment in the GATT articles, and the GATT's supporters worried about the growth of GDAs. The theoretical point that mutually beneficial FTAs will be continuously formed until the whole world is a single FTA (the Kemp–Wan proposition) was dismissed as irrelevant by economists interested in the real world.

The conventional wisdom was challenged in the early 1990s by several US economists, who argued not only that GDAs might be welfare-improving over the status quo, but also that they might smooth the way to eventual global free trade. Summers (1991) was the most influential of these writers, although his original arguments are unconvincing.[12] The possibility that RTAs might be building blocks rather than stumbling blocks to global trade liberalization entered into the regionalism-versus-multilateralism debate, although the case was rarely spelled out. Economic theorists developed models, but these offered little practical guidance (Winters, 1996b). Petri and Plummer (1996) provide the fullest collation and synthesis of arguments why RTAs might promote 'MFNization'. The building block case may be divided into resource allocation (trade diversion/trade creation) arguments, political economy arguments, negotiating arguments, and experimentation arguments.

Discrimination involves welfare-reducing trade diversion which will prompt countermeasures. Members of a free trade area experiencing trade diversion will be tempted to reduce MFN tariff barriers (compare Fig. 8.2), although as described in Part I a more common response has been to exit from the GDA (as did Honduras from the CACM, and Tanzania from the EAC). Trade diversion will encourage affected non-members to join the RTA, as happened with three EFTA countries' EU accession in 1995, although this has not been the normal reason for RTA expansion. (For example, the EC's first two enlargements and ASEAN's expansion do not fit this pattern.) Trade diversion concerns may also encourage outsiders with no prospect of membership to press for MFN tariff reductions; for example, the Rome Treaty may have encouraged the USA to promote the Kennedy Round, and

[12] Summers was influential because he was the top economist at the World Bank and soon to become a high-ranking member of the Clinton administration; also, he had an impressive academic record (although not in this area). His arguments were that in plausible RTAs trade creation is more likely than trade diversion, that trade diversion is not necessarily harmful, that RTAs have other beneficial effects (mainly pro-competitive stimuli to efficiency), and that RTAs reduce the number of distinct participants in multilateral trade negotiations, making agreement easier to reach. The downplaying of trade diversion and emphasis on other benefits from RTAs are typical of the new regionalism (see Ch. 10), but are not strongly supported by the empirical evidence reviewed in Part III. The point about the number of negotiators is dealt with later in this section of Ch. 18.

the transformation of CUSTA into NAFTA may have encouraged other countries to participate more actively in the Uruguay Round. None of these arguments is conclusive, and where they are valid their impact is marginal rather than dramatic, suggesting that, even if RTAs are building blocks, the construction of a liberal international trade regime would be a very slow process following this road.

Trade creation resulting from preferential tariff reduction may encourage further trade liberalization via a demonstration effect. This argument is close in spirit to the Kemp–Wan proposition, but is of doubtful practical importance. The numerous RTAs established in Latin America and Africa in the 1960s, partly in imitation of the EC, were not sustained. No other RTA has been even vaguely the kind of success that might prompt imitation. The successful unilateral trade liberalization by the high-performing East Asian economies has been a more convincing model.

The importance for policymaking of the political economy arguments outlined in the previous chapter has become widely accepted, and many advocates of the building block argument have emphasized the role of RTAs in reducing internal opposition to further (i.e. MFN) trade liberalization. Internal competition within a RTA will weed out some of the unproductive companies that resist trade liberalization. This argument is, however, not fully convincing; preferential access to partners' markets will create interest groups which benefit from the RTA and which will consequently resist MFNization, which would eliminate their preferential advantage. The exact balance of interests may change in any direction. Petri and Plummer also argue that RTA-induced direct foreign investment will create a broader constituency favouring multilateral trade liberalization because transnational corporations dislike impediments to moving their inputs around the globe. Again, this may be true in some cases, but there are counter-arguments; TNCs like to segment markets in order to operate as discriminating monopolists, and if the DFI has been diverted because of the RTA then the operations are not at their least-cost locations and the TNCs will resist being exposed to competition from producers at the global least-cost location.

The negotiating arguments centre on the presumption that multilateral trade negotiations would be easier with fewer independent participants. In fact, the number of negotiators in multilateral trade negotiations did not matter much in the GATT era. GATT rounds increased in length because the issues became more complex, not because the number of GATT signatories increased. At every round since the early 1960s, the key to completion was reaching US–EU agreement on a package acceptable to both parties; any additional new members since the previous round were irrelevant to the closure decision. The counter-argument that regional arrangements distract top-level trade policy-makers from multilateral negotiations has also been made, although it too is not supported by the historical record; in the end, neither the EC92 programme nor NAFTA prevented successful completion of the Uruguay Round.

In sum, the trade consequences of a RTA neither directly nor indirectly (via changes in the political economy equation) provide building blocks for global liberalization, while they may just as likely provide stumbling blocks. The negotiating arguments are also ambiguous, and are weak in either direction. Thus, with respect to tariffs, the simple conventional wisdom that discriminatory trade policies undermine the non-discrimination principle remains a good guide.

A stronger building block argument can be made with respect to the new areas discussed in Section 10.3. In these intrinsically more complex areas, agreement may be easier among a subset of like-minded countries than in a global forum. RTAs also offer opportunities for experimentation on a sub-global scale, with regulatory competition facilitating selection of the best codes for eventual global adoption. Both of these arguments have merit, although a tension exists in so far as likeminded partners may produce codes biased in favour of their particular interests or views of the world. If codes are not just a technical matter but involve choices over what is desirable or important, then the superior approach to devising global codes will be to establish appropriate global forums.

The stumbling block-versus-building block debate is difficult to evaluate because the few pieces of evidence can be interpreted to support either side. On balance, the evidence with respect to traditional trade barriers such as tariffs or QRs is not supportive of the building block view. Not only were RTAs major stumbling blocks in the 1930s, but in the GATT era both the EU and the GSP have delayed the global trade liberalization process by creating beneficiaries from discriminatory trade policies. A more plausible building block argument concerns the new areas of trade diplomacy, where regional arrangements can provide testing grounds for alternative regulatory regimes, although it is possible that countries not in RTAs will consider this an unacceptable process. A better analogy appears to be that discriminatory trading arrangements end up as millstones rather than stepping stones.

6. GATT's Unfinished Business

The GATT era, 1947–94, was distinguished by a huge dismantling of conventional barriers to international trade (i.e. tariffs, QRs, and exchange controls) and by widespread agreement not to replace these by equivalent measures. The record was imperfect; tariffs and QRs remain widespread, and many grey area measures sprang up to compensate for reduced tariffs. Nevertheless, world trade was considerably freer by the 1990s than it had been half a century earlier. The significance in the present context is that the lower the trade barriers are, the less scope there is for discriminatory application.

The outcome was a close-run thing. During the 1980s GATT was discredited in the eyes of many observers, especially in the USA,[13] and ignored by others, especially in Western Europe. Progress reports on the Uruguay Round fretted over its iminent collapse. The turning point came in 1993. Although NAFTA negotiations captured most US media attention during that year, the crucial actions of President Clinton were to reverse the shift from multilateralism towards bilateralism which had characterized Reagan–Bush trade policy.

In Asia, the USA had initially given its support to APEC as a defensive measure to forestall the establishment an Asian regional bloc (as envisaged by the EAEC). The positive component of US economic diplomacy in Asia was extremely limited under President Bush, whose most memorable action was to collapse over a meal in Japan during a trip intended to open

[13] The loss of credibility of the non-discrimination principle in the USA is captured in the observation by Weintraub (1986, 364): 'Anyone advocating non-discrimination in the face of the rampant discrimination that exists and is in the making must sound like the village idiot.'

Japanese markets to *inter alia* US auto makers. Secretary of State Baker was best-known in Asia for his hunting trip to Mongolia in search of trophies from rare animals. Although East Asian targets of super 301 were less pugnacious than Brazil or India, US aggressive unilateralism was widely resented.

President Clinton signalled the end of the policy of Asian neglect by declaring 1993 the Year of Asia in US policy.[14] The USA assumed an active role in APEC, culminating in hosting the first APEC summit at Blake Island, near Seattle. Blake Island symbolized US commitment to Asia, and also sent a strong signal (as the NAFTA negotiations were being concluded) that the USA was not retreating into a Western Hemispheric exclusive trading bloc. Owing to differing perceptions of insiders and outsiders, the 1993 APEC summit may have had a double impact in facilitating completion of the Uruguay Round; APEC members saw the summit as an affirmation of US good faith in multilateral fora, while the excluded Europeans feared that without successful conclusion of the Uruguay Round the USA would turn to pan-Pacific regionalism.

In late 1993, the USA and the EU reached agreement on the outstanding issues in the Uruguay Round. The final act of the Uruguay Round was signed in December, paving the way for the official concluding conference in Marakesh in April 1994. Much groundwork had of course been done before 1993, but US leadership was still required to ensure completion of the last GATT round.

The WTO has inherited GATT trade law and has been endowed with stronger enforcement mechanisms. The areas most closely connected with discriminatory trade policies were analysed in Chapter 7. How the WTO actually functions is yet to be determined, but the most positive sign is the widespread commitment to a liberal international trading regime, in contrast to the situation even as recently as the 1970s when many countries were suspicious of unregulated international trade. Unfinished

[14] One of Clinton's first acts as president was to abandon the most obnoxious of all the aggressive unilateralism measures, which had aimed at opening up Asian cigarette markets. In several countries the USA demanded not only market access but also advertising practices (to enable US tobacco firms to establish their brands) that were illegal in the USA, and which dramatically increased the number of young Asian smokers (Chaloupka and Laixuthai, 1996).

business remains, however, in the conventional trade policy areas of tariffs and QRs, which retain potential for conflict and for discrimination.

What are the prospects for eliminating trade taxes and QRs? For the first time, this idea was seriously proposed in the mid-1990s (Bergsten, 1996). An important catalyst has been APEC, through the 1994 Bogor Declaration, which called on APEC members to reduce their MFN tariffs to zero by 2010, with a ten-year grace period for less developed countries. This target was echoed by Western Hemisphere leaders at the December 1994 Summit of the Americas in Miami.

Declarations are not the same as actions. This was exemplified by the international conferences of the 1920s (see Section 2.3). Yet, 2010 is not far off, and the commitments given in Bogor and Miami were made by heads of government. The biggest cause for optimism is that tariff elimination makes economic sense. Trade taxes normally cause welfare-reducing price distortions. Although there are several situations where tariffs may improve national welfare, they are seldom the first-best policies.[15] The practical experience is that the theoretically valid arguments in support of tariffs have been hijacked by vested interests to justify tariffs which benefit themselves but not the nation as a whole. There is no well-documented case of a trade tax improving national economic welfare in the long run. Moreover, when tariffs are as low as they became after the Uruguay Round (Table 7.1), they are of less value to the gainers, and even the direct administrative costs become significant relative to any benefits.

The EU is the major stumbling block in the path to global free trade, because of its commitment to preferential tariffs. Many EU policy-makers continue to see the customs union, with its preferential treatment of EU products, as the bedrock of economic integration, which is in turn the basis for political integration. European integration has progressed beyond this point, with some elements of economic union already in place; monetary union

[15] Tariffs are blunt instruments because they do too much; support for domestic production and discouragement of consumption of a good are better provided by separate subsidies and sales taxes. Trade measures are first-best when the market failure is in international markets; e.g. if a country has market power then the use of trade taxes may increase national welfare at the expense of trading partners. Irwin (1996) provides a history of the doctrine of free trade and challenges to it.

should reinforce the point that tariff preferences are no longer essential glue needed to hold the union together.

The EU's external trade policy remains the principal source of trouble. When faced with a new situation in Eastern Europe after 1989, the EU adopted a policy that was directly descended from the Global Mediterranean Policy of two decades earlier, despite the poor record of that policy. When APEC and Western Hemisphere leaders declared their support for tariff elimination by 2010/2020, the EU responded with a similar target in the Euro–Med agreement, except that the Euro–Med agreement calls for free trade within the EU and the Mediterranean Basin, and not for zero MFN tariffs.

EU policy-makers remain wedded to discriminatory tariffs because they have few alternative foreign policy instruments. Despite repeated attempts to construct a common foreign policy, EU national leaders have not progressed beyond the consultation stage, and even this lapses in difficult situations. In 1989/90 Germany progressed rapidly with reunification, paying less attention to its EU partners than to US or USSR leaders. In the Gulf War, France and the UK acted as global powers with permanent seats on the UN Security Council rather than as EU members. Most dramatically of all, the EU failed to pursue a successful common policy towards the disintegration of Yugoslavia, to the extent that by the mid-1990s Bosnia became the symbol of EU foreign policy failure.[16]

Will the EU change its spots, renounce its attachment to discriminatory trade policies, and board the global free trade bandwagon? One cause for optimism is a new twist on the recurring theme that those who feel most affected by GDAs come from among the excluded. The 1993 APEC summit brought together leaders from all of the major trading nations outside Europe. It was the first important international trade summit since the Treaty of Kadesh at which European leaders were not represented.[17] The EU reaction was to promote its own links with East Asia and

[16] The EU has achieved better co-ordination elsewhere in Eastern Europe and the former Soviet Union. Technical and financial assistance have been chanelled through the Partners in Transition and other programmes with less unfortunate acronyms. In some capitals, e.g. Almaty, the EU members with embassies share common premises, but this is exceptional.

[17] Ramses II of Egypt and the Hittite ruler Muwatalis delimited spheres of influence in 1268 BC, after 17 years of negotiations following the battle of Kadesh.

with North America. The first Asia–Europe summit in Bangkok in March 1996 made little impact, and proposals for a Transatlantic Free Trade Area (TAFTA) received little encouragement from the US government.[18] One result might be to bring home to the EU the disadvantages of pursuing exclusionary trade policies. The EU's conversion could be eased by the fact that the first head of the WTO is European. On the other hand, 'zero' is always a difficult target for EU policy, which is ultimately determined by fifteen veto-yielding delegations on the Council who typically reach important decisions by compromise.

7. Concluding Remarks on the Role of Economists

Economists do not make trade policy, but they do play a part. The gains from trade and the probable costs of barriers to international trade are among the issues on which there is most general agreement among academic economists. This consistently held position has contributed to the climate in which trade taxes and quantitative restrictions have fallen substantially during the second half of the twentieth century. Exposure to graduate study in economics directly influenced key policy-makers in Latin America and India, who reversed the most protectionist trade regimes in the Third World.

On discriminatory trade policies, the role of economists is less clear because the economic consequences are ambiguous and complex. Where RTAs are seen as primarily economic (as in CUSTA and NAFTA) rather than political (as in Western Europe or ASEAN), economists have contributed significantly to policy formation. Some leading experts on discriminatory trade policies have influenced policy-makers directly as advisers, e.g. Lipsey in Canada or Bhagwati at GATT. Others have become involved in the public debate, although unfortunately this has been at the expense of simplifying the economic arguments.

During the CUSTA debates most economists weighed in on the side of free trade. Potential trade diversion costs of CUSTA could be downplayed because they were likely to be unimportant. Continued support for 'free trade' was less justified with

[18] The TAFTA proposal is discussed by Frost (1997), Preeg (1996), and Siebert *et al.* (1996).

respect to NAFTA, and some economists (such as Krueger) began to emphasize the trade diversion potential that lay in the details. Nevertheless, the general economists' view, exemplified by Dornbusch (1990) and Summers (1991), represented a return to the pre-Vinerian simplification that all tariff reductions are good, whether they are bilateral, plurilateral, or multilateral. Bhagwati (1993) has criticized this funereal approach to GATT's non-discrimination principle, based on poor information and poor analysis,[19] but there is no doubt that NAFTA became identified with free trade in the US policy debate.

A similar distortion has occurred when empirical results have been presented as contributions to policy debates. The Cecchini Report published, and the EU subsequently publicized, wildly upper-bound estimates of the benefits from EC92 based on acceptable but not-conclusive techniques. The Washington-based Institute for International Economics gained wide publicity for its NAFTA study (Hufbauer and Schott, 1993), which focused on the potential job cration impact of NAFTA on the US economy. As Krugman (1995b) emphasized in his review of the Hufbauer–Schott study, the method was so shaky that its abuse could undermine the future credibility of economists' empirical contributions to policy debates. The underlying problem is the pressure for simple answers to complex questions and for empirical results which unambiguously support the right policies.

The suspicion arises that not only are economists' views and empirical results abused by policy advocates (that is inevitable and is not the economists' fault), but also, some economists have been seduced by the limelight into abusing their own intellectual heritage. Such temptations are especially strong in the second-best world of comparing preferential tariff reductions with a tariff-ridden alternative.[20] In the comparison of free trade

[19] Bhagwati dubs it the 'funereal' school because many of its members are associated with the Massachusetts Institute of Technology, whose address is Memorial Drive in Cambridge, Mass.

[20] When economists hold genuinely differing views, advocacy groups may select their advisers non-randomly. In-house economists tend to have biases in perspective; when the IMF and OECD reacted to the regionalism-versus-multilateralism debate by publishing surveys of the issue (de la Torre and Kelly, 1992; OECD, 1995), these covered fairly standard ground, but the global organization saw regionalisnm as a stumbling block to global liberalization while the plurilateral organization was more sanguine about the complementarity of regionalism and multilateralism.

with protective tariffs and QRs, economists are in less ambiguous agreement and empirical estimates are firmly based, with arguments over the size rather than the sign of net welfare effects. Thus, as the policy debate shifts towards the global elimination of tariffs and QRs, the role of economists may return to being both stronger and less ambiguous.

There are regional variations in the impact of economists. All governments prefer to listen to economists whose positions confirm their own prejudices, but some are more open to independent advice than others. In the USA, Germany, Australia, and elsewhere this has been institutionalized in independent and influential advisory bodies. In many developing and transition economies economic technocrats have often been granted great influence in designing new policies to replace discredited development strategies or allocative mechanisms. Other countries have relied to a greater extent on in-house economic advisers, who are often conservative (in the sense of resistent to change), or have ignored professional economic advice.

The EU has fallen into this last category, with policy implementation in the hands of professional Eurocrats rather than specialized economists. The EU leadership is also hypersensitive to criticism, perhaps because of its own lack of democratic legitimacy. Thus, although the EU makes some use of outside economic advisers, it tends to be highly selective in choosing economists who emphasize the EU's achievements and share its predilection for dealing with regulatory issues; the EU remains impervious to criticisms of its ongoing tariff and quantitative restrictions to trade, and of its continued efforts to maintain a pyramid of preferences in its external trade relations.[21]

[21] To give some examples from this book's bibliography, EU representatives frequently quote the work of Pelkmans, Sapir, Venables, or Richard Baldwin, at least selectively, but ignore contributions of Hindley, Messerlin, Langhammer, or Winters, which are critical of anti-dumping policies, internal trade restrictions, or preferential external trade policies.

19

Summary and Prospects

In this book I have analysed discriminatory trade policies using history, international trade theory, and public choice theory. Economic analysis can explain the impact on trade patterns and the welfare consequences of such policies. Thus, Part II is the core of the book, but standard economists' tools are insufficient to explain the proliferation of discriminatory trade policies and their full long-term implications. Political considerations (both domestic power relations and foreign policy matters) often enter into the calculus behind a discriminatory policy's introduction. Moreover, the historical record clearly indicates dynamic processes at work, which are poorly captured by comparative static analysis or taxonomies.

The subject is complicated by the layers of direct, indirect, and systemic consequences of discriminatory trade policies. It is also complicated by issues raised in Chapter 1 of defining the appropriate unit of analysis, distinguishing between regionalism and regionalization, and differentiating between alternative forms of discriminatory policies, including most recently the distinction between regional trading arrangements and regional integration. I have focused on regionalism using traditional trade policy instruments of trade taxes and quantitative restrictions, and have taken existing nation states as the units. The last point is most debatable with respect to the EU, which in the 1960s was a fairly conventional customs union but is now well on the path to economic union. No book on regional trading arrangements can ignore the EU, but it is a special case in that it is explicitly moving towards some yet-to-be-determined form of economic and political integration.

The most celebrated theoretical conclusion about GDAs is that discriminatory trade policies belong in the world of second-best, and valid generalizations are rarely possible. This is in part why the GATT had difficulty in distinguishing between permissible and non-permissible exceptions to MFN treatment; even Article

XXIV's superficially attractive distinction between GDAs with internal free trade and other GDAs has no economic basis as a guide to good versus bad GDAs.[1] Nevertheless, the theory of second-best is not a blanket justification for agnosticism about the desirability of discriminatory trade policies. From an economic perspective, free trade is a fairly robust prescription for improving global resource allocation, and free trade subsumes no discrimination among trading partners.

In a world of trade barriers and market imperfections, there are costs and benefits of discriminatory trade policies, but actual GDAs have tended to be designed in such ways as to increase sectional rather than global economic welfare. The empirical literature reviewed in Part III offers support for the proposition. Western European integration is a possible exception, although even in this case special treatment of agriculture and other sensitive sectors has led to substantial trade diversion; whether trade creation or trade diversion dominated is difficult to say, owing to the problem of specifying the counterfactual. One-way preferential trading arrangements are invariably implemented in forms that preclude significant trade creation and either lead to trade diverison or, more typically, have no large impact. Reciprocal arrangements also tend to be constructed to favour trade diversion rather than trade creation; this is apparent from comparison of *ex ante* studies estimating the effects of proposed thoroughgoing schemes with estimates of the imperfect PTAs actually implemented (e.g. NAFTA or AFTA).

Political economy considerations can explain the proliferation of discriminatory trade arrangements and their bias towards trade diversion. The costs of trade diversion fall on outside producers and domestic taxpayers, whereas the costs of trade creation are concentrated on specific factors of production in domestic industries. The latter groups are often better organized and able to influence policy. The complexity of tailor-made GDAs also reduces transparency as agreements are negotiated by government officials, who may themselves relish the discretionary powers that arise. Complexity is itself a source of higher net costs.

Theory, and practice, also yield strong conclusions about various forms of discriminatory arrangements. Pure free trade areas

[1] Ethier and Horn (1984) set out a model in which small internal tariffs are Pareto-superior to internal free trade.

are, under most plausible circumstances, unstable because of trade deflection. The only significant FTA in recent decades was EFTA, in which the trade deflection problem was minimized by low external tariffs on manufactures and by excluding agriculture from internal free trade. In general, FTAs can be expected to lead to a race to the bottom (i.e. to non-discriminatory free trade) or to be replaced by customs unions, or to break down. Apparent exceptions, characterized by long sets of rules on intra-area trade or product exclusions, are not FTAs. Among recent examples, the first ASEAN FTA collapsed while AFTA appears to be heading towards non-discriminatory trade liberalization, and NAFTA does not have true internal free trade.

Customs unions are more stable, but require political agreement on external trade policy and revenue sharing. Historically this has been accomplished in one of two ways. A small partner has accepted the commercial and fiscal policy decisions of a dominant partner (e.g. San Marino or Monaco) or the customs union has been a prelude to, or a component of, political integration (e.g. the German Zollverein, Canada, or Australia).[2] The EU's destination is still unknown, but past experience suggests that it is difficult to stop for long at the customs union stage.

One-way preferences are easy to analyse economically, but they also have important political and international relations aspects. They invariably benefit the small preference recipient, while having a trivial (and ambiguously signed) impact on the large 'donor' country. Their longevity mainly depends upon whether the large country sees political benefits from what is typically a transfer of tariff revenue to a client. The impact of such arrrangements is often restricted, owing to the political economy pressure from competing producers in the donor country (leading to product exclusions) and to the low tariffs on items which the recipient can export (leading to narrow preference margins). Nevertheless, they do have adverse systemic effects as the recipients' competitors feel harmed by the discrimination, and rivals of the donor may feel that it is gaining an edge in creating an influence sphere. Viner's comment still seems appropriate:

[2] Proposals for customs unions in the CIS and in southern Africa have encountered problems arising from the dominant partner not being sufficiently dominant to impose its commercial and financial policy decision on its smaller neighbours.

Tariff discriminations are invariably resented by the countries which are discriminated against, and three centuries of experience demonstrates that under all circumstances they operate to poison international relations and to make more difficult the task of maintaining international harmony. (Viner, 1951, 355)

Such poisonous consequences clearly arose from the EU's Mediterranean policy in the 1970s, and are associated in the 1990s with the EU's preferential trading arrangements with Eastern European countries and with the especially putative PTAs with Russia and Ukraine.

The systemic consequences of discriminatory trade policies are difficult to evaluate because there is no adequate way to test competing theories. The historically unique evolution of the international trading system between the 1860s and the Second World War provides the only evidence of the long-run systemic consequences of discriminatory trade policies. After 1870 there was a gradual erosion of faith in and adherence to the unconditional MFN clause, culminating in large-scale resort to bilateral and regional trading arrangements in the 1930s. The architects of the postwar international economic order were strongly influenced by this experience and, in order to avoid the disastrous political consequences as well as the economic costs of the 1930s trade regime, they made non-discrimination the cornerstone of the GATT. Between the 1950s and 1980s there was again a gradual erosion of faith in and adherence to the unconditional MFN clause, raising the prospect that the 1870–1939 historical pattern might be repeated with discriminatory trade policies inexorably proliferating until the system broke down. This did not happen in the 1990s, as a co-operative solution was found to shore up the multilateral trading system, symbolically with the establishment of the World Trade Organization in 1995.

Why was the 1930s outcome not repeated in the 1990s? Institutions matter. The existence of the GATT as a set of rules placed limits on the proliferation and design of GDAs, and as a forum GATT enabled national policy-makers to meet and ultimately to reach a co-operative solution.[3] Ideas matter even more. The spread

[3] Chance might also matter. The widely held view of the world economy consolidating into three huge blocs was given pause by the disintegration of Yugoslavia and the Soviet Union in the early 1990s. Preeg (1995) argues that

of GDAs in the 1960s and 1970s was fostered by structuralist views of economic development which encouraged inward-looking economic integration and demands for special treatment which were met by GSP. When these policies failed, they were succeeded not by more illiberal trade policies, as in the 1930s, but by a global trend towards trade liberalization. The nemesis of discriminatory trade policies is free trade.

The novel argument in favour of GDAs in the 1990s is that they can be building blocks towards global free trade. Some proponenets still argue that GDAs promote trade cration rather than trade diversion, although this is not supported by the empirical evidence. Stronger building block arguments focus on non-trade aspects of regional arrangements.[4] The outcome of these ongoing debates remains inconclusive, but there is a strong case for making the primary forums for discussion of new trade-related issues the appropriate multilateral non-trade organization, while the WTO maintains a watching brief. On narrowly defined border measures such as tariffs, quantitative restrictions on imports or exports, customs valuation and clearance procedures, etc., there is little scope for regional measures, and discriminatory practices have little to recommend them.

What are the prospects for eliminating discriminatory border measures? Given the widespread and increasing recognition among policy-makers that trade taxes are inefficient (and non-tariff barriers are at least as distortionary), and given that discriminatory trade policies add a further level of distortion, the time is ripe for the adoption of free trade, which would eliminate discriminatory border measures. The practical problem is the lack of leadership from the USA and EU. The EU remains wedded to discriminatory tariffs, not just to create Community preference on internal trade but also as a tool of foreign policy. The USA continues to insist on reciprocity in trade liberalization. In both

individuals matter too; in his account, the Uruguay Round was on the brink of failure until Kantor and Brittan provided an unlikely but highly effective negotiating pair in the final stretch.

[4] I have scarcely addressed the argument that RTAs help to cement commitment to trade liberalization and wider reforms. This is usually made in the context of Mexico's accession to NAFTA or of Mercosur, but RTAs are neither necessary (East Asia has many counter-examples) nor sufficient (as shown by the exits from the EAC and CACM) to enforce trade liberalization.

the EU and the USA, the need for political compromise among member states or branches of government makes 'zero' a difficult target to achieve. These obstacles are, however, not insuperable; the EU may develop a more coherent foreign policy with alternative instruments, and the USA could revise its constitutional ban on export taxes to include all trade taxes. This assumes a role reversal as medium-sized trading nations, which are major beneficiaries of free trade, will need to provide leadership to obtain change in the countries that led during the GATT era. If that happens, then this book's subject matter will become history rather than the stuff of currnt trade policy debates, as it has been throughout the twentieth century.

APPENDIX

Discriminatory Trading Arrangements between the USA and Canada before CUSTA

To assess the prospects of preferential trading arrangements between the United States and Canada, we can use the theory, empirical evidence, and public choice analysis presented in this book. Past experience of US–Canadian trade relations is also worth examining because, despite an apparently positive-sum game, North American preferential trading arrangements have been rare and this case illustrates why discriminatory trading arrangements may not come into existence.

The distribution of economic costs and benefits from a USA–Canada free trade area is easy to predict. Given the relative size of the two economies, the lion's share of the economic gains should accrue to Canada. Some of the Canadian gains could be obtained by unilateral tariff elimination, but there are significant additional benefits from the removal of American tariffs.[1] For the United States the benefits are likely to be minor, and the possibility of trade diversion rules out any presumption of net gain. Of course, with any preferential arrangement less than bilateral free trade, the magnitude and even the distribution of economic costs and benefits will depend upon the specific arrangement.

The national effects just described explain why the economic motivation for a preferential trade agreement has been strongest on the Canadian side. The USA has shown real concern about the efficiency gains from bilaterally negotiated trade liberalization only when US–Canadian trade relations have seriously deteriorated, while under normal conditions any American interest in a trade agreement has been subsidiary to other economic or political objectives. In both countries the internal distribution of costs and benefits has been important in forestalling or limiting the coverage of a trade agreement; import-competing producers such as the American lumber and dairy industries or most of the Canadian manufacturing sector were often sufficiently powerful to prevent breaches in the tariff wall. The political consequences of wide-ranging North American free trade have figured strongly in policy debates, although these consequences have been perceived in varying (and contradictory) ways; in particular, there has been dispute over whether free trade with

[1] In the studies by the Wonnacotts and by Harris and Cox, described in Ss. 9.4 and 13.1, these additional benefits are estimated to be the larger source of Canadian gains.

the USA would strengthen the Canadian economy so that Canada could better retain political independence or whether a free trade agreement would lead inexorably to annexation. Finally, North American trade policies are not formed in a vacuum; before the Second World War, Britain's commercial policies were vital as the UK was the most important overseas market for both North American countries and the main competitor to US manufacturers in the Canadian market, while since 1945 other countries' commercial policies have influenced US attitudes towards the GATT.

The Nineteenth Century

During the first half of the nineteenth century, the British North American colonies were part of the British imperial economic system. The mainland colonies benefited particularly through the diversion of British timber imports from closer Baltic suppliers to preferred colonial suppliers. After the 1846 Repeal of the Corn Laws, it was evident that Imperial Preference would soon vanish and the North American colonies would lose much of their lucrative transatlantic trade; a free trade agreement with the USA was seen as a way to reorient their exports.

The British and American positions were crucial for the realization of the colonies' goal. Although the colonies had introduced small revenue tariffs after 1846, their tariff-setting autonomy was not yet clearly established, and even with the later 1858–9 Canadian tariffs there was some concern as to whether they might be disallowed in Westminster. Thus, particularly for a trade treaty involving all the North American colonies, the British government was their negotiator, and it had its own interests. In the early 1850s these centred on resolving fishing disputes which had lingered since 1812 to the detriment of Anglo-American relations. New England politicians were willing to make commercial policy concessions in return for a satisfactory settlement of the fisheries issue, and northern US politicians generally favoured freer trade with Canada as a means of strengthening ties. Southern US politicians had strongly opposed closer ties with Canada for fear they would lead to annexation and thereby increase the anti-slavery majority among states. However, after Lord Elgin's visit to Washington in 1854 they were convinced that freer trade and the consequent increased Canadian prosperity was necessary to forestall annexation: 'Thus was afforded the amazing spectacle of two groups of men, the North and the South, sitting in the same House and supporting the same measure for contradictory reasons' (Masters, 1937/1963 edn., 43). The measure's success was also helped by an ebbing of US protectionism; the tariff was at its lowest level since 1815 and lower than it would be at any later date until after the Second World

War. These reasons were, however, facilitating rather than crucial; the fundamental reason for the 1854 Reciprocity Treaty was the British and American desire to settle the fisheries issue, and neither's objection to a limited free trade agreement being included in the package to satisfy the colonies.

The Reciprocity Treaty provided for free trade in natural products between the USA and the British North American colonies (Canada, New Brunswick, Nova Scotia, and Prince Edward Island, plus Newfoundland after December 1855), initially for ten years and then subject to one year's notice of termination. There seems no doubt that the Reciprocity Treaty increased trade, but the magnitude of this impact is difficult to measure because of contemporaneous events (especially the mid-1850s Canadian railway boom and the American Civil War) and poor data quality.[2] Despite some differences in detail, however, the studies of Masters (1937), Officer and Smith (1968), and Ankli (1971) all point to similar conclusions: the Reciprocity Treaty had a positive but small effect on Canadian exports.[3]

Any economic benefits from the Reciprocity Treaty were swamped by other considerations after its first few years, and the USA abrogated it after the minimum eleven-year term. In Canada the crucial step away from the spirit of reciprocity was the 1858–9 tariff on manufactures. The tariff increases reflected revenue concerns after overambitious railway subsidies and the 1857 recession had left the government heavily indebted, but more fundamentally they reflected the growing power of protectionist interests in Canada. American manufacturers denounced the closing of the Canadian market, and rising revenue requirements (and Anglo-American political tension) during the Civil War and growing protectionism in the northern states reinforced the pressure for abrogation. Non-renewal of the Treaty was inevitable well before its termination in 1866, and illustrates not so much the treaty's failure to

[2] Officer and Smith (1968) point out the inconsistencies in the North American trade data of the time. They also quote reports of large-scale smuggling of agricultural goods and livestock in the early 1850s, suggesting that some of the increase in recorded trade (which they found to be concentrated in the first year of the treaty's operation) was simply a legitimization of previously unrecorded trade.

[3] Masters is more enthusiastic at some points in his book, but in the key chapter on economic effects he plays them down, ascribing most of the increased trade to 'commerce of convenience', i.e. intra-industry trade (1937/1963 edn., 109–10). Officer and Smith identify an impact only on Canadian exports of wheat and oats, and, because these covered less than 15% of Canadian exports and cost differentials between the two partners were small, welfare gains must have been limited (1968, 619). Ankli (1971) found instead that barley, rye, and perhaps lumber were the only exports that were unambiguously helped by the Reciprocity Treaty.

meet its objectives but rather its unimportance in the wider frame of Anglo-American–Canadian relations.

After Confederation in 1867, Canadian tariff laws carried formal offers of reciprocity in some products, but the USA was increasingly cool. A new fisheries settlement in 1871 gave Canada financial compensation rather than a new Reciprocity Treaty. Canada continued to lobby for the latter and a treaty was negotiated in 1874, but failed to obtain ratification in the US Senate. Continuing overtures during the 1880s, as the fisheries dispute dragged on, met ever stronger resistance in the US Senate where New England, the border states, and lumber interests blocked any move to reduce tariffs on imports from Canada. Faced with a negative US response to reciprocity and continuing US tariff increases (notably in 1890 and 1897), the offer was deleted from Canadian tariff legislation in 1894 and British Empire preferences were unilaterally reintroduced in 1897. Imperial Preference was an attempt both to reorient Canadian trade (Australia, New Zealand, and South Africa responded by reintroducing Imperial Preferences, although Britain remained committed to free trade) and to retaliate against the 1897 US tariff without raising Canada's general tariff rate. In sum, although Canada remained committed at least on paper to a preferential trade arrangement with the USA after 1866,[4] growing American protectionism ruled it out.

1911

The 1907 Canadian tariff revision established a three-tier schedule, with Imperial Preference rates set at one-third of the general rate and intermediate tariff rates established for countries granting trade favours to Canada. In the USA the 1909 Payne–Aldrich Act required the government to impose maximum tariff rates on imports from any country discriminating against US exports. In 1910 a Franco–Canadian trade agreement was negotiated by which French goods would enter Canada at the intermediate tariff rate in return for some tariff reductions on Canadian exports to France. Since US exports to Canada faced the general tariff rate, the scene was set for a USA–Canada trade war—an eventuality that was averted by negotiations which led in January 1911 to an executive-level Reciprocity Agreement providing for tariff reductions on a limited range of raw and processed products and a few manufactured items.[5]

[4] There is, however, some doubt as to whether Canadian commitment to reciprocity would have stood up to a practical test by the 1890s. In the 1891 election the Liberal Party included it prominently in its programme and lost, partly because this permitted the Conservations to identify themselves with loyalty to the British connection.

[5] Percy *et al.* (1982, 414) estimate the coverage to have been 17% of Canadian exports and 9% of Canadian imports.

President Taft obtained congressional approval for the agreement (with some difficulty in the Senate), but in Canada after a lengthy parliamentary debate Laurier took the issue to the people and lost the election.

The 1911 episode was a seminal event in US–Canadian trade relations. The Canadian desire for reciprocal free trade and the less positive American attitude during the previous 65 years are easy to explain in economic terms, but in 1911 Canada turned down a concrete proposal already approved by the USA. Acceptance might have led to a more thoroughgoing trade agreement; rejection ended prospects for special bilateral trade relations for over half a century.[6]

Three sets of reasons, which turn out to be mutually reinforcing, explain the Canadian voters' rejection of the 1911 Reciprocity Agreement. First, in the Westminster system, victory depends upon a party's overall appeal and organizational strength. In 1911 the Liberals had held office for fifteen years and the government had lost its dynamism, while the Conservatives had built up strong provincial bases (especially in Ontario and British Columbia) for victory in the federal election. Thus, a Conservative victory was likely, even before Laurier seized on Reciprocity as a potential trump card. Secondly, the Conservatives were identified with the British connection and they successfully linked the Reciprocity issue to imperial loyalty. Whatever the potential economic gains from freer trade with the USA, there was widespread apprehension that it might lead to annexation.[7] Thirdly, strong vested interests opposed any reductions in the Canadian tariff; orchard-owners and mixed farmers faced immediate competition if the 1911 Agreement took effect,[8] while manufacturers feared it would be the thin end of the wedge. These interests were influential in determining Conservative Party policy and cultivating concerns about American political intentions (L. E. Ellis, 1939/1968 edn., 196).

[6] This ignores the close cross-border co-operation during wartime, when North American supplies were obtained regardless of national origin. These were, however, explicitly temporary arrangements which ceased immediately with the end of hostilities.

[7] There were also wider cultural fears of being forced to conform to alien commercial, legal, financial, social, and ethical standards. This loss of the 'national soul' was emphasized by Rudyard Kipling in an interview with the *Montreal Star* (7 September 1911): 'Whatever the United States may gain and I presume that the United States proposals are not wholly altruistic, I see nothing for Canada in reciprocity except a little ready money, which she does not need, and a very long repentance' (quoted in L. Ellis, 1939/1968 edn., 182).

[8] The general equilibrium model of Percy *et al.* (1982) identifies more complex distributional effects, e.g. the potential losses to skilled labour in the Prairies, which explains the swing to the Conservatives in urban constituencies while the rural constituencies in the region swung to the Liberals.

The econometric study by Johnston and Percy (1980) found evidence to support all three sets of reasons, but the 'economic' variables were the most important determinants of voting patterns. The main economic gainers from Reciprocity (and from any more extensive move toward free trade) were the wheat farmers, and the Liberals actually gained votes in the Prairies, but for the other beneficiaries (including consumers) the gains were too small to determine their voting patterns. In the fruit-growing, livestock and manufacturing regions there was a pronounced swing to the Conservatives. Nationwide, religion (as a proxy for imperialist sentiment) helped to explain the swing, as did the provincial government's party affiliation in some regions.

The 1911 Canadian vote on Reciprocity fits well with the interest group model of trade barriers, allowing for specific institutional conditions. The main difference from US-based analyses is the importance in a Westminster parliamentary system of influencing a major political party and then helping that party to get elected, which can lead to apparently sudden major trade policy changes (the 1931 UK tariff is another example), rather than the ebb and flow of protectionism characteristic of the US system.

Between the Wars

The threatened US–Canadian tariff war failed to materialize despite the 1911 defeat of the Reciprocity Agreement. The 1913 Underwood tariff introduced many of the American tariff cuts envisaged in the 1911 agreement, and further US liberalization occurred during the war (e.g. removal of the American duty on Canadian wheat). Other wartime trends, however, confirmed that preferential North American trade arrangements were off the agenda, as British imperial links were tightened (and the UK introduced minor preferences for Empire goods) and the USA championed the unconditional MFN clause.

During the 1920s American tariffs began to rise once more and Canada, along with the rest of the world, became increasingly worried about the non-negotiable high US tariffs. The 1930 Hawley–Smoot tariff hurt exports from every region of Canada (Isaacs, 1948, 236–7), and led to immediate retaliation which, as in 1897, was accompanied by wider Imperial Preference margins. After Britain's abandonment of free trade in 1932, Canada (together with Australia) pressed for establishing greater Imperial Preference by raising tariffs on foreign goods, although at the Ottawa Conference this approach was resisted by the UK, who favoured reducing intra-Empire tariffs instead, and Canada only partially implemented general tariff increases (e.g. on iron and steel, drugs and chemicals, and textiles).

The main loser from Canadian tariff hikes and increased discrimination against non-Empire trade was the USA. American exports to Canada fell dramatically between 1929 and 1933 (from $1000 million to $210 million) and, although it is difficult to separate the policy-induced causes of this drop from the impact of depression and falling prices, the tough Canadian reaction to the Hawley–Smoot tariff was seen by contemporaries as a significant cause; for example, J. Jones (1934, 176) refers to '[the] mutilation of the billion dollar market that was Canada . . . as the most deplorable and the most costly single fruit of the Hawley–Smoot tariff'. Canadian reaction took the form of non-tariff as well as tariff barriers to imports from the USA, and arbitrary customs valuation procedures were in American eyes the most obnoxious innovation. The situation during the first half of the 1930s was in effect an 'unofficial trade war' (Kottman, 1968, 79).

As in 1911, neither side desired a full-scale trade war. The 1934 US Reciprocal Trade Agreements Act paved the way for commercial agreements with Canada in 1935 and 1938. The two agreements were of great symbolic importance in lowering trade tensions, but their precise terms were limited and the second agreement was a subsidiary outcome of trilateral US–UK–Canadian negotiations.

In both Canada and the USA, conditions were propitious for a trade agreement in 1935, as there was widespread support for promoting exports as a way out of recession. Nevertheless, both governments were wary of arousing domestic opposition from sheltered producers, and the agreement concentrated on guarantees of more co-operative trade policy implementation rather than on wide-ranging tariff reductions. Canada granted MFN treatment to US goods, guaranteed existing free entry, reduced or bound tariffs on 180 additional items, and agreed to alter customs valuation procedures. The USA granted Canada MFN status, guaranteed existing free entry; and reduced tariffs subject to quantitative limits on five important Canadian exports and without ceilings on other primary products.

For the American government, an added motive behind the 1935 agreement was to undermine the Imperial Preference system and prepare the way for a trade agreement with Britain.[9] The British response was lukewarm, and British insistence that the dominions must be compensated for any erosion of Imperial Preference arising from an Anglo-American

[9] Apart from American dislike of Imperial Preferences and Secretary of State Hull's fervent commitment to trade liberalization as the antidote to rising international tension, the US government sought a trade agreement with the UK to assuage agricultural interests whose support of the Reciprocal Trade Agreements programme was lukewarm as long as agreements were signed only with primary product exporting nations. Kottman (1968) describes the Anglo-American-Canadian negotiations.

trade agreement brought Canada into the negotiations. Within North America, opposition to trade liberalization came from the US textile and lumber industries, although the latter also wanted easier access to the British market, and from Canadian fruit-growers and lumber interests, who feared US competition in their home market or loss of preference margins in the British market. In 1938 US–UK and US–Canadian trade agreements were signed because a show of solidarity between the three nations at a time of world crisis was considered essential, but as in 1935 the actual provisions of the US–Canadian agreement were conservative. Some tariffs were reduced, and Canada abolished the 3 per cent tax which had plagued US exporters since 1932, while the USA changed some quotas on Canadian lumber exports. The net effect of the two agreements was a retreat from the bitterness of the early 1930s and an easing of the most contentious trade restrictions, but no dramatic change from the pre-1930 situation.

The Postwar Period

The 1940s saw a dramatic shift in US–Canadian trade policy relations as both countries became leading supporters of the GATT system, and as multilateral trade negotiations largely superseded bilateral (or trilateral) negotiations as the forum for North American trade policy-making. For the next four decades, this situation served both countries' interests sufficiently well that the few initiatives for North American PTAs were soon abandoned, apart from the special case of the 1965 Autopact. Only in the mid-1980s, when American adherence to GATT principles had become less certain, did a North American PTA make a serious return to policy-makers' agenda.

During the Second World War the two North American economies had been closely linked,[10] and Britain's economic decline emphasized that Canadian trade would be oriented more than ever towards the USA after the war. In 1944 Canadian exports to the USA were valued at $1335 million and imports from the US at $1447 million, while trade with the UK consisted of $1238 million in exports and $111 million in imports; without loans and credit from the Canadian government, trade with Britain would have been close to zero, and, given the state of the British economy, the same situation was likely to continue in the immediate postwar years (Bothwell *et al.*, 1981, 9). Canadian policy-makers were therefore first and foremost concerned with nurturing a liberal US postwar trade policy. Supporting American advocacy of an

[10] A joint declaration in December 1941 suspended any barriers which impeded the free flow of war supplies between the two countries, although the situation had been implicit in the April 1941 Hyde Park Declaration even before the USA entered the war (Cuff and Granatstein, 1978, 6–7).

early establishment of a liberal non-discriminatory world trading system also served Canada's own interests as one of the strong postwar economies, and multilateralism offered some prospect of countering over-reliance on US markets for Canadian exports.

The political ties between Canada and Britain remained strong during and after the war. Although Canadian policy-makers no longer placed much store on Imperial Preference,[11] they had no wish to break Commonwealth links and their special relationship gave them a better understanding of the magnitude of the European reconstruction problem than most American policy-makers had. In this situation the Canadians could use what influence they had to convince Britain that multilateralism need not be too distant and to convince America that Imperial Preferences should be treated as negotiable rather than anathema. Between 1945 and 1947, Canada played some role in achieving the GATT compromise on Imperial Preference and participated enthusiastically in the Geneva tariff reductions. The latter move was encouraged by substantial US tariff cuts, but was also helped by favourable domestic factors such as the internationalism of the political parties and the quiescence of potentially protectionist forces.

The 1947 tariff cuts were the first step in the sweeping dismantlement of North American trade barriers on an MFN basis in the next six GATT rounds, but in the winter of 1947–8 this future pattern was far from assured. Between 1945 and 1947 Canada had contributed to European economic reconstruction with a $1.25 billion loan to Britain, about $600 million in authorized credits to other countries, and an agreement to supply specified quantities of wheat to Britain for four years at less than world prices. This generosity brought on a Canadian balance of payments crisis as hard currency earnings from overseas were no longer forthcoming to settle the Canadian dollar deficit, and temporary controls on imports from the USA were introduced in November 1947. One way out of the crisis was to construct a North American regional bloc, and, after Canadian overtures, US State Department officials proposed a modified customs union which was enthusiastically received by Canadian officials and supported by Prime Minister Mackenzie King. Secret negotiations proceeded for several months but were aborted when King reversed his

[11] This was formalized in Canada's uncontested acceptance in 1942 of the multilateralism in Art. 7 of the US–UK Lend-Lease Agreement. Canada would readily abandon Imperial Preferences altogether as long as compensatory tariff reductions were made by the USA and the UK (Cuff and Granatstein, 1978, 25). Failure of the Ottawa Conference agreements to yield major benefits played a part in this policy change, but more fundamentally Britain's portion of Canadian trade was in dramatic secular decline; in 1867, at Confederation, 60% of Canada's imports came from the UK and 32% from the USA, but by 1938, despite Imperial Preference, the shares were 18% and 63%, respectively.

position in mid-March, apparently out of concern for the electoral consequences.[12] Nevertheless, US–Canadian relations remained amicable and the Canadian BOP crisis resolved itself in 1948.[13]

After 1947, North American trade liberalization was achieved by MFN tariff reductions negotiated in GATT rounds. The American average tariff fell from over 50 per cent in the early 1930s to 5 per cent in the early 1980s.[14] Canadian tariffs fell less rapidly[15] and stood slightly above US levels after the Tokyo Round, but still at historically very low rates. By the 1980s, over 95 per cent of US–Canadian trade was either duty-free or subject to tariffs of 5 per cent or less. One interesting feature of this long trade liberalization episode was the growth of intra-industry trade, so that increased Canadian exports to the USA came to a large extent from the same industries as were facing greater US competition at home (Lipsey, 1986).

The one significant exception to the liberalization of North American trade in a multilateral framework was the 1965 Autopact, a bilaterally negotiated sectoral trade agreement. During the late 1950s Canada had become concerned about the health of the automobile industry, which had come under increasing European competition and showed a large trade deficit on components. The Canadian government tried to encourage greater export orientation by measures such as import-duty remissions conditional on export performance, but such 'subsidies' ran the risk of liability to mandatory countervailing duties in the USA, and when a test case was brought up in 1964 American and Canadian policy-makers sought a negotiated solution. The January 1965 Autopact provided for elimination of US tariffs on Canadian-made cars and parts, while Canada allowed auto makers to import cars and parts duty-free from the US

[12] King himself was about to retire and did not want to have a political epitaph as the man who sold Canada's British connection, but he was also unwilling to set his Liberal Party up for a repeat of 1911 in the 1949 federal election (Cuff and Granatstein, 1978, 64–82). Even if Canada had accepted the US proposals, it is unlikely that they would have passed through Congress unscathed.

[13] Amicable relations were underlined by the American decision to allow Marshall Aid to be spent on Canadian as well as US goods. This decision helped to raise Canadian hard currency earnings, while the temporary import restrictions cut imports substantially; in 1948 Canada's US dollar reserves increased by $496 m, after a loss of $743 m in the previous year (Cuff and Granatstein, 1978, 83).

[14] The figures are the ratio of duties collected to dutiable imports (USTR, *Annual Report*, 1983, 187); this is a downward-biased measure of the average tariff and, as with an average, it ignores the dispersion of tariff rates, but it provides an indication of the dramatic magnitude of postwar tariff cuts.

[15] Canada has successfully argued for special treatment in the later GATT rounds (i.e. the right to make smaller tariff reductions than trading partners), because as a primary product exporter she could expect less benefits from other countries' tariff cuts.

subject to certain conditions about the level of output in their Canadian plant. The Autopact did not introduce sectoral free trade, because consumers could not import cars duty-free into Canada (and thus a price differential between US and Canadian markets could persist) and because producers' decisions were constrained. Thus, although it met one principal objective as the Big Three US car firms rationalized North American production, the Autopact aroused controversy over the 'fairness' of its terms, and swings in the sectoral trade balance, first in favour of Canada and then in favour of the USA, have given ammunition to critics on both sides of the border. Because it has essentially involved three large firms whose investment decisions and distribution of productive activities[16] become national political issues, the Autopact is a rather special case of a discriminatory trade policy.

Despite the countries' ever-increasing bilateral trade, US–Canadian political relations deteriorated for two decades after 1965. The original disputes were not economic, but they spilled over into economic relations when Canada was not exempted from President Nixon's 1971 import surcharge and when the Canadian External Affairs Minister proposed in 1972 the Third Option for Canadian foreign policy.[17] The Third Option involved strengthening links with other countries in order to counter over-dependence on the USA, but it failed to make much progress; the EC was not interested in any special relationship with Canada, and a Pacific preferential trading area with Japan, discriminating against US exports to the two countries, was politically impossible. More irritating to the USA were Canada's nationalist policies (especially the 1974 Foreign Investment Review Agency and the 1980 National Energy Program) which discriminated against American businesses operating in Canada. By the early 1980s trade between the USA and Canada was freer than ever before, but the potential for trade conflict was growing as protectionist sentiment revived in the USA.

Several forces converged to bring a North American preferential trading arrangement back on to the political agenda in the 1980s: US interest

[16] For example, allegations that Autopact-induced rationalization reduced the skill content of Canadian car operations fuelled more general criticisms of foreign firms' activity in Canada during the 1970s.

[17] In 1957 Prime Minister Diefenbaker, also worried about dependence on US markets, had announced a similar reorientation of Canadian trade towards Britain, but when the UK responded by offering a GATT-consistent Anglo-Canadian free trade area the Canadian government realized that new discriminatory policies against American goods were a non-starter (Bothwell *et al.*, 1981, 205). Although Imperial Preferences ended only in 1979, they were moribund from the time Britain applied for EC membership, and meanwhile Britain became a less and less important market for Canadian exporters. By 1980 Japan had replaced the UK as Canada's second largest market, and by the mid-1980s a mere 2% of Canadian exports were going to the UK.

in new bilateral trade policy avenues to supplement the GATT approach, Canadian disillusionment with the Third Option and fear of resurgent US protectionism, and on both sides a desire to end niggling economic disputes. In Canada proposals for bilateral free trade had been discussed with increasing seriousness during the late 1970s, and it was recommended by a Senate Committee in 1982 and in the Final Report of the Macdonald Commission in 1985. More importantly, closer economic ties with the USA were part of the platform of the Conservative Party which came to power in late 1984. At the March 1985 summit between President Reagan and Prime Minister Mulroney, the political decision to proceed was taken, and US congressional approval for negotiations was granted early in 1986.

The prospects for a USA–Canada free trade area were brighter in the late 1980s than at any previous time. There were few remaining tariff barriers to US–Canadian trade, although some remaining tariffs still provided substantial effective protection, and it would be easy to justify further bilateral liberalization as compatible with GATT Article XXIV. Non-tariff measures were more significant trade barriers, and they provided some scope for conflict, which could undermine an agreement; for example, Canadian provincial governments are able to prevent complete free trade even within Canada by preferential procurement or by regulation, and these barriers would not be removed by national government negotiations. A more important obstacle to a North American free trade agreement was Canada's greater social preference for welfare state and other interventionist policies, which could be construed as indirect subsidies and hence be subject to countervailing duties on exports to the USA. Finally, there are 'nationalist' opponents of any closer Canadian links with the USA. Surprisingly, Canadian producers' organizations supported the free trade proposals, perhaps because of a growing confidence in their ability to compete in American markets after the experience of increased intra-industry trade following the Kennedy and Tokyo Rounds of trade liberalization. On the American side, there was little discussion of the proposal, which corresponded to the amount of economic impact it was likely to have there (Weintraub, 1984).

Despite the ups and downs of US–Canadian trade relations, the forces determining these relations have remained fairly constant. American interest has been limited, and, especially at times when protectionism has been strong in the USA, there has been little impetus for a PTA with Canada. Support has been forthcoming only when a PTA was part of a package, when it offered a way out of deteriorating bilateral trade relations, or in the special circumstances of the North American automobile industry. Since the economic gains from a PTA would accrue mainly to Canada, the Canadian government has been more positive, but it is important to remember the distribution of gains, which would go to

Canadian consumers and to firms exporting to the USA while import-competing industries would lose from freer trade—and the latter have since the 1860s been a politically powerful group in Canada. Their influence placed a brake on Canadian trade liberalization, whether on a general or on a regional basis, at least until the 1970s. On the other hand, Canadian exporters are numerous and have some political influence, receiving widespread support for the idea that Canada must enjoy good access to key export markets even if this involves some sacrifices on other matters. During the 1980s renewed bilateralism appeared an attractive solution to Canadian economic problems and to the political balancing act, because it offered continued protection from European and Asian competition while opening up the US market for Canadian exports. Finally, political forces have been intertwined with economic considerations as both countries' governments have used economic agreements to promote political harmony or, more commonly on the Canadian side, have identified deleterious political consequences with closer economic ties.[18]

[18] Confusion in mapping economic and political results continued, from the joint North–South US support for Reciprocity in 1854 to the situation in the 1980s when Canadian supporters of bilateral free trade saw no threat to political or cultural identity (e.g. Lipsey, 1986), whereas opponents saw dire consequences.

References

Agarwal, Jamuna P., Dippl, Martin, and Langhammer, Rolf J. (1985): *EC Trade Policies towards Associated Developing Countries: Barriers to success*, Kieler Studien 193. Tübingen: JCB Mohr.

Ahmad, Jaleel (1978): Tokyo Round of Trade Negotiations and the Generalized System of Preferences. *Economic Journal*, **88**, 285–95.

Aitken, Norman D. (1973): The Effect of the EEC and EFTA on European Trade: A temporal cross-section analysis. *American Economic Review*, **63**, 881–92.

Alesina, Alberto, and Spolaore, Enrico (1995): On the Number and Size of Nations. National Bureau of Economic Research, Working Paper no. 5050, March.

Amelung, Torsten (1990): Explaining Regionalization of Trade in Asia Pacific. *Kieler Arbietspapier* no. 423, Kiel Institut für Weltwirtschaft, June.

Anderson, James E. (1979): A Theoretical Foundation for the Gravity Equation. *American Economic Review*, **69**, 106–16.

Anderson, Kym (1992): Europe 1992 and the Western Pacific Economies. *Economic Journal*, **101**, 1538–52.

—— and Blackhurst, Richard (eds.) (1993): *Regional Integration and the Global Trading System*. Hemel Hempstead, Herts: Harvester Wheatsheaf.

—— and Norheim, Hege (1993): From Imperial to Regional Trade Preferences: Its effect on Europe's intra- and extra-regional trade. *Weltwirtschaftliches Archiv*, **128**, 78–101.

—— and Snape, Richard (1994): Europe and American Regionalism: Effects on and options for Asia. *Journal of the Japanese and International Economies*, **8**, 454–77.

Ankli, Robert E. (1971): The Reciprocity Treaty of 1854. *Canadian Journal of Economics*, **4**, 1–20.

Ariff, Mohamed, and Tan, Gerald (1992): ASEAN–Pacific Trade Relations. *ASEAN Economic Bulletin*, **8**, 258–83.

Arndt, Sven W. (1968): On Discriminatory *v.* Non-Preferential Tariff Policies. *Economic Journal*, **78**, 971–9.

—— (1969): Customs Unions and the Theory of Tariffs. *American Economic Review*, **59**, 108–18.

Artis, Michael J., and Taylor, Mark P. (1988): Exchange Rates, Interest Rates, Capital Control and the European Monetary System: Assessing the track record. In Francesco Giavazzi, Stefano Micossi, and Marcus Miller (eds.), *The European Monetary System*. Cambridge University Press, 185–206.

Aw, Bee Yan, and Roberts, Mark J. (1986): Measuring Quality Change in Quota-Constrained Import Markets: The case of US footwear. *Journal of International Economics*, **21**, 45–60.

Badgett, L. D. (1978): Preferential Tariff Reductions: The Philippine response. *Journal of International Economics*, **8**, 79–92.

Bairoch, Paul (1989): European Trade Policy, 1815–1914. In Peter Mathias and Sidney Pollard (eds.), *The Cambridge Economic History of Europe*, viii, *The Industrial Economies: The development of economic and social policies*. New York: Cambridge University Press, 1–160.

Balassa, Bela (1961): *The Theory of Economic Integration*. Homewood, Ill: Richard D. Irwin.

—— (1966): Tariff Reductions and Trade in Manufactures among the Industrial Countries. *American Economic Review*, **56**, 466–72.

—— (1967): Trade Creation and Trade Diversion in the European Common Market. *Economic Journal*, **77**, 1–21.

—— (ed.) (1975): *European Economic Integration*. Amsterdam: North-Holland.

—— (1980): The Tokyo Round and the Developing Countries. *Journal of World Trade Law*, **14**, 93–118.

—— and Balassa, Carol (1984): Industrial Protection in the Developed Countries. *The World Economy*, **7**, 179–96.

Baldwin, David A. (1985): *Economic Statecraft*. Princeton University Press.

Baldwin, Richard (1989): On the Growth Effect of 1992. *Economic Policy*, **9**, 3–54.

—— (1992): Measurable Dynamic Gains from Trade. *Journal of Political Economy*, **100**, 162–74.

—— (1994): *Towards an Integrated Europe*. London: Centre for Economic Policy Research.

—— (1995): A Domino Theory of Regionalism. In Richard Baldwin, Pertti Haaparanta, and Jaakko Kiander (eds.), *Expanding Membership of the European Union*. Cambridge University Press for the Centre for Economic Policy Research, 25–48.

—— and Krugman, Paul (1988): Market Access and International Competition: A simulation study of 16K random access memories. In Rob Feenstra (ed.), *Empirical Methods for International Trade*, Cambridge, Mass.: MIT Press, 171–97.

—— and Venables, Anthony (1995): Regional Economic Integration. In Gene M. Grossman and Kenneth Rogoff (eds.), *Handbook of International Economics*, iii. Amsterdam: North-Holland, 1597–1644.

Baldwin, Robert E. (1985): *The Political Economy of US Import Policy*. Cambridge, Mass.: MIT Press.

—— (1993): Comment on Bhagwati (1993), 51–4.

—— and Murray, Tracy (1977): MFN Tariff Reductions and Developing Country Trade Benefits under the GSP. *Economic Journal*, **87**, 30–46.

Basevi, Giorgio (1970): Domestic Demand and Ability to Export. *Journal of Political Economy*, **78**, 330–7.

—— and Grassi, Silvia (1993): The Crisis of the European Monetary System and its Consequences for Agricultural Trade. *Review of Economic Conditions in Italy*, January, 81–104.

Bayard, Thomas O., and Elliott, Kimberly Ann (1994): *Reciprocity and Retaliation in US Trade Policy*. Washington DC: Institute for International Economics.

Bayoumi, Tamim, and Eichengreen, Barry (1995): Is Regionalism Simply a Diversion? Evidence from the evolution of the EC and EFTA. IMF Working Paper WP/95/109, Washington DC.

Beckett, Grace (1941): *The Reciprocal Trade Agreements Program*. New York: Columbia University Press.

Bello, Judith H., and Holmer, Alan (1990): The Heart of the 1988 Trade Act: A legislative history of the amendments to Section 301. In Jagdish Bhagwati and Hugh Patrick (eds.), *Aggressive Unilateralism: America's 301 trade policy and the world trading system*. Ann Arbor: University of Michigan Press.

Ben-David, Dan (1993): Equalizing Exchange: Trade liberalization and income convergence. *Quarterly Journal of Economics*, **108**, 653–79.

Benedek, Wolfgang (1986): The Caribbean Basin Economic Recovery Act: A new type of preference in GATT. *Journal of World Trade Law*, **20**, 29–46.

Benham, Frederic (1940): The Terms of Trade. *Economica*, **7**, 360–76.

—— (1941): *Great Britain under Protection*. New York: Macmillan.

Berglas, Eitan (1979): Preferential Trading Theory: The *n* commodity case. *Journal of Political Economy*, **87**, 315–31.

—— (1983): The Case for Unilateral Tariff Reductions: Foreign tariffs rediscovered. *American Economic Review*, **73**, 1141–2.

Bergson, Abraham (1980): The Geometry of COMECON Trade. *European Economic Review*, **14**, 291–306.

Bergsten, C. Fred (1996): Globalizing Free Trade. *Foreign Affairs*, **75**, 105–20.

Bergstrand, Jeffrey H. (1985): The Gravity Equation in International Trade: Some microeconomic foundations and empirical evidence. *Review of Economics and Statistics*, **67**, 474–81.

—— (1989): The Generalized Gravity Equation: Monopolistic competition and the factor-proportions theory in international trade. *Review of Economics and Statistics*, **71**, 143–53.

Bhagwati, Jagdish N. (1971): Trade-Diverting Customs Unions and Welfare Improvement: A clarification. *Economic Journal*, **81**, 580–7.

—— (1973): Reply to Professor Kirman. *Economic Journal*, **83**, 895–7.

—— (1988): Export Promoting Protection: Endogenous monopoly and price disparity. *Pakistan Development Review*, **27**(1), 1–5; reprinted in

Jagdish Bhagwati, *Political Economy and International Economics* (ed. Douglas Irwin), Cambridge, Mass.: MIT Press, 1992, 110–5.

—— (1990): Aggressive Unilateralism: An overview. In Jagdish Bhagwati and Hugh Patrick (eds.), *Aggressive Unilateralism: America's 301 Trade Policy and the World Trading System*. Ann Arbor: University of Michigan Press.

—— (1991): *The World Trading System at Risk*. London: Harvester Wheatsheaf.

—— (1993): Regionalism and Multilateralism: An overview. In Jaime de Melo and Arvind Panagariya (eds.), *New Dimensions in Regional Integration*. Cambridge University Press, 22–51.

—— (1995): Trade Liberalisation and 'Fair Trade' Demands: Addressing the environmental and labour standards issues. *The World Economy*, **18**, 745–59.

—— and Hudec, Robert E. (eds.) (1996): *Fair Trade and Harmonization: Prerequisites for Free Trade?* (2 vols.) Cambridge, Mass.: MIT Press.

—— and Panagariya, Arvind (1996): Preferential Trading Areas and Multilateralism: Strangers, friends or foes? In Jagdish Bhagwati and Arvind Panagariya (eds.), *Free Trade Areas or Free Trade? The Economics of Preferential Trading Arrangements*. Washington DC: AEI Press.

Blackhurst, Richard (1971): Tariff Preferences for LDC Exports: A note on the welfare component of additional earnings. *Rivista Internazionale di Scienze Economiche e Commerciali*, **18**, 1180–8.

—— (1972): General versus Preferential Tariff Reduction for LDC Exports: An analysis of the welfare effects. *Southern Economic Journal*, **38**, 350–62.

Bofinger, Peter (1995): The Political Economy of the Eastern Enlargement of the EU. Centre for Economic Policy Research Discussion Paper no. 1234 (London), August.

Borrell, B., and M-C. Yang (1990): EC Bananarama 1992. World Bank Working Paper WPS 523, Washington DC.

—— —— (1992): EC Bananarama 1992: The sequel. World Bank Working Paper WPS 958, Washington DC.

Bothwell, Robert, Drummond, Ian, and English, John (1981): *Canada since 1945*. University of Toronto Press.

Brada, Josef C. (1985): Soviet Subsidization of Eastern Europe: The primacy of economics over politics? *Journal of Comparative Economics*, **9**, 80–92.

—— (1993): Regional Integration in Eastern Europe: Prospects for integration within the region and with the European Community. In Jaime de Melo and Arvind Panagariya (eds.), *New Dimensions in Regional Integration*. Cambridge University Press, 319–47.

—— and Mendez, J. A. (1985): Economic Integration among Developed, Developing and Centrally Planned Economies: A comparative analysis. *Review of Economics and Statistics*, **67**, 549–56.

Breton, Albert (1995): A Comment. In Michael J. Trebilcock and Daniel Schwanen (eds.), *Getting There: An assessment of the agreement on internal trade.* Toronto: C. D. Howe Institute, 90–4.

Brittan, Leon (1995): How to make Trade Liberalisation Popular. *The World Economy*, **18**, 761–7.

Brown, Drusilla (1987): General Equilibrium Effects of the US Generalized System of Preferences. *Southern Economic Journal*, **54**, 27–47.

—— (1992): The Impact of a North American Free Trade Area: Applied general equilibrium models. In Nora Lustig, Barry P. Bosworth, and Robert Z. Lawrence (eds.), *North American Free Trade: Assessing the impact*. Washington DC: Brookings Institution, 26–68.

—— and Stern, Robert (1987): A Modeling Perspective. In Robert Stern, P. H. Trezise, and John Whalley (eds.), *Perspectives on a US–Canadian Free Trade Agreement*. Washington DC: Brookings Institution, 155–90.

—— —— (1989a): USA–Canada Bilateral Tariff Elimination: The role of product differentiation and market structure. In Robert C. Feenstra (ed.), *Trade Policies for International Competitiveness*. University of Chicago Press, 217–53.

—— —— (1989b): Computable General Equilibrium Estimates of the Gains from US–Canadian Trade Liberalisation. In David Greenaway, Thomas Hyclak, and Robert Thornton (eds.), *Economic Aspects of Regional Trading Arrangements*. Hemel Hempstead, Herts: Harvester Wheatsheaf, 69–108.

Brunner, Karl (ed.) (1981): *The Great Depression Revisited*. Boston: Martinus Nijhoff.

Buchanan, James, and Tullock, Gordon (1962): *The Calculus of Consent*. Ann Arbor: University of Michigan Press.

Caballero, Ricardo J., and Lyons, Richard K. (1990): Internal versus External Economies in European Industry. *European Economic Review*, **34**, 805–26.

—— —— (1991): External Effects and Europe's Integration. In L. Alan Winters and Anthony J. Venables (eds.), *European Integration: Trade and Industry*. Cambridge University Press, 34–50.

Camps, Miriam (1964): *Britain and the European Community 1955–1963*. Princeton University Press.

Canadian Department of Finance (1988): *The Canada–USA Free Trade Agreement: An Economic Assessment*. Ottawa: CDF.

Capie, Forrest (1983): *Depression and Protectionism: Britain between the Wars*. London: George Allen and Unwin.

Carnoy, Martin (1970): A Welfare Analysis of Latin American Economic Union: Six industry studies. *Journal of Political Economy*, **78**, 626–54.

—— (1972): *Industrialization in a Latin American Common Market*. Washington: Brookings Institution.

Casella, Alessandra (1995): Large Countries, Small Countries and the Enlargement of Trade Blocs. National Bureau of Economic Research, Working Paper 5365, Cambridge, Mass.

Caves, Richard E. (1974): The Economics of Reciprocity: Theory and evidence on bilateral trading arrangements. In Willy Sellekaerts (ed.), *International Trade and Finance, Essays in Honour of Jan Tinbergen*. London: Macmillan, 17–54.

—— (1985): Review of Owen (1983). *Journal of International Economics*, **19**, 385–7.

—— and Johnson, Harry G. (eds.) (1968): *Readings in International Economics*. Homewood, Ill.: Richard D. Irwin.

Cecchini, Paolo, Catinat, Michel, and Jacquemin, Alexis (1988): *The European Challenge 1992: The Benefits of a Single Market*, Aldershot, Hants: Wildwood House.

Chaloupka, Frank, and Adit Laixuthai (1996): US Trade Policy and Cigarette Smoking in Asia. National Bureau of Economic Research, Working Paper 5543, Cambridge, Mass.

Cheh, John H. (1974): United States Concessions in the Kennedy Round and Short-Run Labor Adjustment Costs. *Journal of International Economics*, **4**, 323–40.

Chen, Pochih (1994): Competitiveness of Taiwan Exports in the United States. In Shu-Chin Yang (ed.), *Manufactured Exports of East Asian Industrializing Countries*. Armonk, NY: M. E. Sharpe, 135–48.

Child, Frank (1958): *The Theory and Practice of Exchange Control in Germany: A Study of Monopolistic Exploitation in International Markets*. The Hague: Martinus Nijhoff.

Clague, Christopher (1971): Tariff Preferences and Separable Utility. *American Economic Review* (Papers and Proceedings), **61**, 188–94.

—— (1972): The Trade Effects of Tariff Preferences. *Southern Economic Journal*, **38**, 379–89.

Clark, Don P. (1985): Protection and Developing Country Exports: The case of vegetable oils. *Journal of Economic Studies*, **12**, 3–18.

—— and Zarrilli, Simonetta (1994): Non-Tariff Measures and United States' Imports of CBERA-Eligible Products. *Journal of Development Studies*, **31**, 214–24.

Cline, William R. (1982): *'Reciprocity': A new approach to world trade policy?* Washington DC: Institute for International Economics.

—— and Delgado, Enrique (eds.) (1978): *Economic Integration in Central America*. Washington DC: Brookings Institution.

Cohen Otrantes, I. (1972): *Regional Integration in Central America*. Lexington, Mass.: Lexington Books.

Collier, Paul (1979): The Welfare Effects of Customs Unions: An anatomy. *Economic Journal*, **89**, 84–95.

Commission of the European Communities (1988): The Economics of 1992. *The European Economy*, **35** (summarizing the 16-volume *Research on the Cost of Non-Europe: Basic Findings*). Brussels: European Commission.

Condliffe, John B. (1950): *The Commerce of Nations*. New York: W. W. Norton.

Connolly, Michael, Devereux, John, and Cortes, Mariluz (1995): The Transhipment Problem: Smuggling and welfare in Paraguay, *World Development*, **23**, 975–85.

Cooper, Charles A., and Massell, Benton F. (1965): A New Look at Customs Unions Theory. *Economic Journal*, **75**, 742–7.

Cooper, Richard N. (1976): Worldwide versus Regional Integration: Is there an optimum size of the integration area? In Fritz Machlup (ed.), *Economic Integration: Worldwide, Regional, Sectoral*. London: Macmillan, for the International Economic Association, 40–53; reprinted in Garnaut and Drysdale (1994, 11–19).

Corden, W. Max (1957): The Calculation of the Cost of Protection. *Economic Record*, **33**, 29–51.

—— (1965): *Recent Developments in the Theory of International Trade*. Special Papers in International Economics, no. 7. Princeton University, International Finance Section.

—— (1972): Economies of Scale and Customs Union Theory. *Journal of Political Economy*, **80**, 465–75.

—— (1976): Customs Union Theory and the Non-uniformity of Tariffs. *Journal of International Economics*, **6**, 98–108.

Cox, David, and Harris, Richard (1985): Trade Liberalization and Industrial Organization: Some estimates for Canada. *Journal of Political Economy*, **93**, 115–45.

Croome, John (1995): *Reshaping the World Trading System: A history of the Uruguay Round*. Geneva: World Trade Organization.

Cuff, Robert D., and Granatstein, J. L. (1978): *American Dollars—Canadian Prosperity: Canadian–American Economic Relations 1945–1950*. Toronto: Samuel Stevens.

Curzon, Gerard (1965): *Multilateral Commercial Diplomacy*. London: Michael Joseph.

Dam, Kenneth W. (1963): Regional Economic Arrangements and the GATT: The legacy of a misconception. *University of Chicago Law Review*, **30**, 615–65.

—— (1970): *The GATT: Law and International Economic Organization*. University of Chicago Press.

Davenport, Michael (1986): *Trade Policy, Protectionism and the Third Word*. London: Croom Helm.

de Janvry, Alain, Sadoulet, Elizabeth, and Gordillo de Anda, Gustavo (1995): NAFTA and Mexico's Maize Producers. *World Development*, **23**, 1349–62.

de la Torre, Augusto, and Kelly, Margaret (1992): *Regional Trade Arrangements*. IMF Occasional Paper no. 93. Washington DC.

Delle-Donne, Ottavio (1929): *European Tariff Policies*. New York: Adelphi.

de Melo, Jaime, and Panagariya, Arvind (eds.) (1993): *New Dimensions in Regional Integration*. Cambridge University Press.

—— —— and Rodrik, Dani (1993): The New Regionalism: A country perspective. In Jaime de Melo and Arvind Panagariya (eds.), *New Dimensions in Regional Integration*. Cambridge University Press, 159–93.

Desai, Padma (1986): Is the Soviet Union Subsidizing Eastern Europe? *European Economic Review*, **30**, 107–16.

Dhar, Sumana, and Panagariya, Arvind (1994): Is East Asia less open than North America and the European Economic Community? No. World Bank Policy Research Working Paper no. 1370, Wahington DC.

Diebold, William (1959): *The Schuman Plan: A study in economic co-operation, 1950–1959*. New York: Praeger.

Donges, Juergen B., *et al.* (1982): *The Second Enlargement of the European Community: Adjustment Requirements and Challenges for Policy Reform*, Kieler Studien 171. Tübingen: JCB Mohr.

Dornbusch, Rudiger (1990): Policy Options for Freer Trade: The case for bilateralism. In Robert Z. Lawrence and Charles L. Schultz (eds.), *An American Trade Strategy: Options for the 1990s*. Washington DC: Brookings Institution, 106–34.

—— (1992): Monetary Problems of Post-Communism: Lessons from the end of the Austro-Hungarian Empire. *Weltwirtschaftliches Archiv*, **128**, 391–424.

Drabek, Zdenek (1985): Foreign Trade Performance and Policy. In M. C. Kaser and E. A. Radice (eds.), *The Economic History of Eastern Europe 1919–1975*; i, *Economic Structure and Performance between the Two Wars*. Oxford: Clarendon Press, 379–531.

Drysdale, Peter, and Garnaut, Ross (1982): Trade Intensities and the Analysis of Bilateral Trade Flows in a Many-Country World: A survey. *Hitotsubashi Journal of Economics*, **22**, 62–84; reprinted in Garnaut and Drysdale (1994, 20–35).

—— —— (1993): The Pacific: An application of a general theory of economic intergation. In C. Fred Bergsten and Marcus Noland (eds.), *Pacific Dynamism and the International Economic System*. Washington DC: Institute for International Economics, 183–223.

Dumke, Rolf H. (1976): *The Political Economy of German Economic Unification: Tariffs, trade and politics of the Zollverein Era*. Ph.D. thesis, University of Wisconsin–Madison.

Eastman, Harry C., and Stykolt, Stefan (1967): *The Tariff and Competition in Canada*. Toronto: Macmillan.

Edwards, Sebastian, and Savastano, Miguel (1989): Latin American Intra-regional Trade: Evolution and future prospects. In David Greenaway,

Thomas Hyclak, and Robert Thornton (eds.), *Economic Aspects of Regional Trading Arrangements*. New York University Press, 189–233.

EFTA (1980): *EFTA: Past and future*. Geneva: EFTA.

Eichengreen, Barry J. (1981): *Sterling and the Tariff 1929–32*. Princeton Studies in International Finance, no. 48. Princeton University International Finance Section.

—— (1993): European Monetary Unification. *Journal of Economic Literature*, **31**, 1321–57.

—— and Irwin, Douglas (1995): Trade Blocs, Currency Blocs, and the Reorientation of World Trade in the 1930s. *Journal of International Economics*, **38**, 1–24.

Einzig, Paul (1941): Why Defend Nazi Trade Methods? *Banker*, **58**, 108–13.

El-Agraa, Ali M. (ed.) (1982; 3rd edn. 1996): *International Economic Integration*. London: Macmillan, and New York: St Martin's Press.

Ellis, Howard S. (1941): *Exchange Controls in Central Europe*. Cambridge, Mass.: Harvard University Press.

Ellis, L. Ethan (1939): *Reciprocity 1911: A study in Canadian–American Relations*. New Haven: Yale University Press; reprinted by Greenwood Press, New York, 1968.

Erzan, Refik, and Yeats, Alexander (1992): Free Trade Agreements with the United States: What's in it for Latin America? World Bank PRE Working Papers no. 827. Washington DC.

Ethier, Wilfred, and Horn, Henrik (1984): A New Look at Economic Integration. In Henryk Kierzkowski (ed.), *Monopolistic Competition and International Trade*. Oxford: Clarendon Press, 207–29.

Faini, Riccardo, and Richard Portes (1995): *European Union Trade with Eastern Europe: Adjustment and opportunities*. London: Centre for Economic Policy Research.

Federal Reserve Bank of Kansas City (1991): *Symposium on the Policy Implications of Trade and Currency Zones*.

Feinberg, Richard E., and Newfarmer, Richard (1984): The Caribbean Basin Initiative: Bold plan or empty promise? In Richard Newfarmer (ed.), *From Gunboats to Diplomacy: New US policies for Latin America*. Baltimore: Johns Hopkins University Press, 210–27.

Fieleke, Norman (1992): One Trading World or Many: The issue of regional trading blocs, *New England Economic Review*, May/June, 3–20.

Finger, J. Michael, and Winters, L. Alan (forthcoming): What Can the WTO Do for Developing Countries? In Anne Krueger (ed.), *Institutional Aspects of the WTO's Effectiveness*.

—— Hall, H. K., and Nelson, D. R. (1982): The Political Economy of Administered Protection, *American Economic Review*, **72**, 452–66.

Fishlow, Albert, and Haggard, Stephan (1992): *The United States and the Regionalisation of the World Economy*. Paris: OECD Development Centre.

Flam, Harry (1995): From EEA to EU: Economic consequences for the EFTA countries. *European Economic Review*, **39**, 457–66.

Fleming, Marcus (1951): On Making the Best of Balance of Payments Restrictions on Imports. *Economic Journal*, **61**, 48–71.

Foroutan, Faezeh (1993): Regional Integration in Sub-Saharan Africa: Past experience and future prospects. In Jaime de Melo and Arvind Panagariya (eds.), *New Dimensions in Regional Integration*. Cambridge University Press, 234–71.

Francois Joseph F., and Shiells, Clinton R. (eds.) (1994) *Modeling Trade Policy: Applied General Equilibrium Assessments in North American Free Trade*. Cambridge University Press.

Frank, Isaiah (1961): *The European Common Market*. London: Stevens and Sons.

Frankel, Jeffrey (1993): Is Japan creating a Yen Bloc in Asia and the Pacific? In Jeffrey Frankel and Miles Kahler (eds.), *Regionalism and Rivalry: Japan and the United States in Pacific Asia*. University of Chicago Press, 53–85; reprinted in Garnaut and Drysdale (1994, 11–19).

Frisch, Ragnar (1947): On the Need for Forecasting a Multilateral Balance of Payments. *American Economic Review*, **37**, 535–51.

—— (1948): Outline of a System of Multicompensatory Trade. *Review of Economics and Statistics*, **30**, 265–71.

Frost, Ellen (1997): A Transatlantic Free Trade Agenda? Prospects for transatlantic co-operation in shaping the future multilateral trade order. In Jens van Scharping (ed.), *Toward Rival Regionalism: US and EU regional economic integration policies and the risk of a transatlantic regulatory rift*. Munich: Nomos Verlag.

Gaines, David B., Sawyer, William C., and Sprinkle, Richard (1981): EEC Mediterranean Policy and US Trade in Citrus. *Journal of World Trade Law*, **15**, 431–9.

Gardner, Richard N. (1956): *Sterling–Dollar Diplomacy*. Oxford University Press; new expanded edn., McGraw-Hill, New York, 1969.

Garnaut, Ross, and Drysdale, Peter (eds.) (1994): *Asia Pacific Regionalism: Readings in international economic relations*. Pymble, NSW: HarperCollins.

Gasiorek, Michael, Smith, Alisdair, and Venables, Anthony J. (1991): Completing the Internal Market in the EC: Factor demands and comparative advantage. In L. Alan Winters and Anthony J. Venables (eds.), *European Integration: Trade and industry*. Cambridge University Press, 9–30.

—— —— —— (1992): '1992': Trade and Welfare—A general equilibrium model. In L. Alan Winters (ed.), *Trade Flows and Trade Policy after '1992'*. Cambridge University Press, 35–63.

GATT (1958): *Trends in International Trade: A report by a panel of experts* [Campos, Haberler, Meade, and Tinbergen]. Geneva: GATT.

Gehrels, Franz (1956–7): Customs Unions from a Single Country's Viewpoint. *Review of Economic Studies*, **24**, 61–4.

Gerig, Benjamin (1930): *The Open Door and the Mandates System: A study of economic equality before and since the establishment of the Mandates System*. London: George Allen and Unwin.

Geroski, Paul (1989): The Choice between Diversity and Scale. In E. Davis *et al., 1992: Myths and realities*. London: Centre for Business Strategy, 29–45.

Glickman, David L. (1947): The British Imperial Preference System. *Quarterly Journal of Economics*, **61**, 439–70.

Goldstein, Judith (1993): *Ideas, Interests and American Trade Policy*. Ithaca, NY: Cornell University Press.

Gordon, Margaret S. (1941): *Barriers to World Trade: A Study of Recent Commercial Policy*. New York: Macmillan.

Grant, Heather A., and Winham, Gilbert R. (1995): Anti-Dumping and Countervailing Duties in a Western Hemisphere Free Trade Agreement. In Inter-American Development Bank and Economic Commission for Latin America and the Caribbean, *Trade Liberalization in the Western Hemisphere*. Washington DC, 283–301.

Greenaway, David (1984): A Statistical Analysis of Fiscal Dependence on Trade Taxes and Economic Development. *Public Finance*, **39**, 70–89.

—— and Milner, Chris (1986): *The Economics of Intra-Industry Trade*. Oxford: Basil Blackwell.

Grilli, Enzo R. (1993): *The European Community and the Developing Countries*. Cambridge University Press.

Grinols, Earl L. (1981): An Extension of the Kemp–Wan Theorum on the Formation of Customs Unions. *Journal of International Economies*, **11**, 259–66.

—— (1984): A Thorn in the Lion's Paw: Has Britain paid too much for Common Market membership? *Journal of International Economies*, **16**, 271–93.

Grossman, Gene, and Helpman, Elhanan (1995): The Politics of Free-Trade Agreements. *American Economic Review*, **85**, 667–90.

—— and Krueger, Alan (1993): Environmental Impacts of a North American Free Trade Area. In Peter M. Garber (ed.), *The Mexico–USA Free Trade Agreement*. Cambridge, Mass.: MIT Press, 13–56.

Grunwald, Joseph, Wionczek, Miguel S., and Carnoy, Martin (1972): *Latin-American Economic Integration and US Policy*. Washington DC: Brookings Institution.

Haaland, Jan (1990): Assessing the Effects of EC Integration on EFTA Countries: The position of Norway and Sweden. *Journal of Common Market Studies*, **28**, 379–400.

Haaland, Jan and Norman, Victor (1992): Global Production Effects of European Integration. In L. Alan Winters (ed.), *Trade Flows and Trade Policy after '1992'*. Cambridge University Press, 67–88.

Haberler, Gottfried von (1936): *The Theory of International Trade*. London: William Hodge (trans. from the 1933 German edn.).

—— (1943): *Quantitative Trade Controls: Their causes and nature*. Geneva: League of Nations.

Haight, Frank A. (1941): *A History of French Commercial Policies*. New York: Macmillan.

Hamilton, Bob, and Whalley, John (1985): Geographically Discriminatory Trade Arrangements. *Review of Economics and Statistics*, **67**, 446–55.

Hamilton, Carl (1985): Voluntary Export Restraints and Trade Diversion. *Journal of Common Market Studies*, **23**, 345–55.

—— (1986): An Assessment of Voluntary Restraints on Hong Kong Exports to Europe and the USA. *Economica*, **53**, 339–50.

—— and Winters, Alan (1992): Opening up International Trade with Eastern Europe, *Economic Policy*, **14**, 77–116.

Hanson, Gordon H. (1996): USA–Mexico Integration and Regional Economies: Evidence from Border-City Pairs. National Bureau of Economic Reaearch Working Paper 5425, Cambridge, Mass.

Harris, Richard G. (1984a): *Trade, Industrial Policy and Canadian Manufacturing*. Toronto: Ontario Economic Council.

—— (1984b): Applied General Equilibrium Analysis of Small Open Economies with Scale Economies and Imperfect Competition. *American Economic Review*, **74**, 1016–32.

—— (1985): Why Voluntary Export Restraints are 'Voluntary'. *Canadian Journal of Economics*, **18**, 799–809.

Havrylyshyn, Ole, and Pritchett, L. (1991): European Trade Patterns after the Transition. World Bank Working Paper WPS 748, Washington DC.

Hay, Keith A. J., and Sulzenco, B. Andrei (1982): US Trade and 'Reciprocity'. *Journal of World Trade Law*, **16**, 471–9.

Hazlewood, Arthur (1979): The End of the East African Community: What are the lessons for regional integration schemes? *Journal of Common Market Studies*, **18**, 40–58.

Helleiner, Gerald K. (1977): The Political Economy of Canada's Tariff Structure: An alternative model. *Canadian Journal of Economics*, **10**, 310–26.

Helliwell, John (1996): Do National Borders Matter for Quebec's Trade? *Canadian Journal of Economics*, **29**, 507–22.

Hellvin, Lisbeth (1994): *Trade and Specialization in Asia*, Lund Economic Studies no. 56.

Herin, Jan (1986): *Rules of Origin and Differences between Tariff Levels in EFTA and in the EC*. European Free Trade Association Occasional Paper no. 13. Geneva: EFTA.

Heuser, Heinrich (1939): *Control of International Trade*. London: George Routledge & Sons.

Hieronymi, Otto (1973): *Economic Discrimination against the United States in Western Europe (1945–1958): Dollar shortage and the rise of regionalism*. Geneva: Librairie Droz.

Hindley, Brian (1986): EC Imports of VCRs from Japan: A costly precedent. *Journal of World Trade Law*, **20**, 168–84.

Hine, Robert C. (1985): *The Political Economy of European Trade: An introduction to the trade policies of the EEC*. Brighton: Wheatsheaf.

Hirschman, Albert O. (1945): *National Power and the Structure of Foreign Trade*. Berkeley, Calif.: University of California Press.

Hoekman, Bernard, and Djankov, Simeon (1996a): Catching Up with Eastern Europe? The European Union's Mediterranean Free Trade Initiative. World Bank Policy Research Working Paper 1562, Washington DC.

—— —— (1996b): The European Union's Mediterranean Free Trade Initiative, *The World Economy*, **19**, 387–406.

—— and Kostecki, Michel (1995): *The Political Economy of the World Trading System: From GATT to WTO*. Oxford University Press.

—— and Mavroidis, Peter (1994): Competition, Competition Policy and the GATT. *The World Economy*, **17**, 121–50.

Holzman, Franklyn D. (1962): Soviet Foreign Trade Pricing and the Question of Discrimination. *Review of Economics and Statistics*, **44**, 134–47.

—— (1976): *International Trade under Communism: Politics and economics*. New York: Basic Books.

—— (1985): Comecon: A 'Trade-Destroying' Customs Union? *Journal of Comparative Economics*, **9**, 410–23.

Hufbauer, Gary C. (1990): *Europe 1992: An American perspective*. Washington DC: Brookings Institution.

—— and Schott, Jeffrey J., assisted by Kimberley A. Elliot (1985): *Economic Sanctions Reconsidered: History and current policy*. Washington DC: Institute for International Economics.

—— —— assisted by Robin Dunnigan and Diana Clark (1993): *NAFTA: An assessment*. Washington DC: Institute for International Economics.

—— —— assisted by Diana Clark (1994): *Western Hemisphere Economic Integration*. Washington DC: Institute of International Economics.

Humphrey, D. C., and Ferguson, C. E. (1960): The Domestic and World Benefits of a Customs Union. *Economia Internazionale*, **13**, 197–213.

Imada, Pearl (1993): Production and Trade Effects of the ASEAN Free Trade Area. *The Developing Economies*, **31**, 3–23.

Ingram, James (1973): The Case for European Monetary Integration. *Princeton Essays in International Finance*, no. 98, Princeton University, International Finance Section.

Irwin, Douglas A. (1993): Multilateral and Bilateral Trade Policies in the World Trading System: An historical perspective. In Jaime de Melo and Arvind Panagariya (eds.), *New Dimensions in Regional Integration*. Cambridge University Press, 90–119.

—— (1996): *Against the Tide: An Intellectual History of Free Trade*. Princeton University Press.

Isaacs, Asher (1948): *International Trade: Tariff and Commercial Policies*. Chicago: Richard D. Irwin.

Jackson, John (1969): *World Trade and the Law of GATT*. Indianapolis: Bobbs Merrill Company.

—— (1995): The World Trade Organization: Watershed innovation or small step forward? *The World Economy*, **18**, 11–31.

Jacquemin, Alexis, and Sapir, André (1991): Competition and Imports in the European Market. In Alan Winters and Anthony Venables (eds.), *European Integration: Trade and Industry*. Cambridge University Press, 82–95.

Janssen, L. H. (1961): *Free Trade, Protection and Customs Union*. Leiden: H. E. Stenfert Kroese N.V.

Johnson, Harry G. (1957): Discriminatory Tariff Reduction: A Marshallian analysis. *Indian Journal of Economics*, **5**, 39–47.

—— (1958a): Marshallian Analysis of Discriminatory Tariff Reductions: An extension. *Indian Journal of Economics*, **6**, 177–82; reprinted in Johnson (1962).

—— (1958b): The Gains from Freer Trade with Europe: An estimate. *Manchester School of Economic and Social Studies*, **26**, 247–55.

—— (1960a): The Economic Theory of Customs Union. *Pakistan Economic Journal*, **10**, 14–30; reprinted in Johnson (1962).

—— (1960b): The Cost of Protection and the Scientific Tariff. *Journal of Political Economy*, **68**, 327–45.

—— (1962): *Money, Trade and Economic Growth*. London: George Allen and Unwin.

—— (1964): The International Competitive Position of the United States and the Balance of Payments Prospects for 1968. *Review of Economics and Statistics*, **46**, 14–32.

—— (1965): An Economic Theory of Protectionism, Tariff Bargaining and the Formation of Customs Unions. *Journal of Political Economy*, **73**, 256–83.

—— (1970): The Efficiency and Welfare Implications of the International Corporation. In Ian A. McDougall and Richard H. Snape (eds.), *Studies in International Economics*. Amsterdam: North-Holland, 83–103.

—— (1974): Trade Diverting Customs Unions: A comment. *Economic Journal*, **84**, 618–21.

Johnston, Richard, and Percy, Michael B. (1980): Reciprocity, Imperial Sentiment, and Party Politics in the 1911 Election. *Canadian Journal of Political Science*, **13**, 709–29.

Jones, Joseph M., (1934): *Tariff Retaliation: Repercussions of the Hawley–Smoot Bill*. Philadelphia: University of Pennsylvania Press.

Jones, Kent (1984): The Political Economy of Voluntary Export Restraint Agreements. *Kyklos*, **37**, 82–101.

—— (1985): Trade in Steel: Another turn in the protectionist spiral. *The World Economy*, **8**, 393–408.

—— (1986): *Politics vs. Economics in World Steel Trade*. London: Allen and Unwin.

—— (1994): *Export Restraint and the New Protectionism: The political economy of discriminatory trade restrictions*. Ann Arbor: University of Michigan Press.

Ju, Jiandong, and Krishna, Kala (1996): Market Access and Welfare Effects of Free Trade Areas without Rules of Origin. National Bureau of Economic Reaearch Working Paper 5480, Cambridge, Mass.

Kaiser, David E. (1980): *Economic Diplomacy and the Origins of the Second World War: Germany, Britain, France and Eastern Europe 1930–1939*. Princeton University Press.

Karsenty, Guy, and Laird, Sam (1987): The Generalized System of Preferences: A quantitative assessment of the direct trade effects and policy options. *Weltwirtschaftliches Archiv*, **123**, 262–96.

Keesing, Donald B., and Wolf, Martin (1980): *Textile Quotas against Developing Countries*, Thames Essay no. 23. London: Trade Policy Research Centre.

Kehoe, Patrick, and Kehoe, Timothy (1995): *Modeling North American Economic Integration*. Dordrecht: Kluwer.

Kellman, Mitchell, and Schroder, Tim (1983): The Export Similarity Index: Some structural tests. *Economic Journal*, **93**, 193–8.

Kemp, Murray C. (1969): *A Contribution to the General Equilibrium Theory of Preferential Trading*. Amsterdam: North-Holland.

—— and Wan, Henry Y. (1976): An Elementary Proposition Concerning the Formation of Customs Unions. *Journal of International Economics*, **6**, 95–7.

Keohane, Robert O. (1984): *After Hegemony*. Princeton University Press.

Keuschnigg, Christian, and Kohler, Wilhelm (1996): Austria in the European Union: Dynamic gains from integration and distributional implications. *Economic Policy*, **22**, 137–211.

Kihl, Young Whan, and Lutz, James M. (1985): *World Trade Issues: Regime, Structure and Policy*. New York: Praeger.

Kindelberger, Charles P. (1951): Group Behaviour and International Trade. *Journal of Political Economy*, **59**, 30–47.

Kindelberger, Charles P. (1975): The Rise of Free Trade in Western Europe 1820–1875. *Journal of Economic History*, **35**, 20–55.

—— (1986): *The World in Depression 1929–1939*, rev. edn. Berkeley, Calif.: University of California Press (first published 1973).

Kirman, Alan P. (1973): Trade Diverting Customs Unions and Welfare Improvement: A comment. *Economic Journal*, **83**, 890–4.

Kleiman, Ephraim (1976): Trade and the Decline of Colonialism. *Economic Journal*, **86**, 459–80.

Klepper, Gernot (1992): Pharmaceuticals: Who's afraid of '1992'? In L. Alan Winters (ed.), *Trade Flows and Trade Policy after '1992'*. Cambridge University Press, 150–69.

Kostecki, Michel (1987): Export Restraint Arrangements and Trade Liberalization, *The World Economy*, **10**, 425–53.

Kottman, Richard N. (1968): *Reciprocity and the North Atlantic Triangle, 1932–1938*. Ithaca, NY: Cornell University Press.

Krause, Lawrence B. (1963): The European Economic Community and the US Balance of Payments. In Walter S. Salant (ed.), *The United States Balance of Payments in 1968*. Washington DC: Brookings Institution, 95–118.

—— (1968): *European Economic Integration and the United States*. Washington DC: Brookings Institution.

Krauss, Melvyn B. (1972): Recent Developments in Customs Union Theory: An interpretative survey. *Journal of Economic Literature*, **10**, 413–36.

Kreinin, Mordechai E. (1964): On the Dynamic Effects of a Customs Union. *Journal of Political Economy*, **72**, 193–5.

—— (1972): Effects of the EEC on Imports of Manufactures. *Economic Journal*, **82**, 897–920.

—— (1973): Some Economic Consequences of Reverse Preferences. *Journal of Common Market Studies*, **11**, 161–72.

—— (1974): *Trade Relations of the EEC: An Empirical Investigation*. New York: Praeger.

—— and Plummer, Michael (1992): Effects of Economic Integration in Industrial Countries on ASEAN and Asian NIEs. *World Development*, **20**, 345–66.

—— —— (1994): 'Natural' Economic Blocs: An alternative formulation. *International Trade Journal*, **8**, 193–205.

Krishna, Kala, and Krueger, Anne O. (1995): Implementing Free Trade Areas: Rules of origin and hidden protection. In Alan Deardorff, James Levinsohn and Robert Stern (eds.), *New Directions in Trade Theory*. Ann Arbor: University of Michigan Press, 149–87.

Krueger, Anne O. (1990): The Political Economy of Controls: American sugar. In Maurice Scott and Deepak Lal (eds.), *Public Policy and*

Economic Development: Essays in honour of Ian Little. Oxford: Clarendon Press, 170–216.

—— (1993): Free Trade Agreements as Protectionist Devices: Rules of origin. National Bureau of Economic Research Working Paper 4342, Cambridge, Rules of Origin as Protectionist Devices. In James Melvin, James Moore, and Ray Riezman (eds.), *International Trade Policy*, forthcoming.

—— (1995): Free Trade Agreements versus Customs Unions. National Bureau of Economic Research Working Paper 5084, Cambridge, Mass.

—— and Roderick Duncan (1993): The Political Economy of Controls: Complexity. National Bureau of Economic Research Working Paper 4351, Cambridge, Mass.

Krugman, Paul (1984): Import Protection as Export Promotion: International competition in the presence of oligopoly and economies of scale. In Henryk Kierzkowski (ed.), *Monopolistic Competition and International Trade*. New York: Oxford University Press, 180–93.

—— (1991a): *Geography and Trade*. Cambridge, Mass.: MIT Press.

—— (1991b): Is Bilateralism Bad? In Elhanan Helpman and Assaf Razin (eds.), *International Trade and Trade Policy*. Cambridge, Mass.: MIT Press, 9–23.

—— (1991c): The Move towards Free Trade Zones. In Federal Reserve Bank of Kansas City, *Symposium on the Policy Implications of Trade and Currency Zones*, 7–42.

—— (1993): Regionalism versus Multilateralism: Analytical notes. In Jaime de Melo and Arvind Panagariya (eds.), *New Dimensions in Regional Integration*. Cambridge University Press, 58–79.

—— (1995a): Increasing Returns, Imperfect Competition, and the Positive Theory of International Trade. In Gene Grossman and Kenneth Rogoff (eds.), *Handbook of International Economics*, iii. Amsterdam: Elsevier/North-Holland, 1243–77.

—— (1995b): Review of Hufbauer and Schott (1993), in *Journal of Economic Literature*, **33**, 849–51.

—— (1995c): Growing World Trade: Causes and consequences, *Brookings Papers on Economic Activity*, **1**, 327–62.

—— and Venables, Anthony J. (1990): Integration and Competitiveness of Peripheral Industry. In Christopher Bliss and Jorge Braga de Macedo (eds.), *Unity with Diversity in the European Economy: The Community's southern frontier*. Cambridge University Press, 56–75.

Laird, Sam, and Sapir, André (1987): Tariff Preferences. In *The World Bank Handbook on Multilateral Trade Negotiations*. Washington DC: World Bank.

—— and Yeats, Alexander (1990): *Quantitative Methods for Trade Barrier Analysis*. London: Macmillan.

Landau, Daniel (1995): The Contribution of the European Common Market to the Growth of its Member Countries: An empirical test. *Weltwirtschaftliches Archiv*, **131**, 774–82.

Langhammer, Rolf J. (1983): Ten Years of the EEC's Generalized System of Preferences for Developing Countries: Success or failure? Kiel Working Paper no. 183, Institut für Weltwirtschaft, Kiel (Germany).

Lavergne, Réal P. (1983): *The Political Economy of US Tariffs: An empirical analysis*. Toronto: Academic Press.

Lawrence, Robert Z. (1991): *Emerging Regional Arrangements: Building blocks or stumbling blocks?* In R. O'Brien (series ed.), *Finance and the International Economy*, No. 5. Oxford University Press, for American Express.

—— (1996): *Regionalism, Multilateralism and Deeper Integration*. Washington DC: Brookings Institution.

League of Nations (1927): *Tariff Level Indices*. Documentation for the International Economic Conference II.34. Geneva: League of Nations, Economic and Financial Section.

—— (1942): *Commercial Policy in the Interwar Period: International proposals and national policies*. Geneva: League of Nations.

Leamer, Edward, and James Levinsohn (1995): International Trade Theory: The evidence. In Gene Grossman and Kenneth Rogoff (eds.), *Handbook of International Economics*, iii. Amsterdam: Elsevier/North-Holland, 1339–94.

—— Guerra, Alfonso, Kaufman, Martin, and Segura, Boris (1995): How Does the North American Free Trade Agreement affect Central America? World Bank Policy Research Working Paper 1464, Washington DC.

Levinsohn, James (1994): Competition Policy and International Trade. National Bureau of Economic Research Working Paper no. 4972, Cambridge, Mass.

Levy, Santiago, and van Wijnbergen, Sweder (1992): Maize and the Free Trade Agreement between Mexico and the United States. *World Bank Economic Review*, **6**, 481–502.

Lewis, William Arthur (1949): *Economic Survey 1919–1939*. London: George Allen and Unwin.

Liepmann, Heinrich (1938): *Tariff Levels and the Economic Unity of Europe*. London: George Allen and Unwin.

Linnemann, Hans (1966): *An Econometric Study of International Trade Flows*. Amsterdam: North-Holland.

Lipsey, Richard G. (1956–7): Mr Gehrels on Customs Unions. *Review of Economic Studies*, **24**, 211–14.

—— (1957): The Theory of Customs Unions: Trade diversion and welfare. *Economica*, **24**, 40–6.

—— (1960): The Theory of Customs Unions: A general survey. *Economic Journal*, **70**, 496–513.

—— (1970): *The Theory of Customs Unions: A general equilibrium analysis*. London: Weidenfeld and Nicholson.

—— (1986): Will There be a Canadian–American Free Trade Association? *The World Economy*, **9**, 217–38.

—— and Lancaster, Kelvin (1956–7): The General Theory of 'Second Best'. *Review of Economic Studies*, **24**, 11–32.

Lloyd, Peter J. (1982): 3 × 3 Theory of Customs Unions. *Journal of International Economics*, **12**, 41–63.

—— (1992): Regionalisation and World Trade. *OECD Economic Studies*, **18**, 7–43.

—— (1993): A Tariff Substitute for Rules of Origin in Free Trade Areas. *The World Economy*, **16**, 699–712.

—— (1996): The Changing Nature of Regional Trading Arrangements. In Bijit Bora and Christopher Findlay (eds.), *Regional Integration and the Asia-Pacific*. Melbourne: Oxford University Press, 25–48.

Lopez de Silanes, Florencio, Markusen, James, and Rutherford, Thomas (1994): The Automobile Industry and the North American Free Trade Agreement: Employment, production and welfare effects. In Joseph F. Francois and Clinton R. Shiells (eds.), *Modeling Trade Policy: Applied General Equilibrium Assessments in North American Free Trade*. Cambridge University Press.

Lorenz, Detlef (1990): Regionale Enwtwicklungslinien in der Weltwirtschaft: Tendenzen zur Bildung von Wachstumspolen? In Erhard Kantzenbach and Otto Mayer (eds.), *Perspektiven der weltwirtschaftlichen Entwicklung und ihre Konsequenzen für die Bundesrepublik Deutschland*. Hamburg: Verlag Weltarchiv, 11–31.

—— (1991): Regionalization versus Regionalism: Problems of change in the world economy. *Intereconomics*, **26**, 3–10.

—— (1992): Economic Geography and the Political Economy of Regionalization: The example of Western Europe. *American Economic Review (Papers and Proceedings)*, **82**, 84–7.

—— (1995): Regionalization in Europe and East Asia: Differences and consequences. In M. Dutta, David Jay Green, Suthiphand Chirathivat, and Paitoon Wiboonchutikula (eds.), *Research in Asian Economic Studies*, vi. Greenwich, Conn.: JAI Press, 31–44.

Lortie, Pierre (1975): *Economic Integration and the Law of GATT*. New York: Praeger.

Low, Patrick, and Subramanian, Arvind (1995): TRIMs in the Uruguay Round: An unfinished business? In Will Martin and L. Alan Winters (eds.), *The Uruguay Round and the Developing Economies*. World Bank Discussion Paper no. 307, Washington DC.

Lustig, Nora, Bosworth, Barry P., and Lawrence, Robert Z. (1992): *North American Free Trade: Assessing the impact*. Washington DC: Brookings Institution.

McCallum, John (1995): National Borders Matter: Canada–USA regional trade patterns. *American Economic Review*, **85**, 615–23.

McCulloch, Rachel, and Pinera, Jose (1977): Trade as Aid: The political economy of tariff preferences for developing countries. *American Economic Review*, **67**, 959–67.

MacDougall, Donald, and Hutt, Rosemary (1954): Imperial Preference: A quantitative analysis. *Economic Journal*, **64**, 233–57.

McKeown, Timothy J. (1983): Hegemonic Stability Theory and Nineteenth-Century Tariff Levels in Europe. *International Organization*, **37**, 73–91.

McKinnon, Ronald (1963): Optimum Currency Areas, *American Economic Review*, **53**, 717–25.

McLean, Ian (1995): Trans-Tasman Trade Relations: Decline and rise. In Richard Pomfret (ed.), *Australia's Trade Policies*. Melbourne: Oxford University Press, 171–89.

McMillan, John (1993) Does Regional Integration Foster Open Trade? Economic theory and GATT Article XXIV. In Kym Anderson and Richard Blackhurst (eds.), *Regional Integration and the Global Trading System*. Hemel Hempstead (UK): Harvester Wheatsheaf, 292–309.

—— and McCann, Ewen (1981): Welfare Effects in Customs Unions. *Economic Journal*, **91**, 697–703.

MacPhee, Craig R. (1984): Evaluation of the Trade Effects of the Generalized System of Preferences. UNCTAD TD/B/C.5/87 January 1984; also collected in UNCTAD *Operation and Effects of the Generalized System of Preferences*. New York: United Nations (1985), 57–86.

McQueen, Matthew (1982): Lomé and the Protective Effect of Rules of Origin. *Journal of World Trade Law*, **16**, 119–32.

Marer, Paul, and Montias, John M. (1982): The Council for Mutual Economic Assistance. In Ali M. El-Agraa (ed.), *International Economic Integration*. New York: St Martin's Press, 102–38.

Markusen, James, and Venables, Anthony (1988): Trade Policy with Increasing Returns and Imperfect Competition: Contradictory results from competing assumptions. *Journal of International Economics*, **24**, 299–316.

—— Rutherford, Thomas, and Hunter, Linda (1995): North American Free Trade and the Production of Finished Automobiles. In Patrick Kehoe and Timothy Kehoe (eds.), *Modeling North American Economic Integration*. Dordrecht (NL): Kluwer, 117–30.

Marrese, Michael (1986): CMEA: Effective but cumbersome political economy. *International Organization*, **40**, 287–327.

—— and Vanous, Jan (1983): *Soviet Subsidization of Trade with Eastern Europe: A Soviet perspective*. Berkeley, Calif.: University of California Institute of International Studies.

Massell, Benton F. (1968): A Reply, and Further Thoughts on Customs Unions. *Economic Journal*, **78**, 979–82.

Masters, Donald (1937): *The Reciprocity Treaty of 1854*. Toronto: McClelland and Stewart (1963 edn.).

Matlekovits, Alexandre von (1906): La Nouvelle Ére de la politique douaniére. *Revue Économique Internationale*, **3**, 243–313.

Mayer, Wolfgang (1981): Theoretical Considerations on Negotiated Tariff Adjustments. *Oxford Economic Papers*, **33**, 135–53.

Mayes, David G. (1978): The Effects of Economic Integration on Trade. *Journal of Common Market Studies*, **17**, 1–25.

Meade, James E. (1951): *The Theory of International Economic Policy*, i, *The Balance of Payments*. Oxford University Press.

—— (1955a): *The Theory of International Economic Policy*, ii, *Trade and Welfare*. Oxford University Press.

—— (1955b): *The Theory of Customs Unions*. Amsterdam: North-Holland.

—— Liesner, H. H., and Wells, S. J. (1962): *Case Studies in European Economic Union: The mechanics of integration*. Oxford University Press.

Meltzer, Allan H. (1976): Monetary and Other Explanations of the Start of the Great Depression. *Journal of Monetary Economics*, **2**, 455–71.

Melvin, James R. (1969): Comments on the Theory of Customs Unions. *Manchester School of Economic and Social Studies*, **37**, 161–8.

Messerlin, Patrick A. (1981): The Political Economy of Protectionism: The bureaucratic case. *Weltwirtschaftliches Archiv*, **117**, 469–96.

—— (1989): The EC Antidumping Regulations: A first economic appraisal, 1980–5. *Weltwirtschaftliches Archiv*, **125**, 563–87.

Michael, Michael S. (1992): International Factor Mobility, Non-traded Goods, Tariffs, and the Terms of Trade. *Canadian Journal of Economics*, **25**, 493–9.

Michaely, Michael (1976): The Assumptions of Jacob Viner's Theory of Customs Unions. *Journal of International Economics*, **6**, 75–93.

—— (1977): *Theory of Commercial Policy*. University of Chicago Press.

Miller, Marcus H., and Spencer, John E. (1977): The Static Economic Effects of the UK Joining the EEC: A general equilibrium approach. *Review of Economic Studies*, **44**, 71–94.

Molle, Willem (1990): *The Economics of European Integration*. Aldershot, Hants: Dartmouth Press.

Moore, Lynden (1985): *The Growth and Structure of International Trade since the Second World War*. Totowa, NJ: Barnes and Noble.

Moss, Joanna (1982): *The Lomé Conventions and their Implications for the United States*. Boulder, Colo.: Westview Press.

Moss, Joanna and Ravenhill, John (1982): Trade Developments during the First Lomé Convention. *World Development*, **10**, 841–56.

—— —— (1983): Trade between the ACP and EEC during Lomé I. In Christopher Stevens (ed.), *EEC and the Third World: A survey, 3*. London: Hodder and Stoughton, 133–51.

Mundell, Robert A. (1961): Theory of Optimum Currency Areas, *American Economic Review*, **51**, 657–65.

—— (1964): Tariff Preferences and the Terms of Trade. *Manchester School of Economic and Social Studies*, **32**, 1–13.

Murray, Tracy (1977): *Trade Preferences for Developing Countries*. London: Macmillan.

—— (1980): Evaluation of the Trade Benefits under the United States Scheme of Generalized Preferences. UNCTAD TD/B/C.5/66 February 1980; also collected in UNCTAD *Operation and Effects of the Generalized System of Preferences*. New York: United Nations (1981), 67–75.

—— Schmidt, Wilson, and Walter, Ingo (1978): Alternative Forms of Protection against Market Disruption. *Kyklos*, **31**, 624–37.

Neal, Larry (1979): The Economics and Finance of Bilateral Clearing Agreements: Germany, 1934–8. *Economic History Review*, **32**, 391–404.

Negishi, Takashi (1969): The Customs Union and the Theory of Second Best. *International Economic Review*, **10**, 391–7.

Newton, Jim, and Tse Lai-hing (1996): Child's Play: The political economy of the China/EU toy trade. Paper presented to the Second Conference on East Asia-EU Business, King's College London, 17–19 April 1996.

Nogués, Julio J., Olechowski, Andrzej, and Winters, L. Alan (1986): The Extent of Nontariff Barriers to Industrial Countries' Imports. *World Bank Economic Review*, **1**, 181–99.

Norheim, Hege, Finger, Karl-Michael, and Anderson, Kym (1993): Trends in the Regionalization of World Trade, 1928 to 1990. In Kym Anderson and Richard Blackhurst (eds.), *Regional Integration and the Global Trading System*. Hemel Hempstead (UK): Harvester Wheatsheaf, 436–86.

Norman, Victor (1989): EFTA and the Internal European Market. *Economic Policy*, **9**, 423–65.

—— (1990): Assessing Trade and Welfare Effects of Trade Liberalization: A comparison of alternative approaches to CGE modelling with imperfect competition. *European Economic Review*, **34**, 725–45.

Norton, Desmond (1986): Smuggling under the Common Agriculural Policy: Northern Ireland and the Republic of Ireland. *Journal of Common Market Studies*, **24**, 297–312.

Nugent, Jeffrey B. (1974): *Economic Integration in Central America*. Baltimore: Johns Hopkins University Press.

O'Brien, Denis (1976): Customs Unions: Trade creation and trade diversion in historical perspective. *History of Political Economy*, **8**, 540–63.

Officer, Lawrence H., and Smith, Lawrence B. (1968): The Canadian–American Reciprocity Treaty of 1855 to 1866. *Journal of Economic History*, **28**, 598–623.

Oguledo, Victor Iwuagwu, and Macphee, Craig R. (1994): Gravity Models: A reformulation and an application to discriminatory trade arrangements. *Applied Economics*, **26**, 107–20.

Ohyama, M. (1972): Trade and Welfare in General Equilibrium, *Keio Economic Studies*, **9**, 37–73.

Olson, Mancur (1982): *The Rise and Fall of Nations: Economic Growth, Stagflation and Social Rigidities*. New Haven: Yale University Press.

Onwuka, Ralph I., and Sesay, Amadu (1985): *The Future of Regionalism in Africa*. New York: St Martin's Press.

Orden, David (1996): Agricultural Interest Groups and the North American Free Trade Agreement. In Anne O. Krueger (ed.), *The Political Economy of American Trade Policy*. University of Chicago Press, 335–82.

Organisation for Economic Co-operation and Development (1995): *Regional Integration and the Multilateral Trading System: Synergy and divergences*. Paris: OECD.

Owen, Nicholas (1976): Scale Economies in the EEC: An approach based on intra-EEC trade. *European Economic Review*, **7**, 143–63.

—— (1983): *Economies of Scale, Competitiveness, and Trade Patterns within the European Community*. Oxford University Press.

Palmeter, N. David (1993): Rules of Origin in Customs Unions and Free Trade Areas. In Kym Anderson and Richard Blackhurst (eds.), *Regional Integration and the Global Trading System*. Hemel Hempstead, Herts: Harvester Wheatsheaf, 326–43.

—— (1995): Rules of Origin in a Western Hemisphere Free Trade Agreement. In Inter-American Development Bank and Economic Commission for Latin America and the Caribbean, *Trade Liberalization in the Western Hemisphere*. Washington DC: 191–206.

Pangestu, Mari, and Bijit Bora (1996): *Evolution of Liberalization Policies affecting Investment Flows in the Asia Pacific*. Centre for International Economic Studies Policy Discussion Paper no. 96/01, University of Adelaide, Australia.

Parmenter, Brian R. (1986): Review of Whalley (1985). *Canadian Journal of Economics*, **19**, 363–6.

Pastor, Robert A. (1992): NAFTA as the Center of an Integration Process: The non-trade issues. In Nora Lustig, Barry P. Bosworth, and Robert Z. Lawrence (eds.), *North American Free Trade: Assessing the impact*. Washington DC: Brookings Institution, 176–209.

—— (1995): The North America Free Trade Agreement: Hemispheric and geopolitical implications. In Inter-American Development Bank and Economic Commission for Latin America and the Caribbean, *Trade Liberalization in the Western Hemisphere*. Washington DC: 53–84.

Patterson, Gardner (1966): *Discrimination in International Trade: The policy issues, 1945–1965*. Princeton University Press.

—— (1983): The European Community as a Threat to the System. In William R. Cline (ed.), *Trade Policy in the 1980s*. Cambridge, Mass.: MIT Press, 223–42.

Pearson, Charles (1983): *Emergency Protection in the Footwear Industry*. Thames Essay no. 36. London: Trade Policy Research Centre.

—— (1995): Regional Free Trade and the Environment. In Inter-American Development Bank and Economic Commission for Latin America and the Caribbean, *Trade Liberalization in the Western Hemisphere*. Washington DC: 303–31.

Pearson, Scott R., and Ingram, William D. (1980): Economies of Scale, Domestic Divergences, and Potential Gains from Economic Integration in Ghana and the Ivory Coast. *Journal of Political Economy*, **88**, 994–1008.

Peck, Merton J. (1989): Industrial Organisation and the Gains from Europe 1992. *Brookings Papers on Economic Activity*, **2**, 277–300.

Pelkmans, Jacques (1984): *Market Integration in the European Community*. The Hague: Martinus Nijhoff.

—— and Gremmen, Hans (1983): The Empirical Measurement of Static Customs Unions Effects. *Rivista Internazionale di Scienze Economiche e Commerciali*, **30**, 612–22.

Pelzman, Joseph (1977): Trade Creation and Trade Diversion in the Council of Mutual Economic Assistance. *American Economic Review*, **67**, 713–22.

Percy, Michael B., Norrie, K. H., and Johnston, R. G. (1982): Reciprocity and the Canadian General Election of 1911. *Explorations in Economic History*, **19**, 409–34.

Petith, Howard C. (1977): European Integration and the Terms of Trade. *Economic Journal*, **87**, 262–72.

Petri, Peter (1993): The East Asian Trading Bloc: An analytical history. In Jeffrey Frankel and Miles Kahler (eds.), *Regionalism and Rivalry*, University of Chicago Press, 21–52.

—— and Michael Plummer (1996): The Multilateralization of Regional Preferences: Evidence from the Asia–Pacific, Brandeis University Department of Economics Working Paper, Waltham, Mass.

Plummer, Michael (1991a): Ex-post Empirical Estimates of the Second Enlargement: The case of Greece. *Weltwirtschaftliches Archiv*, **127**, 171–82.

—— (1991b): Efficiency Effects of the Accession of Spain and Portugal to the EC. *Journal of Common Market Studies*, **29**, 317–25.

Plumptre, A. F. Wynne (1977): *The Decades of Decision: Canada and the world monetary system*. Toronto: McClelland and Stewart.

Pomfret, Richard (1975): Some Interrelationships between Import Substitution and Export Promotion in a Small Economy. *Weltwirtschaftliches Archiv*, **111**, 714–27.

—— (1978): The Economic Consequences for Israel of Free Trade in Manufactured Goods with the EEC. *Weltwirtschaftliches Archiv*, **114**, 526–39.

—— (1981): The Impact of EEC Enlargement on Non-Member Countries' Exports to the EEC. *Economic Journal*, **91**, 726–9.

—— (1982a): Trade Preferences and Foreign Investment in Malta. *Journal of World Trade Law*, **16**, 236–50.

—— (1982b): Trade Effects of European Community Preferences to Mediterranean Countries. *World Development*, **10**, 857–62.

—— (1984): The Quiet Shift in US Trade Policy. *Challenge*, **27**, 61–4.

—— (1985a): Discrimination in International Trade: Extent, motivation, and implications. *Economia Internazionale*, **38**, 3–19.

—— (1985b): The Trade Diversion due to EC Enlargement: A comment on Sawyer's estimate. *Weltwirtschaftliches Archiv*, **121**, 560–1.

—— (1986a): *Mediterranean Policy of the European Community: A study of discrimination in trade*. London: Macmillan.

—— (1986b): MFN Tariff Reductions and Developing Country Trade Benefits under the GSP: A comment. *Economic Journal*, **96**, 534–6.

—— (1986c): The Effects of Trade Preferences for Developing Countries. *Southern Economic Journal*, **53**, 18–26.

—— (1986d): The Theory of Preferential Trading Agreements. *Weltwirtschaftliches Archiv*, **122**, 439–65.

—— (1986e): The Trade-Diverting Bias of Preferential Trading Arrangements. *Journal of Common Market Studies*, **25**, 109–17.

—— (1987): Long-Term Consequences of Temporary Trade Measures. *Challenge*, **30** (November), 57–9.

—— (1988): *Unequal Trade*. Oxford: Basil Blackwell.

—— (1989): Voluntary Export Restraints in the Presence of Monopoly Power. *Kyklos*, **42**, 61–72.

—— (1991): What is the Secret of the EMS's Longevity? *Journal of Common Market Studies*, **29**, 623–33.

—— (1992): *International Trade Policy with Imperfect Competition*. Special Papers in International Economics, no. 17. Princeton University: International Finance Section.

—— (1993): Measuring the Effects of Economic Integration on Third Countries. *World Development*, **21**, 1435–7.

—— (ed.) (1995a): *Australia's Trade Policies*. Melbourne: Oxford University Press.

—— (1995b): *The Economies of Central Asia*. Princeton University Press.

Pomfret, Richard (1996a): Sub-regional Economic Zones. In Bijit Bora and Christopher Findlay (eds.), *Regional Integration and the Asia Pacific*. Melbourne: Oxford University Press, 207–22.

—— (1996b): The Association of South-East Asian Nations. In Ali M. El-Agraa (ed.), *Economic Integration Worldwide*, 3rd edn. London: Macmillan, 297–318.

—— (1996c): *Asian Economies in Transition*. Cheltenham, Glos.: Edward Elgar.

—— (1997): The Economic Co-operation Organization: Current status and future prospects. *Europe–Asia Studies* (formerly *Soviet Studies*), **49**, 000–00.

Preeg, Ernest H. (1995): *Traders in a Brave New World: The Uruguay Round and the future of the international trading system*. University of Chicago Press.

—— (1996): Policy Forum: Transatlantic free trade. *Washington Quarterly*, **19(2)**, 105–33.

Prestowitz, Clyde V., *et al.* (1991): *The New North American Order: A win–win strategy for US–Mexican trade.* Washington DC: Economic Strategy Institute.

Prewo, Wilfried E. (1974): Integration Effects in the EEC: An attempt at quantification in a general equilibrium framework. *European Economic Review*, **5**, 379–405.

Price, Victoria Curzon (1982): The European Free Trade Association. In Ali M. El-Agraa (ed.), *International Economic Integration*. New York: St Martin's Press, 77–101.

Primo Braga, Carlos A. (1992): NAFTA and the Rest of the World. In Nora Lustig, Barry P. Bosworth, and Robert Z. Lawrence (eds.), *North American Free Trade: Assessing the impact*. Washington DC: Brookings Institution, 210–49.

—— Safadi, Raed, and Yeats, Alexander (1994): NAFTA's Implications for East Asian Exports. World Bank Policy Research Working Paper 1351, Washington DC.

Prusa, Thomas J. (1992): Why Are So Many Anti-Dumping Petitions Withdrawn? *Journal of International Economics*, **33**, 1–20.

Raboy, David, Teri Simpson, and Bing Xu (1995): A Transition Proposal for Lomé Convention Trade Preferences: The case of the EU banana regime, *The World Economy*, **18**, 565–81.

Read, Robert (1994): The EC Banana Market: The issues and the dilemma, *The World Economy*, **17**, 219–35.

Resnick, Stephen A., and Truman, Edwin M. (1974): The Distribution of West European Trade under Alternative Tariff Policies. *Review of Economics and Statistics*, **56**, 83–91.

Richardson, Martin (1995): Tariff Revenue Competition in a Free Trade Area. *European Economic Review*, **39**, 1429–37.

Riedel, James (1977): Tariff Concessions in the Kennedy Round the Structure of Protection in West Germany. *Journal of International Economics*, **7**, 133–43.

—— (1987): Trade Policy in the United States: from multilateralism to bilateralism? In Herbert Giersch (ed.), *Free Trade in the World Economy: Towards an opening of markets*. Tübingen: JCB Mohr.

Riezman, Raymond (1979): A 3 × 3 Model of Customs Unions. *Journal of International Economics*, **9**, 341–54.

—— (1985): Customs Unions and the Core. *Journal of International Economics*, **19**, 355–65.

Robbins, Lionel (1958): *Robert Torrens and the Evolution of Classical Economics*. London: Macmillan.

Robson, Peter (1983): *Integration, Development and Equity: Economic integration in West Africa*. London: George Allen and Unwin.

—— (1984): *The Economics of International Integration*, 2nd edn. London: George Allen and Unwin.

Röpke, Wilhelm (1934): *German Commercial Policy*. London: Longmans, Green.

—— (1942): *International Economic Disintegration*. London: William Hodge.

Rooth, Tim J. T. (1984): Limits of Leverage: The Anglo-Danish trade agreement of 1933. *Economic History Review*, **37**, 211–28.

—— (1986): Tariffs and Trade Bargaining: Anglo-Scandinavian economic relations in the 1930s. *Scandinavian Economic History Review*, **34**, 54–71.

Rosendorff, B. Peter (1996): Voluntary Export Restraints, Antidumping Procedure, and Domestic Politics. *American Economic Review*, **86**, 544–61.

Safadi, Raed, and Alexander Yeats (1993): The North American Free Trade Agreement: Its effect on South Asia. World Bank Working Paper 1119, Washington DC.

Sampson, Gary P., and Snape, Richard H. (1980): Effects of the EEC's Variable Import Levies. *Journal of Political Economy*, **88**, 1026–40.

Sapir, André (1981): Trade Benefits under the EEC Generalized System of Preferences. *European Economic Review*, **15**, 339–55.

—— (1992): Regional Integration in Europe. *Economic Journal*, **102**, 1491–1506.

—— (1993): Comment [on Winters (1993a)], 230–3.

—— and Lundberg, Lars (1984): The US GSP and its Impacts. In Robert E. Baldwin and Anne O. Krueger (eds.), *The Structure and Evolution of Recent US Trade Policy*. University of Chicago Press.

Sawyer, Charles W. (1984): The Effects of the Second Enlargement of the EC on US Exports to Europe. *Weltwirtschaftliches Archiv*, **120**, 572–9.

—— and Sprinkle, Richard L. (1984): Caribbean Basin Economic Recovery Act: Export Expansion Effects. *Journal of World Trade Law*, **18**, 429–36.

Sawyer, Charles W. and Sprinkle, Richard L. (1986): USA–Israel Free Trade Area: Trade Expansion Effects of the Agreement. *Journal of World Trade Law*, **20**, 526–39.

Scaperlanda, Anthony, and Balough, Robert S. (1983): Determinants of US Direct Investment in the EEC, Revisited. *European Economic Review*, **21**, 381–90.

Schachmurove, Yochanan, and Spiegel, Uriel (1995): Labor-managed Firms in Transition Economies. *Comparative Economic Studies*, **37**, 39–53.

Schattschneider, E. E. (1935): *Politics, Pressures and the Tariff: A study of free private enterprise in pressure politics, as shown in the 1929–1930 revision of the tariff*. New York: Prentice-Hall.

Schott, Jeffrey J. (ed.) (1989): *Free Trade Areas and US Trade Policy*. Washington DC: Institute for International Economics.

Scitovsky, Tibor (1956): Economies of Scale, Competition, and European Integration. *American Economic Review*, **46**, 71–91.

—— (1958): *Economic Theory and Western European Integration*. Stanford, Calif.: Stanford University Press.

Scollay, Rob (1996): Australia–New Zealand Closer Economic Relations Agreement. In Bijit Bora and Christopher Findlay (eds.), *Regional Integration and the Asia Pacific*. Melbourne: Oxford University Press, 184–96.

Sereghová, Jana (1995): Trade Policy in Central and Eastern Europe. In Jens Hölscher, Anke Jacobsen, Horst Tomann, and Hans Weisfeld (eds.), *Bedingungen ökonomischer Entwicklung in Zentralosteuropa*. Marburg (Germany): Metropolis-Verlag, 253–77.

Shibata, H. (1967): The Theory of Economic Unions: A comparative analysis of customs unions, free trade areas, and tax unions. In Carl S. Shoup (ed.), *Fiscal Harmonization in Common Markets*, i, *Theory*. New York: Columbia Univeristy Press, 145–264.

Siebert, Horst, Langhammer, Rolf, and Piazola, Daniel (1996): The Transatlantic Free Trade Area: Fuelling trade discrimination or global liberalization? *Journal of World Trade*, **30**, 45–61.

Smith, Adam (1776): *An Inquiry into the Nature and Causes of the Wealth of Nations*. London.

Smith, Alasdair (1990): The Market for Cars in the Enlarged European Community. In Christopher Bliss and Jorge Braga de Macedo (eds.), *Unity with Diversity in the European Economy: The Community's southern frontier*. Cambridge University Press, 78–103.

—— and Venables, Anthony J. (1988): Completing the Internal Market in the European Community: Some industry simulations. *European Economic Review*, **32**, 1501–25.

Snape, Richard H. (1996): Trade Discrimination: Yesterday's problem? *Stockholm School of Economics Working Paper no. 100*, February; subsequently published in *Economic Record*, **72**, 381–96.

Spraos, John (1964): The Condition for a Trade-Creating Customs Union. *Economic Journal*, **74**, 101–8.

Srinivasan, T. N. (1993): Comment on Krugman (1993), 84–9.

—— and Whalley, John (eds.) (1986): *General Equilibrium Trade Policy Modelling*. Cambridge, Mass.: MIT Press.

Stevens, Christopher (1981): *EEC and the Third World: A Survey*, 1. London: Hodder and Stoughton.

—— (1984): *EEC and the Third World: A Survey*, 4. London: Hodder and Stoughton.

Stigler, George J. (1974): The Theory of Economic Regulation. *Bell Journal of Economics and Management Science*, **2**, 3–21.

Stordel, Harry (1977): Trade Cooperation: Preferences in the Lomé Convention, the Generalized System of Preferences and the World Trade System. In Frans Alting von Geusau (ed.), *The Lomé Convention and a New International Economic Order*. Leyden: A. W. Sijthoff, 63–80.

Summers, Lawrence H. (1991): Regionalism and the World Trading System. In Federal Reserve Bank of Kansas City, *Symposium on the Policy Implications of Trade and Currency Zones*, 295–303; reprinted in Garnaut and Drysdale (1994, 194–8).

Taussig, Frank W. (1892): Reciprocity. *Quarterly Journal of Economics*, **7**, 26–39.

Taylor, Robert (1980): *Implications for the Southern Mediterranean Countries of the Second Enlargement of the European Community*. Europe Information: Development X/225/80-EN. Brussels.

Thant, Myo, Min Tang, and Hiroshi Kakazu (eds.) (1994): *Growth Triangles in Asia*. Oxford University Press, for the Asian Development Bank.

Thorbecke, Erik (1960): *The Tendency towards Regionalization in International Trade 1928–1956*. The Hague: Martinus Nijhoff.

Thursby, Jerry G., and Thursby, Marie C. (1987): Bilateral Trade Flows, the Linder Hypothesis, and Exchange Risk. *Review of Economics and Statistics*, **69**, 488–95.

Tinbergen, Jan (1954): *International Economic Integration*, 2nd edn. Amsterdam: Elsevier.

Toh Mun Heng and Linda Low (eds.) (1993): *Regional Cooperation and Growth Triangles in ASEAN*. Singapore: Times Academic Press.

Torrens, Robert (1844): *The Budget: A Series of Letters on Financial Commercial and Colonial Policy*. London: Smith Elder.

Tovias, Alfred (1977): *Tariff Preferences in Mediterranean Diplomacy*. London: Macmillan.

—— (1979): *EEC Enlargement: The Southern Neighbours*. Brighton: Sussex European Research Centre.

Trebilcock, Michael J., and Schwanen, Daniel (1995): *Getting There: An assessment of the agreement on internal trade*. Toronto: C. D. Howe Institute.

Trefler, Daniel (1995): The Case of the Missing Trade and other Mysteries, *American Economic Review*, **85**, 1029–46.

Triffin, Robert (1957): *Europe and the Money Muddle*. New Haven: Yale University Press.

Truman, Edwin M. (1969): The European Economic Community: Trade creation and trade diversion. *Yale Economic Essays*, **9**, 199–257.

Tsoukalis, Loukas (1977): The EEC and the Mediterranean: Is 'global' policy a misnomer? *International Affairs*, **53**, 422–38.

—— (1993): *The New European Economy: The politics and economics of integration*. Oxford University Press.

Twitchett, Carol Cosgrove (1978): *Europe and Africa*. Farnborough, Hants: Saxon House.

Ulph, David T. (1991): Technology Policy in the Completed European Market. In L. Alan Winters and Anthony J. Venables (eds.), *European Integration: Trade and Industry*. Cambridge University Press, 142–61.

UNCTAD (1987): *Protectionism and Structural Adjustment*. UNCTAD T/B/1126 (Part I), Geneva.

Ungerer, Horst, Evans, Owen, Mayer, Thomas, and Young, Philip (1986): *The European Monetary System: Recent Developments*. IMF Occasional Paper no. 48, Washington DC.

United States Tariff Commission (1919): *Reciprocity and Commercial Treaties*. Washington DC: USTC.

—— (1941): *Italian Commercial Policy and Foreign Trade 1922–1940*. Washington DC: USTC.

Vaitsos, Constantine (1978): The Crisis in Regional Economic Cooperation (Integration) among Developing Countries. *World Development*, **6**, 719–69.

Vanek, Jaroslav (1965): *General Equilibrium of International Discrimination: The case of customs unions*. Cambridge, Mass.: Harvard University Press.

Venables, Anthony J., and Smith, Alasdair (1986): Trade and Industrial Policy under Imperfect Competition. *Economic Policy*, **3**, 622–72.

Verdoorn, P. J. (1960): The Intra-Bloc Trade of Benelux. In E. A. G. Robinson (ed.), *Economic Consequences of the Size of Nations*. London: Macmillan, 291–329.

—— and Meyer zu Schlochtern, F. J. M. (1964): Trade Creation and Trade Diversion in the Common Market. In H. Brugmans (ed.), *Intégration Européenne et realité economique*. Bruges: de Tempel, 96–137.

—— and Schwartz, A. N. R. (1972): Two Alternative Estimates of the Effects of EEC and EFTA on the Pattern of Trade. *European Economic Review*, **3**, 291–335.

—— and van Bochove, C. A. (1972): Measuring Integration Effects: A survey. *European Economic Review*, **3**, 337–49.

Vermulst, Edwin, Waer, Paul, and Bourgeois, Jacques (eds.) (1994): *Rules of Origin in International Trade: A comparative study*. Ann Arbor: University of Michigan Press.

Viner, Jacob (1924): The Most-Favored-Nation Clause in American Commercial Treaties. *Journal of Political Economy*, **32**, 101–29; reprinted in Viner (1951).

—— (1931): The Most-Favored-Nation Clause. *Index VI*, no. 61, 2–17. (Stockholm); reprinted in Viner (1951).

—— (1943): *Trade Relations between Free-Market and Controlled Economies*. Geneva: League of Nations.

—— (1944): Peace as an Economic Problem. In *New Perspectives on Peace: Charles R. Walgreen Foundation lectures*. University of Chicago Press; reprinted in Viner (1951).

—— (1950): *The Customs Union Issue*. New York: Carnegie Endowment for International Peace.

—— (1951): *International Economics*. Glencoe, Ill.: Free Press.

—— (1965): Letter to W. M. Corden of 13 March 1965 (published in *Journal of International Economics*, **6**, February 1976, 107–8).

Vousden, Neil (1990): *The Economics of Trade Protection*. Cambridge University Press.

Waelbroeck, Jean (1984): The Logic of EC Commercial and Industrial Policy Making. In Alexis Jacquemin (ed.), *European Industry: Public Policy and Corporate Strategy*. Oxford: Clarendon Press, 99–125.

Wang, Z-K., and Winters, Alan (1991): The Trading Potential of Eastern Europe. CEPR Discussion Paper 610, Centre for Economic Policy Research, London.

Wei Shang-Jin (1996): Intra-national versus International Trade: How stubborn are nations in global integration? National Bureau of Economic Research Working Paper 5531, Cambridge, Mass.

—— and Frankel, Jeffrey (1995): Open Regionalism in a World of Continental Trade Blocs. Ms. (11/15/95; revised version of National Bureau of Economic Research Working Paper 5272).

Weintraub, Sidney (1984): USA–Canada Free Trade: What's in it for the US? *Journal of Interamerican Studies and World Affairs*, **26**, 225–44.

—— (1985): Selective Trade Liberalization and Restriction. In Ernest H. Preeg (ed.), *Hard Bargaining Ahead: US trade policy and developing countries*. New Brunswick, NJ: Transaction Books, 167–84.

—— (1986): A Note on Trade Discrimination. *Rivista Internazionale di Scienze Economiche e Commerciali*, **33**, 353–70.

Welk, William (1937): League Sanctions and Foreign Trade Restrictions in Italy. *American Economic Review*, **27**, 96–107.

Whalley, John (1985): *Trade Liberalization among Major World Trading Areas*. Cambridge, Mass.: MIT Press.

Whalley, John (1993): Regional Trade Arrangements in North America: CUSTA and NAFTA. In Jaime de Melo and Arvind Panagariya (eds.), *New Dimensions in Regional Integration*. Cambridge University Press, 352–82.

—— with Roderick Hill (1985): *The Collected Research Studies*, xi, *Canada–United States Free Trade*. University of Toronto Press, for the Royal Commission on the Economic Union and Development Prospects for Canada.

Wigle, Randall (1988): General Equilibrium Evaluation of Canada–USA Trade Liberalization in a Global Context. *Canadian Journal of Economics*, **21**, 39–64.

Wilcox, Clair (1949): *A Charter for World Trade*. New York: Macmillan.

Wilford, D. Sykes, and Wilford, Walton T. (1978): On Revenue Performance and Revenue–Income Stability in the Third World. *Economic Development and Cultural Change*, **26**, 505–23.

Wilford, Walton T. (1970): Trade Creation in the Central American Common Market. *Western Economic Journal*, **8**, 61–9.

Williamson, John, and Bottrill, Anthony (1971): The Impact of Customs Unions on Trade in Manufactures. *Oxford Economic Papers*, **23**, 323–51.

Willmore, Larry N. (1972): Free Trade in Manufactures among Developing Countries: The Central American experience. *Economic Development and Cultural Change*, **20**, 659–70.

—— (1976): Trade Creation, Trade Diversion and Effective Protection in the Central American Common Market. *Journal of Development Studies*, **12**, 396–414.

—— (1978): The Industrial Economics of Intra-Industry Trade and Specialization. In Herbert Giersch (ed.), *On the Economics of Intra-Industry Trade*. Tübingen: JCB Mohr, 185–209.

Winters, L. Alan (1984): British Imports of Manufactures and the Common Market. *Oxford Economic Papers*, **36**, 103–18.

—— (1987): Britain in Europe: A survey of quantitative trade studies. *Journal of Common Market Studies*, **25**, 315–35.

—— (ed.) (1992a): *Trade Flows and Trade Policy after '1992'*. Cambridge University Press.

—— (1992b): Integration, Trade Policy and European Footwear Trade. In Winters (1992a), 175–209.

—— (1993a): The European Community: A case of successful integration? In Jaime de Melo and Arvind Panagariya (eds.), *New Dimensions in Regional Integration*. Cambridge University Press, 202–28.

—— (1993b): Expanding EC Membership and Association Accords: Recent experience and future prospects. In Kym Anderson and Richard Blackhurst (eds.), *Regional Integration and the Global Trading System*. Hemel Hempstead, Herts: Harvester Wheatsheaf, 104–25.

—— (1994): The EC and Protection: The political economy. *European Economic Review*, **38**, 596–603.

—— (1996a): Regionalism and the Rest of the World. CEPR Discussion Paper 1316, Centre for Economic Policy Research, London.

—— (1996b): Regionalism versus Multilateralism. Paper presented at the CEPR Conference on Regional Integration in La Coruna, Spain, 26–7 April 1996 (conference volume forthcoming, London: Centre for Economic Policy Research).

—— and Venables, Anthony J. (eds.) (1991): *European Integration: Trade and Industry*. Cambridge University Press.

Wionczek, Miguel S. (1972): The Central American Common Market. In Peter Robson (ed.), *International Economic Integration: Selected readings*. Harmondsworth, Middx: Penguin, 403–13.

Wonnacott, Paul, and Lutz, Mark (1989): Is There a Case for Free Trade Areas? In Jeffrey J. Schott (ed.), *Free Trade Areas and US Trade Policy*. Washington DC: Institute for International Economics, 59–84.

—— and Wonnacott, Ronald (1981): Is Unilateral Tariff Reduction Preferable to a Customs Union? The curious case of the missing foreign tariffs. *American Economic Review*, **71**, 704–14.

—— —— (1982): Free Trade between the United States and Canada: Fifteen years later. *Canadian Public Policy* (Supplement), **8**, 412–17.

Wonnacott, Ronald J. (1996): Trade and Investment in a Hub-and-Spoke System versus a Free Trade Area. *The World Economy*, **19**, 237–52.

—— and Wonnacott, Paul (1967): *Free Trade between the United States and Canada: The potential economic effects*. Cambridge, Mass.: Harvard University Press.

Wooton, Ian (1988): Towards a Common Market: Factor mobility in a customs union, *Canadian Journal of Economics*, **21**, 525–38.

World Trade Organization (WTO) (1995): *Regionalism and the World Trading System*. Geneva: World Trade Organization.

Yamazawa, Ippei (1992): On Pacific Economic Integration, *Economic Journal*, **102**, 1519–29.

Young, John H. (1957): *Canadian Commercial Policy*. Ottawa: Royal Commission on Canada's Economic Prospects.

Index